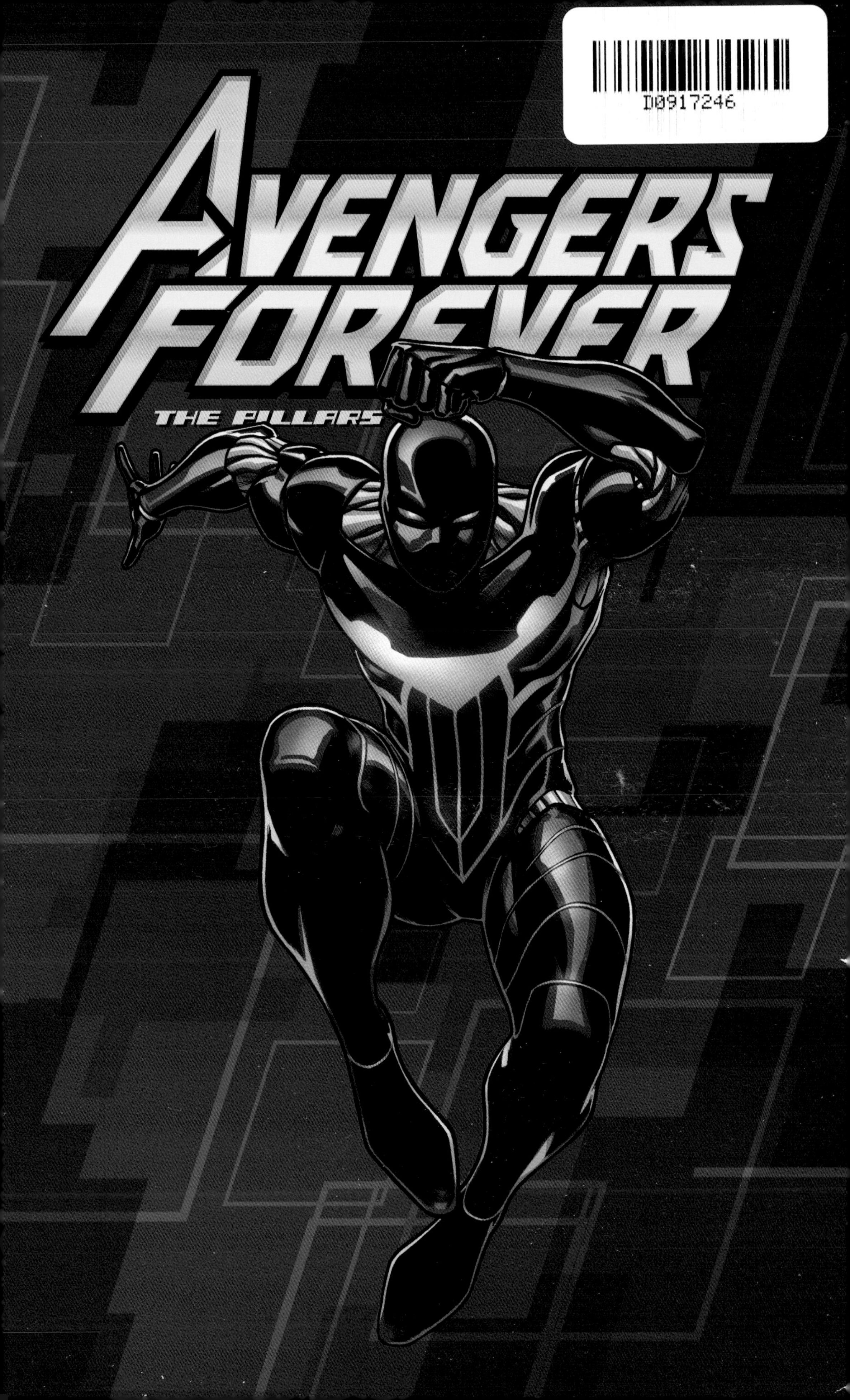
AVENGERS FOREVER
THE PILLARS

THE MULTIVERSAL MASTERS OF EVIL, A GROUP COMPRISED OF THE DEADLIEST VILLAINS OF THEIR RESPECTIVE WORLDS, HAVE BEEN MAKING THEIR WAY THROUGH THE MULTIVERSE, CONQUERING COUNTLESS WORLDS. AMONG THEIR MEMBERS IS *KING KILLMONGER*, WHO WEARS A MODIFIED VERSION OF THE ASGARDIAN *DESTROYER* ARMOR.

AN UNLIKELY GROUP OF *AVENGERS* FROM DIFFERENT REALITIES HAS FORMED TO OPPOSE THE VILLAINS: *ROBBIE REYES, THE ALL-RIDER* FROM *EARTH-616*, A *DEATHLOK* DISPATCHED BY THE MYSTERIOUS *AVENGER PRIME* AND *TONY STARK, THE ANT-MAN* OF *EARTH-818*.

GHOST RIDER

ANT-MAN

DEATHLOK

T'CHALLA

THOR

CAROL DANVERS

STEVE ROGERS

STEVE ROGERS

STEVE ROGERS

STEVE

IRON MAN

TONY STARK

IRON MAN

TONY STARK

AVENGERS FOREVER VOL. 2: THE PILLARS. Contains material originally published in magazine form as AVENGERS FOREVER (2021) #6-11 and AVENGERS FOREVER INFINITY COMIC (2022) #1-4. First printing 2022. ISBN 978-1-302-93261-9. Published by MARVEL WORLDWIDE, INC., a subsidiary of MARVEL ENTERTAINMENT, LLC. OFFICE OF PUBLICATION: 1290 Avenue of the Americas, New York, NY 10104. © 2022 MARVEL No similarity between any of the names, characters, persons, and/or institutions in this book with those of any living or dead person or institution is intended, and any such similarity which may exist is purely coincidental. *Printed in the U.S.A.* KEVIN FEIGE, Chief Creative Officer; DAN BUCKLEY, President, Marvel Entertainment; DAVID BOGART, Associate Publisher & SVP of Talent Affairs; TOM BREVOORT, VP, Executive Editor; NICK LOWE, Executive Editor, VP of Content, Digital Publishing; DAVID GABRIEL, VP of Print & Digital Publishing; SVEN LARSEN, VP of Licensed Publishing; MARK ANNUNZIATO, VP of Planning & Forecasting; JEFF YOUNGQUIST, VP of Production & Special Projects; ALEX MORALES, Director of Publishing Operations; DAN EDINGTON, Director of Editorial Operations; RICKEY PURDIN, Director of Talent Relations; JENNIFER GRÜNWALD, Director of Production & Special Projects; SUSAN CRESPI, Production Manager; STAN LEE, Chairman Emeritus. For information regarding advertising in Marvel Comics or on Marvel.com, please contact Vit DeBellis, Custom Solutions & Integrated Advertising Manager, at vdebellis@marvel.com. For Marvel subscription inquiries, please call 888-511-5480. *Manufactured between 12/9/2022 and 1/10/2023 by SEAWAY PRINTING, GREEN BAY, WI, USA.*

10 9 8 7 6 5 4 3 2 1

AND THERE CAME A DAY, A DAY UNLIKE ANY OTHER, WHEN THE MIGHTIEST AVENGERS OF MANY EARTHS FOUND THEMSELVES UNITED AGAINST A COMMON THREAT — TO FIGHT THE FOES NO SINGLE UNIVERSE COULD WITHSTAND!

AVENGERS FOREVER

THE PILLARS

WRITER
JASON AARON

PENCILERS
JIM TOWE (#6, #10-11) & **AARON KUDER** (#7-9)

INKERS
JIM TOWE (#6, #10-11) & **CAM SMITH** (#7-9)

COLOR ARTISTS
GURU-eFX (#6-10) & **FRANK MARTIN** (#11)

LETTERER
VC's **CORY PETIT**

COVER ART
AARON KUDER & **JASON KEITH** (#6-10) &
AARON KUDER & **ALEX SINCLAIR** (#11)

"THE AVENGING"

WRITER	**ARTIST**
JASON AARON	**KEV WALKER**
COLOR ARTIST	**LETTERER**
DEAN WHITE	VC's **JOE SABINO**

ASSISTANT EDITOR	**ASSOCIATE EDITOR**	**EDITOR**
MARTIN BIRO	**ANNALISE BISSA**	**TOM BREVOORT**

AVENGERS CREATED BY STAN LEE & JACK KIRBY

COLLECTION EDITOR
JENNIFER GRÜNWALD

ASSISTANT EDITOR
DANIEL KIRCHHOFFER

ASSISTANT MANAGING EDITOR
MAIA LOY

ASSOCIATE MANAGER, TALENT RELATIONS
LISA MONTALBANO

VP PRODUCTION & SPECIAL PROJECTS
JEFF YOUNGQUIST

SVP PRINT, SALES & MARKETING
DAVID GABRIEL

BOOK DESIGNERS
ADAM DEL RE WITH **CARLOS LAO**

EDITOR IN CHIEF
C.B. CEBULSKI

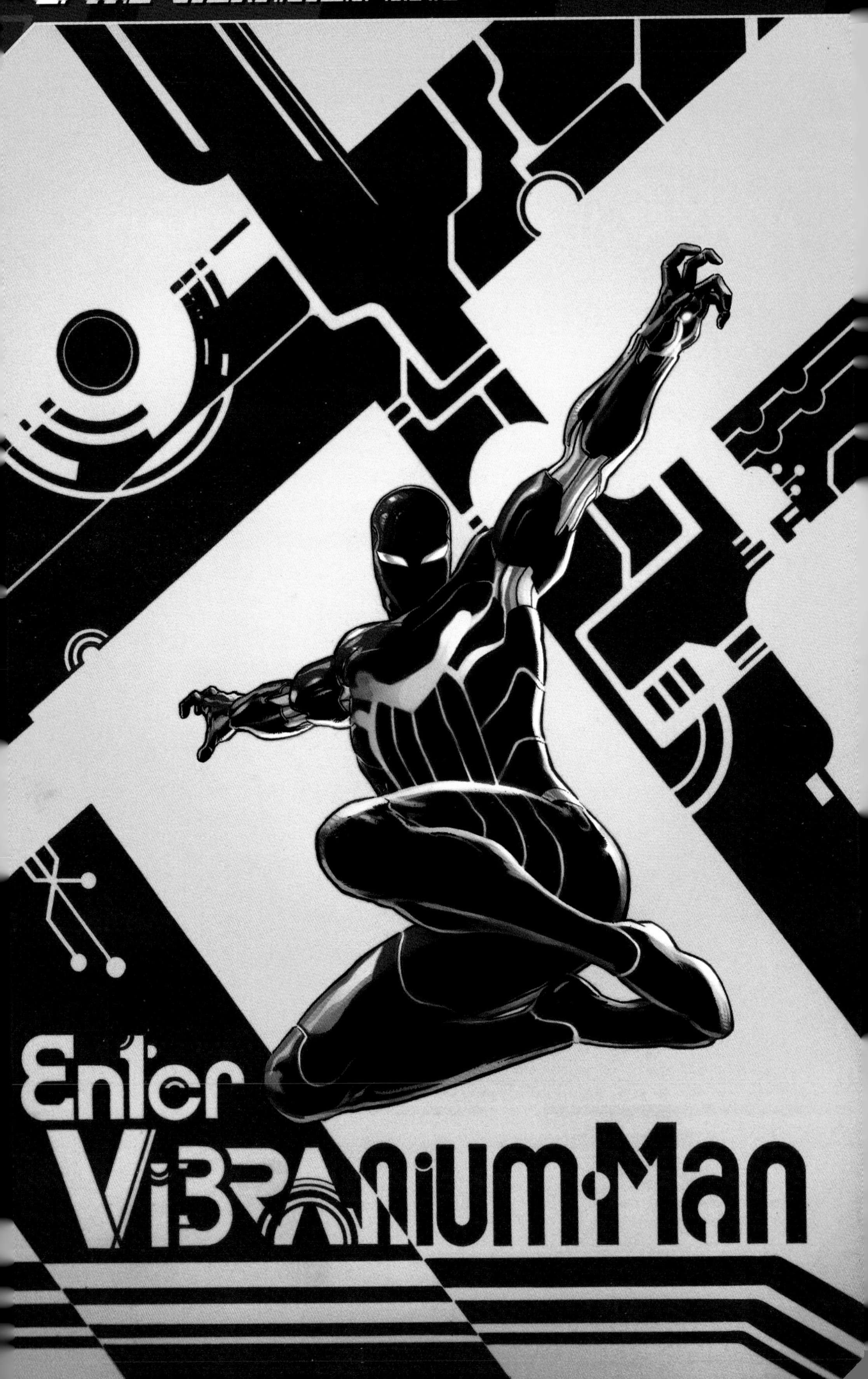
Enter
Vibranium-Man

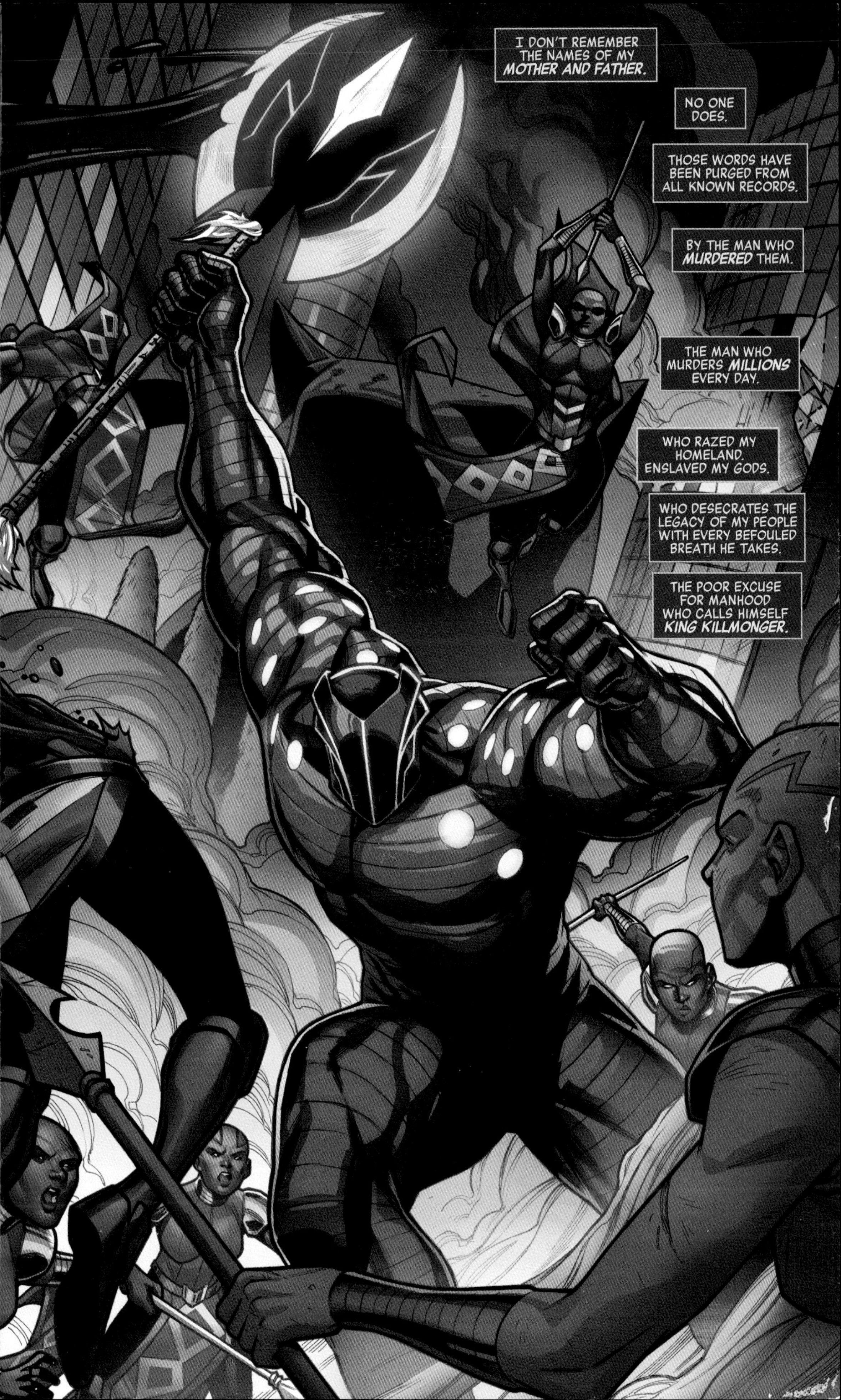
I DON'T REMEMBER THE NAMES OF MY MOTHER AND FATHER.
NO ONE DOES.
THOSE WORDS HAVE BEEN PURGED FROM ALL KNOWN RECORDS.
BY THE MAN WHO MURDERED THEM.
THE MAN WHO MURDERS MILLIONS EVERY DAY.
WHO RAZED MY HOMELAND. ENSLAVED MY GODS.
WHO DESECRATES THE LEGACY OF MY PEOPLE WITH EVERY BEFOULED BREATH HE TAKES.
THE POOR EXCUSE FOR MANHOOD WHO CALLS HIMSELF KING KILLMONGER.

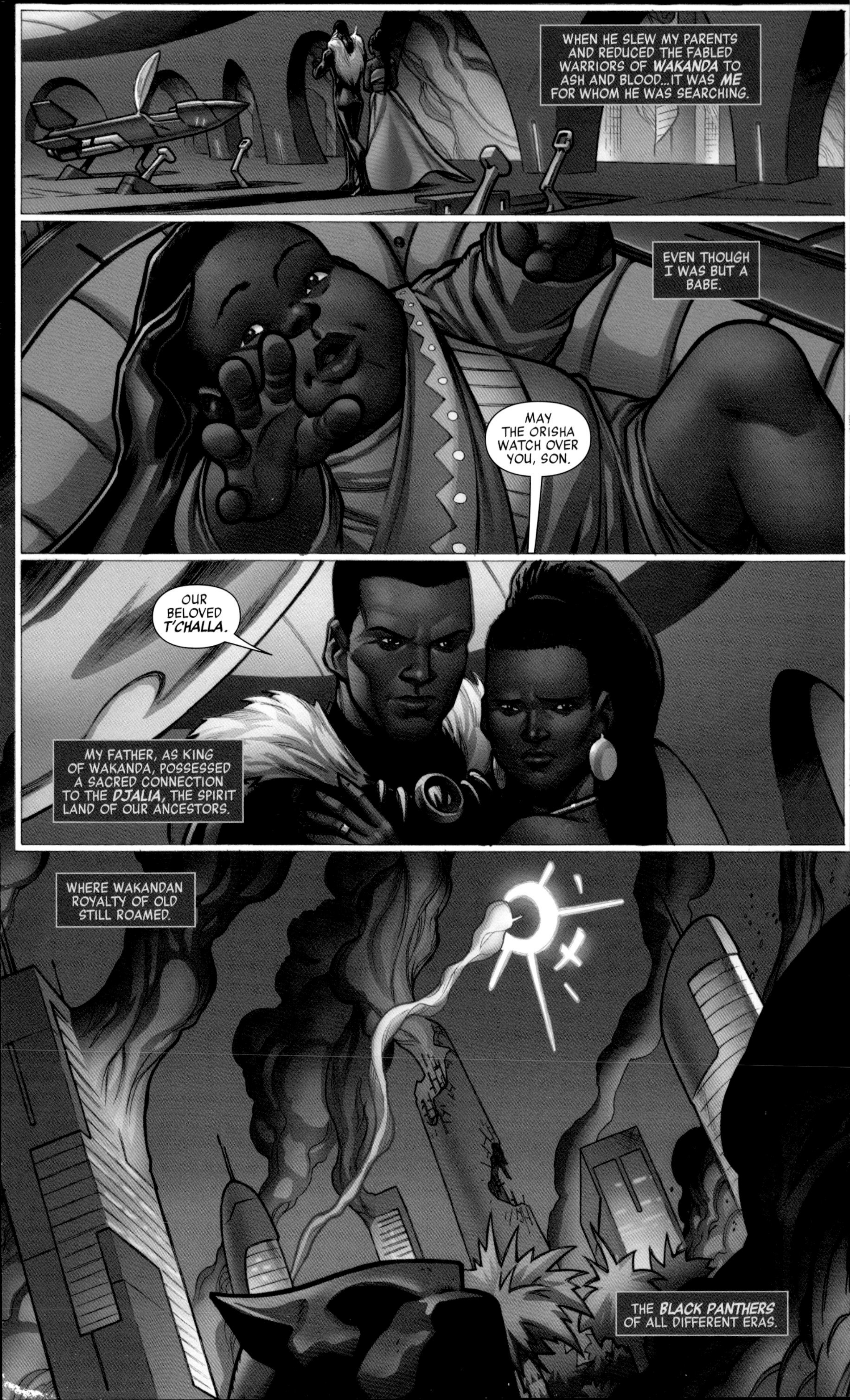

WHEN HE SLEW MY PARENTS AND REDUCED THE FABLED WARRIORS OF **WAKANDA** TO ASH AND BLOOD...IT WAS **ME** FOR WHOM HE WAS SEARCHING.
EVEN THOUGH I WAS BUT A BABE.
MAY THE ORISHA WATCH OVER YOU, SON.
OUR BELOVED **T'CHALLA.**
MY FATHER, AS KING OF WAKANDA, POSSESSED A SACRED CONNECTION TO THE **DJALIA,** THE SPIRIT LAND OF OUR ANCESTORS.
WHERE WAKANDAN ROYALTY OF OLD STILL ROAMED.
THE **BLACK PANTHERS** OF ALL DIFFERENT ERAS.

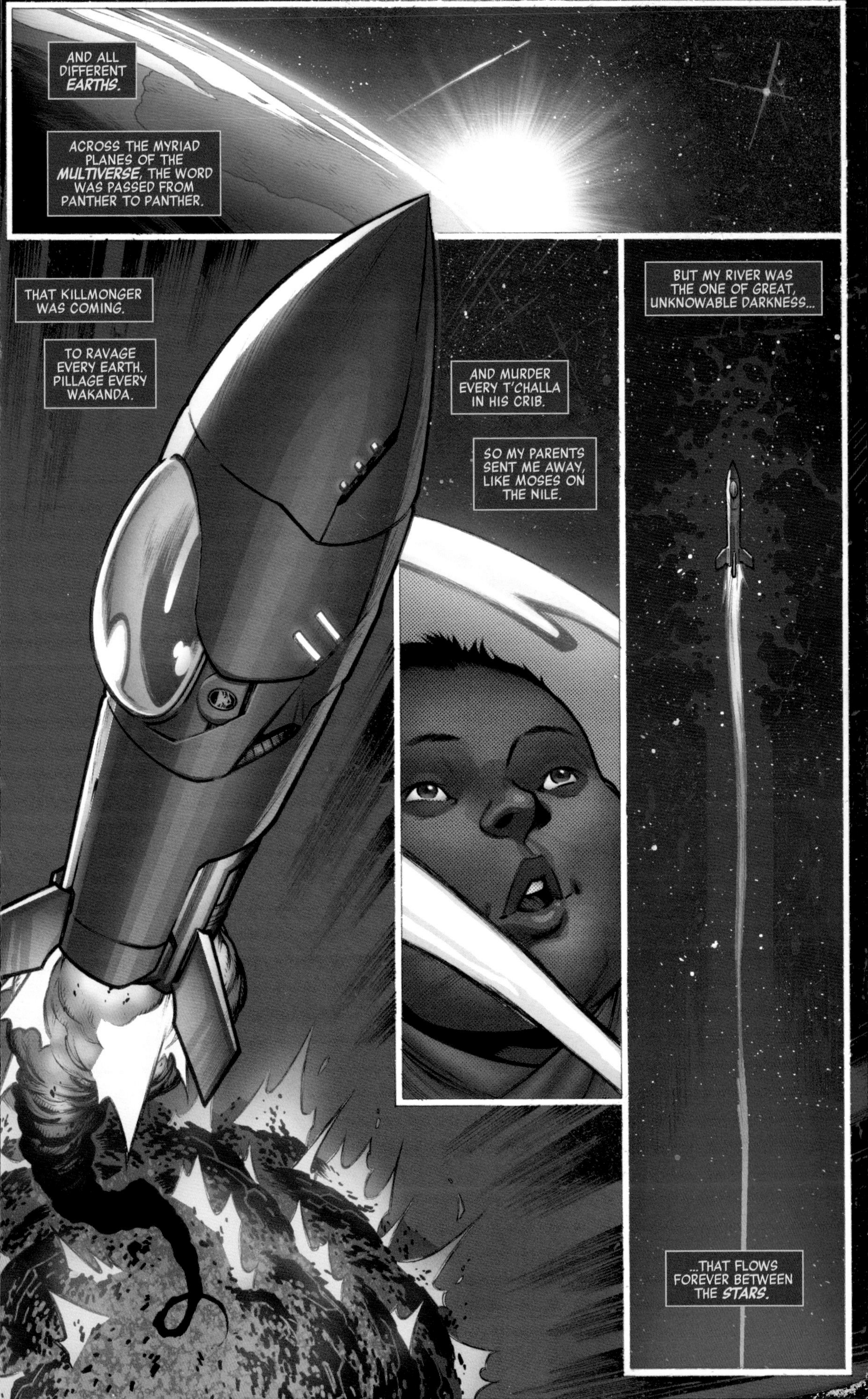
AND ALL DIFFERENT *EARTHS*.
ACROSS THE MYRIAD PLANES OF THE *MULTIVERSE*, THE WORD WAS PASSED FROM PANTHER TO PANTHER.
THAT KILLMONGER WAS COMING.
TO RAVAGE EVERY EARTH. PILLAGE EVERY WAKANDA.
AND MURDER EVERY T'CHALLA IN HIS CRIB.
SO MY PARENTS SENT ME AWAY, LIKE MOSES ON THE NILE.
BUT MY RIVER WAS THE ONE OF GREAT, UNKNOWABLE DARKNESS...
...THAT FLOWS FOREVER BETWEEN THE *STARS*.

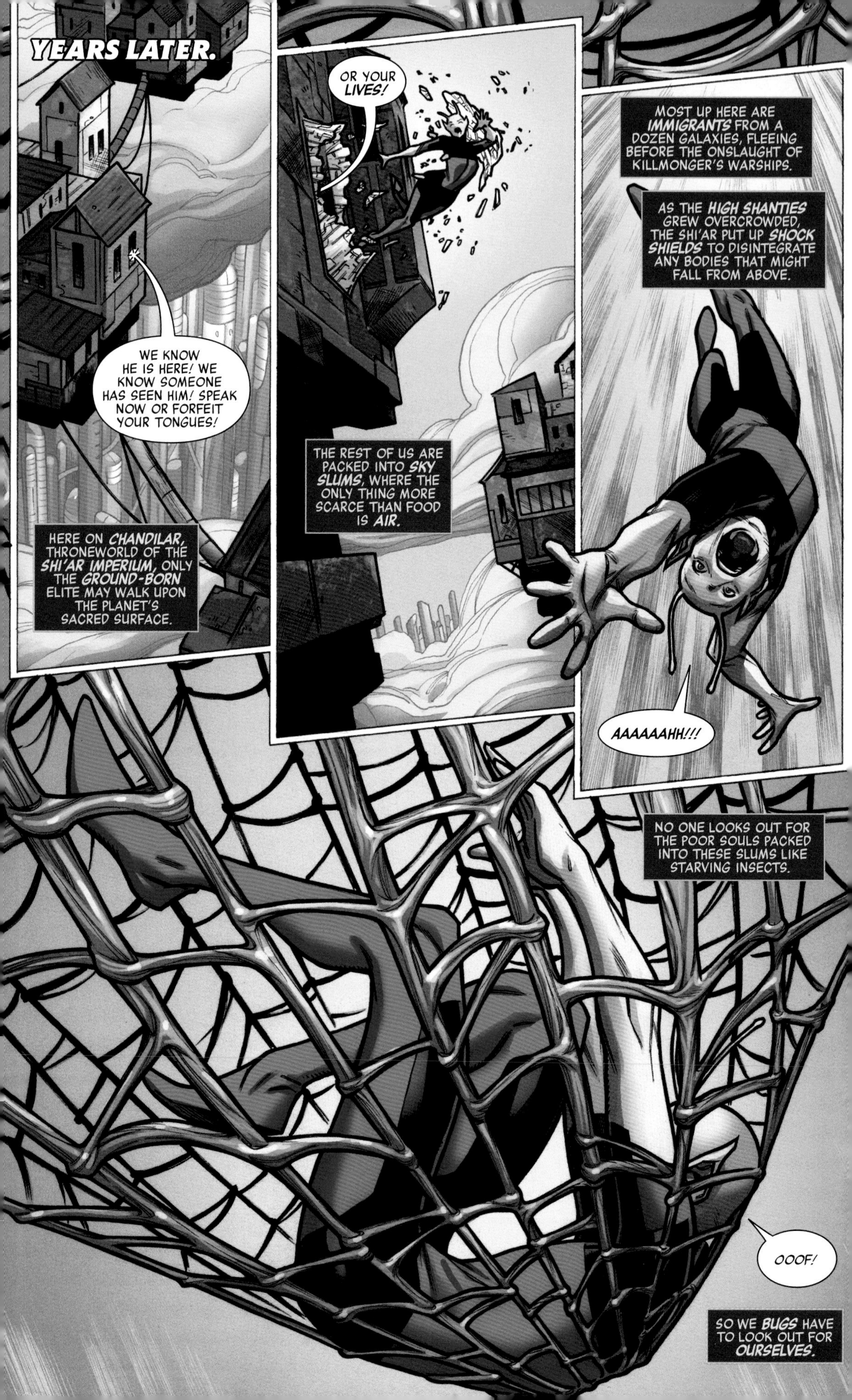
YEARS LATER.
WE KNOW HE IS HERE! WE KNOW SOMEONE HAS SEEN HIM! SPEAK NOW OR FORFEIT YOUR TONGUES!
HERE ON CHANDILAR, THRONEWORLD OF THE SHI'AR IMPERIUM, ONLY THE GROUND-BORN ELITE MAY WALK UPON THE PLANET'S SACRED SURFACE.
OR YOUR LIVES!
THE REST OF US ARE PACKED INTO SKY SLUMS, WHERE THE ONLY THING MORE SCARCE THAN FOOD IS AIR.
MOST UP HERE ARE IMMIGRANTS FROM A DOZEN GALAXIES, FLEEING BEFORE THE ONSLAUGHT OF KILLMONGER'S WARSHIPS.
AS THE HIGH SHANTIES GREW OVERCROWDED, THE SHI'AR PUT UP SHOCK SHIELDS TO DISINTEGRATE ANY BODIES THAT MIGHT FALL FROM ABOVE.
AAAAAAHH!!!
NO ONE LOOKS OUT FOR THE POOR SOULS PACKED INTO THESE SLUMS LIKE STARVING INSECTS.
OOOF!
SO WE BUGS HAVE TO LOOK OUT FOR OURSELVES.

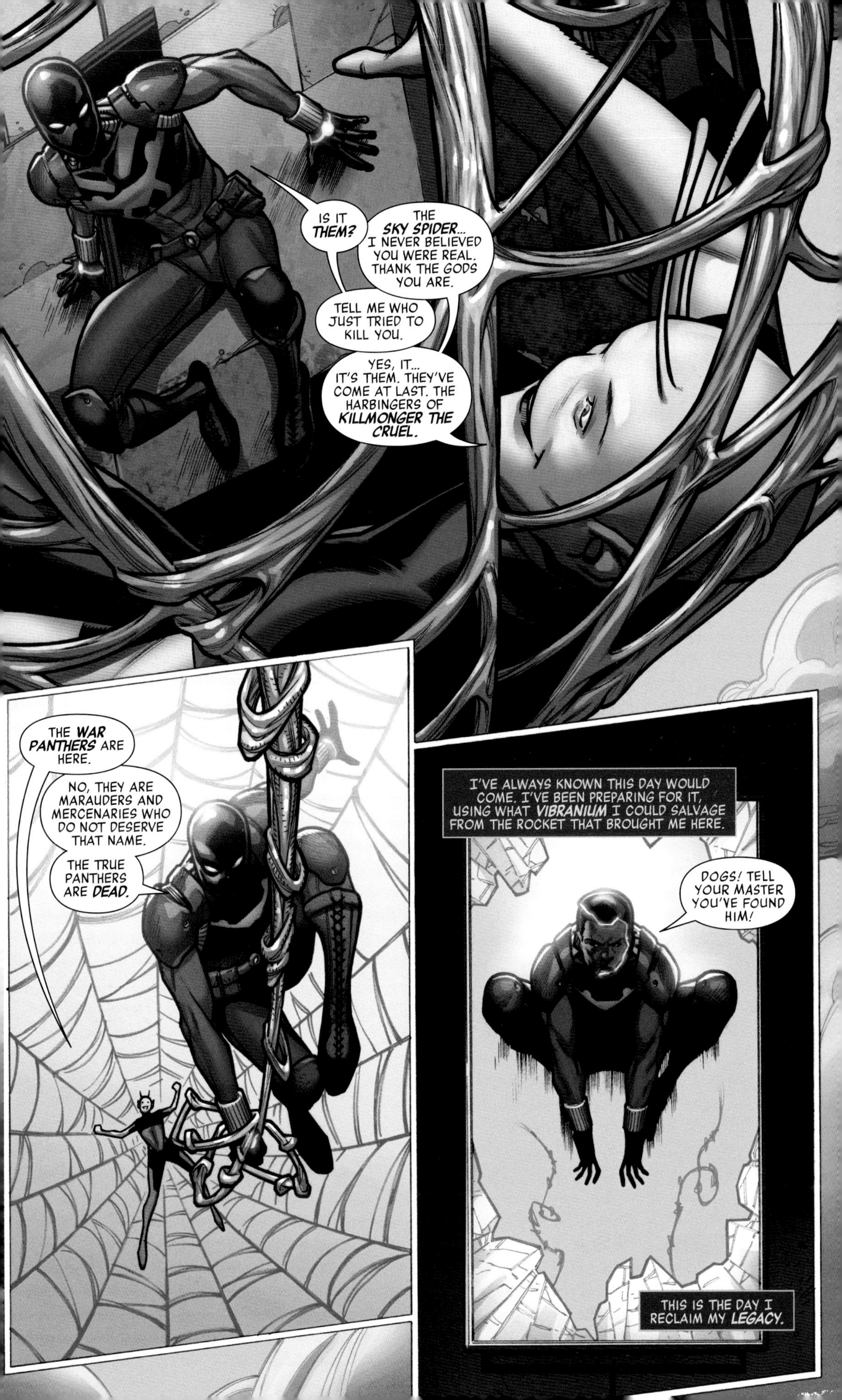

IS IT THEM?
THE SKY SPIDER... I NEVER BELIEVED YOU WERE REAL. THANK THE GODS YOU ARE.
TELL ME WHO JUST TRIED TO KILL YOU.
YES, IT... IT'S THEM. THEY'VE COME AT LAST. THE HARBINGERS OF KILLMONGER THE CRUEL.
THE WAR PANTHERS ARE HERE.
NO, THEY ARE MARAUDERS AND MERCENARIES WHO DO NOT DESERVE THAT NAME.
THE TRUE PANTHERS ARE DEAD.
I'VE ALWAYS KNOWN THIS DAY WOULD COME. I'VE BEEN PREPARING FOR IT, USING WHAT VIBRANIUM I COULD SALVAGE FROM THE ROCKET THAT BROUGHT ME HERE.
DOGS! TELL YOUR MASTER YOU'VE FOUND HIM!
THIS IS THE DAY I RECLAIM MY LEGACY.

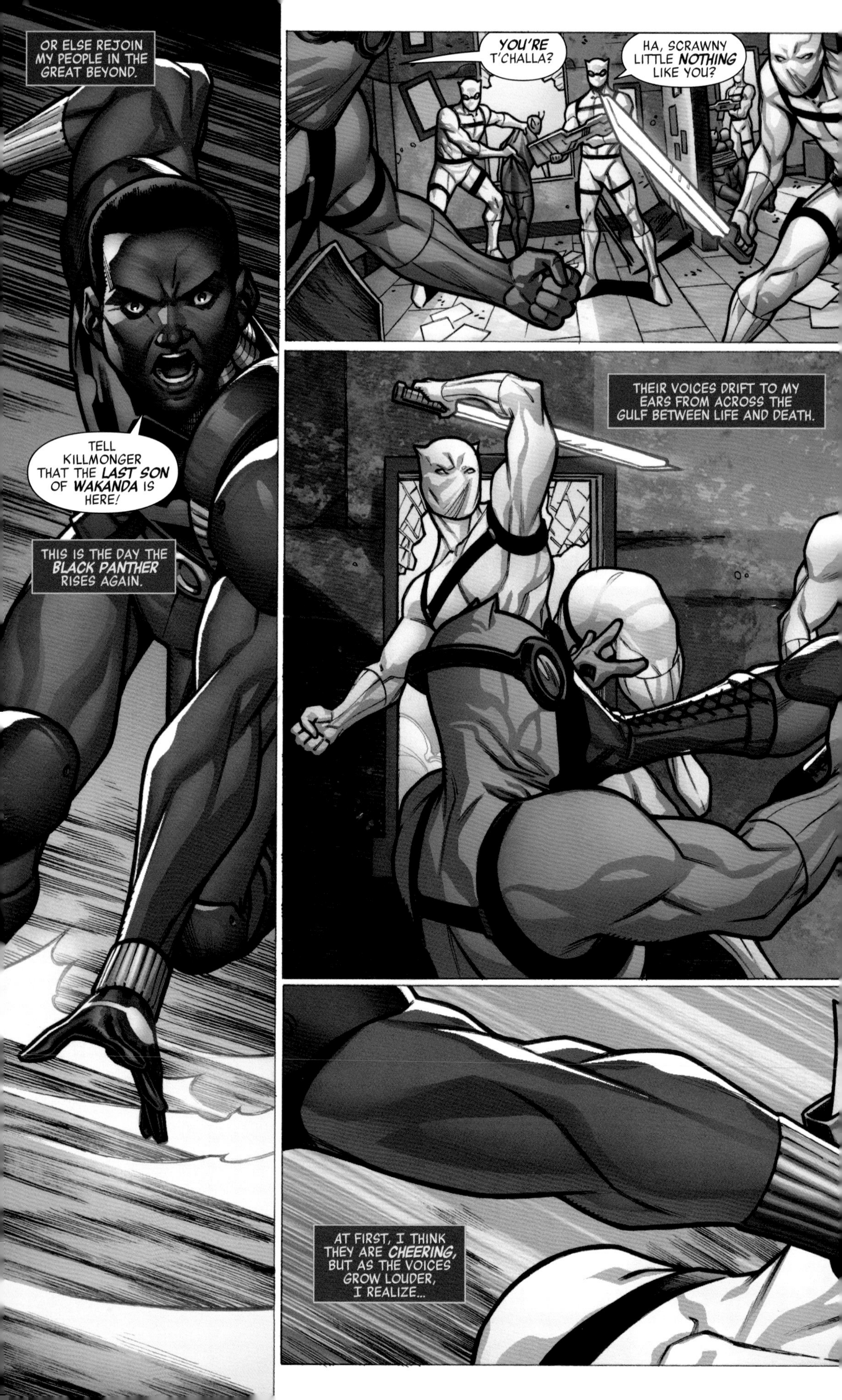
OR ELSE REJOIN MY PEOPLE IN THE GREAT BEYOND.
TELL KILLMONGER THAT THE LAST SON OF WAKANDA IS HERE!
THIS IS THE DAY THE BLACK PANTHER RISES AGAIN.
YOU'RE T'CHALLA?
HA, SCRAWNY LITTLE NOTHING LIKE YOU?
THEIR VOICES DRIFT TO MY EARS FROM ACROSS THE GULF BETWEEN LIFE AND DEATH.
AT FIRST, I THINK THEY ARE CHEERING, BUT AS THE VOICES GROW LOUDER, I REALIZE...

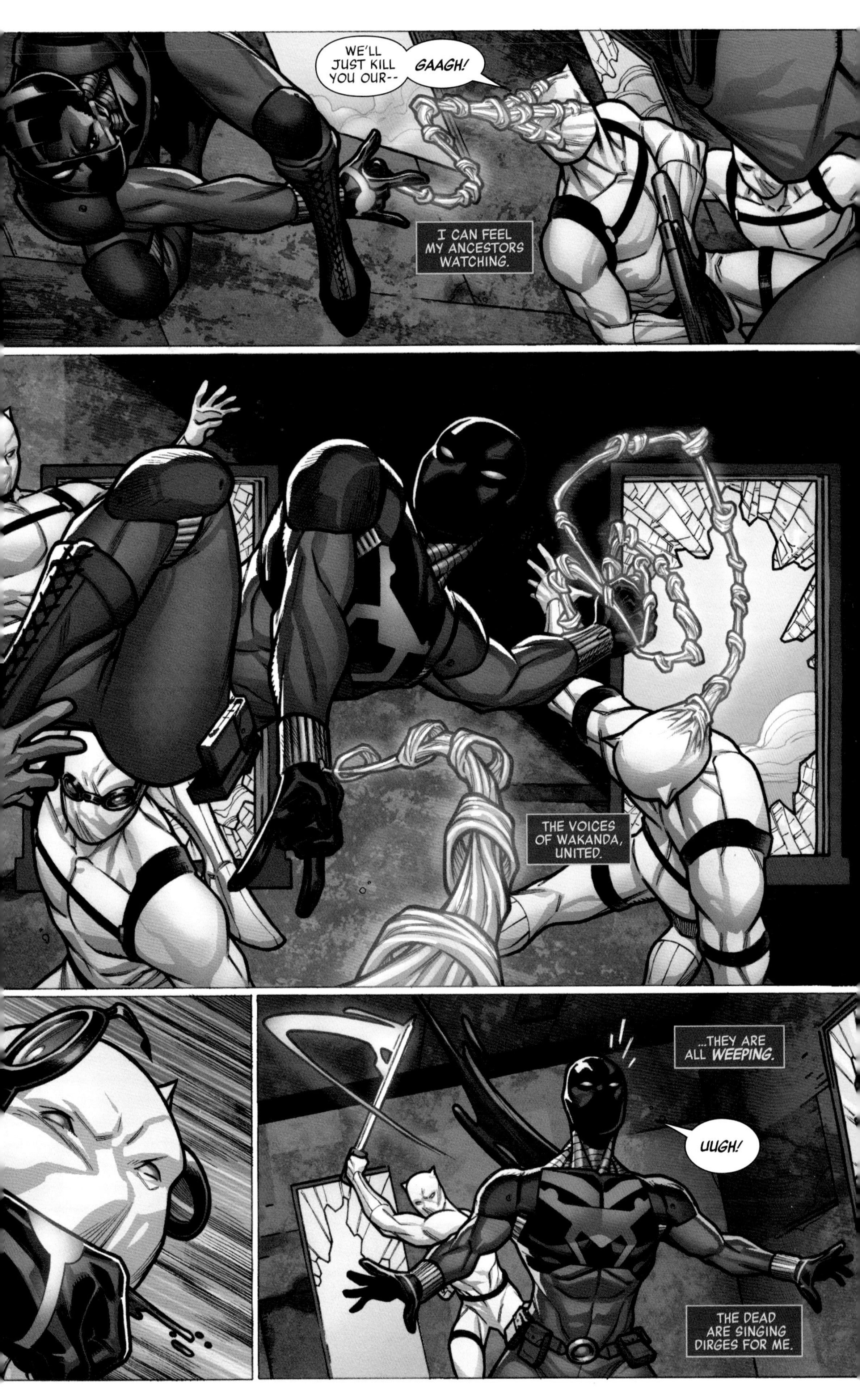

WE'LL JUST KILL YOU OUR--
GAAGH!
I CAN FEEL MY ANCESTORS WATCHING.
THE VOICES OF WAKANDA, UNITED.
...THEY ARE ALL WEEPING.
UUGH!
THE DEAD ARE SINGING DIRGES FOR ME.

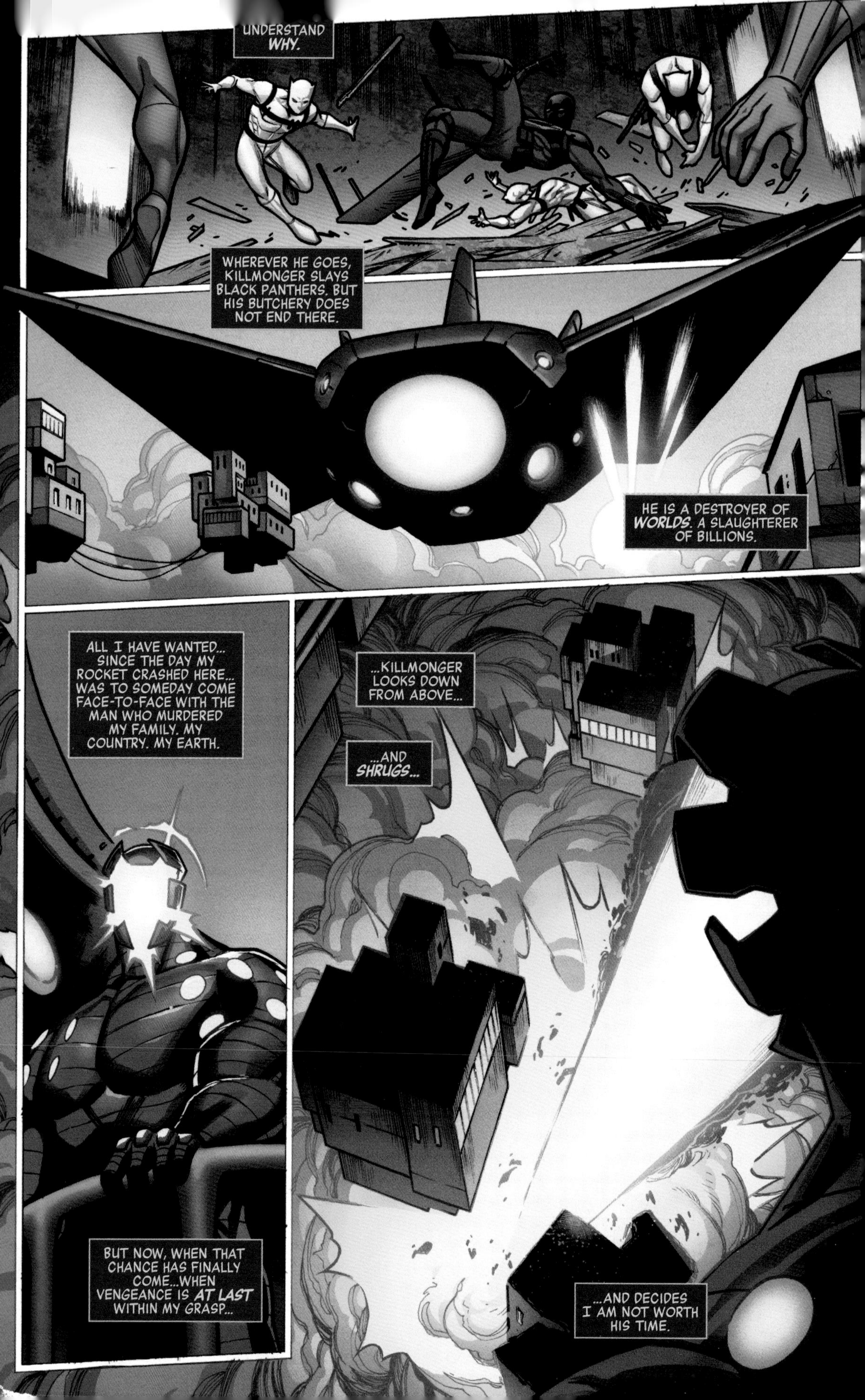
UNDERSTAND WHY.
WHEREVER HE GOES, KILLMONGER SLAYS BLACK PANTHERS. BUT HIS BUTCHERY DOES NOT END THERE.
HE IS A DESTROYER OF WORLDS. A SLAUGHTERER OF BILLIONS.
ALL I HAVE WANTED... SINCE THE DAY MY ROCKET CRASHED HERE... WAS TO SOMEDAY COME FACE-TO-FACE WITH THE MAN WHO MURDERED MY FAMILY. MY COUNTRY. MY EARTH.
BUT NOW, WHEN THAT CHANCE HAS FINALLY COME...WHEN VENGEANCE IS AT LAST WITHIN MY GRASP...
...KILLMONGER LOOKS DOWN FROM ABOVE...
...AND SHRUGS...
...AND DECIDES I AM NOT WORTH HIS TIME.

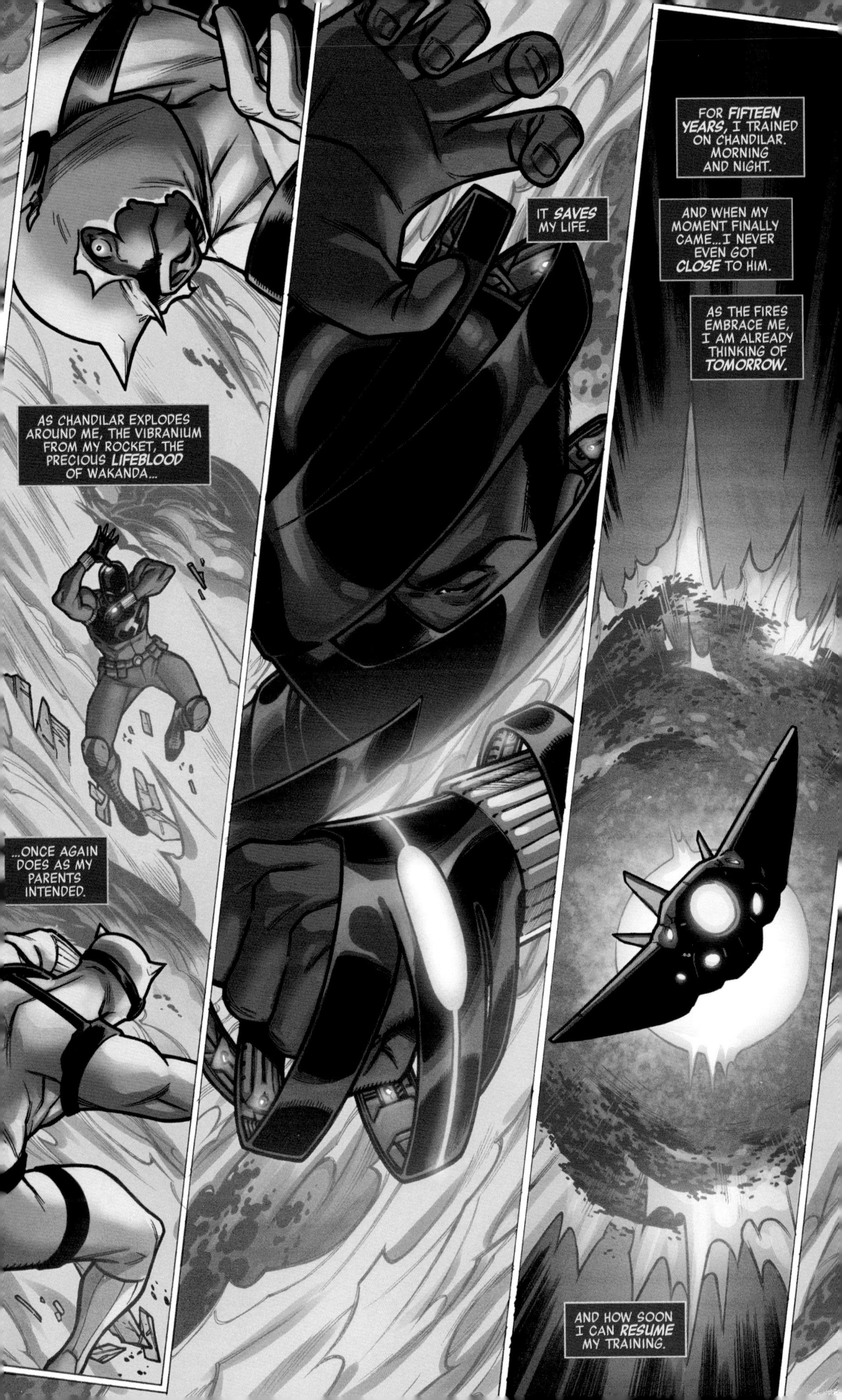
AS CHANDILAR EXPLODES AROUND ME, THE VIBRANIUM FROM MY ROCKET, THE PRECIOUS LIFEBLOOD OF WAKANDA...
...ONCE AGAIN DOES AS MY PARENTS INTENDED.
IT SAVES MY LIFE.
FOR FIFTEEN YEARS, I TRAINED ON CHANDILAR. MORNING AND NIGHT.
AND WHEN MY MOMENT FINALLY CAME...I NEVER EVEN GOT CLOSE TO HIM.
AS THE FIRES EMBRACE ME, I AM ALREADY THINKING OF TOMORROW.
AND HOW SOON I CAN RESUME MY TRAINING.

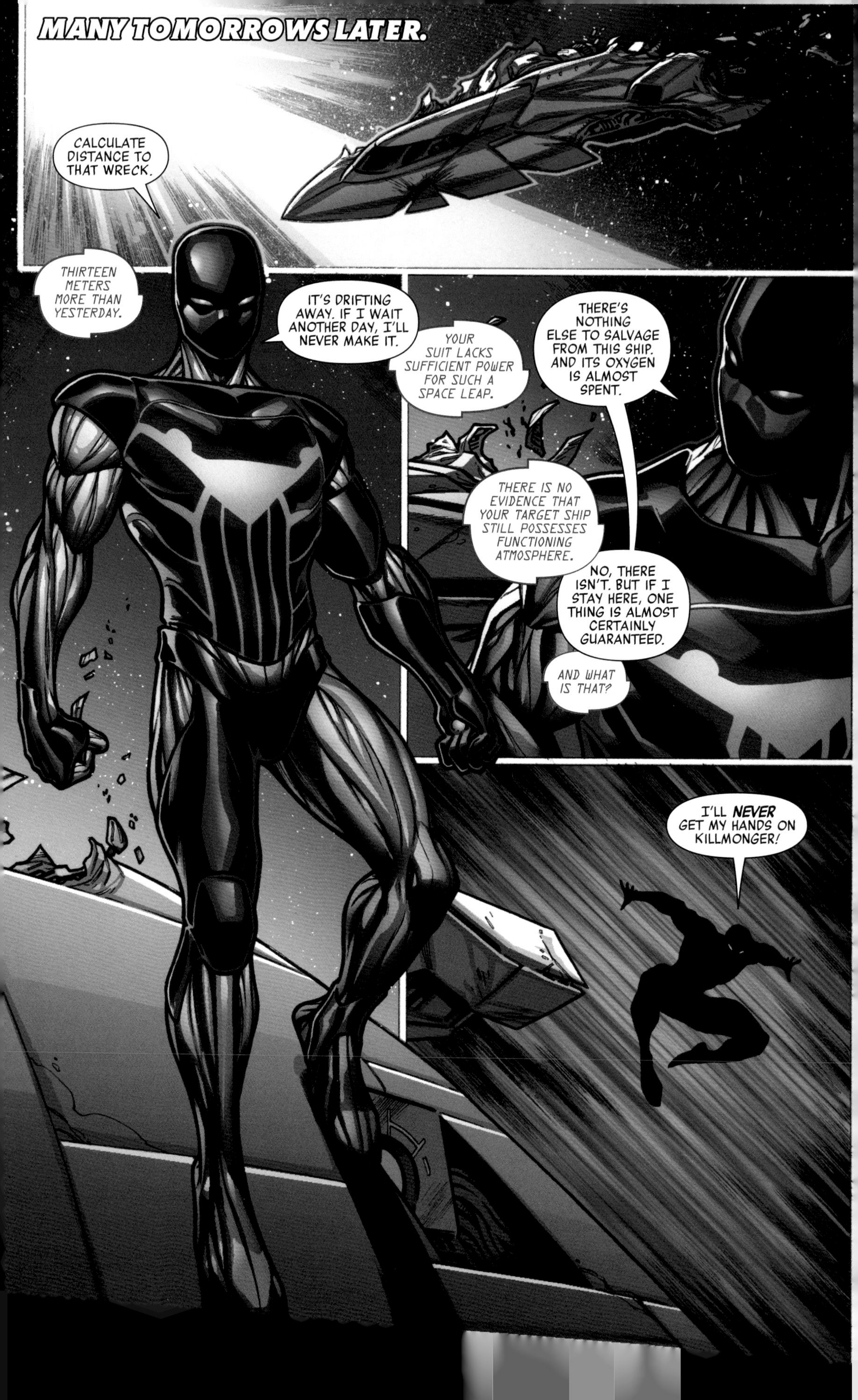
MANY TOMORROWS LATER.
CALCULATE DISTANCE TO THAT WRECK.
THIRTEEN METERS MORE THAN YESTERDAY.
IT'S DRIFTING AWAY. IF I WAIT ANOTHER DAY, I'LL NEVER MAKE IT.
YOUR SUIT LACKS SUFFICIENT POWER FOR SUCH A SPACE LEAP.
THERE'S NOTHING ELSE TO SALVAGE FROM THIS SHIP. AND ITS OXYGEN IS ALMOST SPENT.
THERE IS NO EVIDENCE THAT YOUR TARGET SHIP STILL POSSESSES FUNCTIONING ATMOSPHERE.
NO, THERE ISN'T. BUT IF I STAY HERE, ONE THING IS ALMOST CERTAINLY GUARANTEED.
AND WHAT IS THAT?
I'LL NEVER GET MY HANDS ON KILLMONGER!

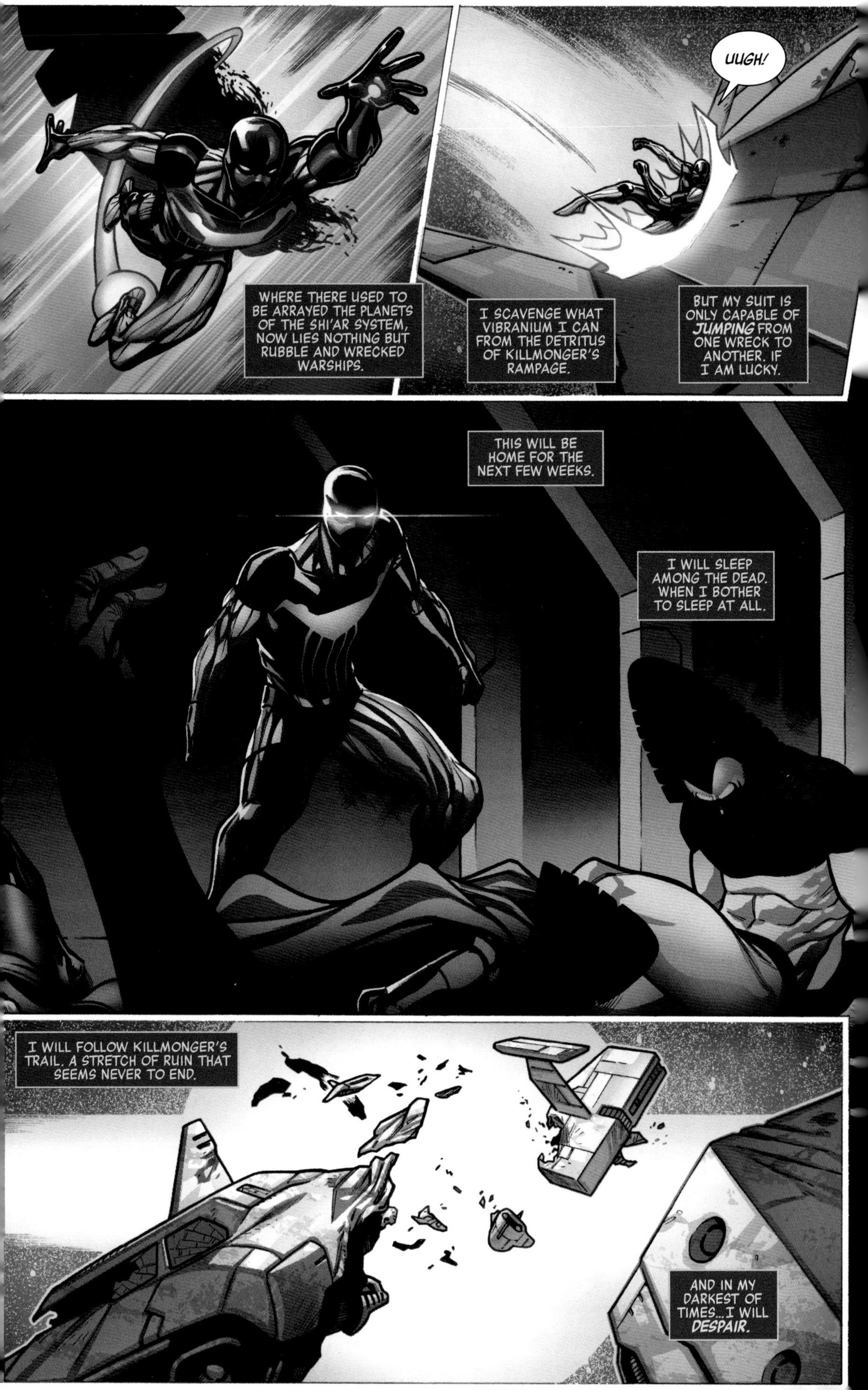
WHERE THERE USED TO BE ARRAYED THE PLANETS OF THE SHI'AR SYSTEM, NOW LIES NOTHING BUT RUBBLE AND WRECKED WARSHIPS.
UUGH!
I SCAVENGE WHAT VIBRANIUM I CAN FROM THE DETRITUS OF KILLMONGER'S RAMPAGE.
BUT MY SUIT IS ONLY CAPABLE OF JUMPING FROM ONE WRECK TO ANOTHER. IF I AM LUCKY.
THIS WILL BE HOME FOR THE NEXT FEW WEEKS.
I WILL SLEEP AMONG THE DEAD. WHEN I BOTHER TO SLEEP AT ALL.
I WILL FOLLOW KILLMONGER'S TRAIL. A STRETCH OF RUIN THAT SEEMS NEVER TO END.
AND IN MY DARKEST OF TIMES...I WILL DESPAIR.

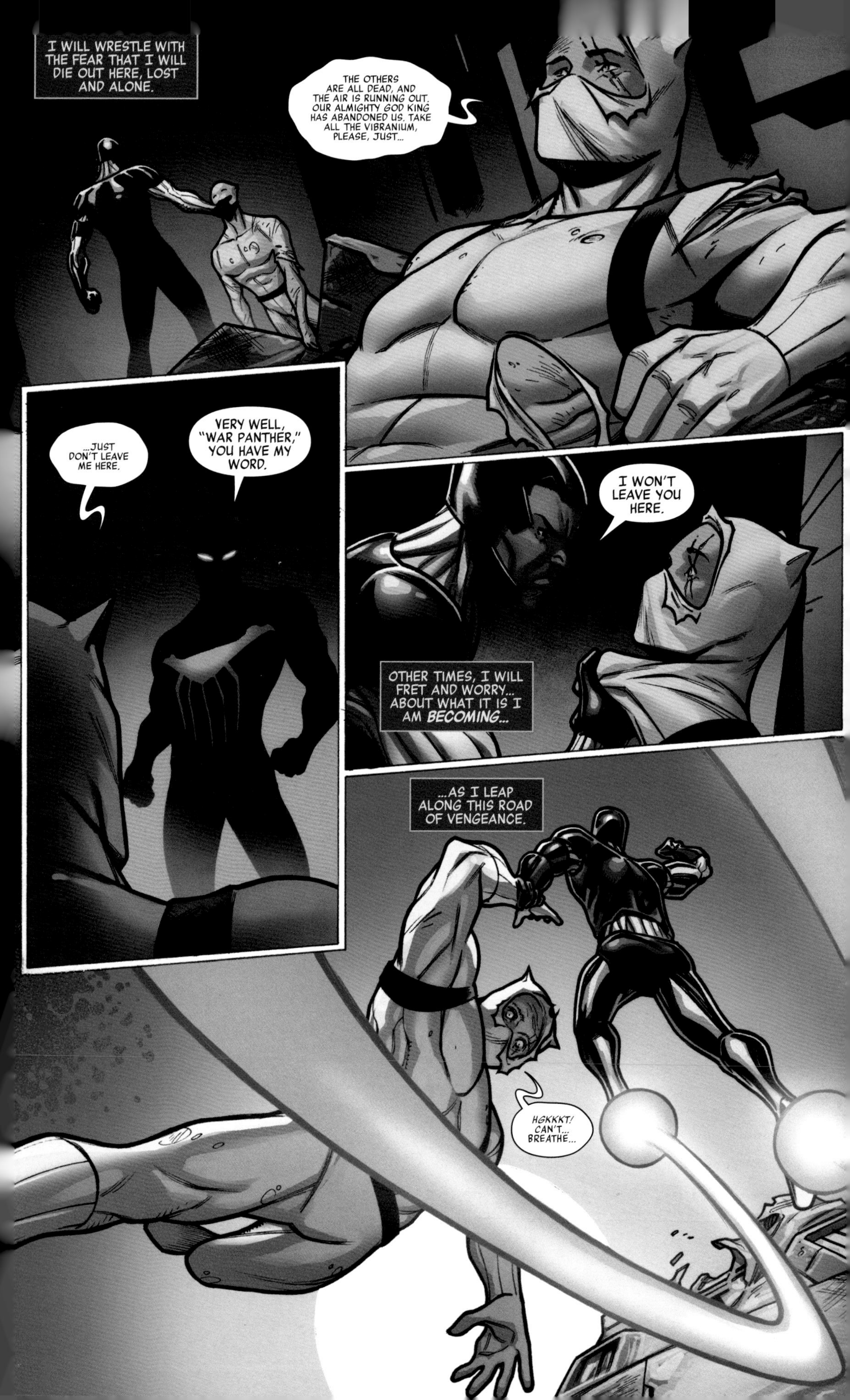
I WILL WRESTLE WITH THE FEAR THAT I WILL DIE OUT HERE, LOST AND ALONE.
THE OTHERS ARE ALL DEAD, AND THE AIR IS RUNNING OUT. OUR ALMIGHTY GOD KING HAS ABANDONED US. TAKE ALL THE VIBRANIUM, PLEASE, JUST...
...JUST DON'T LEAVE ME HERE.
VERY WELL, "WAR PANTHER," YOU HAVE MY WORD.
I WON'T LEAVE YOU HERE.
OTHER TIMES, I WILL FRET AND WORRY... ABOUT WHAT IT IS I AM BECOMING...
...AS I LEAP ALONG THIS ROAD OF VENGEANCE.
HGKKKT! CAN'T... BREATHE...

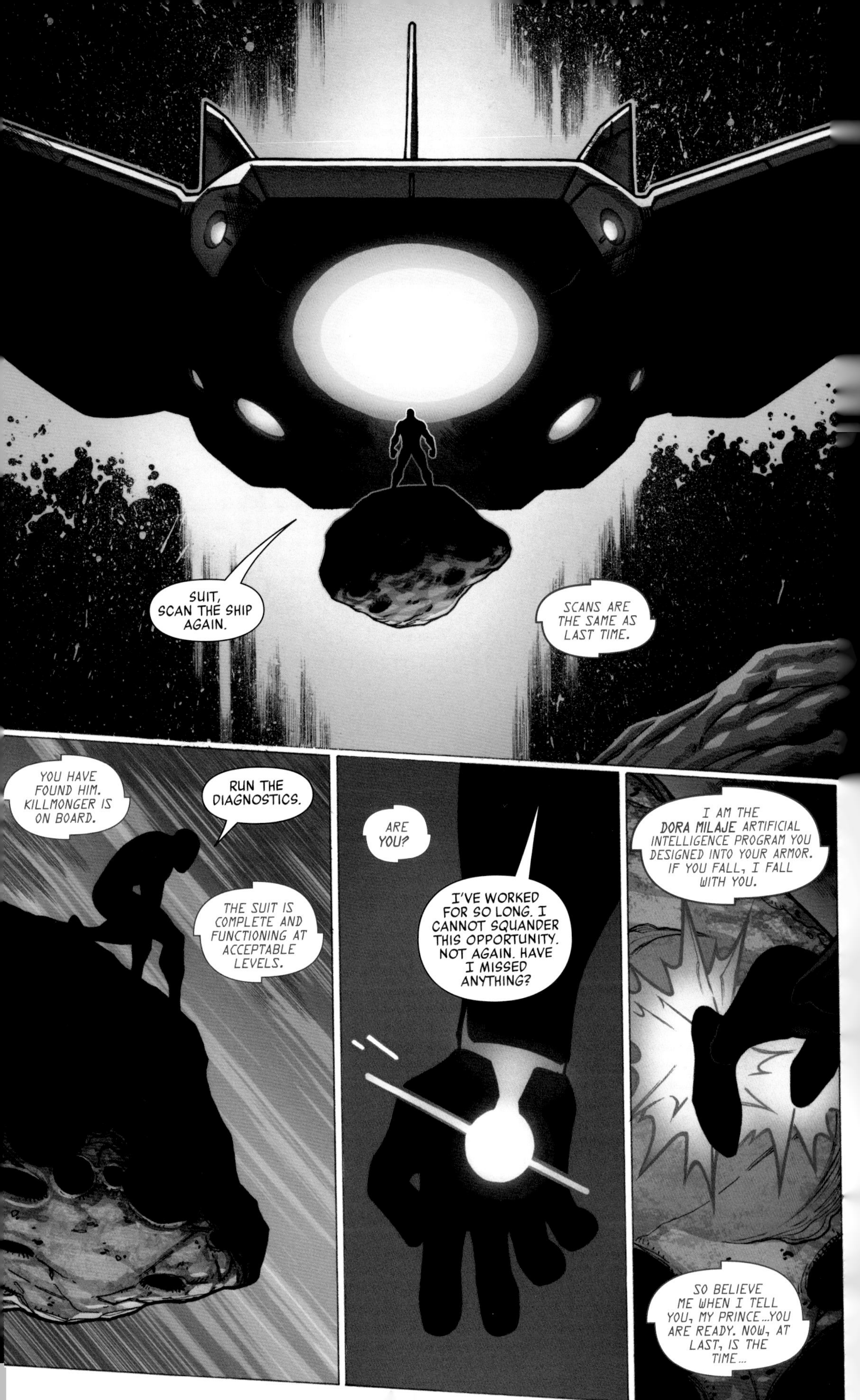
SUIT, SCAN THE SHIP AGAIN.
SCANS ARE THE SAME AS LAST TIME.
YOU HAVE FOUND HIM. KILLMONGER IS ON BOARD.
RUN THE DIAGNOSTICS.
THE SUIT IS COMPLETE AND FUNCTIONING AT ACCEPTABLE LEVELS.
ARE YOU?
I'VE WORKED FOR SO LONG. I CANNOT SQUANDER THIS OPPORTUNITY. NOT AGAIN. HAVE I MISSED ANYTHING?
I AM THE DORA MILAJE ARTIFICIAL INTELLIGENCE PROGRAM YOU DESIGNED INTO YOUR ARMOR. IF YOU FALL, I FALL WITH YOU.
SO BELIEVE ME WHEN I TELL YOU, MY PRINCE...YOU ARE READY. NOW, AT LAST, IS THE TIME...

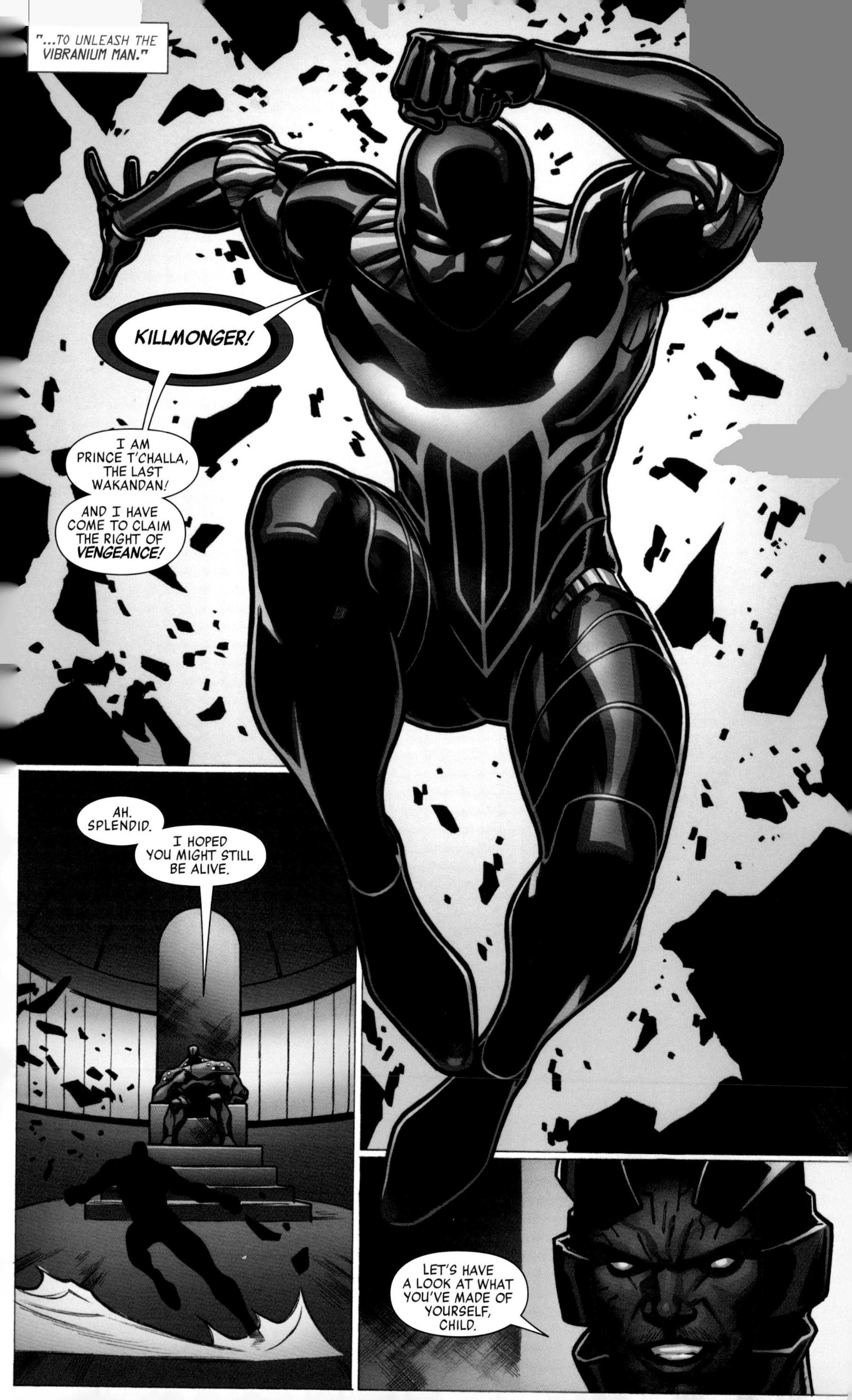
"...TO UNLEASH THE VIBRANIUM MAN."
KILLMONGER!
I AM PRINCE T'CHALLA, THE LAST WAKANDAN!
AND I HAVE COME TO CLAIM THE RIGHT OF VENGEANCE!
AH. SPLENDID.
I HOPED YOU MIGHT STILL BE ALIVE.
LET'S HAVE A LOOK AT WHAT YOU'VE MADE OF YOURSELF, CHILD.

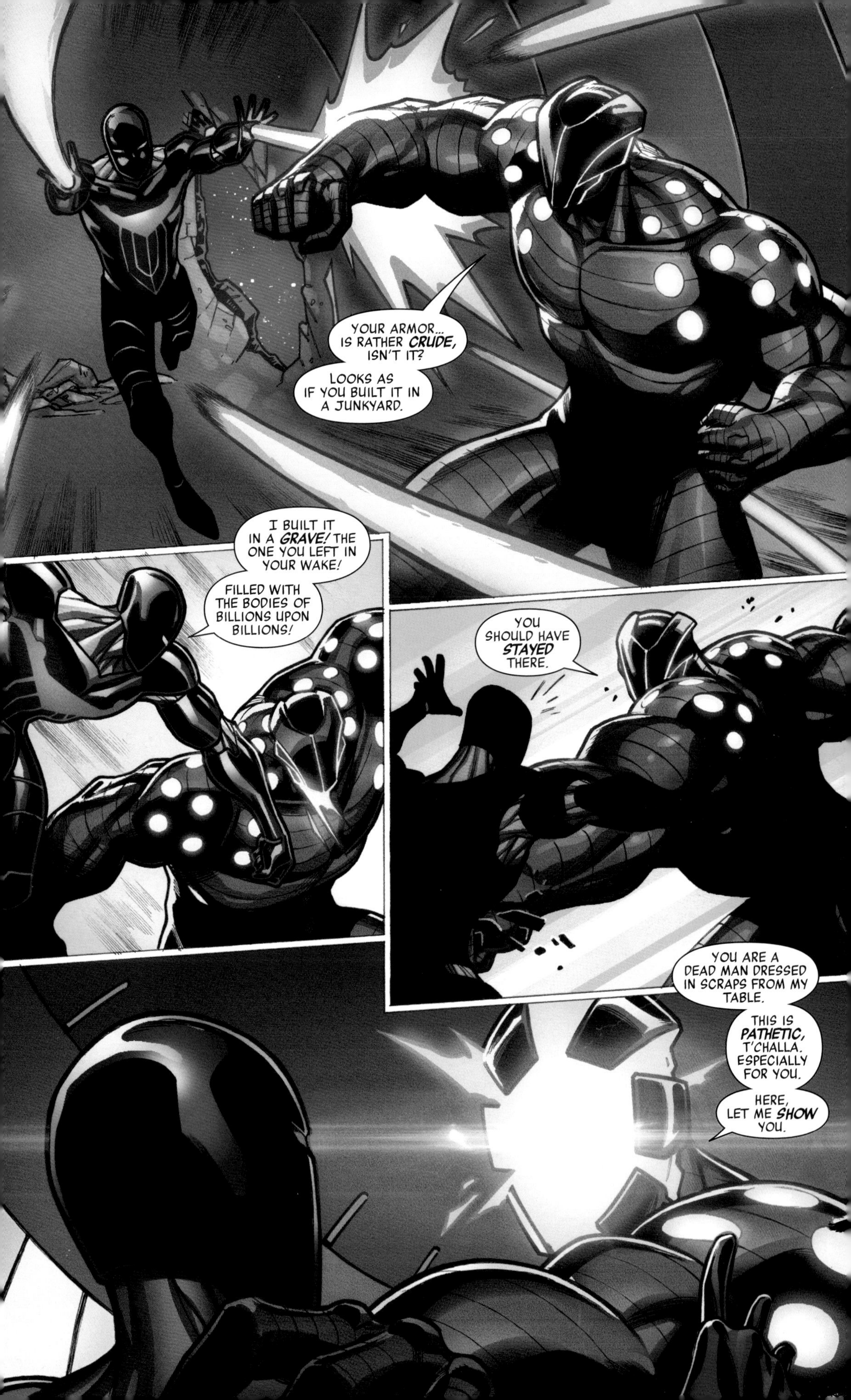
YOUR ARMOR... IS RATHER CRUDE, ISN'T IT?
LOOKS AS IF YOU BUILT IT IN A JUNKYARD.
I BUILT IT IN A GRAVE! THE ONE YOU LEFT IN YOUR WAKE!
FILLED WITH THE BODIES OF BILLIONS UPON BILLIONS!
YOU SHOULD HAVE STAYED THERE.
YOU ARE A DEAD MAN DRESSED IN SCRAPS FROM MY TABLE.
THIS IS PATHETIC, T'CHALLA. ESPECIALLY FOR YOU.
HERE, LET ME SHOW YOU.

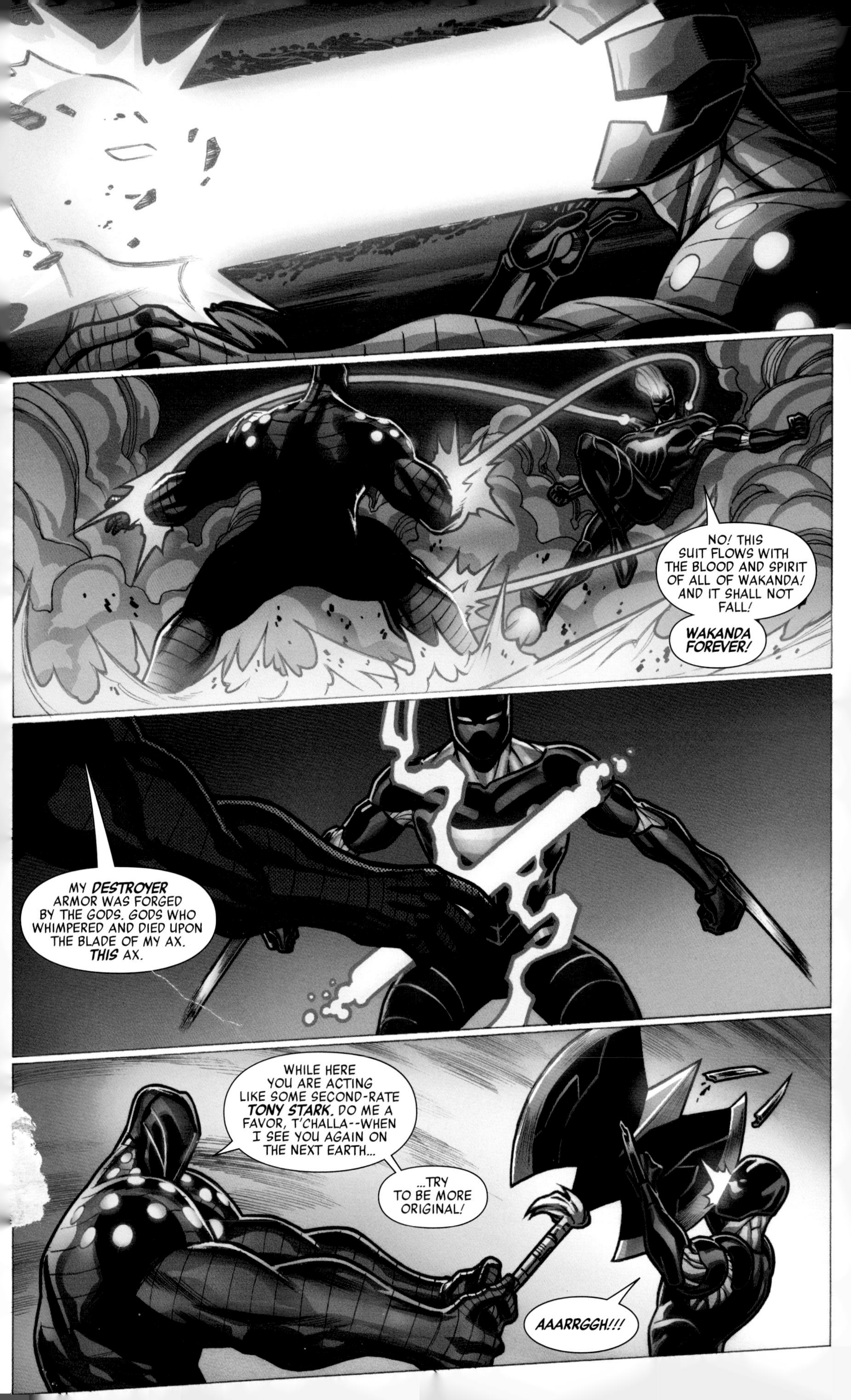
NO! THIS SUIT FLOWS WITH THE BLOOD AND SPIRIT OF ALL OF WAKANDA! AND IT SHALL NOT FALL!
WAKANDA FOREVER!
MY DESTROYER ARMOR WAS FORGED BY THE GODS. GODS WHO WHIMPERED AND DIED UPON THE BLADE OF MY AX. THIS AX.
WHILE HERE YOU ARE ACTING LIKE SOME SECOND-RATE TONY STARK. DO ME A FAVOR, T'CHALLA--WHEN I SEE YOU AGAIN ON THE NEXT EARTH...
...TRY TO BE MORE ORIGINAL!
AAARRGGH!!!

HHHRRGGH!

WAKANDA...

...NEVERMORE!

NO!!!

I HEAR THE DEAD AGAIN. I HEAR THEIR DIRGES.

GAAGGH!

IT IS TIME, THEY SAY. MY VOICE IS MEANT TO JOIN WITH THEIRS.

AAAARRRGH!

BUT I DO MY DAMNDEST....

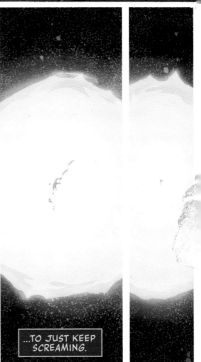

...TO JUST KEEP SCREAMING.

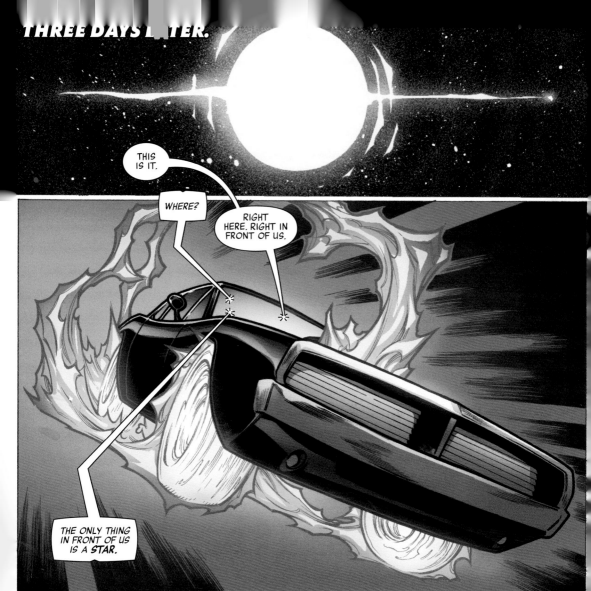

THIS IS IT.

WHERE?

RIGHT HERE. RIGHT IN FRONT OF US.

THE ONLY THING IN FRONT OF US IS A *STAR.*

THIS IS THE EXACT RIGHT SPOT, I'M TELLING YOU.

YOU'RE SAYING HE'S *INSIDE* A STAR? THEN HE'S *DEAD,* LET'S GO.

LOOK, I DON'T KNOW WHAT THE TONY STARKS ARE LIKE WHERE YOU COME FROM, *DEATHLOK,* BUT THIS ONE HERE IS PRETTY MUCH THE SMARTEST DUDE EVER, AND HE'S TELLING YOU...

...THE TRAIL OF T'CHALLA'S ENERGY SIGNATURE LEADS RIGHT HERE!

AND THE SIGNAL IS STILL ACTIVE!

YOU'RE READING IT WRONG.

I *BUILT* IT!

ONE WAY TO FIND OUT.

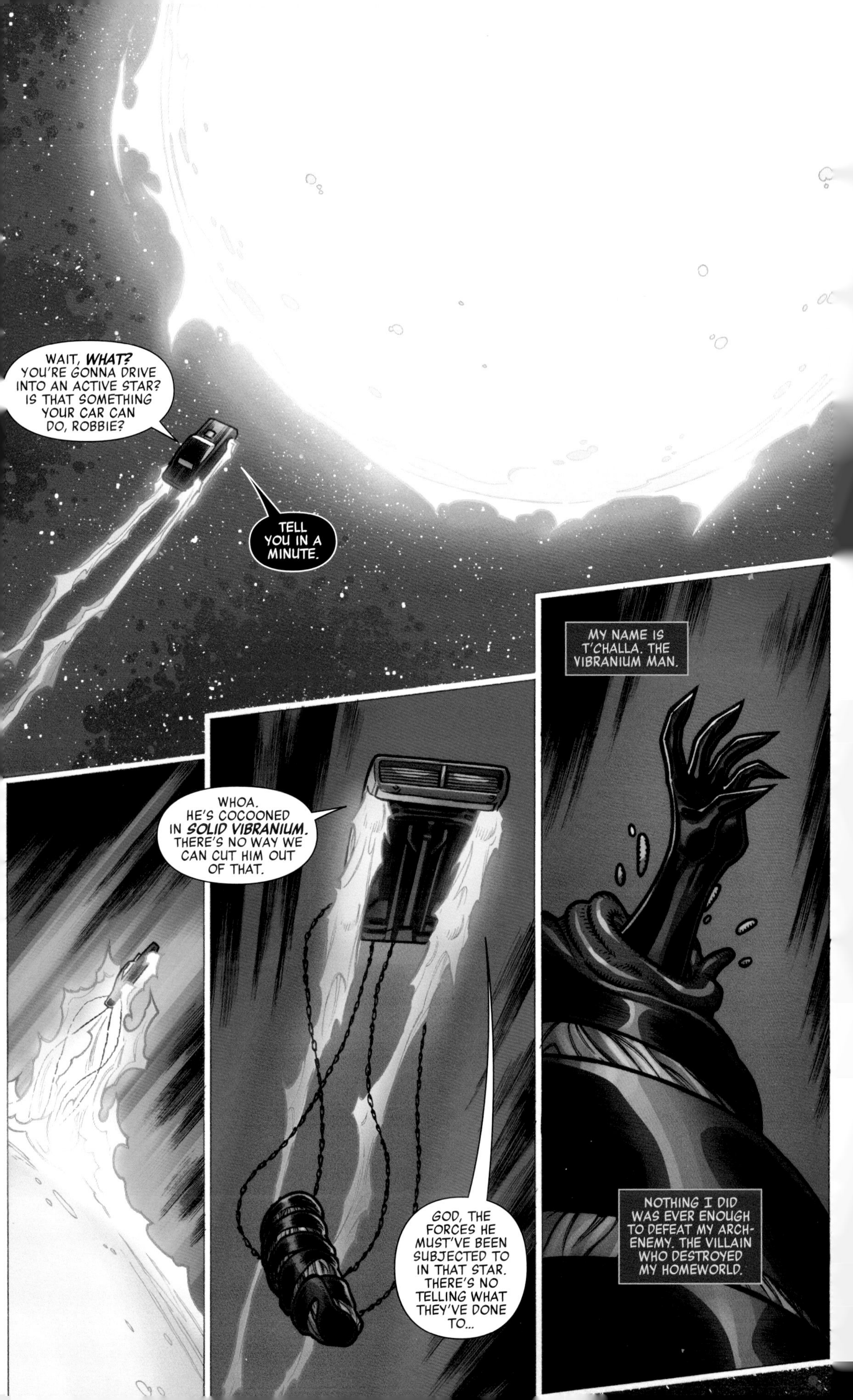
WAIT, WHAT? YOU'RE GONNA DRIVE INTO AN ACTIVE STAR? IS THAT SOMETHING YOUR CAR CAN DO, ROBBIE?
TELL YOU IN A MINUTE.
WHOA. HE'S COCOONED IN SOLID VIBRANIUM. THERE'S NO WAY WE CAN CUT HIM OUT OF THAT.
GOD, THE FORCES HE MUST'VE BEEN SUBJECTED TO IN THAT STAR. THERE'S NO TELLING WHAT THEY'VE DONE TO...
MY NAME IS T'CHALLA. THE VIBRANIUM MAN.
NOTHING I DID WAS EVER ENOUGH TO DEFEAT MY ARCH-ENEMY. THE VILLAIN WHO DESTROYED MY HOMEWORLD.

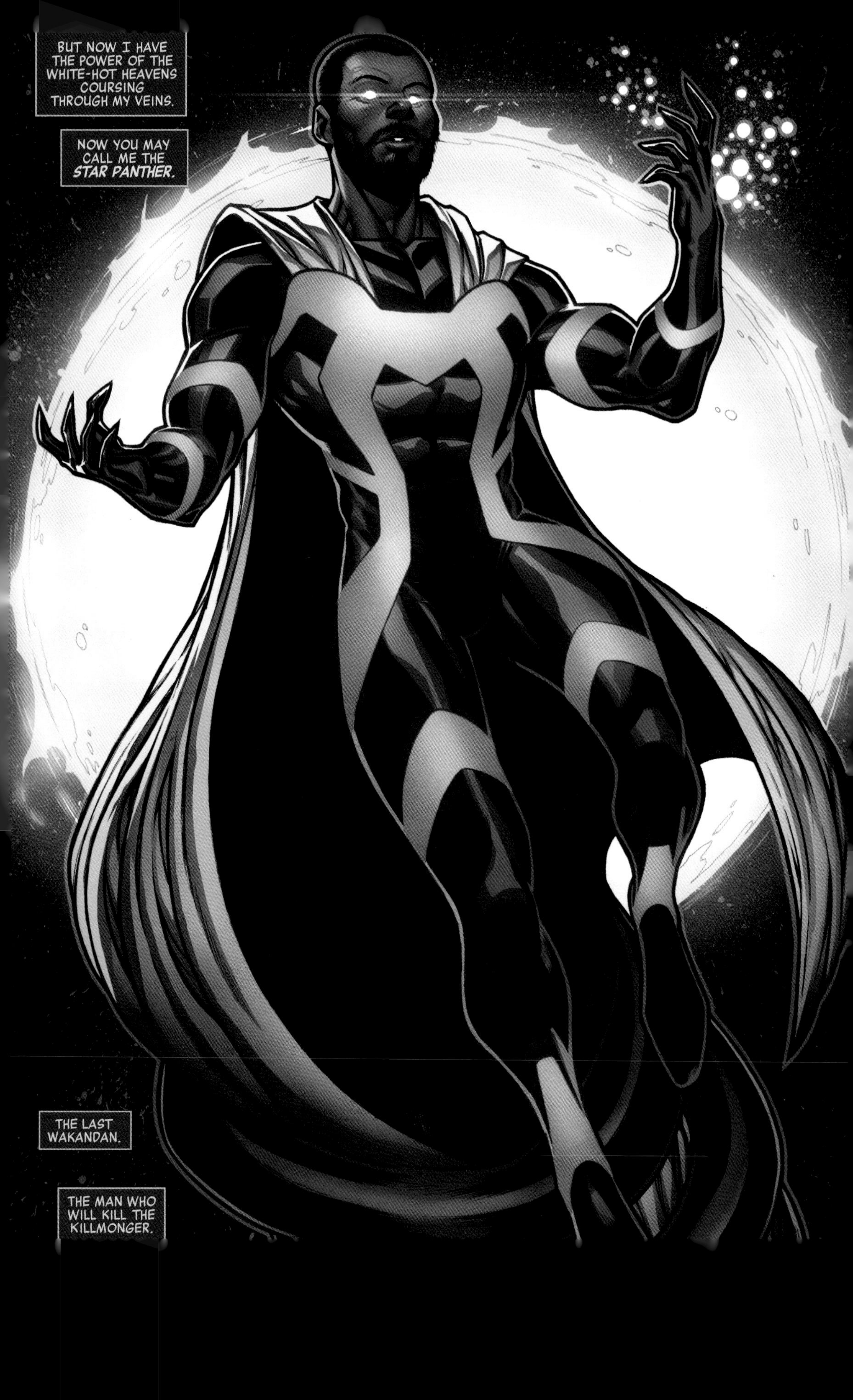
BUT NOW I HAVE THE POWER OF THE WHITE-HOT HEAVENS COURSING THROUGH MY VEINS.
NOW YOU MAY CALL ME THE STAR PANTHER.
THE LAST WAKANDAN.
THE MAN WHO WILL KILL THE KILLMONGER.

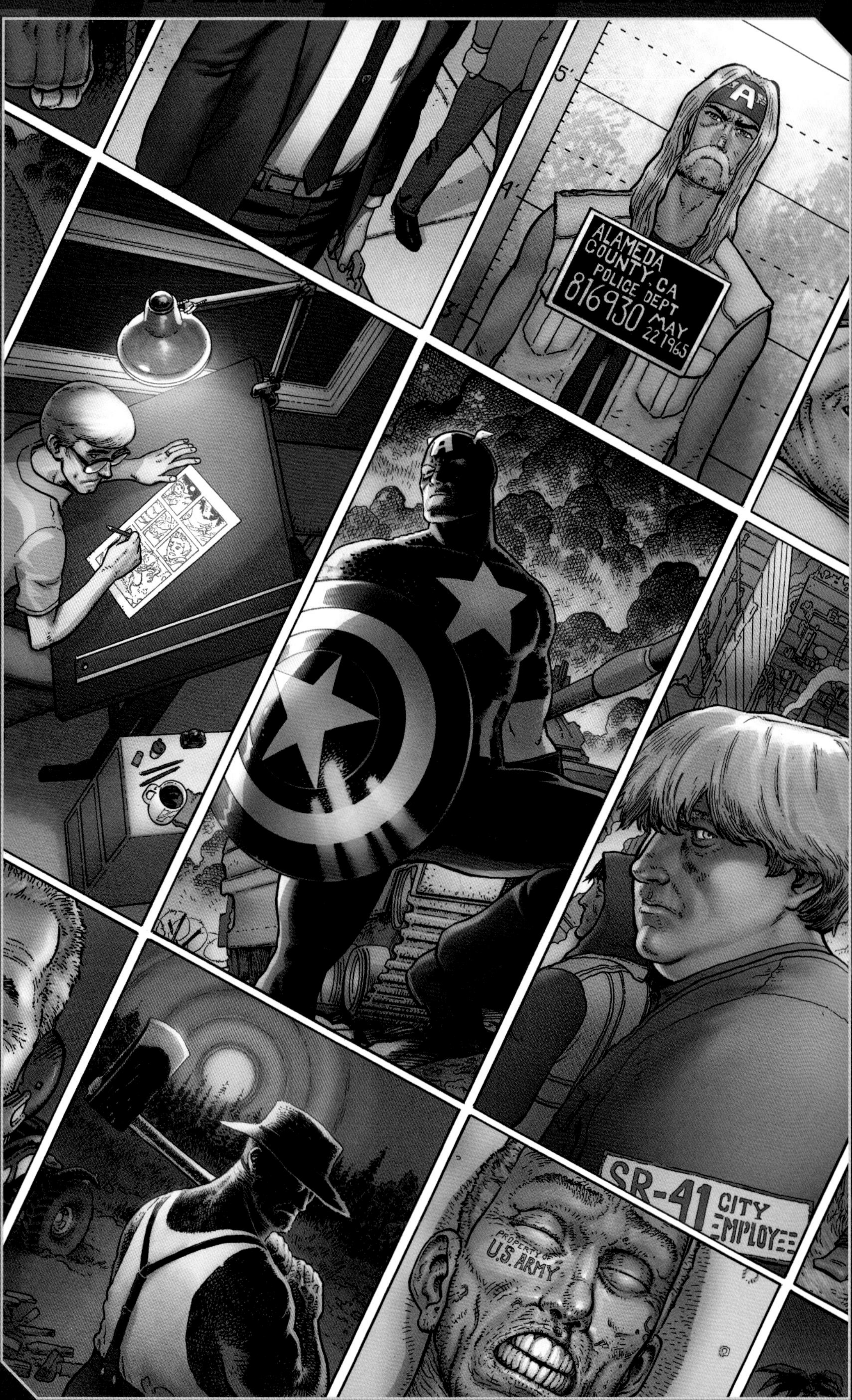
ALAMEDA
COUNTY, CA
POLICE DEPT
816930 MAY
22 1965
SR-41 CITY
EMPLOYEE
PROPERTY OF
U.S. ARMY

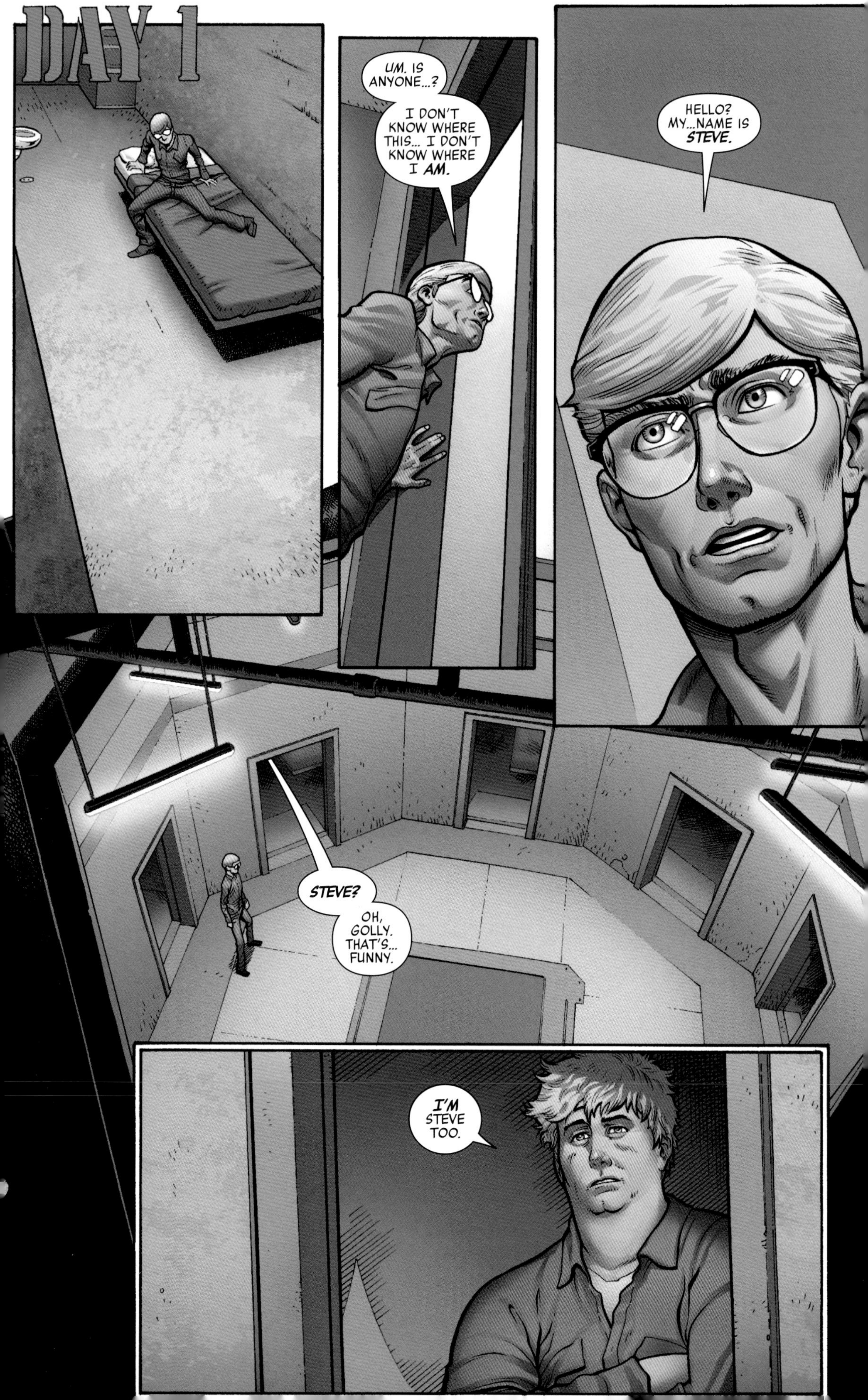
DAY 1
UM. IS ANYONE...?
I DON'T KNOW WHERE THIS... I DON'T KNOW WHERE I AM.
HELLO? MY...NAME IS STEVE.
STEVE?
OH, GOLLY. THAT'S... FUNNY.
I'M STEVE TOO.

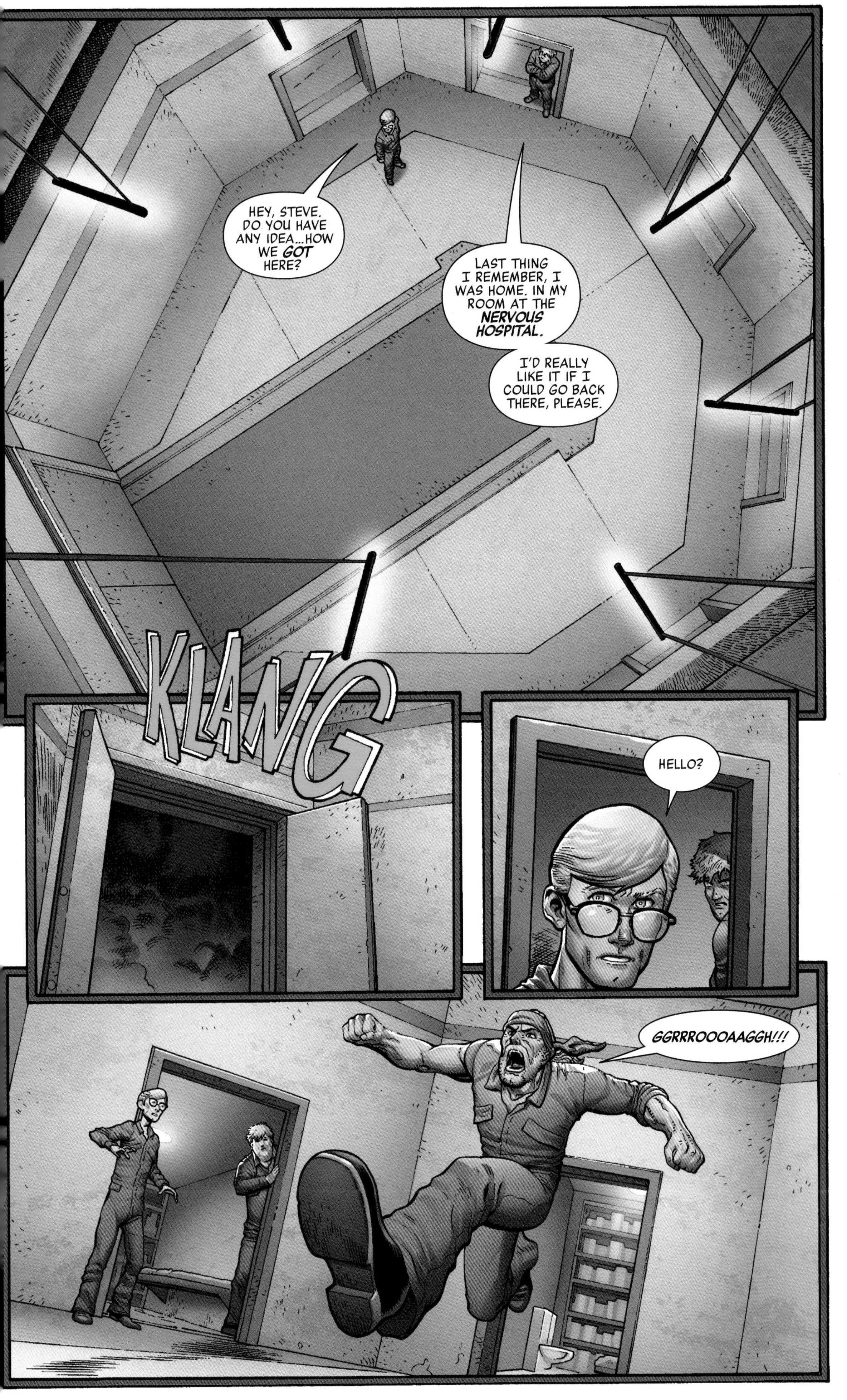
HEY, STEVE. DO YOU HAVE ANY IDEA...HOW WE GOT HERE?
LAST THING I REMEMBER, I WAS HOME. IN MY ROOM AT THE NERVOUS HOSPITAL.
I'D REALLY LIKE IT IF I COULD GO BACK THERE, PLEASE.
KLANG
HELLO?
GGRRROOOAAGGH!!!

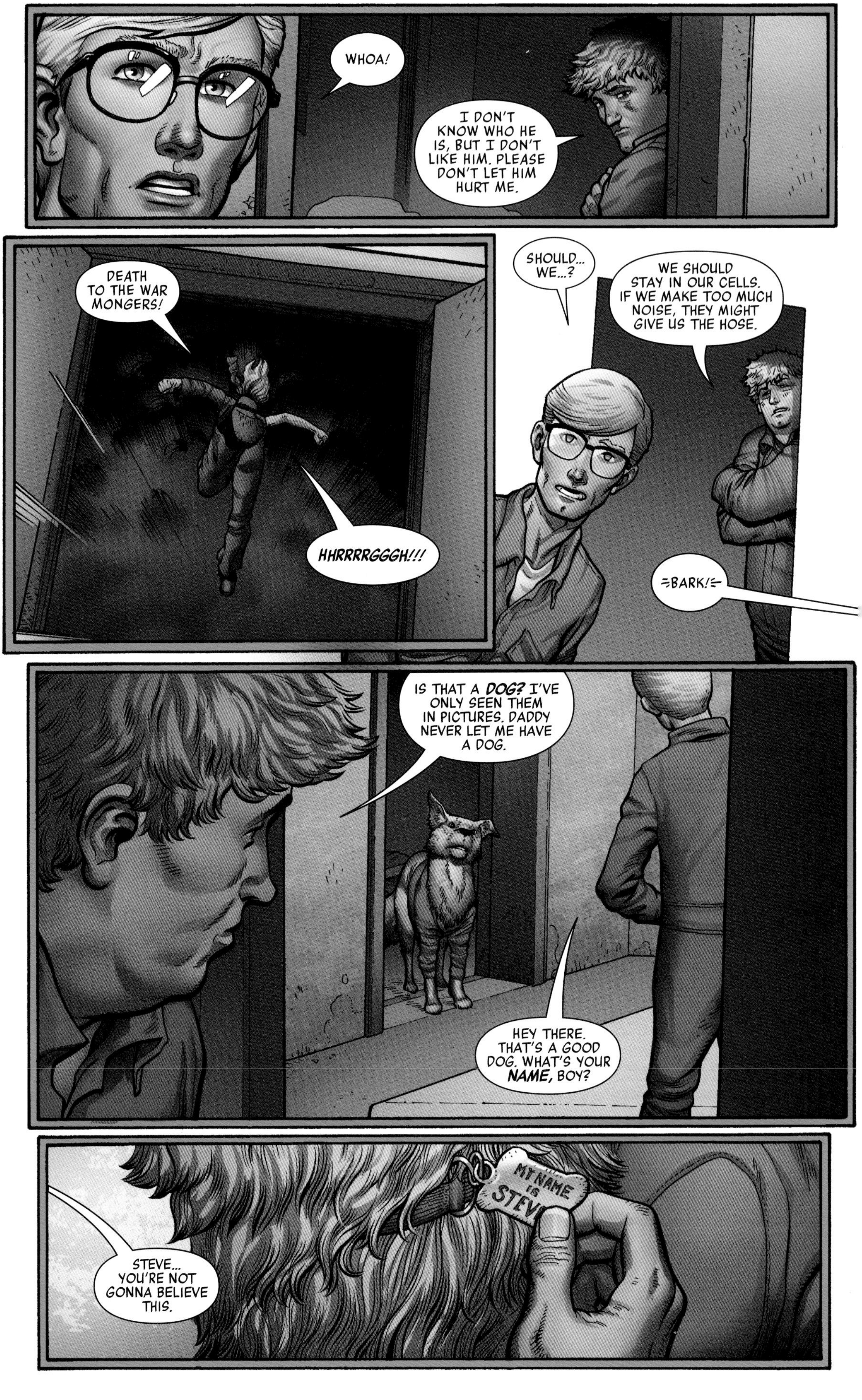
WHOA!
I DON'T KNOW WHO HE IS, BUT I DON'T LIKE HIM. PLEASE DON'T LET HIM HURT ME.
DEATH TO THE WAR MONGERS!
HHRRRRGGGH!!!
SHOULD... WE...?
WE SHOULD STAY IN OUR CELLS. IF WE MAKE TOO MUCH NOISE, THEY MIGHT GIVE US THE HOSE.
BARK!
IS THAT A DOG? I'VE ONLY SEEN THEM IN PICTURES. DADDY NEVER LET ME HAVE A DOG.
HEY THERE. THAT'S A GOOD DOG. WHAT'S YOUR NAME, BOY?
MY NAME IS STEV
STEVE... YOU'RE NOT GONNA BELIEVE THIS.

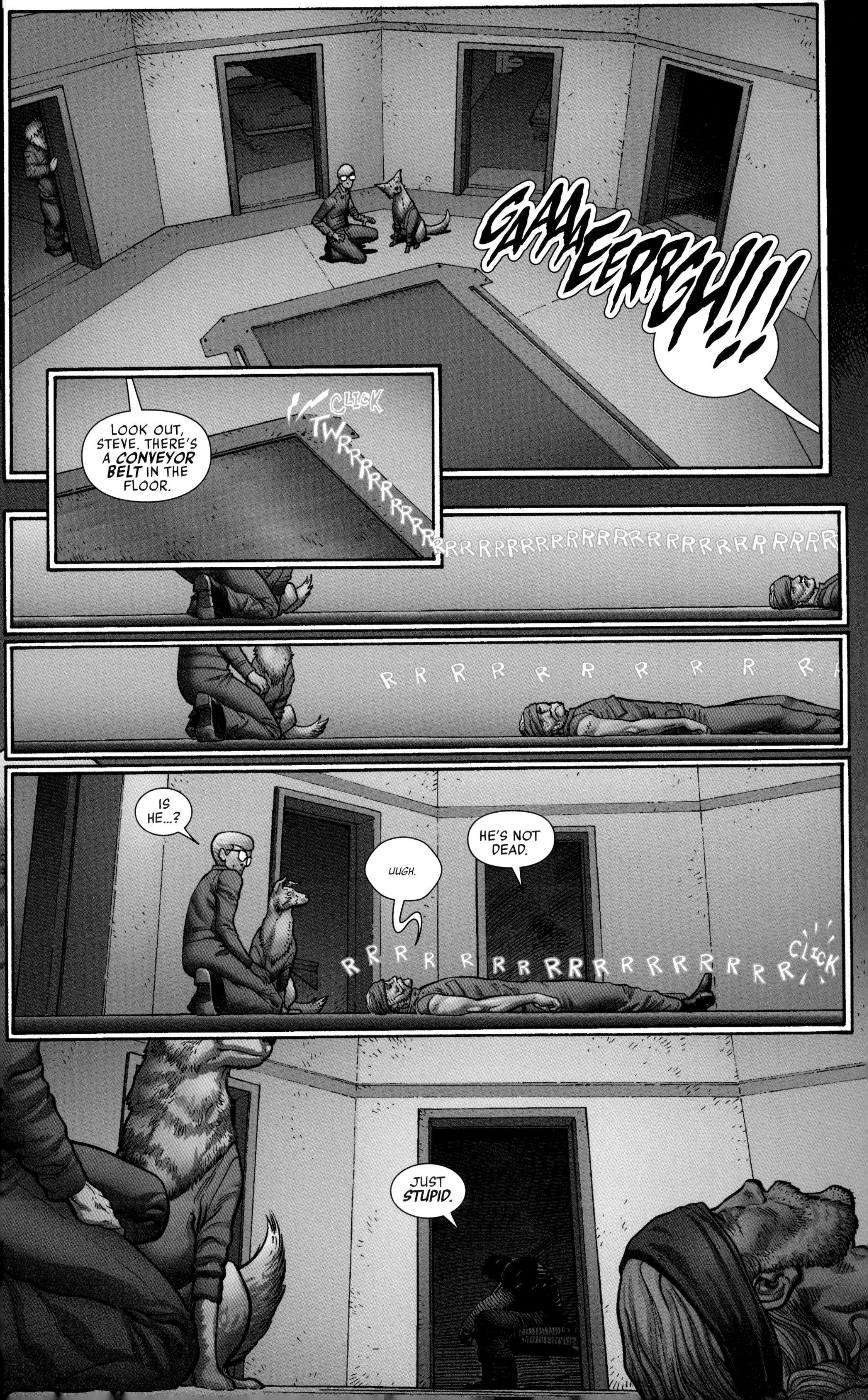
GAAAEERRGH!!!
LOOK OUT, STEVE. THERE'S A CONVEYOR BELT IN THE FLOOR.
CLICK
TWRRRRRRRRRRRRRRRRRRRRRRRRRRRRRRRR
R R R R R R R R R R R
IS HE...?
UUGH.
HE'S NOT DEAD.
R R R R R R R R R R R R R R R R R
CLICK
JUST STUPID.

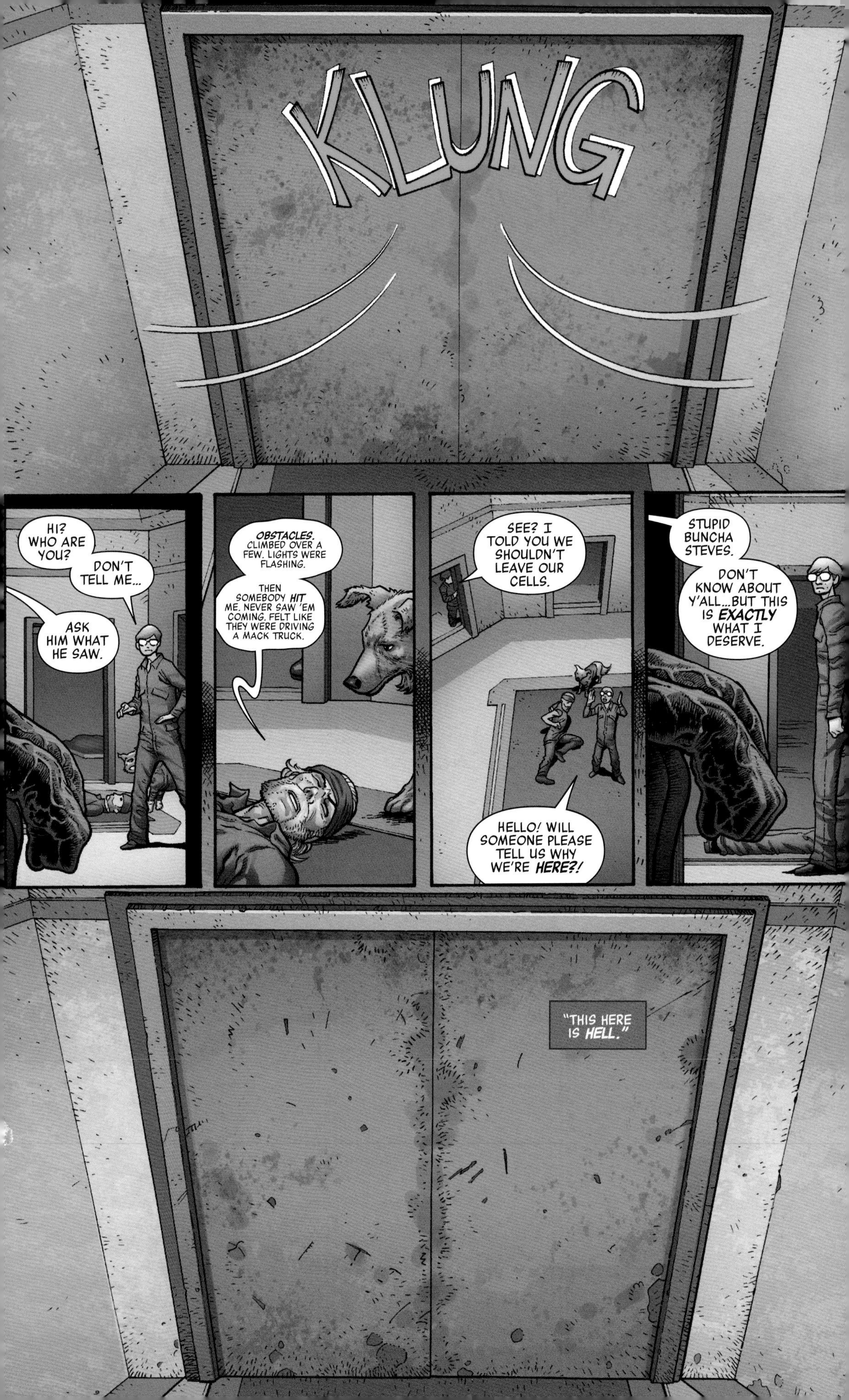
KLUNG
HI? WHO ARE YOU?
DON'T TELL ME...
ASK HIM WHAT HE SAW.
OBSTACLES. CLIMBED OVER A FEW. LIGHTS WERE FLASHING.
THEN SOMEBODY HIT ME. NEVER SAW 'EM COMING. FELT LIKE THEY WERE DRIVING A MACK TRUCK.
SEE? I TOLD YOU WE SHOULDN'T LEAVE OUR CELLS.
HELLO! WILL SOMEONE PLEASE TELL US WHY WE'RE HERE?!
STUPID BUNCHA STEVES.
DON'T KNOW ABOUT Y'ALL...BUT THIS IS EXACTLY WHAT I DESERVE.
"THIS HERE IS HELL."

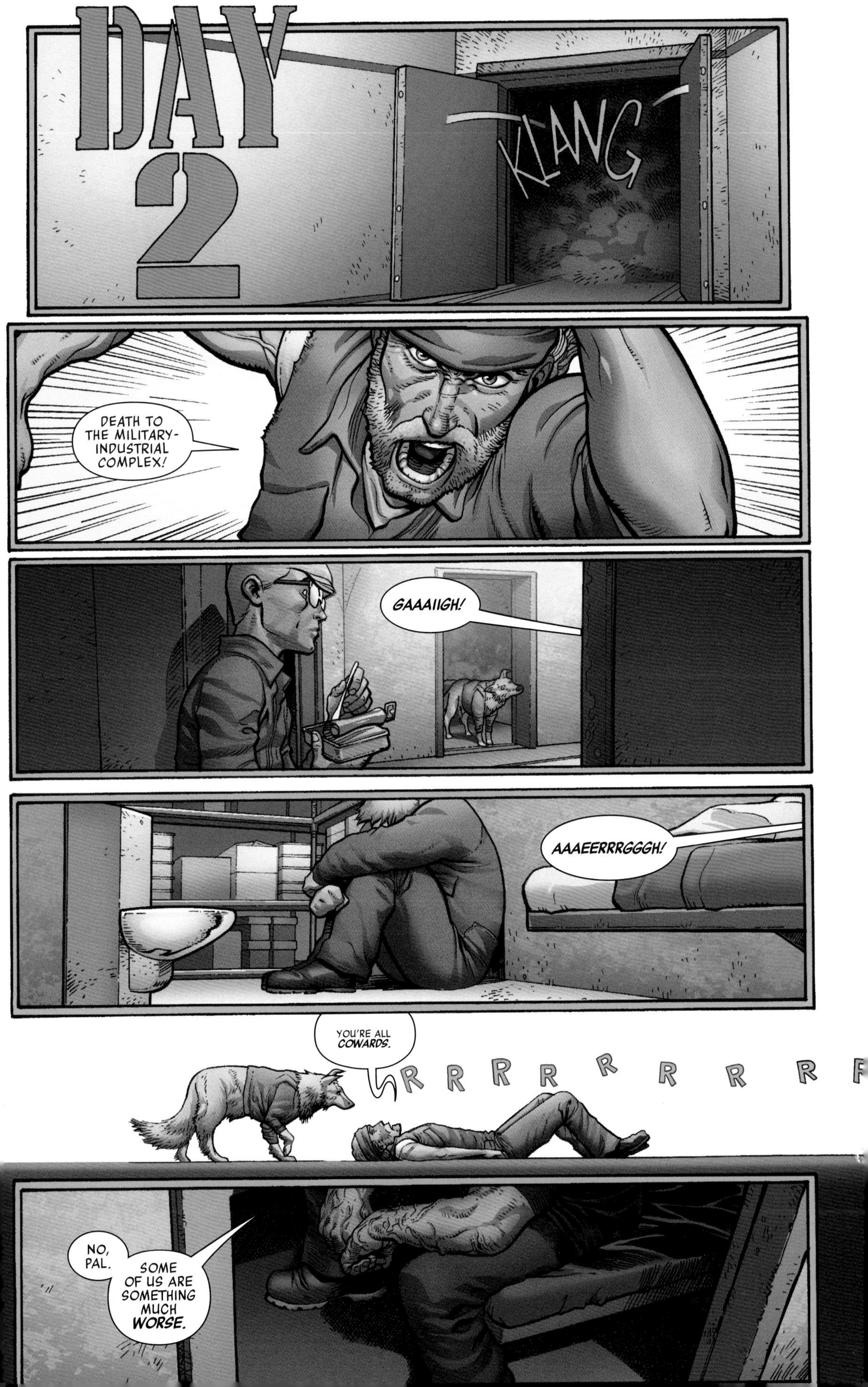
DAY 2
KLANG
DEATH TO THE MILITARY-INDUSTRIAL COMPLEX!
GAAAIIGH!
AAAEERRRGGGH!
YOU'RE ALL COWARDS.
RRRRRRRRR
NO, PAL.
SOME OF US ARE SOMETHING MUCH WORSE.

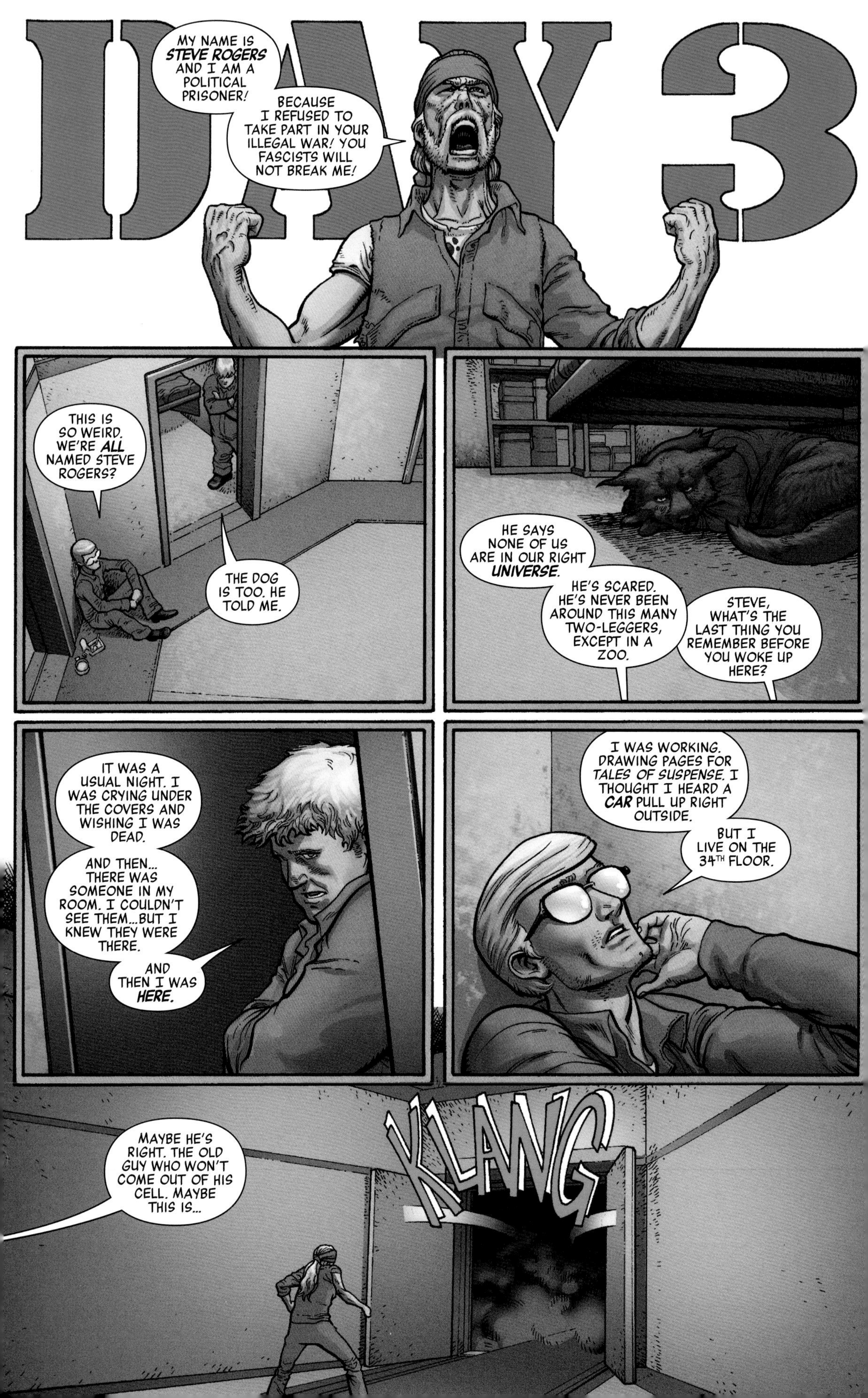
DAY 3
MY NAME IS STEVE ROGERS AND I AM A POLITICAL PRISONER!
BECAUSE I REFUSED TO TAKE PART IN YOUR ILLEGAL WAR! YOU FASCISTS WILL NOT BREAK ME!
THIS IS SO WEIRD. WE'RE ALL NAMED STEVE ROGERS?
THE DOG IS TOO. HE TOLD ME.
HE SAYS NONE OF US ARE IN OUR RIGHT UNIVERSE.
HE'S SCARED. HE'S NEVER BEEN AROUND THIS MANY TWO-LEGGERS, EXCEPT IN A ZOO.
STEVE, WHAT'S THE LAST THING YOU REMEMBER BEFORE YOU WOKE UP HERE?
IT WAS A USUAL NIGHT. I WAS CRYING UNDER THE COVERS AND WISHING I WAS DEAD.
AND THEN... THERE WAS SOMEONE IN MY ROOM. I COULDN'T SEE THEM...BUT I KNEW THEY WERE THERE.
AND THEN I WAS HERE.
I WAS WORKING. DRAWING PAGES FOR TALES OF SUSPENSE. I THOUGHT I HEARD A CAR PULL UP RIGHT OUTSIDE.
BUT I LIVE ON THE 34TH FLOOR.
MAYBE HE'S RIGHT. THE OLD GUY WHO WON'T COME OUT OF HIS CELL. MAYBE THIS IS...
KLANG

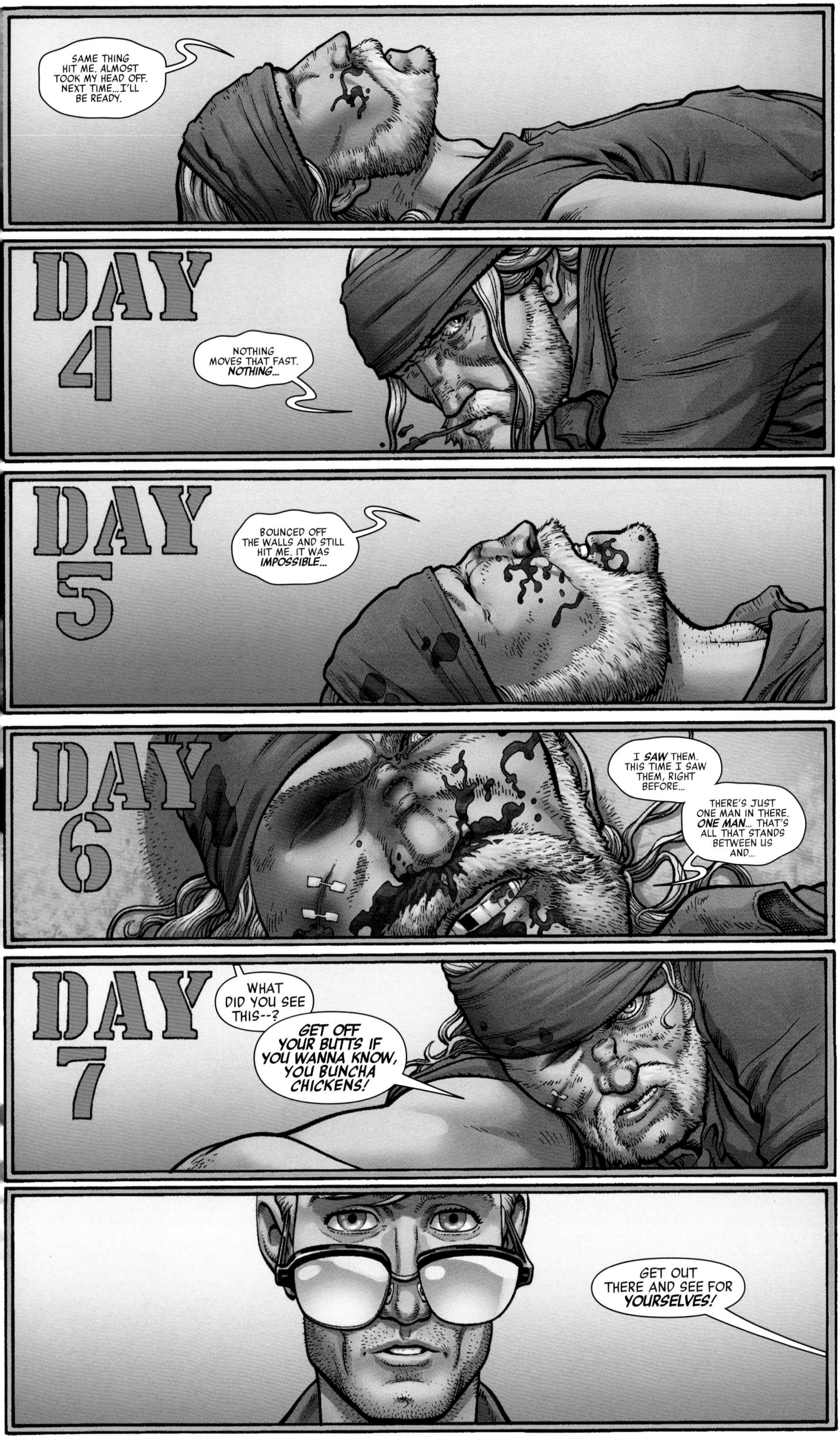

SAME THING HIT ME. ALMOST TOOK MY HEAD OFF. NEXT TIME... I'LL BE READY.
DAY 4
NOTHING MOVES THAT FAST. NOTHING...
DAY 5
BOUNCED OFF THE WALLS AND STILL HIT ME. IT WAS IMPOSSIBLE...
DAY 6
I SAW THEM. THIS TIME I SAW THEM, RIGHT BEFORE...
THERE'S JUST ONE MAN IN THERE. ONE MAN... THAT'S ALL THAT STANDS BETWEEN US AND...
DAY 7
WHAT DID YOU SEE THIS--?
GET OFF YOUR BUTTS IF YOU WANNA KNOW, YOU BUNCHA CHICKENS!
GET OUT THERE AND SEE FOR YOURSELVES!

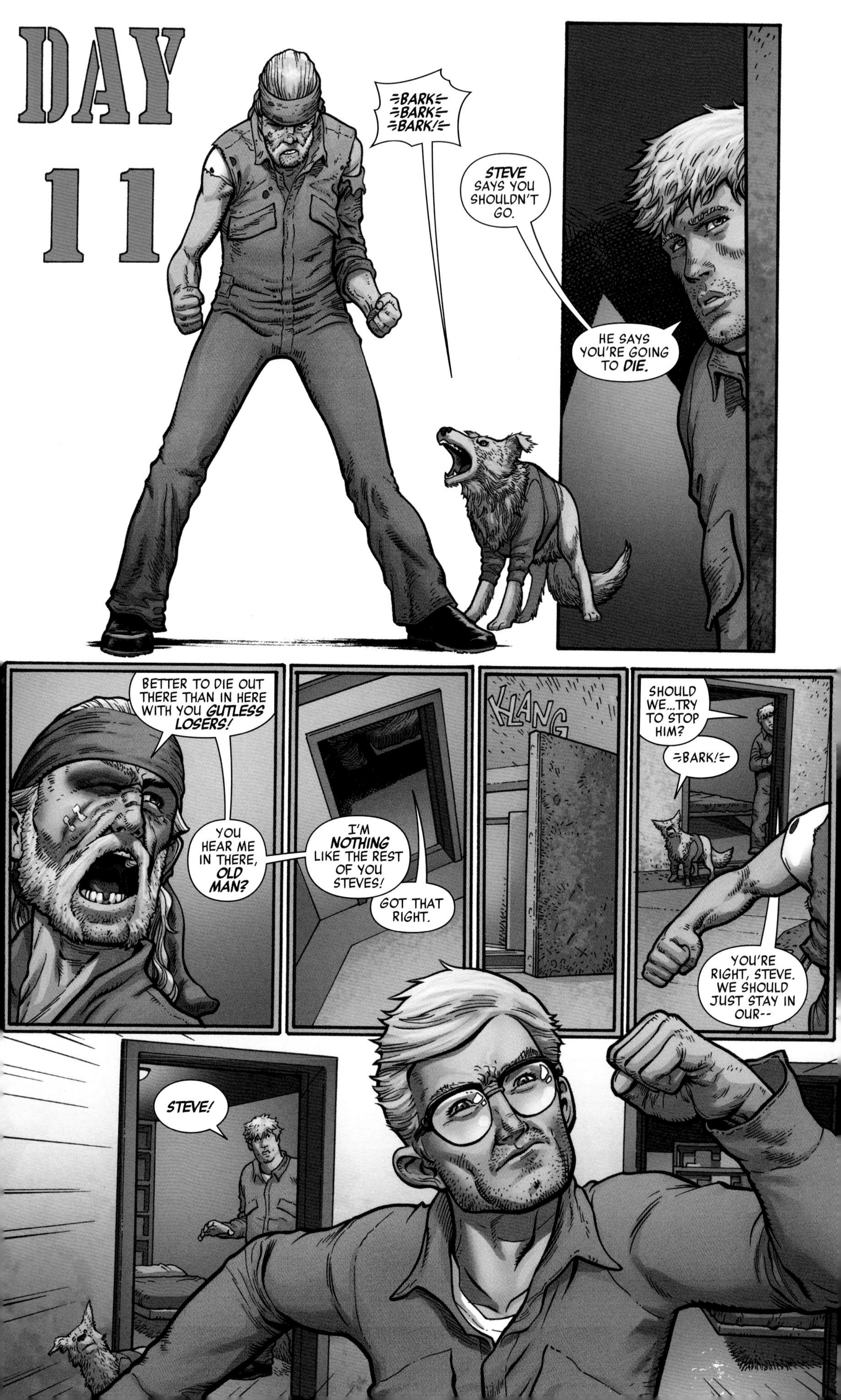

DAY 11
BARK BARK BARK!
STEVE SAYS YOU SHOULDN'T GO.
HE SAYS YOU'RE GOING TO DIE.
BETTER TO DIE OUT THERE THAN IN HERE WITH YOU GUTLESS LOSERS!
YOU HEAR ME IN THERE, OLD MAN?
I'M NOTHING LIKE THE REST OF YOU STEVES!
GOT THAT RIGHT.
KLANG
SHOULD WE...TRY TO STOP HIM?
BARK!
YOU'RE RIGHT, STEVE. WE SHOULD JUST STAY IN OUR--
STEVE!

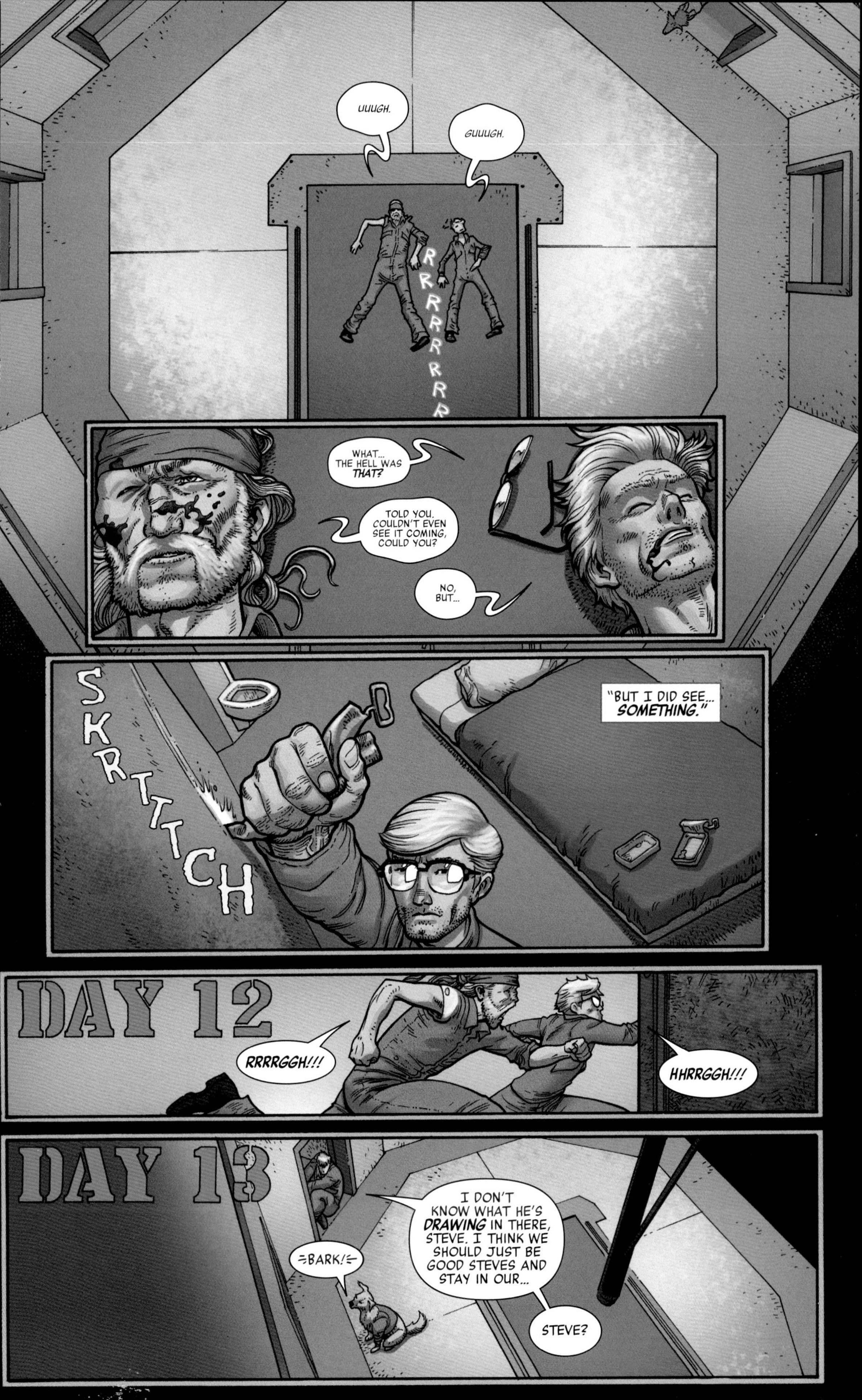
UUUGH.
GUUUGH.
RRRRRRRR
WHAT... THE HELL WAS THAT?
TOLD YOU. COULDN'T EVEN SEE IT COMING, COULD YOU?
NO, BUT...
"BUT I DID SEE... SOMETHING."
SKRTTTCH
DAY 12
RRRRGGH!!!
HHRRGGH!!!
DAY 13
I DON'T KNOW WHAT HE'S DRAWING IN THERE, STEVE. I THINK WE SHOULD JUST BE GOOD STEVES AND STAY IN OUR...
BARK!
STEVE?

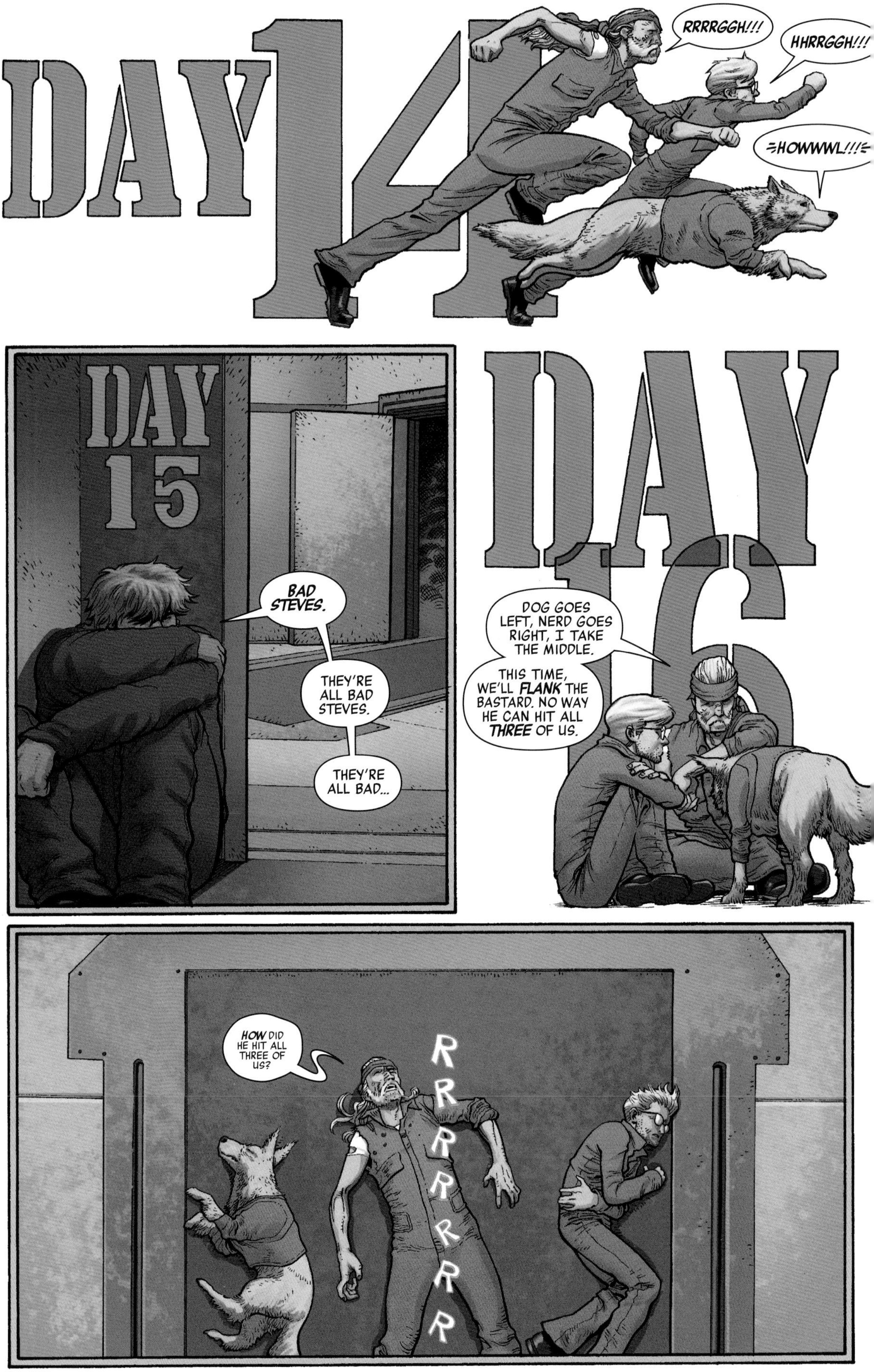
DAY 14
RRRRGGH!!!
HHRRGGH!!!
HOWWWL!!!
DAY 15
BAD STEVES.
THEY'RE ALL BAD STEVES.
THEY'RE ALL BAD...
DAY 16
DOG GOES LEFT, NERD GOES RIGHT, I TAKE THE MIDDLE.
THIS TIME, WE'LL FLANK THE BASTARD. NO WAY HE CAN HIT ALL THREE OF US.
HOW DID HE HIT ALL THREE OF US?
RRRRRRR

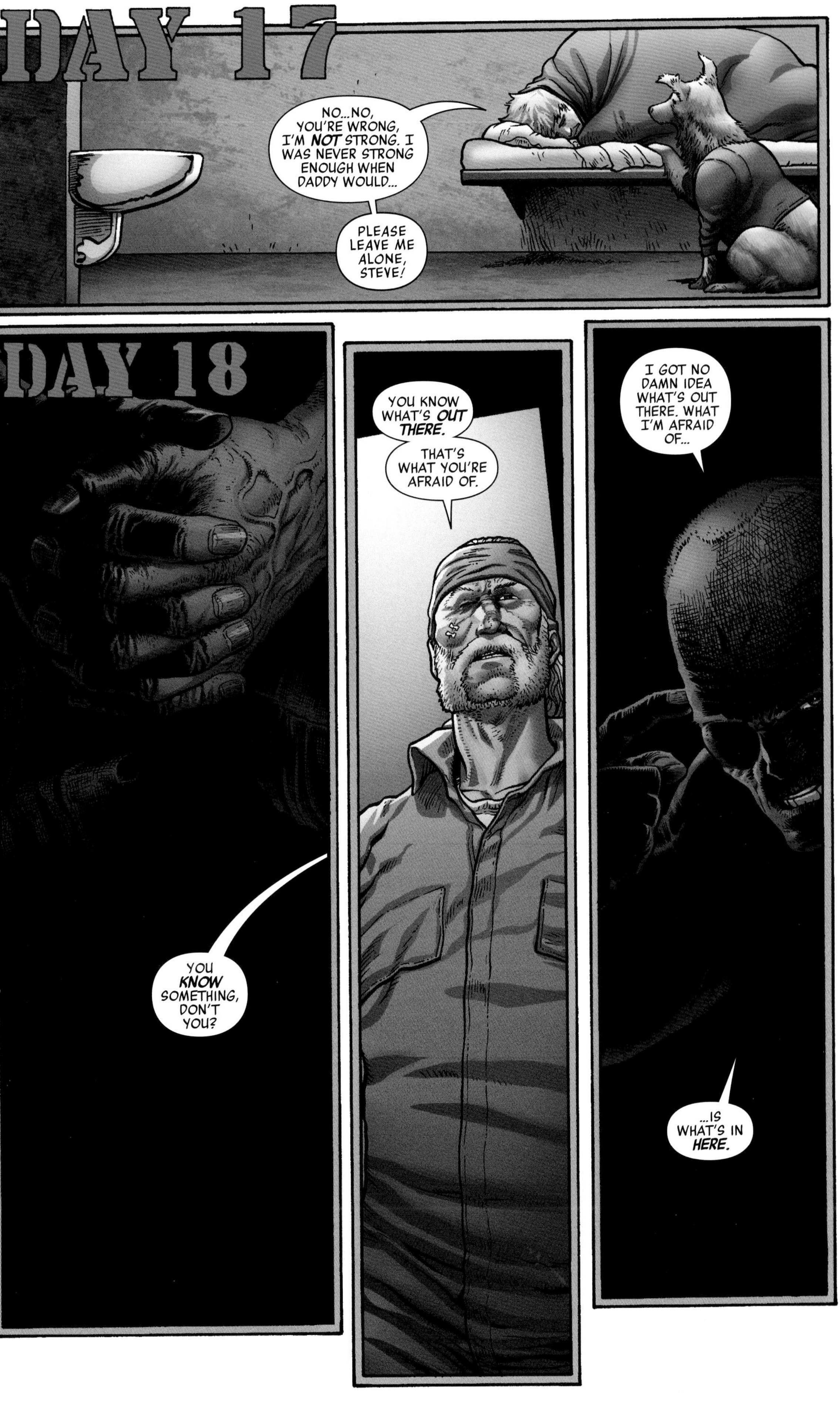
DAY 17
NO...NO, YOU'RE WRONG, I'M NOT STRONG. I WAS NEVER STRONG ENOUGH WHEN DADDY WOULD...
PLEASE LEAVE ME ALONE, STEVE!
DAY 18
YOU KNOW SOMETHING, DON'T YOU?
YOU KNOW WHAT'S OUT THERE.
THAT'S WHAT YOU'RE AFRAID OF.
I GOT NO DAMN IDEA WHAT'S OUT THERE. WHAT I'M AFRAID OF...
...IS WHAT'S IN HERE.

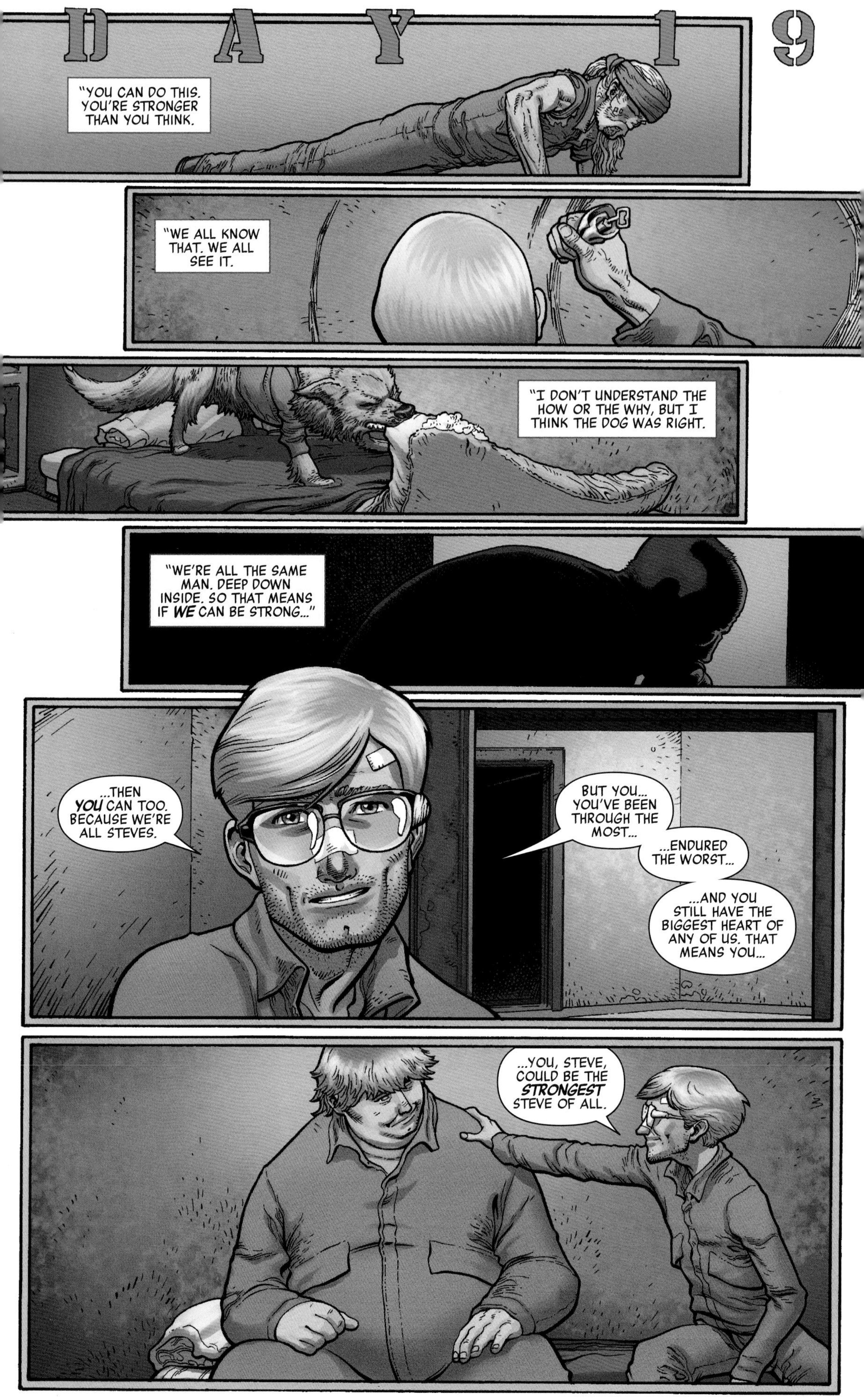
DAY 19
"YOU CAN DO THIS. YOU'RE STRONGER THAN YOU THINK.
"WE ALL KNOW THAT. WE ALL SEE IT.
"I DON'T UNDERSTAND THE HOW OR THE WHY, BUT I THINK THE DOG WAS RIGHT.
"WE'RE ALL THE SAME MAN. DEEP DOWN INSIDE. SO THAT MEANS IF WE CAN BE STRONG..."
...THEN YOU CAN TOO. BECAUSE WE'RE ALL STEVES.
BUT YOU... YOU'VE BEEN THROUGH THE MOST...
...ENDURED THE WORST...
...AND YOU STILL HAVE THE BIGGEST HEART OF ANY OF US. THAT MEANS YOU...
...YOU, STEVE, COULD BE THE STRONGEST STEVE OF ALL.

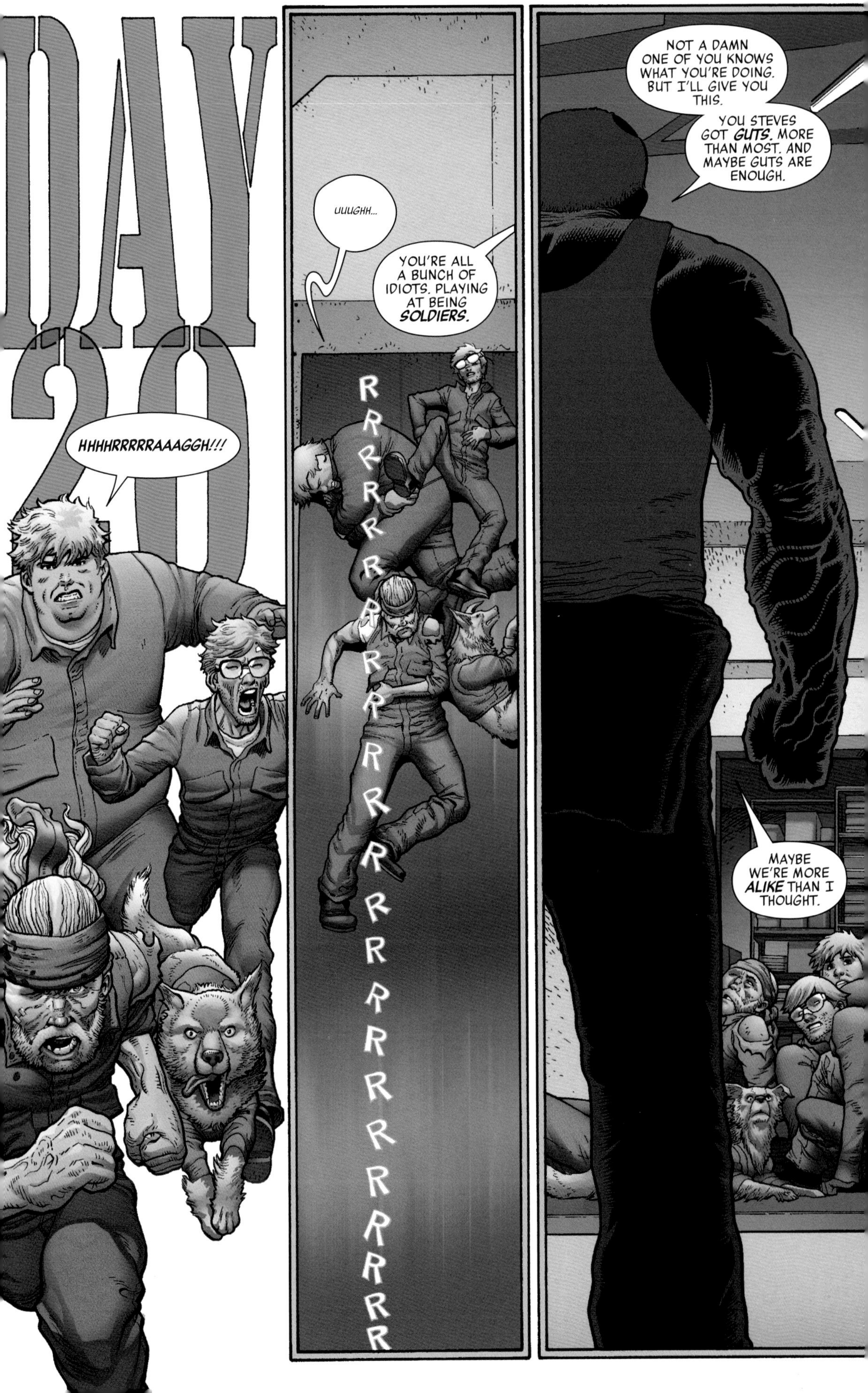
DAY 20
HHHHRRRRRAAAGGH!!!
UUUGHH...
YOU'RE ALL A BUNCH OF IDIOTS. PLAYING AT BEING SOLDIERS.
RRRRRRRRRRRRRRRRRRRR
NOT A DAMN ONE OF YOU KNOWS WHAT YOU'RE DOING. BUT I'LL GIVE YOU THIS.
YOU STEVES GOT GUTS. MORE THAN MOST. AND MAYBE GUTS ARE ENOUGH.
MAYBE WE'RE MORE ALIKE THAN I THOUGHT.

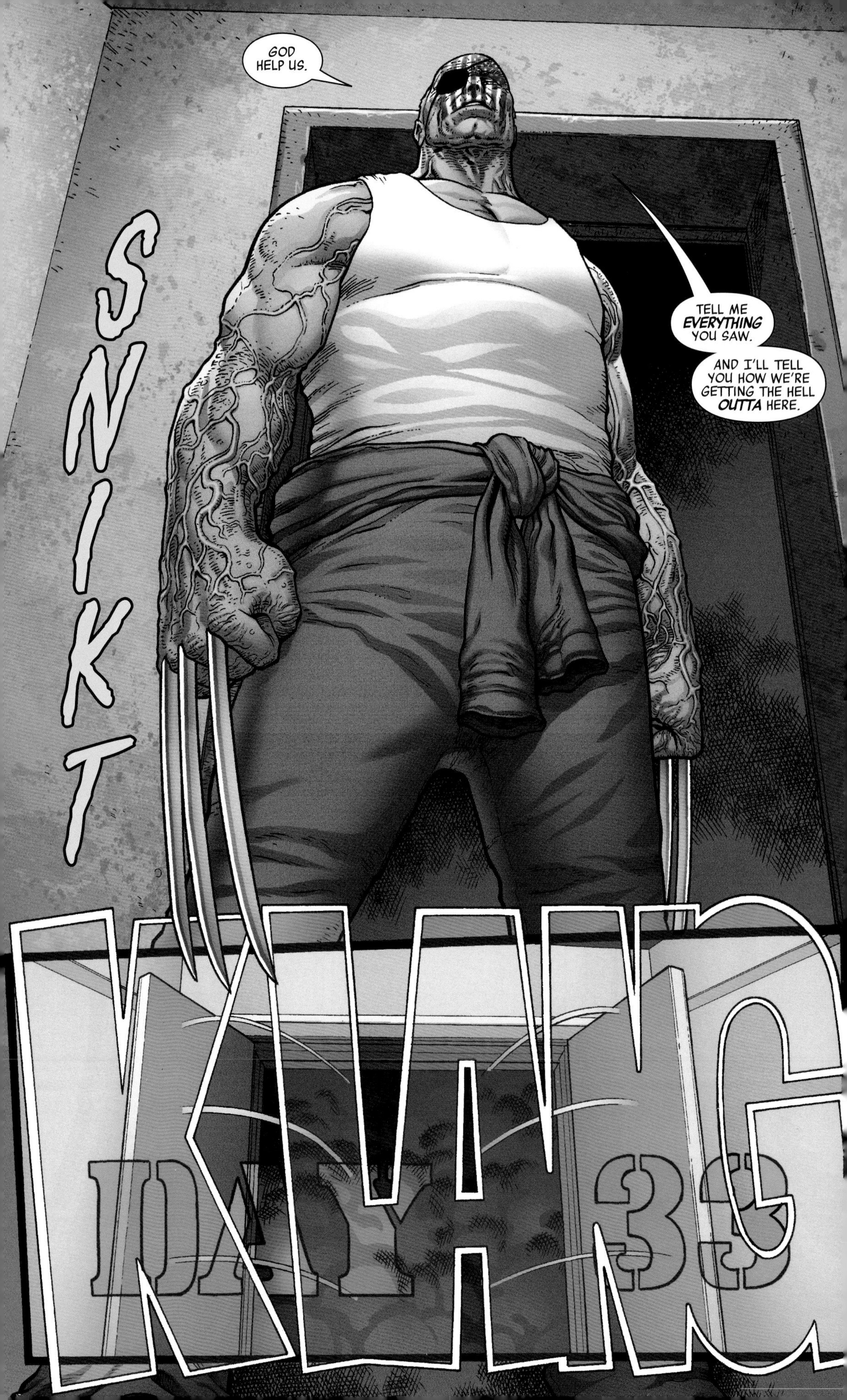

GOD HELP US.
SNIKT
TELL ME **EVERYTHING** YOU SAW.
AND I'LL TELL YOU HOW WE'RE GETTING THE HELL **OUTTA** HERE.
KLANG
DAY 39

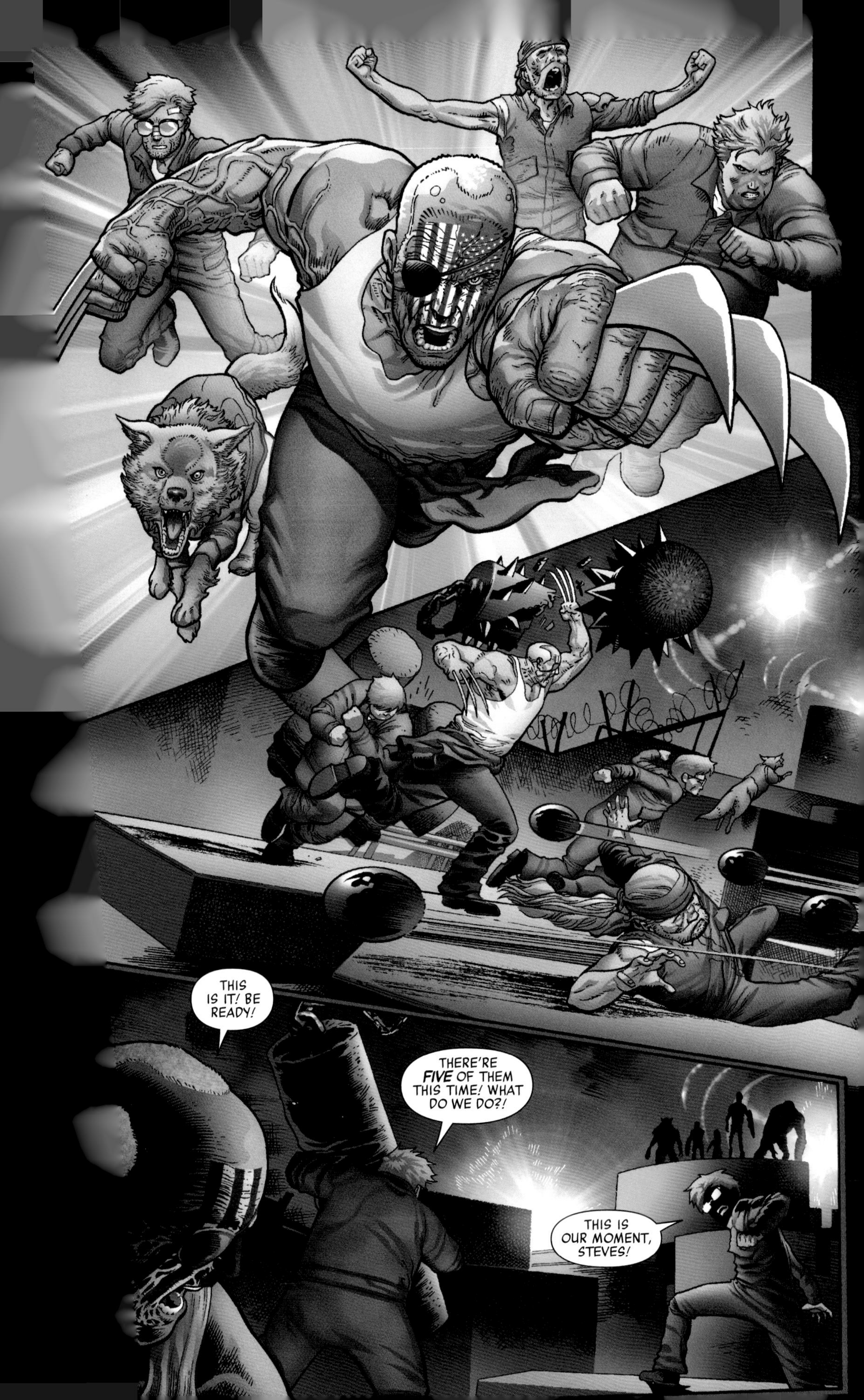
THIS IS IT! BE READY!
THERE'RE FIVE OF THEM THIS TIME! WHAT DO WE DO?!
THIS IS OUR MOMENT, STEVES!

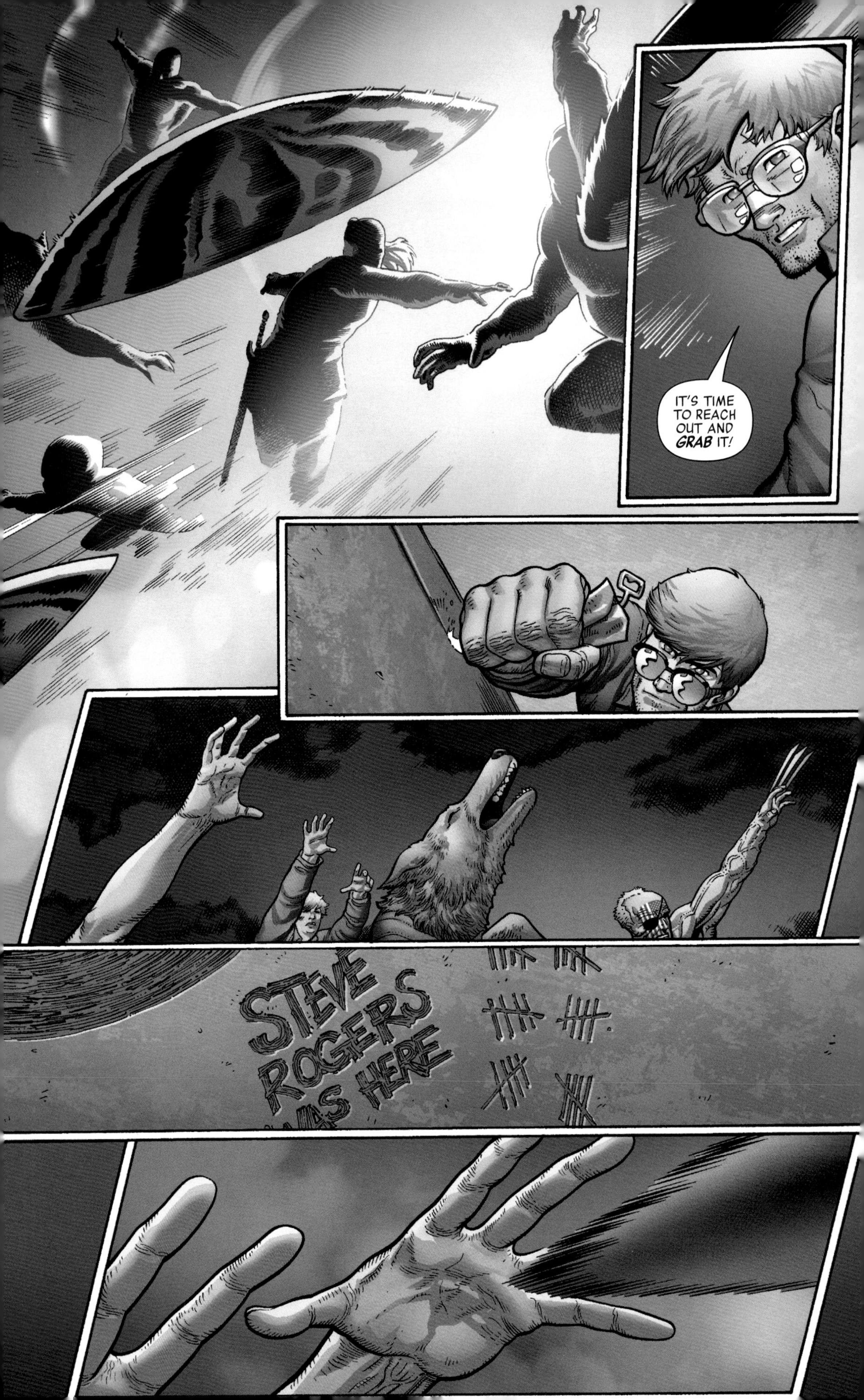
IT'S TIME TO REACH OUT AND GRAB IT!
STEVE ROGERS WAS HERE

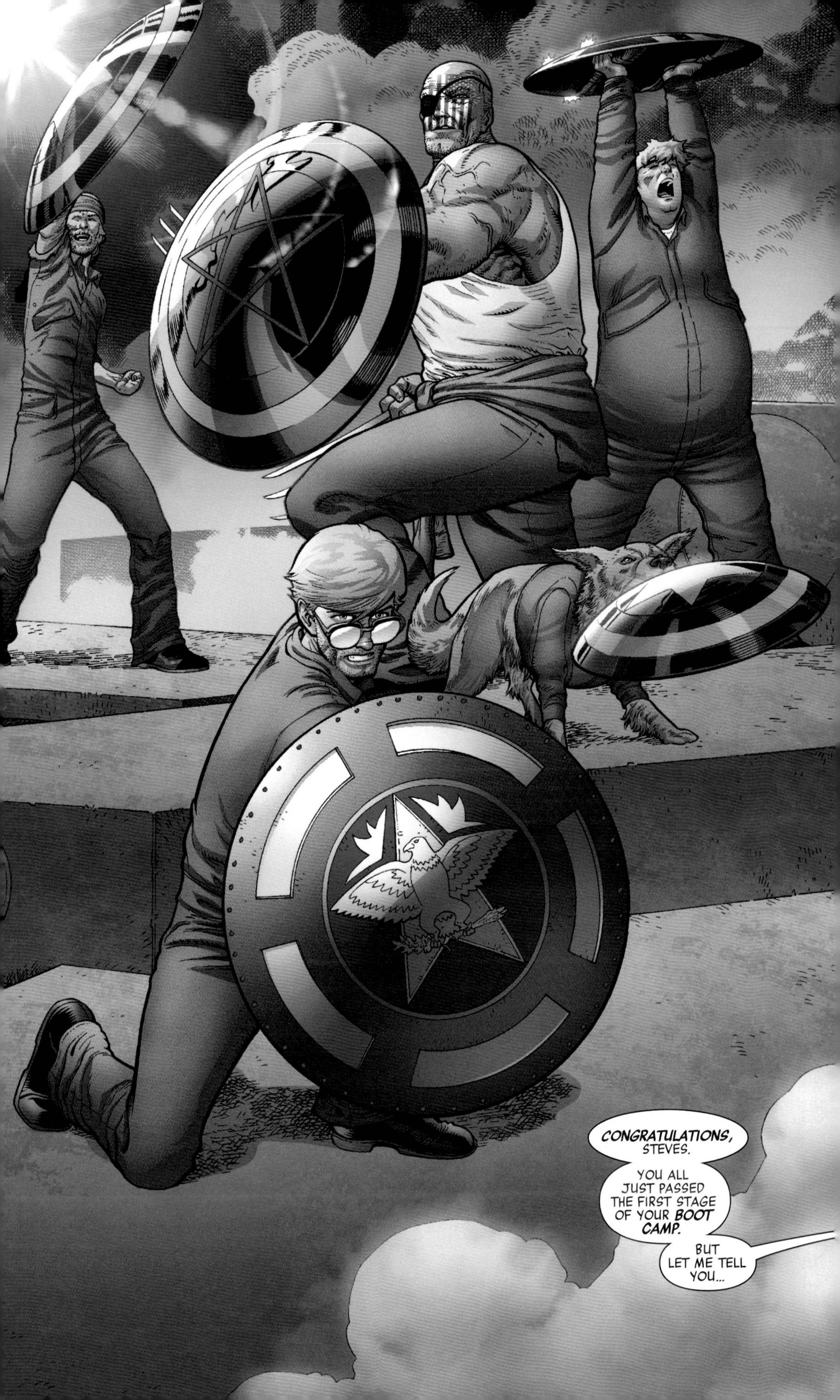

CONGRATULATIONS, STEVES.
YOU ALL JUST PASSED THE FIRST STAGE OF YOUR BOOT CAMP.
BUT LET ME TELL YOU...

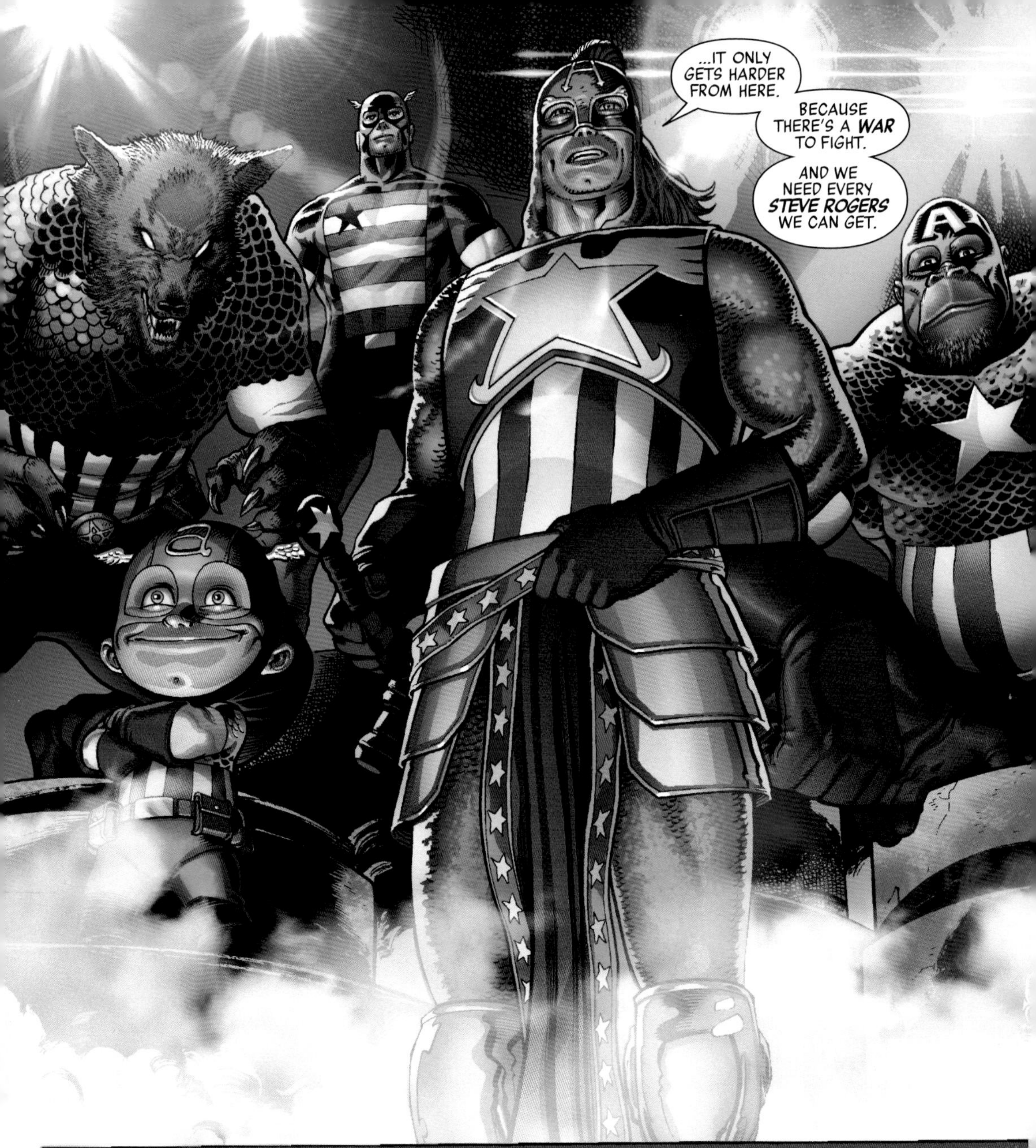
...IT ONLY GETS HARDER FROM HERE.
BECAUSE THERE'S A WAR TO FIGHT.
AND WE NEED EVERY STEVE ROGERS WE CAN GET.

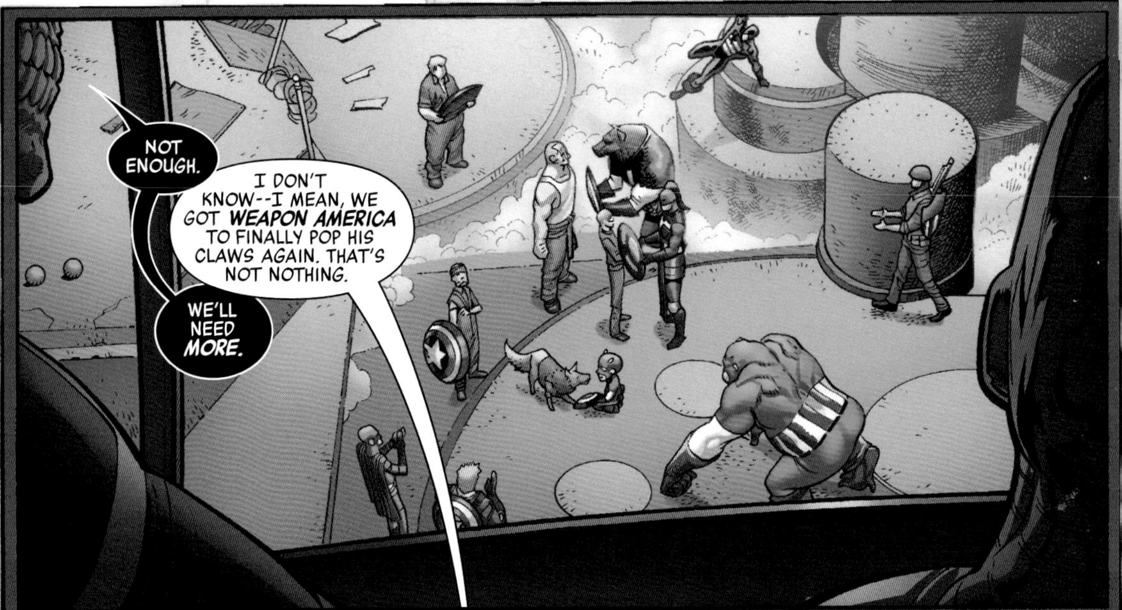
NOT ENOUGH.
I DON'T KNOW--I MEAN, WE GOT WEAPON AMERICA TO FINALLY POP HIS CLAWS AGAIN. THAT'S NOT NOTHING.
WE'LL NEED MORE.

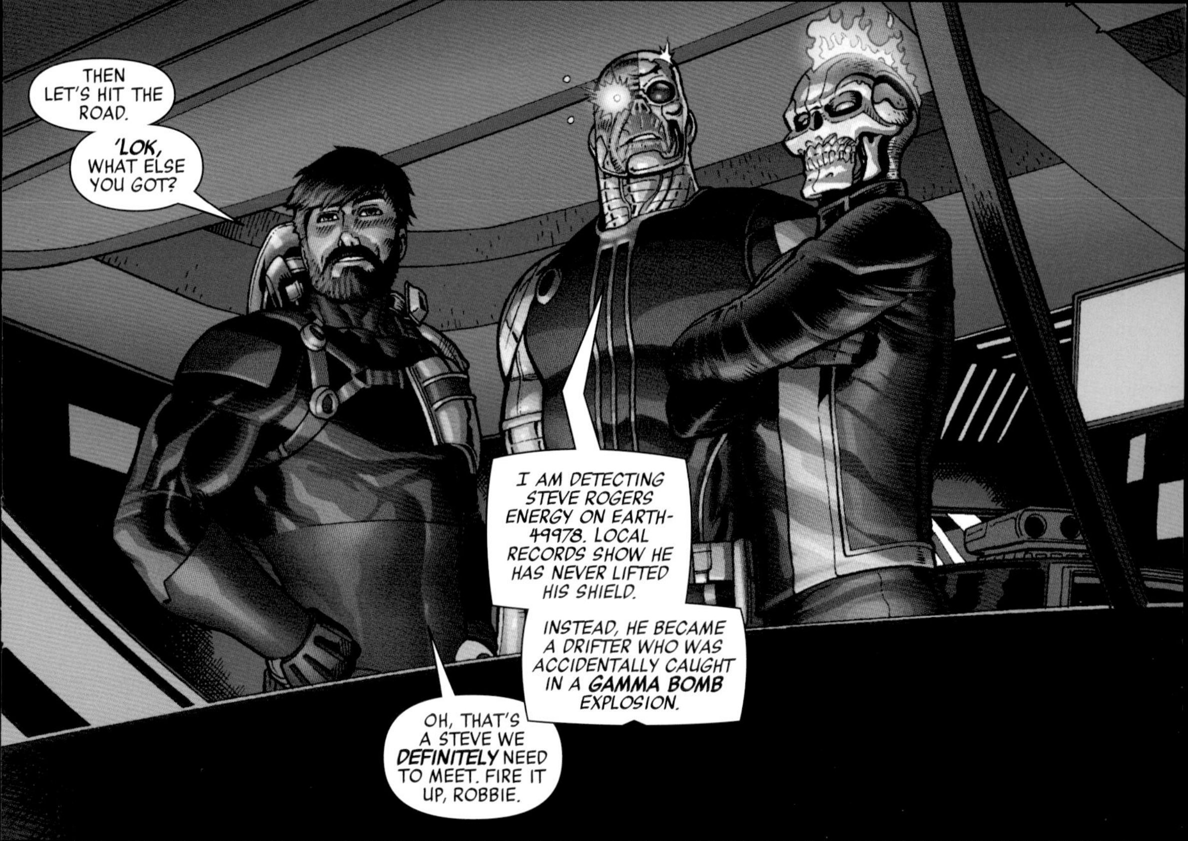
THEN LET'S HIT THE ROAD.
'LOK, WHAT ELSE YOU GOT?
I AM DETECTING STEVE ROGERS ENERGY ON EARTH-49978. LOCAL RECORDS SHOW HE HAS NEVER LIFTED HIS SHIELD.
INSTEAD, HE BECAME A DRIFTER WHO WAS ACCIDENTALLY CAUGHT IN A GAMMA BOMB EXPLOSION.
OH, THAT'S A STEVE WE DEFINITELY NEED TO MEET. FIRE IT UP, ROBBIE.

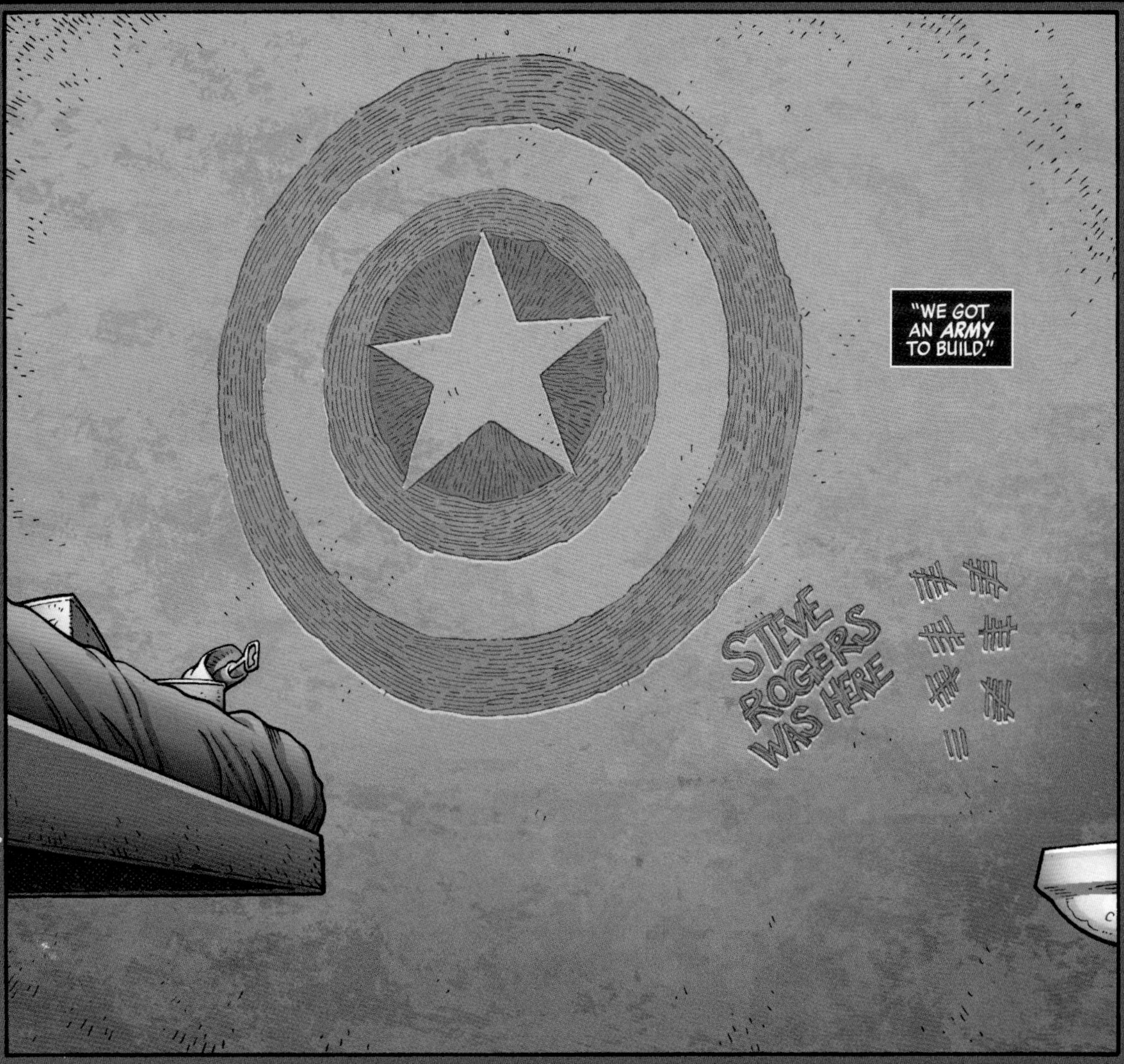
"WE GOT AN ARMY TO BUILD."
STEVE ROGERS WAS HERE

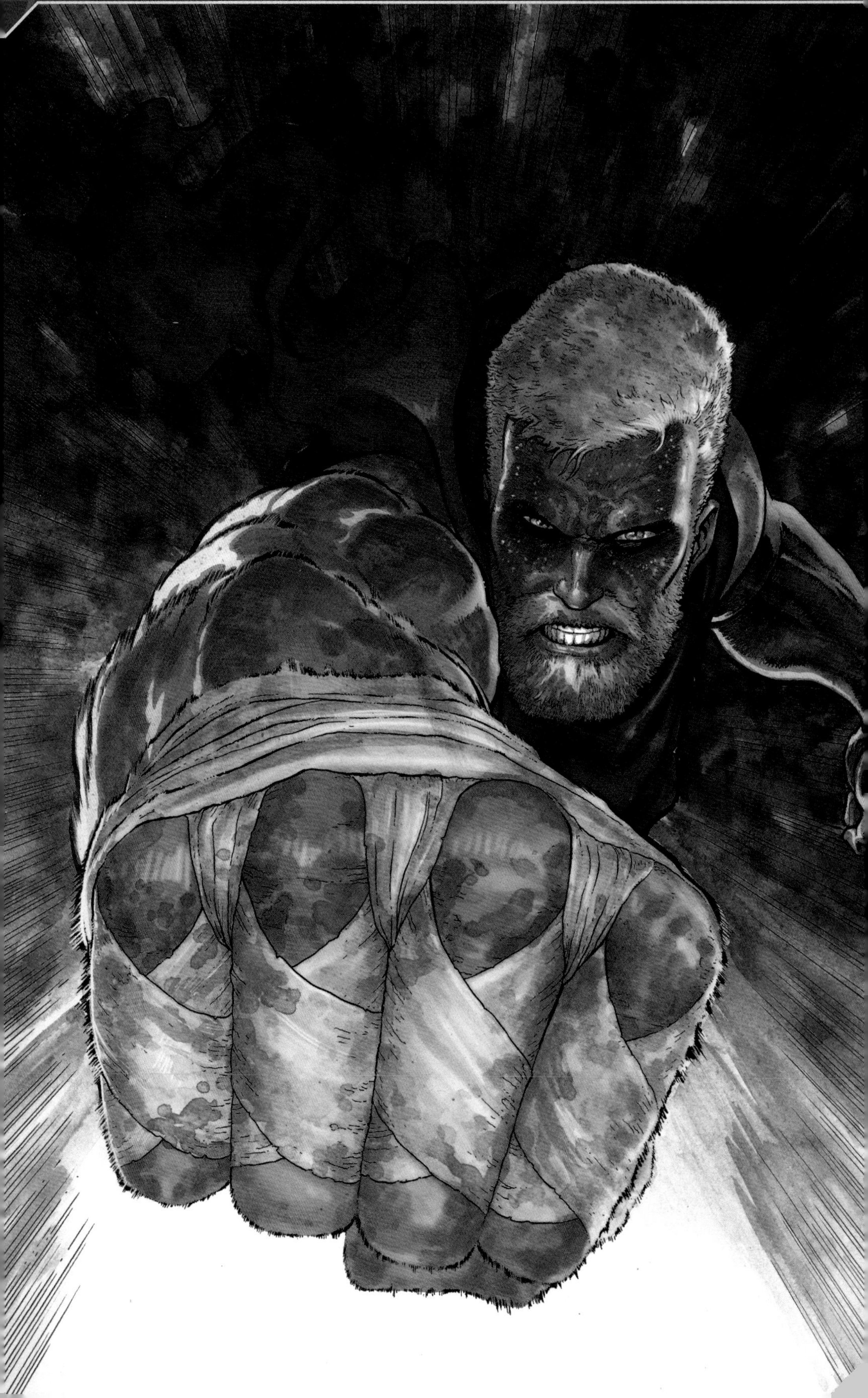

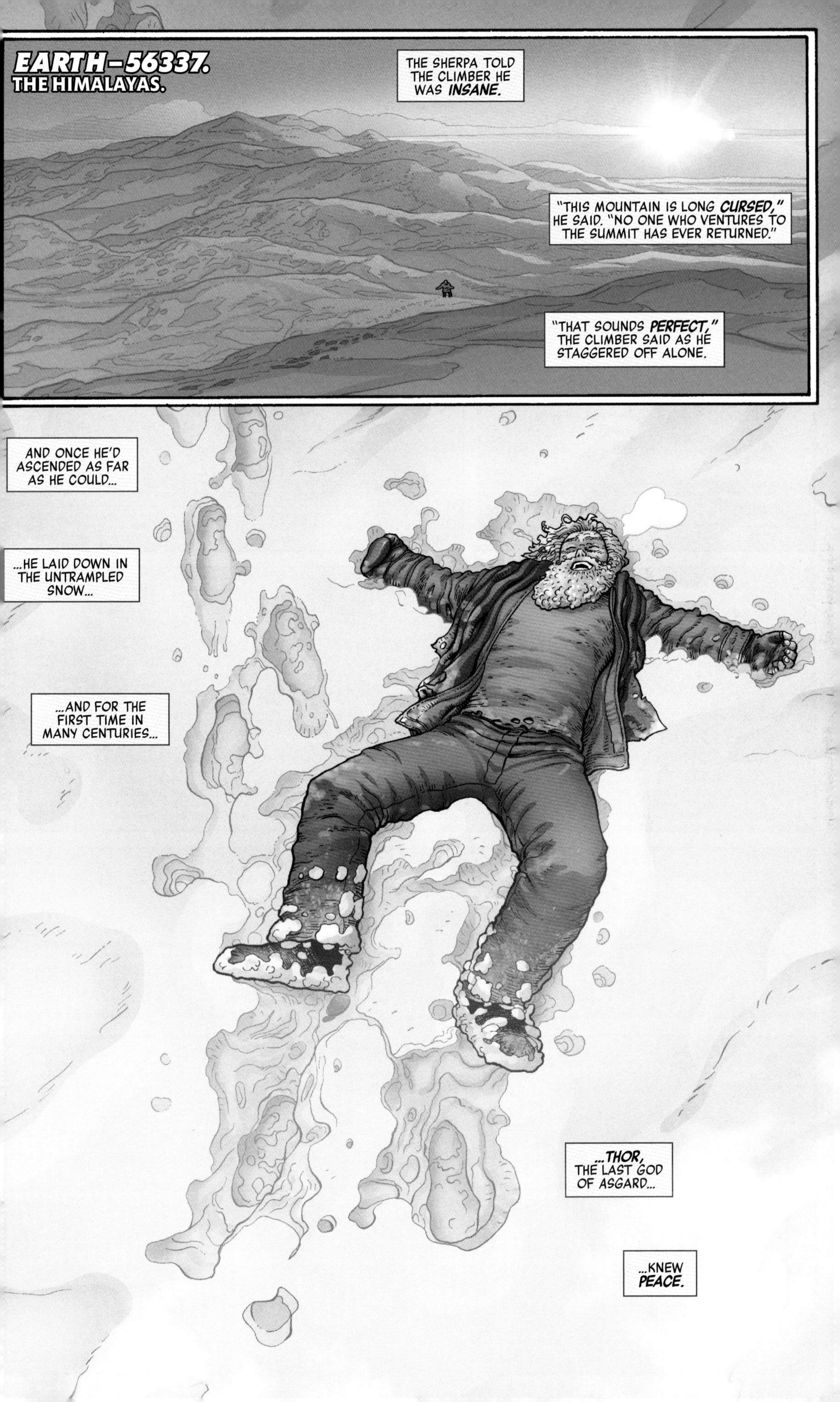
EARTH-56337.
THE HIMALAYAS.
THE SHERPA TOLD THE CLIMBER HE WAS INSANE.
"THIS MOUNTAIN IS LONG CURSED," HE SAID. "NO ONE WHO VENTURES TO THE SUMMIT HAS EVER RETURNED."
"THAT SOUNDS PERFECT," THE CLIMBER SAID AS HE STAGGERED OFF ALONE.
AND ONCE HE'D ASCENDED AS FAR AS HE COULD...
...HE LAID DOWN IN THE UNTRAMPLED SNOW...
...AND FOR THE FIRST TIME IN MANY CENTURIES...
...THOR, THE LAST GOD OF ASGARD...
...KNEW PEACE.

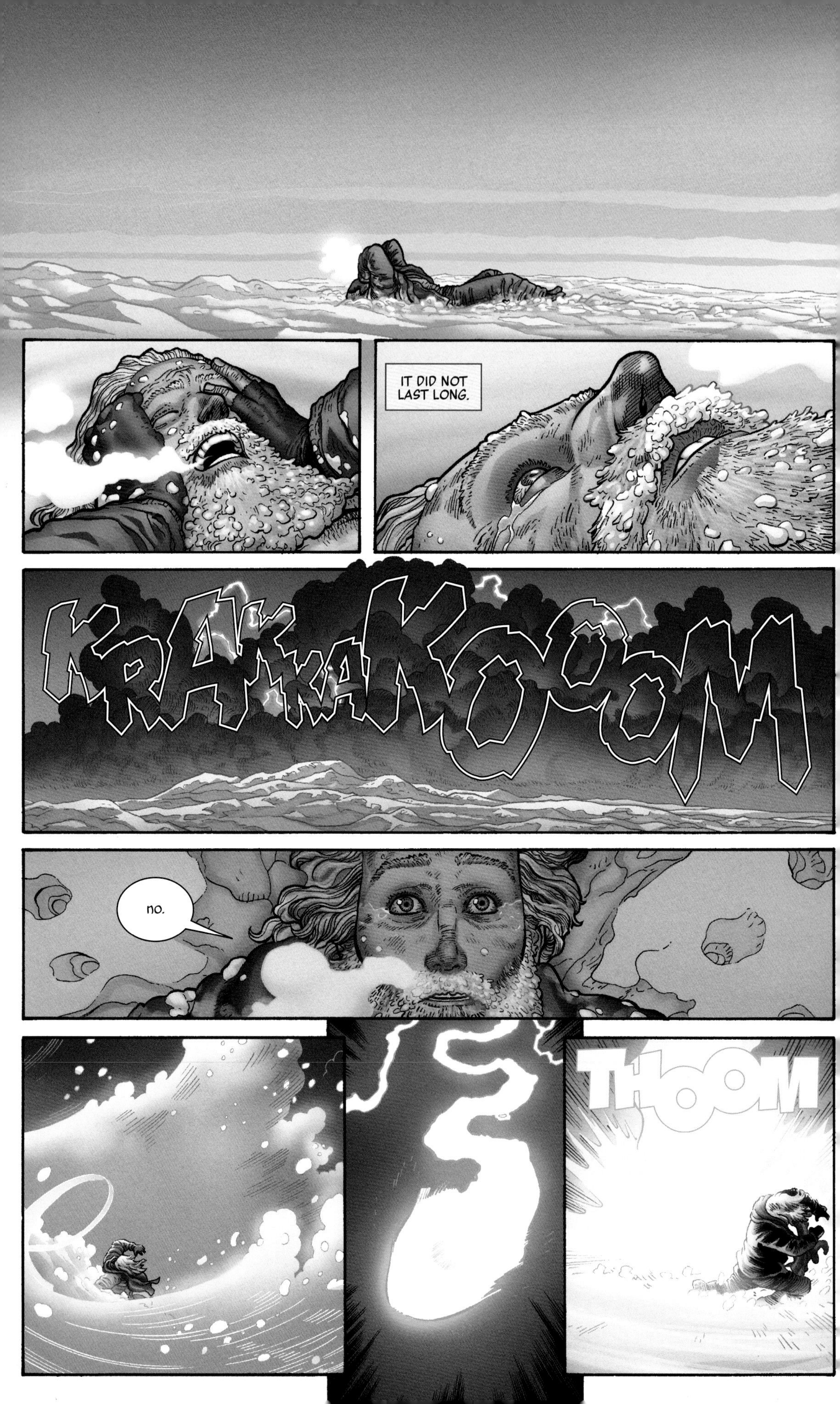
IT DID NOT LAST LONG.
KRAKKAKOOOOM
no.
THOOM

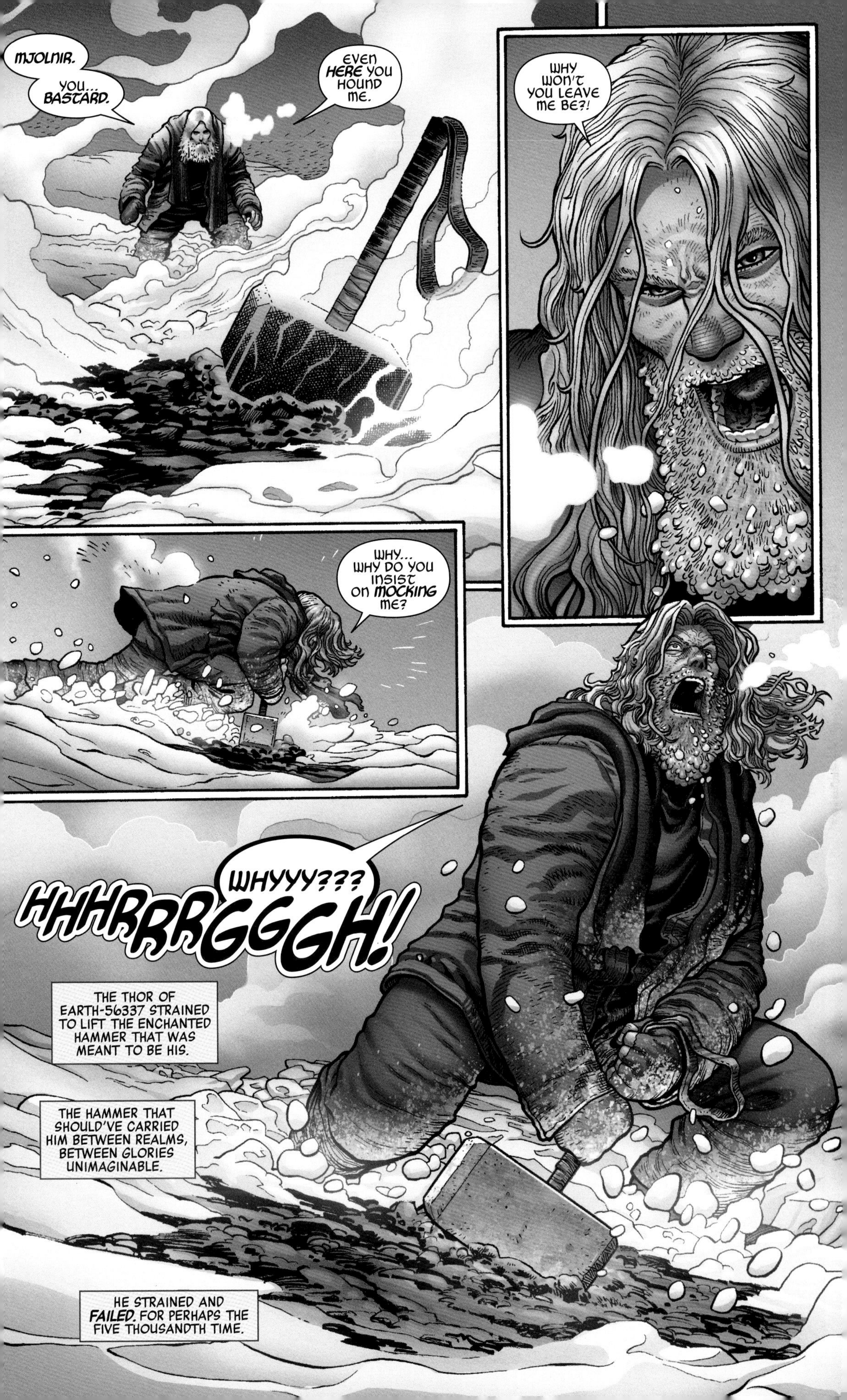

MJOLNIR.
YOU... BASTARD.
EVEN HERE YOU HOUND ME.
WHY WON'T YOU LEAVE ME BE?!
WHY... WHY DO YOU INSIST ON MOCKING ME?
WHYYY???
HHHRRRGGGH!
THE THOR OF EARTH-56337 STRAINED TO LIFT THE ENCHANTED HAMMER THAT WAS MEANT TO BE HIS.
THE HAMMER THAT SHOULD'VE CARRIED HIM BETWEEN REALMS, BETWEEN GLORIES UNIMAGINABLE.
HE STRAINED AND FAILED, FOR PERHAPS THE FIVE THOUSANDTH TIME.

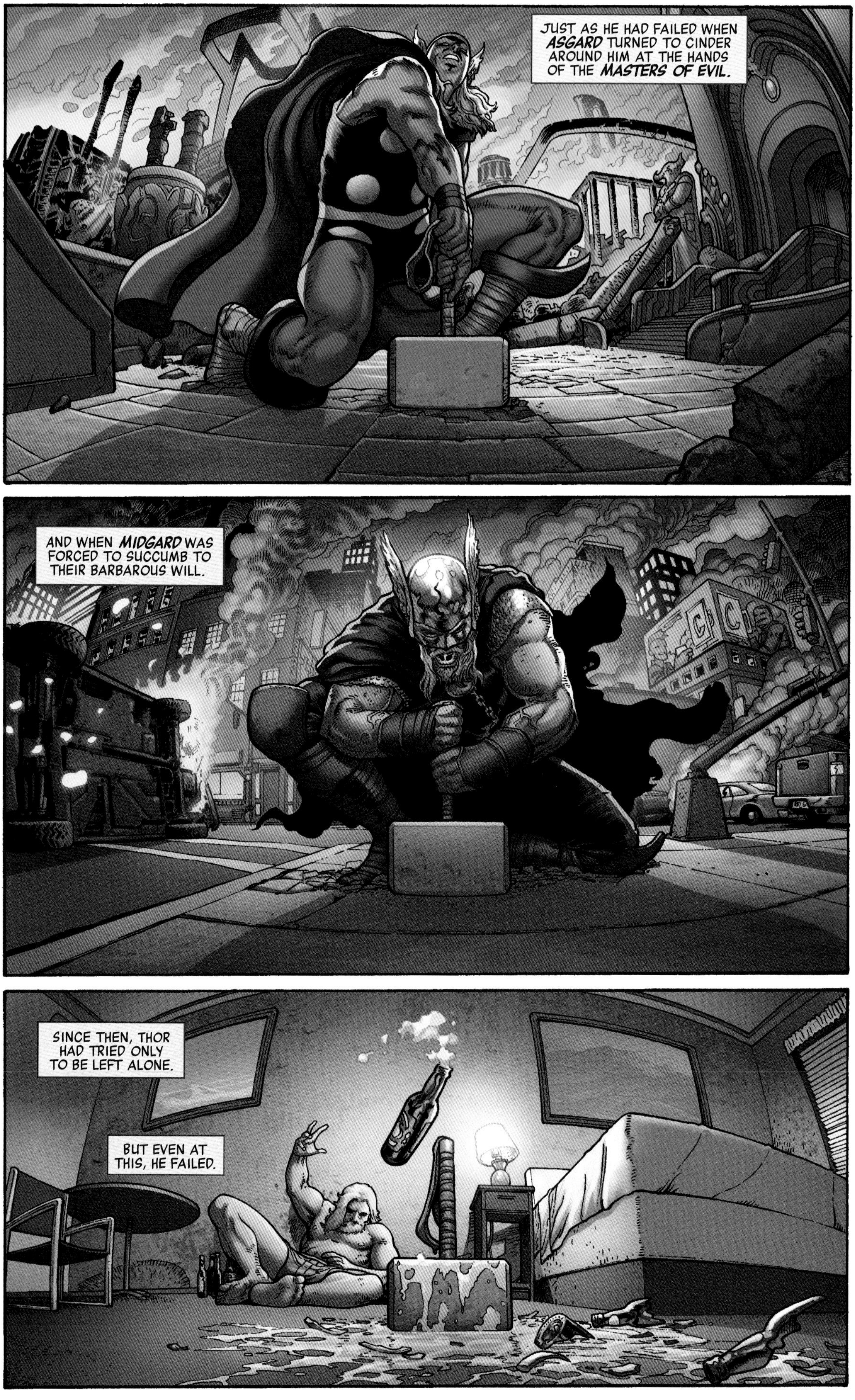
JUST AS HE HAD FAILED WHEN ASGARD TURNED TO CINDER AROUND HIM AT THE HANDS OF THE MASTERS OF EVIL.
AND WHEN MIDGARD WAS FORCED TO SUCCUMB TO THEIR BARBAROUS WILL.
SINCE THEN, THOR HAD TRIED ONLY TO BE LEFT ALONE.
BUT EVEN AT THIS, HE FAILED.

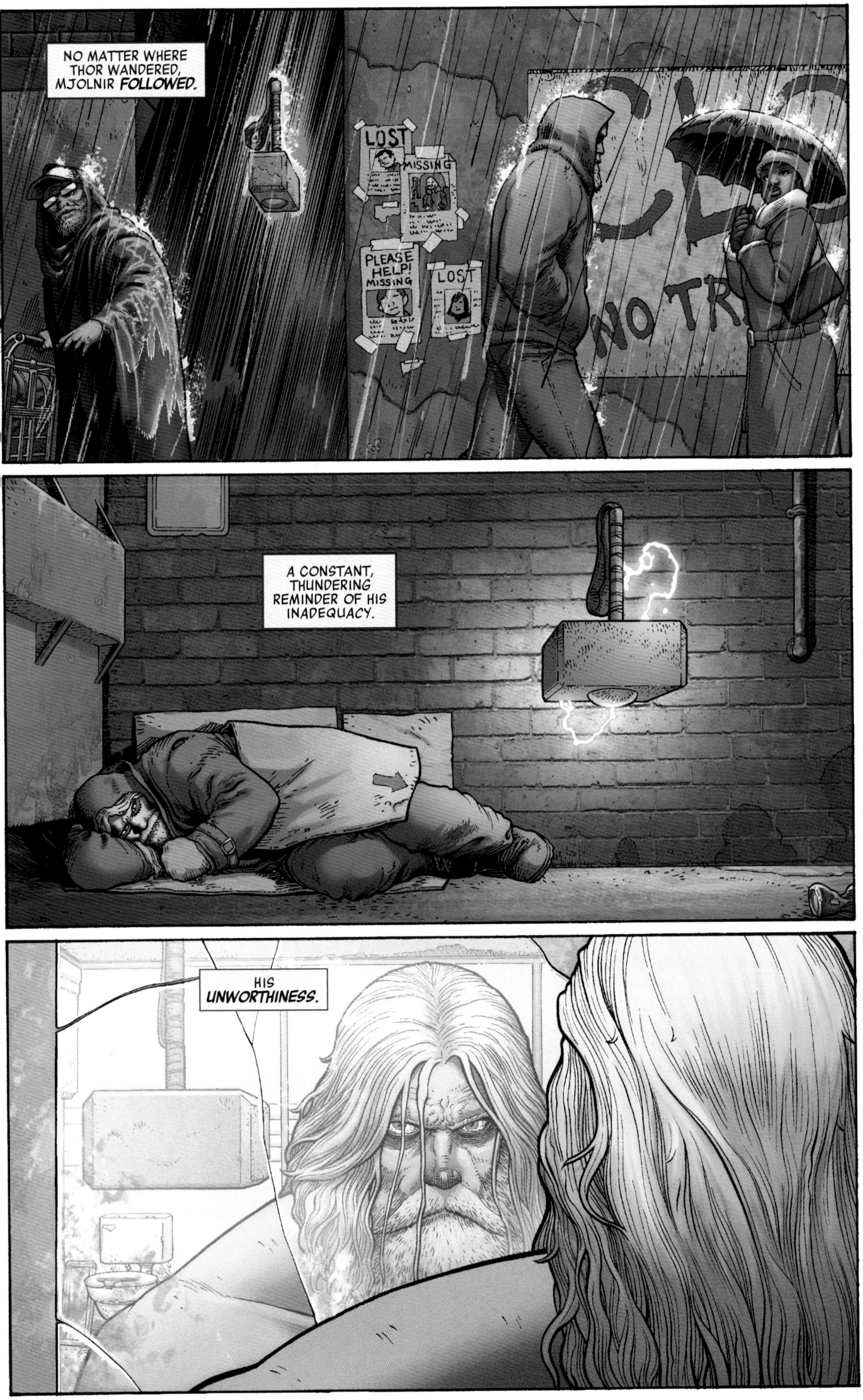
NO MATTER WHERE THOR WANDERED, MJOLNIR **FOLLOWED**.
LOST
MISSING
PLEASE HELP! MISSING
LOST
A CONSTANT, THUNDERING REMINDER OF HIS INADEQUACY.
HIS **UNWORTHINESS**.

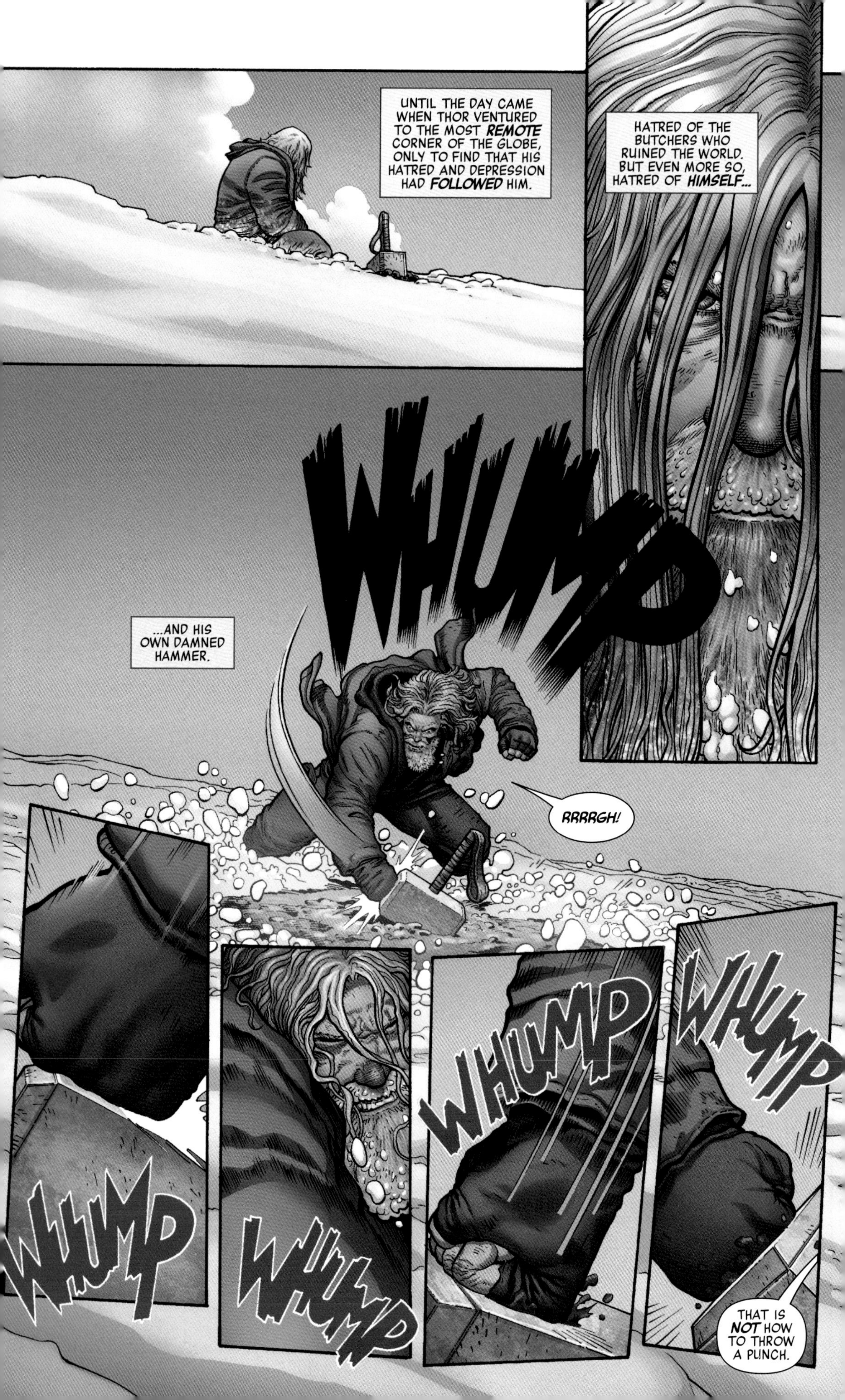
UNTIL THE DAY CAME WHEN THOR VENTURED TO THE MOST REMOTE CORNER OF THE GLOBE, ONLY TO FIND THAT HIS HATRED AND DEPRESSION HAD FOLLOWED HIM.
HATRED OF THE BUTCHERS WHO RUINED THE WORLD. BUT EVEN MORE SO, HATRED OF HIMSELF...
WHUMP
...AND HIS OWN DAMNED HAMMER.
BRRRGH!
WHUMP
WHUMP
WHUMP
WHUMP
THAT IS NOT HOW TO THROW A PUNCH.

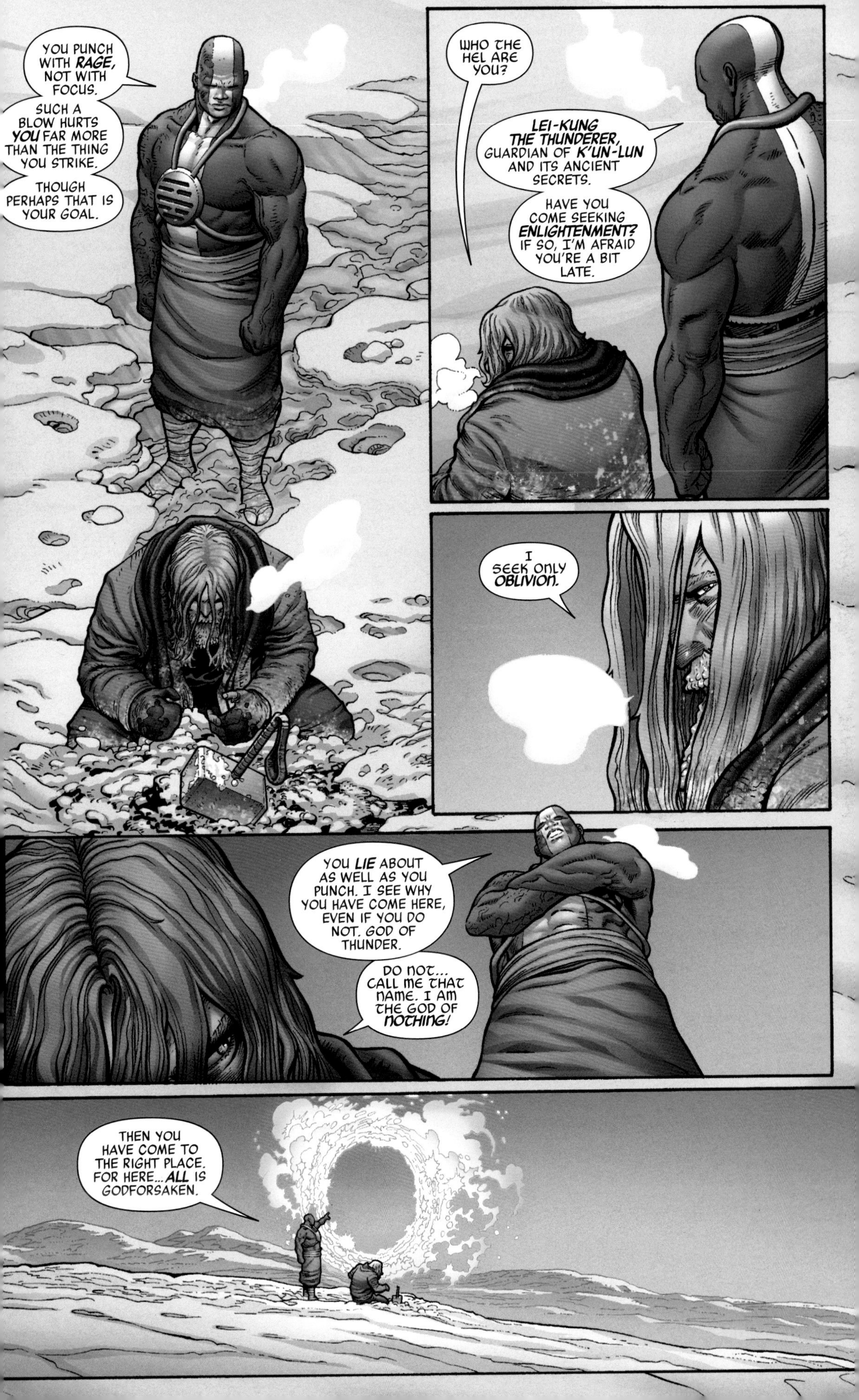
YOU PUNCH WITH RAGE, NOT WITH FOCUS.
SUCH A BLOW HURTS YOU FAR MORE THAN THE THING YOU STRIKE.
THOUGH PERHAPS THAT IS YOUR GOAL.
WHO THE HEL ARE YOU?
LEI-KUNG THE THUNDERER, GUARDIAN OF K'UN-LUN AND ITS ANCIENT SECRETS.
HAVE YOU COME SEEKING ENLIGHTENMENT? IF SO, I'M AFRAID YOU'RE A BIT LATE.
I SEEK ONLY OBLIVION.
YOU LIE ABOUT AS WELL AS YOU PUNCH. I SEE WHY YOU HAVE COME HERE, EVEN IF YOU DO NOT. GOD OF THUNDER.
DO NOT... CALL ME THAT NAME. I AM THE GOD OF NOTHING!
THEN YOU HAVE COME TO THE RIGHT PLACE. FOR HERE... ALL IS GODFORSAKEN.

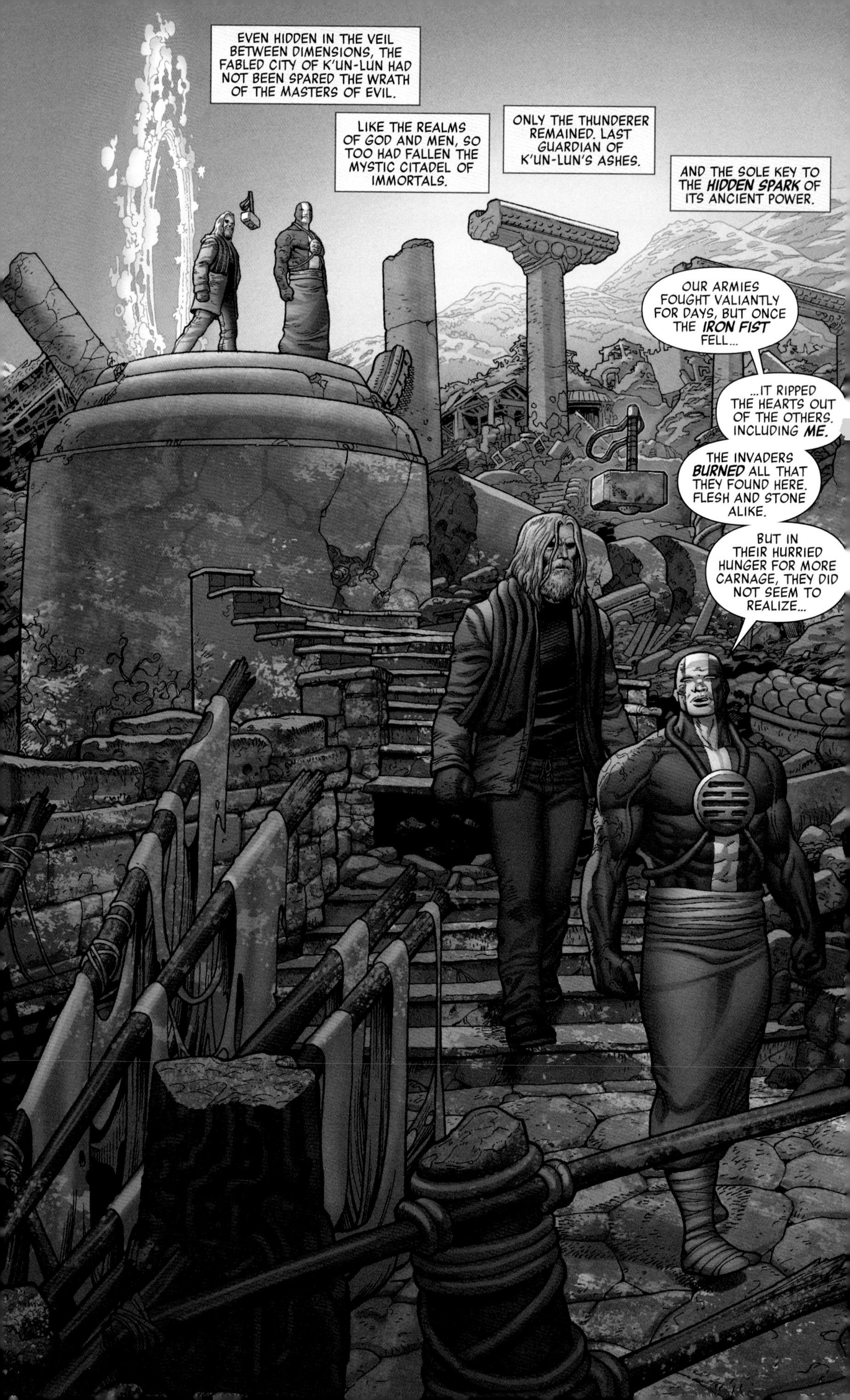

EVEN HIDDEN IN THE VEIL BETWEEN DIMENSIONS, THE FABLED CITY OF K'UN-LUN HAD NOT BEEN SPARED THE WRATH OF THE MASTERS OF EVIL.
LIKE THE REALMS OF GOD AND MEN, SO TOO HAD FALLEN THE MYSTIC CITADEL OF IMMORTALS.
ONLY THE THUNDERER REMAINED. LAST GUARDIAN OF K'UN-LUN'S ASHES.
AND THE SOLE KEY TO THE HIDDEN SPARK OF ITS ANCIENT POWER.
OUR ARMIES FOUGHT VALIANTLY FOR DAYS, BUT ONCE THE IRON FIST FELL...
...IT RIPPED THE HEARTS OUT OF THE OTHERS. INCLUDING ME.
THE INVADERS BURNED ALL THAT THEY FOUND HERE. FLESH AND STONE ALIKE.
BUT IN THEIR HURRIED HUNGER FOR MORE CARNAGE, THEY DID NOT SEEM TO REALIZE...

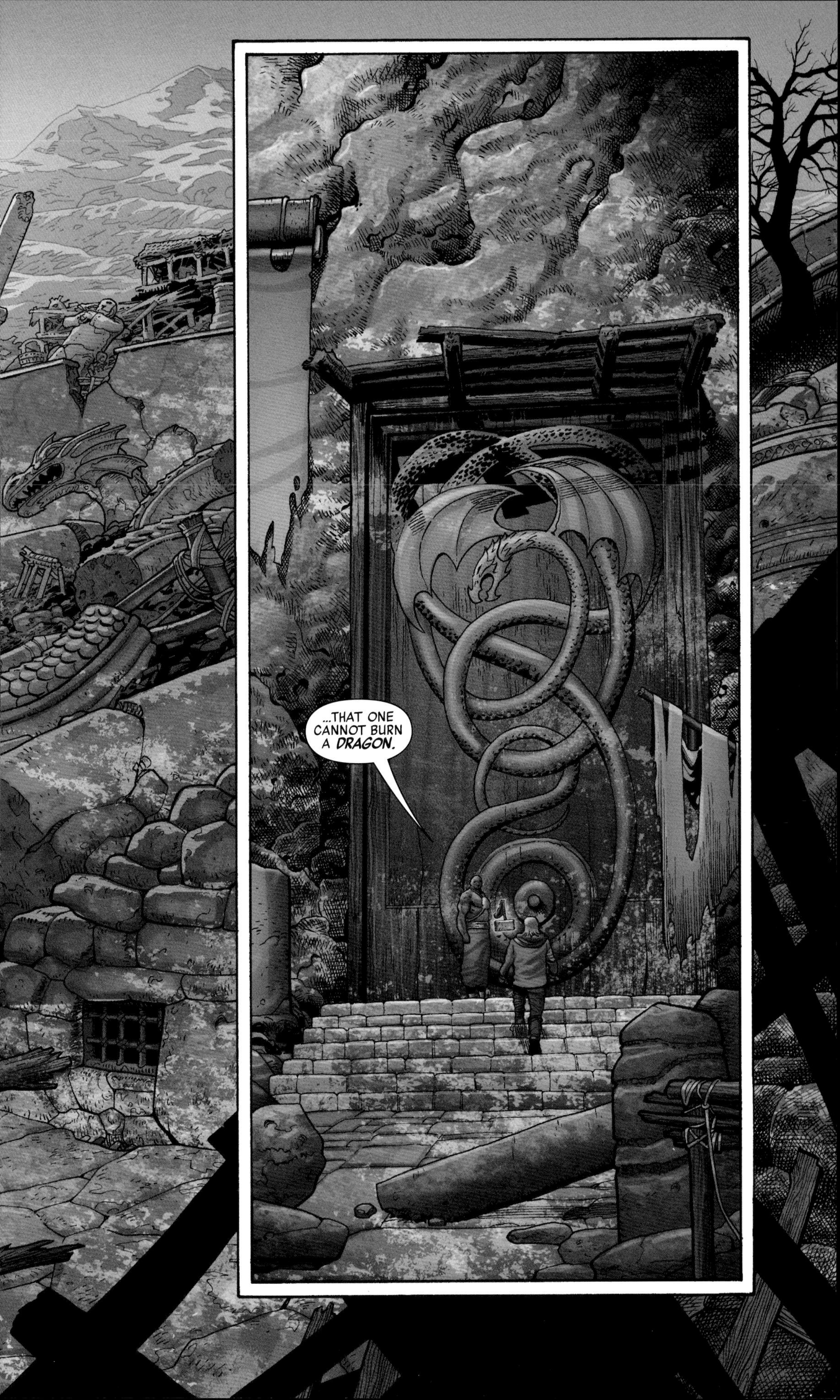
...THAT ONE CANNOT BURN A DRAGON.

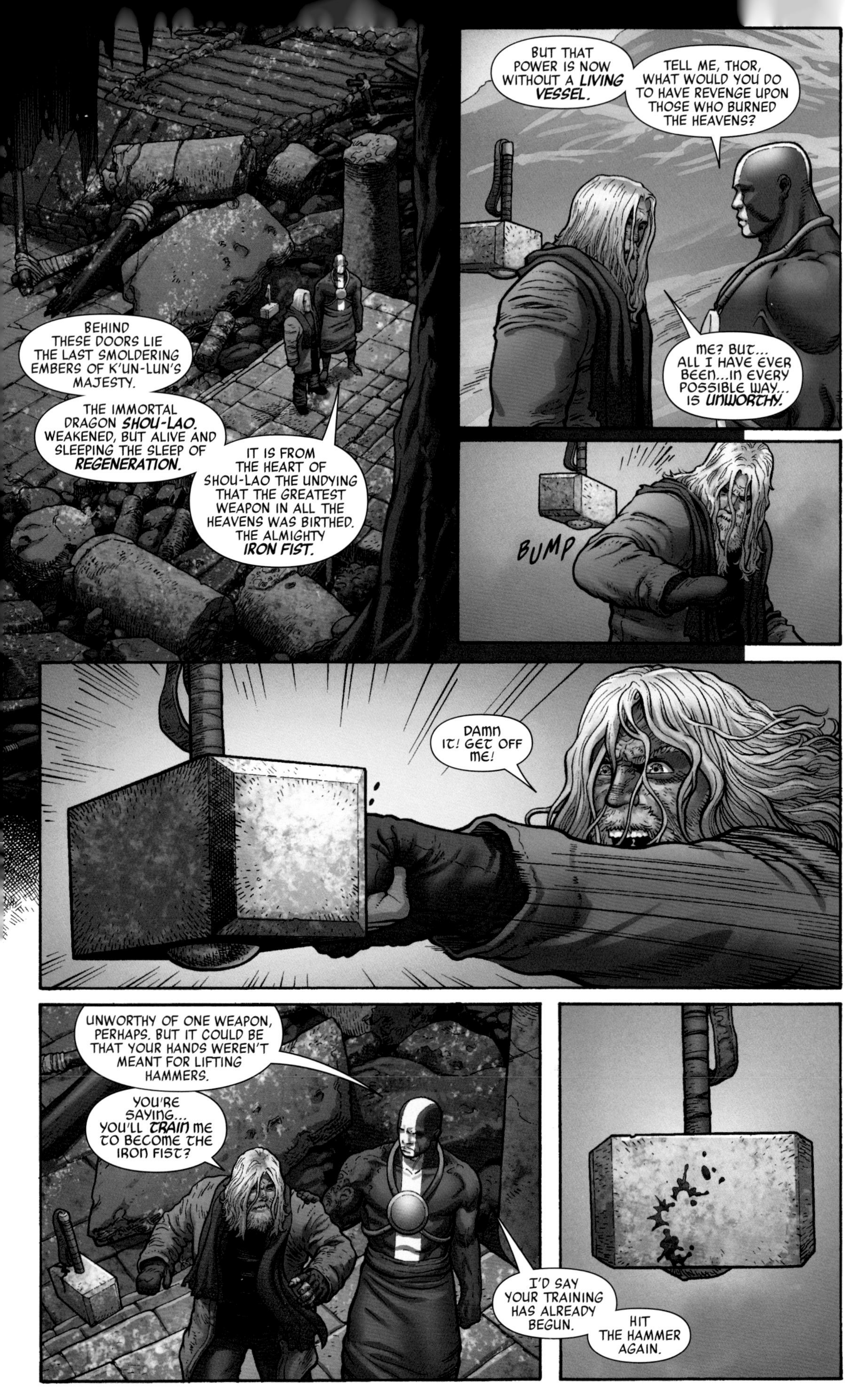

BEHIND THESE DOORS LIE THE LAST SMOLDERING EMBERS OF K'UN-LUN'S MAJESTY.
THE IMMORTAL DRAGON SHOU-LAO. WEAKENED, BUT ALIVE AND SLEEPING THE SLEEP OF REGENERATION.
IT IS FROM THE HEART OF SHOU-LAO THE UNDYING THAT THE GREATEST WEAPON IN ALL THE HEAVENS WAS BIRTHED. THE ALMIGHTY IRON FIST.
BUT THAT POWER IS NOW WITHOUT A LIVING VESSEL.
TELL ME, THOR, WHAT WOULD YOU DO TO HAVE REVENGE UPON THOSE WHO BURNED THE HEAVENS?
ME? BUT... ALL I HAVE EVER BEEN...IN EVERY POSSIBLE WAY... IS UNWORTHY.
BUMP
DAMN IT! GET OFF ME!
UNWORTHY OF ONE WEAPON, PERHAPS. BUT IT COULD BE THAT YOUR HANDS WEREN'T MEANT FOR LIFTING HAMMERS.
YOU'RE SAYING... YOU'LL TRAIN ME TO BECOME THE IRON FIST?
I'D SAY YOUR TRAINING HAS ALREADY BEGUN.
HIT THE HAMMER AGAIN.

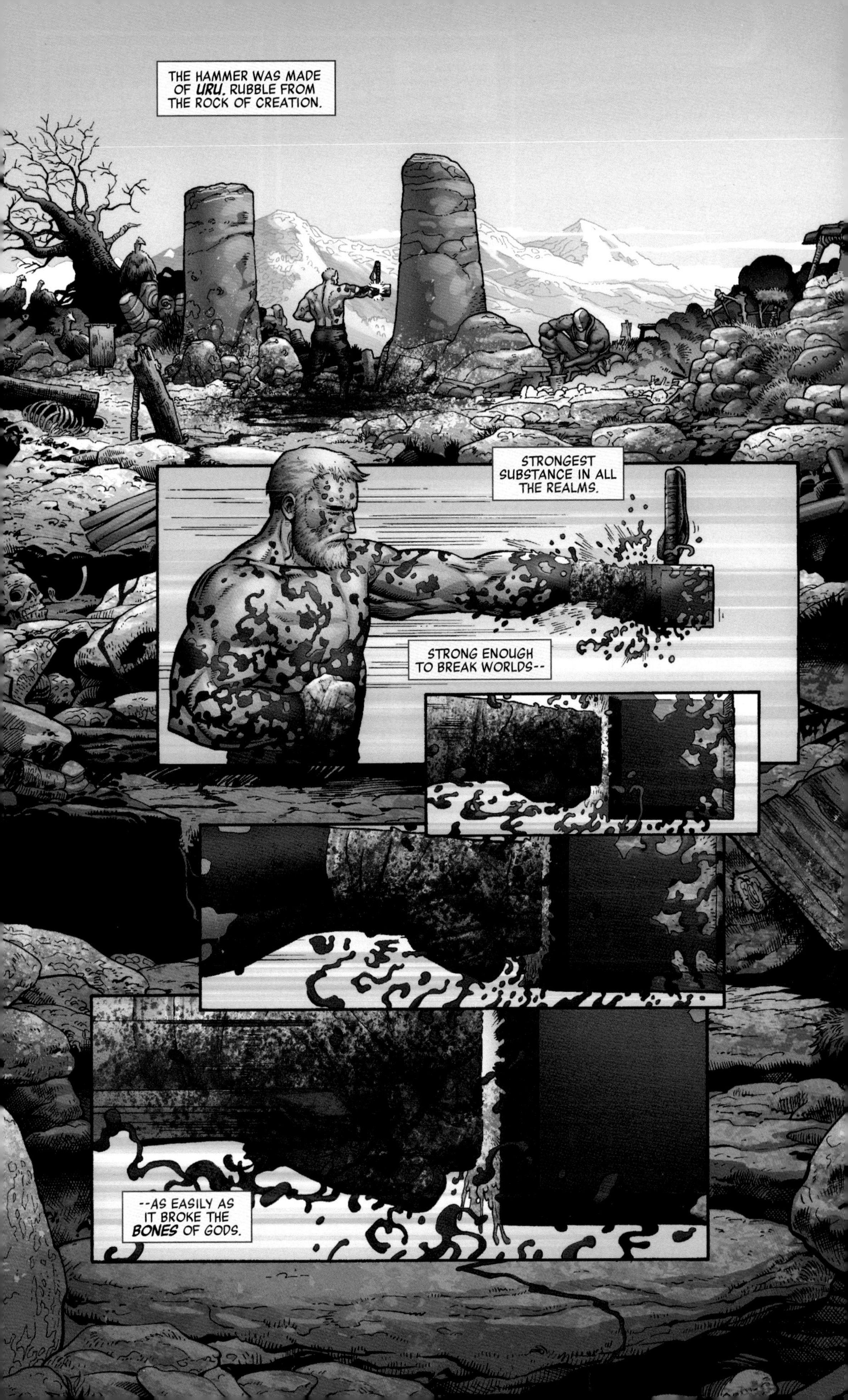
THE HAMMER WAS MADE OF URU. RUBBLE FROM THE ROCK OF CREATION.
STRONGEST SUBSTANCE IN ALL THE REALMS.
STRONG ENOUGH TO BREAK WORLDS--
--AS EASILY AS IT BROKE THE BONES OF GODS.

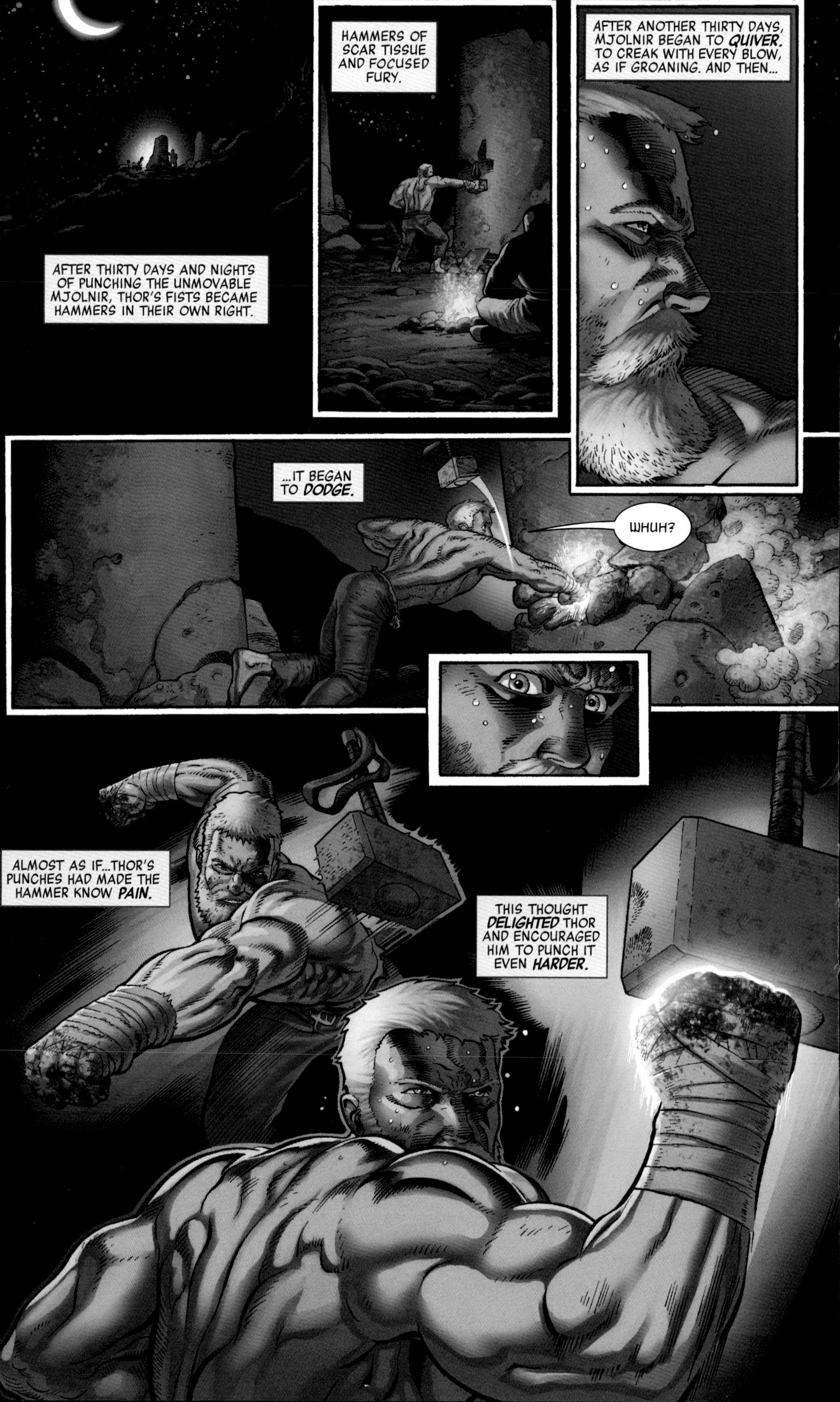
AFTER THIRTY DAYS AND NIGHTS OF PUNCHING THE UNMOVABLE MJOLNIR, THOR'S FISTS BECAME HAMMERS IN THEIR OWN RIGHT.
HAMMERS OF SCAR TISSUE AND FOCUSED FURY.
AFTER ANOTHER THIRTY DAYS, MJOLNIR BEGAN TO QUIVER. TO CREAK WITH EVERY BLOW, AS IF GROANING. AND THEN...
...IT BEGAN TO DODGE.
WHUH?
ALMOST AS IF...THOR'S PUNCHES HAD MADE THE HAMMER KNOW PAIN.
THIS THOUGHT DELIGHTED THOR AND ENCOURAGED HIM TO PUNCH IT EVEN HARDER.

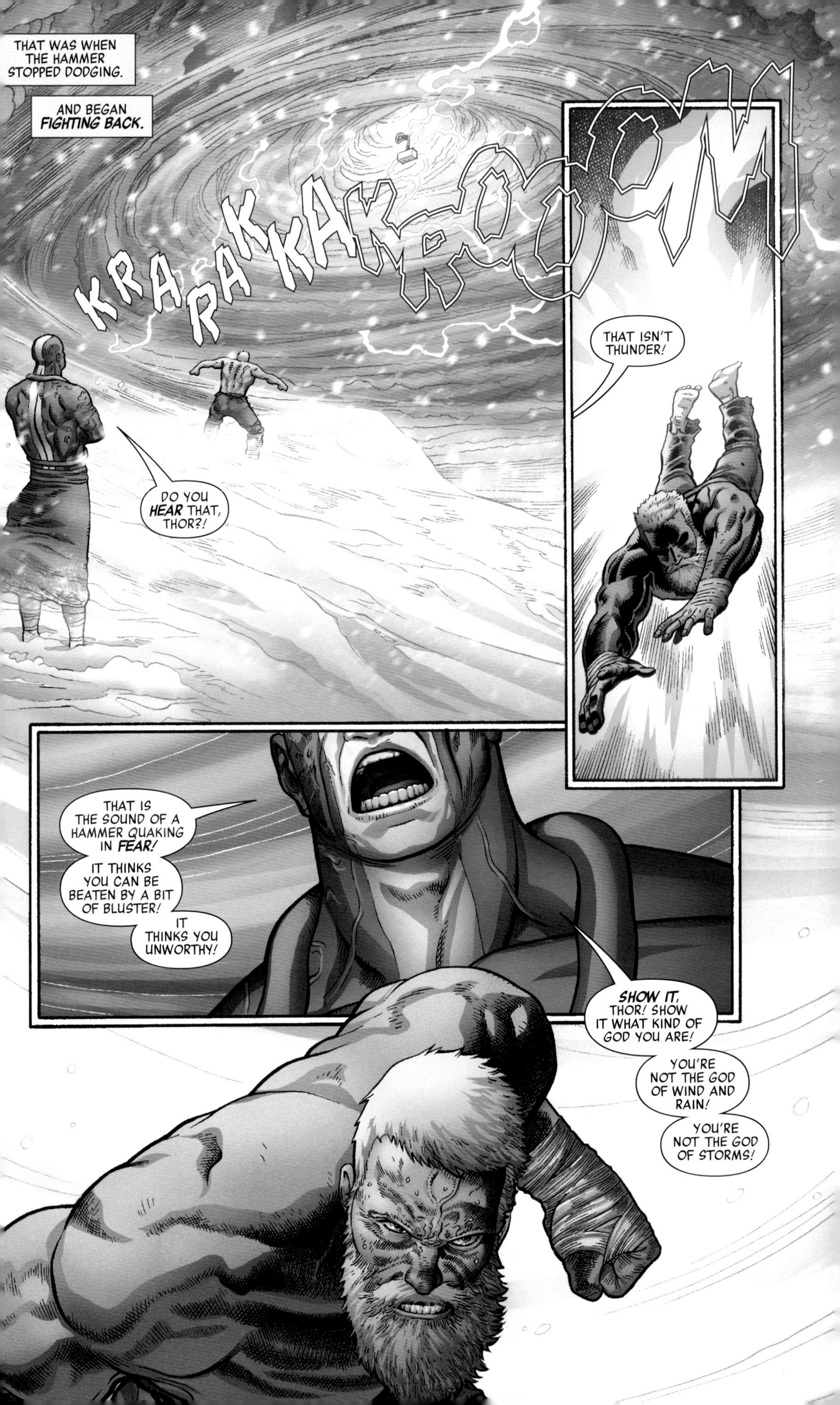

THAT WAS WHEN THE HAMMER STOPPED DODGING.
AND BEGAN FIGHTING BACK.
KRAKAKRAKAKA-KOOM
DO YOU HEAR THAT, THOR?!
THAT ISN'T THUNDER!
THAT IS THE SOUND OF A HAMMER QUAKING IN FEAR!
IT THINKS YOU CAN BE BEATEN BY A BIT OF BLUSTER!
IT THINKS YOU UNWORTHY!
SHOW IT, THOR! SHOW IT WHAT KIND OF GOD YOU ARE!
YOU'RE NOT THE GOD OF WIND AND RAIN!
YOU'RE NOT THE GOD OF STORMS!

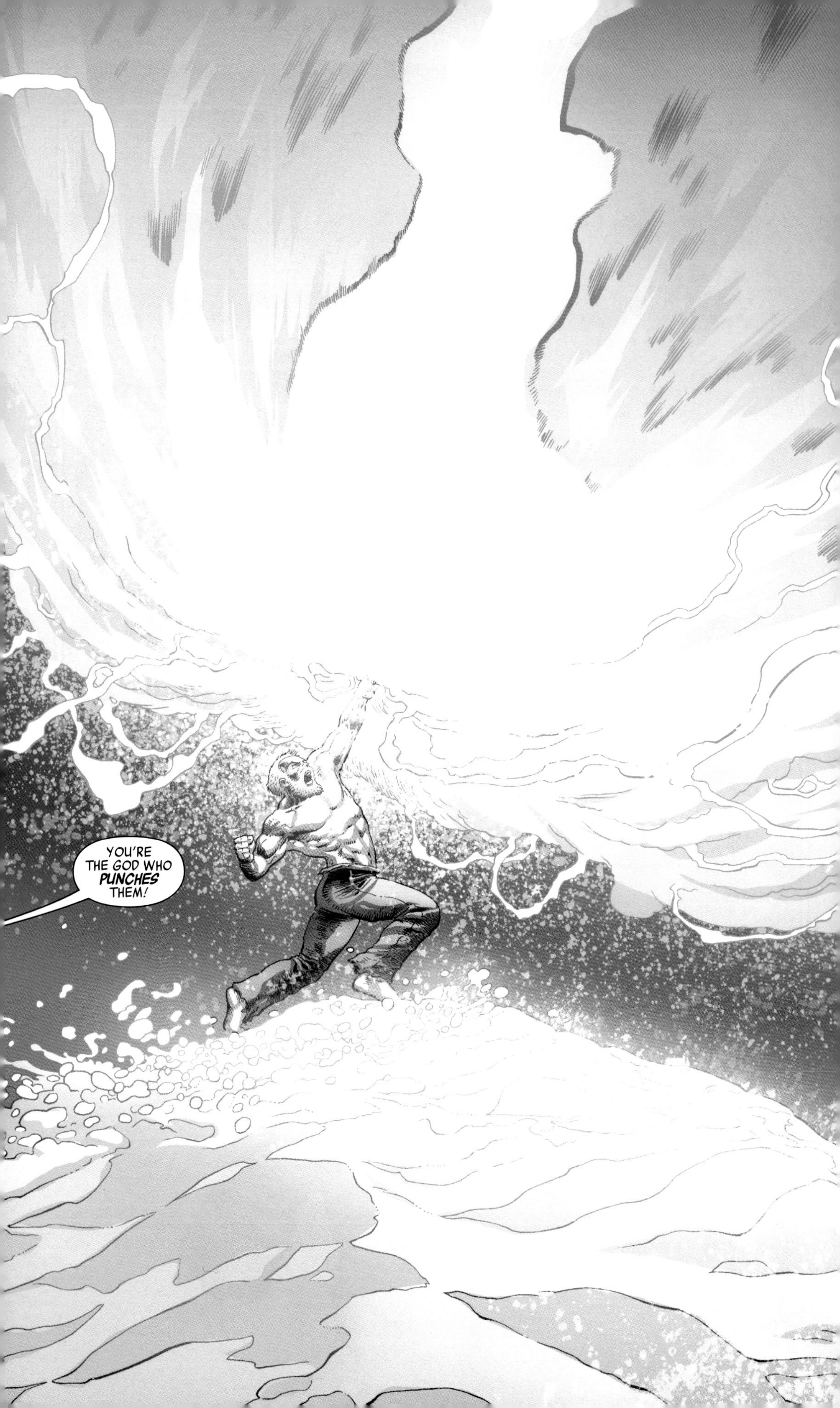
YOU'RE THE GOD WHO PUNCHES THEM!

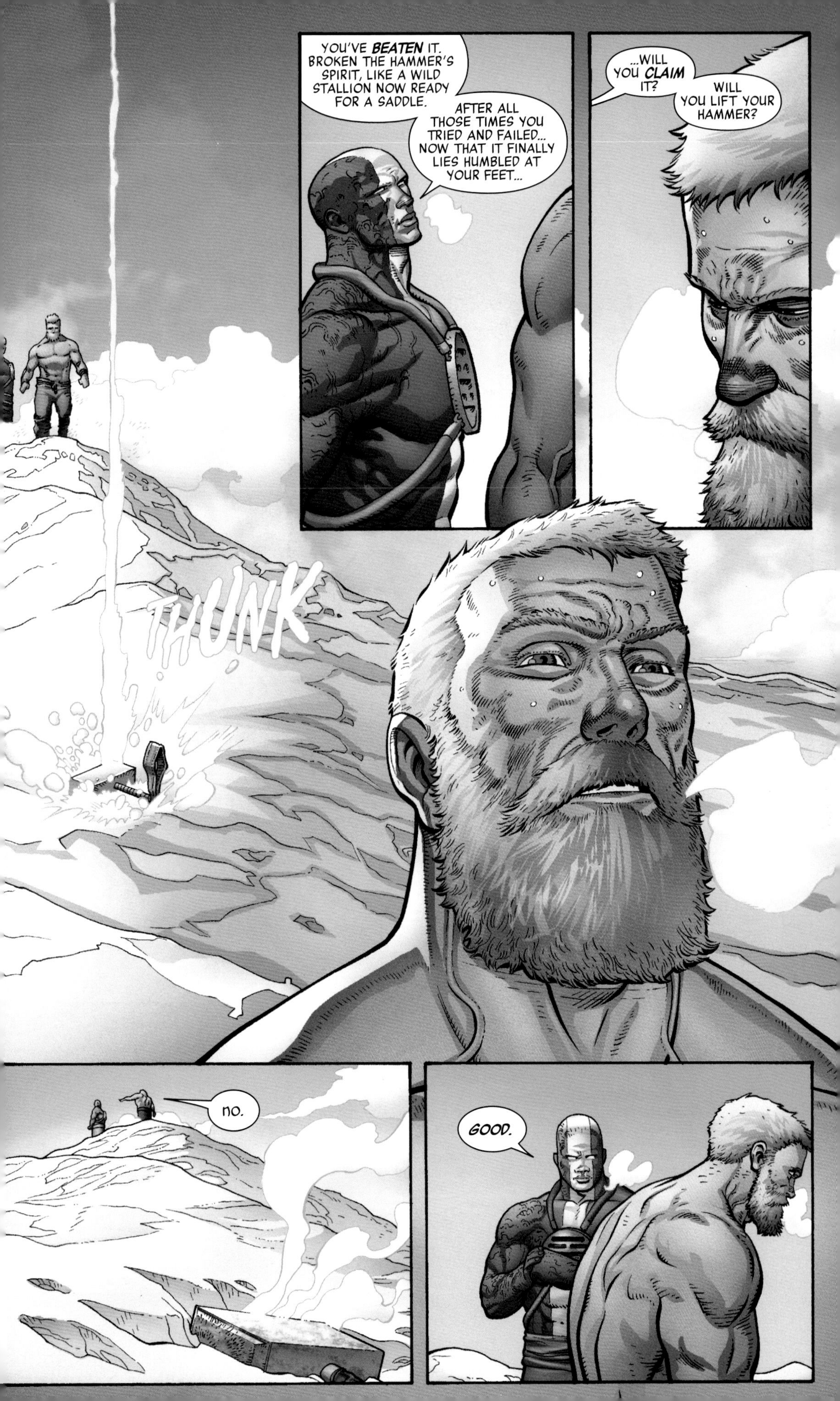
YOU'VE **BEATEN** IT. BROKEN THE HAMMER'S SPIRIT, LIKE A WILD STALLION NOW READY FOR A SADDLE.
AFTER ALL THOSE TIMES YOU TRIED AND FAILED... NOW THAT IT FINALLY LIES HUMBLED AT YOUR FEET...
...WILL YOU **CLAIM** IT?
WILL YOU LIFT YOUR HAMMER?
THUNK
no.
GOOD.

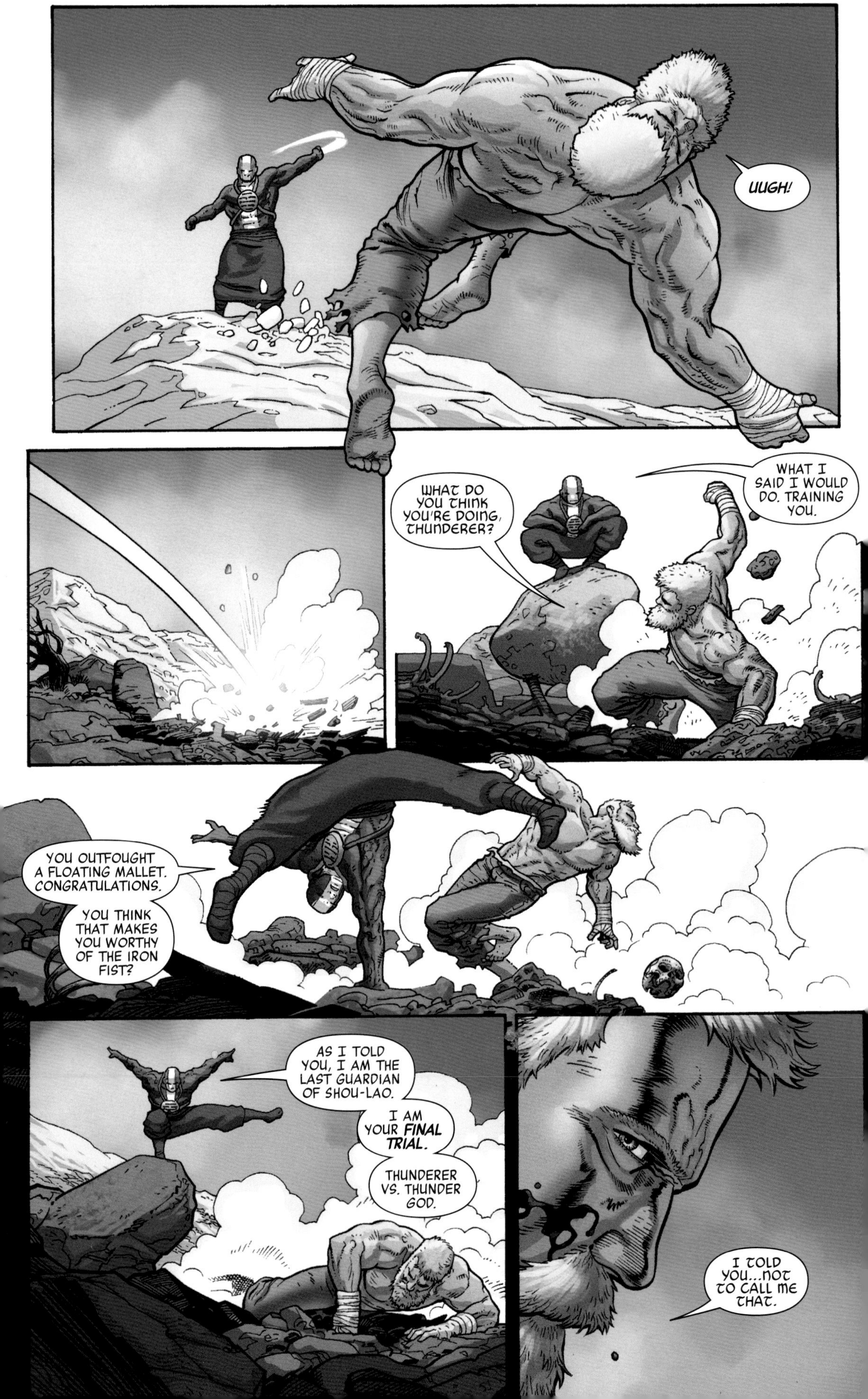
UUGH!
WHAT DO YOU THINK YOU'RE DOING, THUNDERER?
WHAT I SAID I WOULD DO. TRAINING YOU.
YOU OUTFOUGHT A FLOATING MALLET. CONGRATULATIONS.
YOU THINK THAT MAKES YOU WORTHY OF THE IRON FIST?
AS I TOLD YOU, I AM THE LAST GUARDIAN OF SHOU-LAO.
I AM YOUR FINAL TRIAL.
THUNDERER VS. THUNDER GOD.
I TOLD YOU...NOT TO CALL ME THAT.

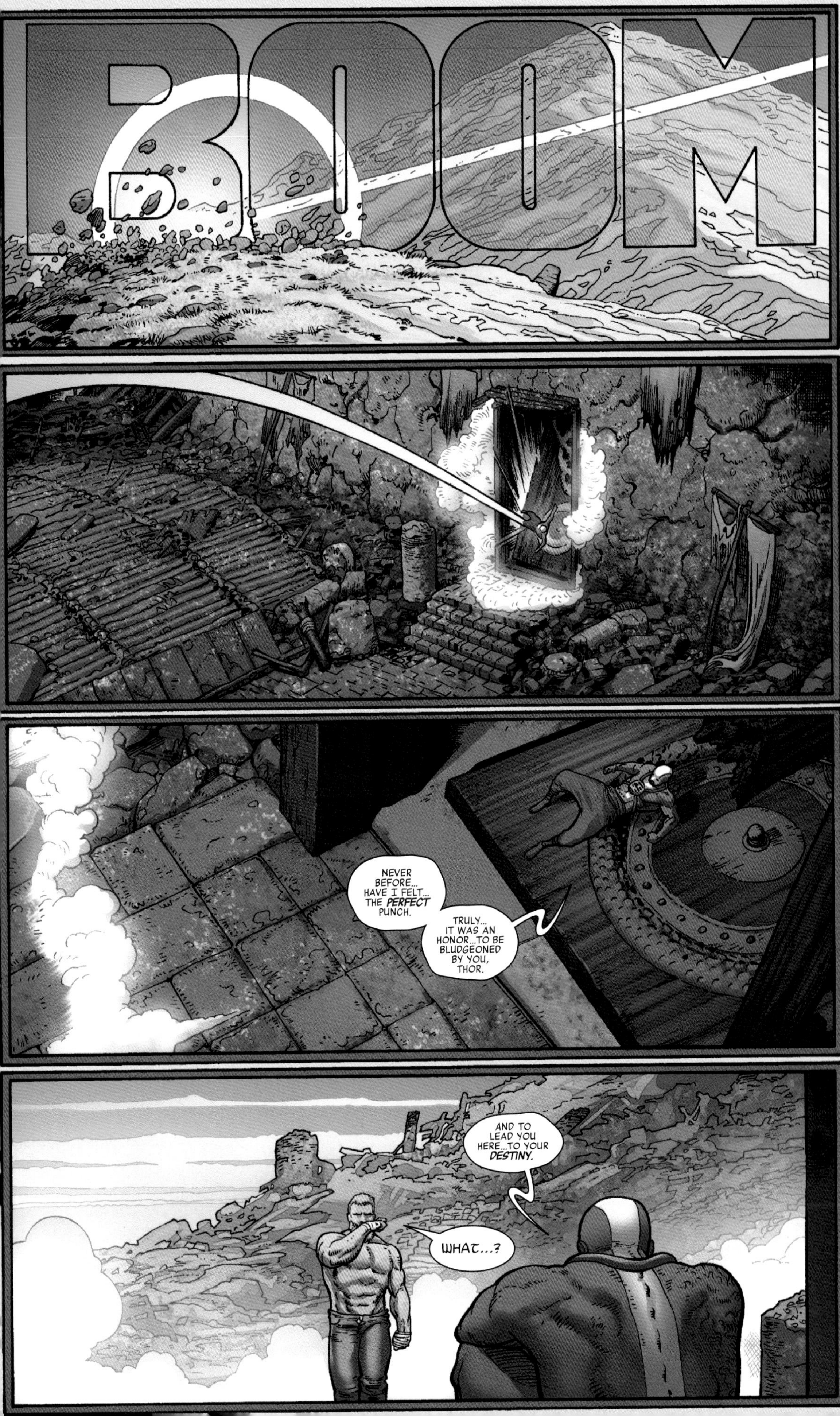
BOOM
NEVER BEFORE... HAVE I FELT... THE PERFECT PUNCH.
TRULY... IT WAS AN HONOR...TO BE BLUDGEONED BY YOU, THOR.
AND TO LEAD YOU HERE...TO YOUR DESTINY.
WHAT...?

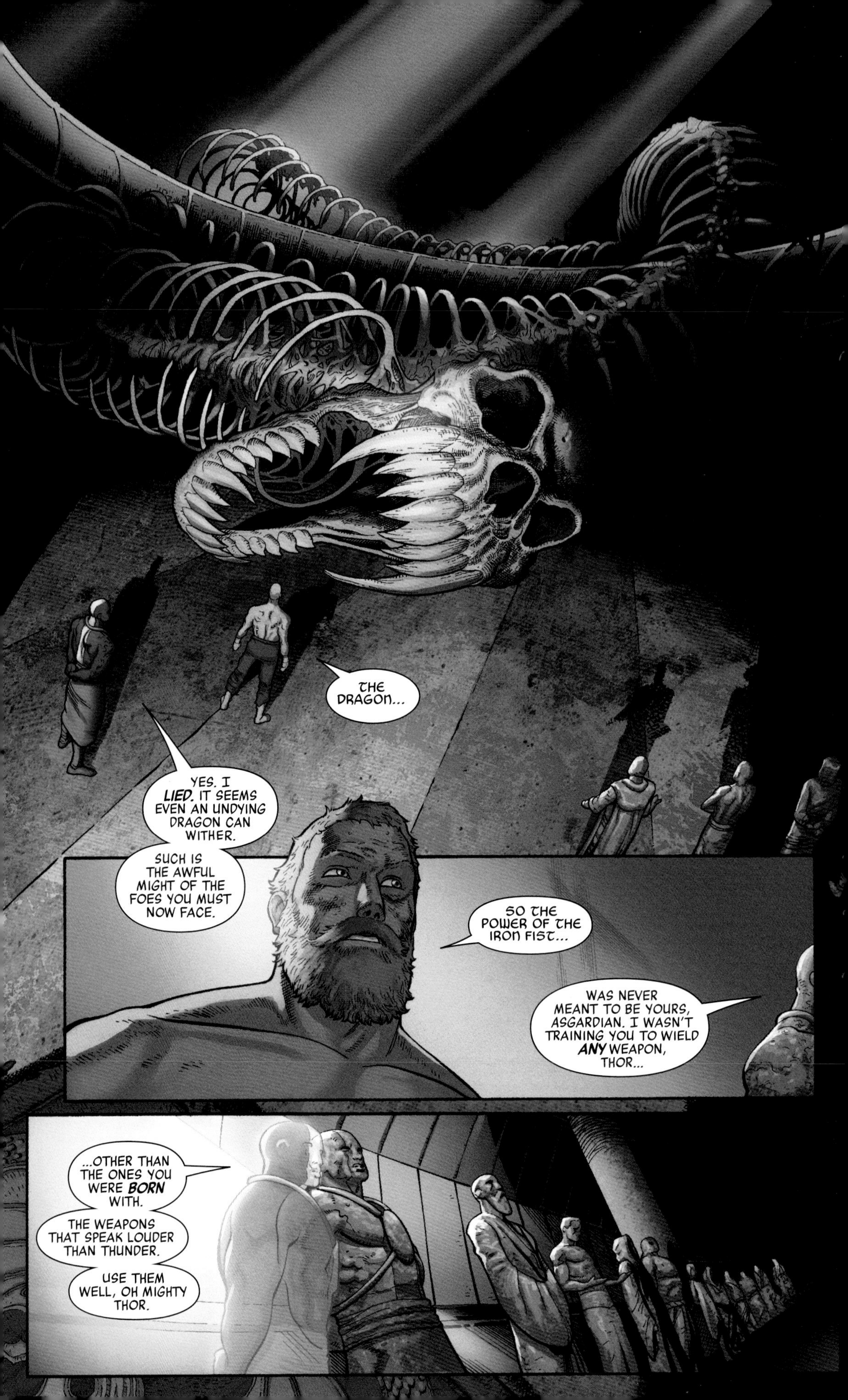
THE DRAGON...
YES. I LIED. IT SEEMS EVEN AN UNDYING DRAGON CAN WITHER.
SUCH IS THE AWFUL MIGHT OF THE FOES YOU MUST NOW FACE.
SO THE POWER OF THE IRON FIST...
WAS NEVER MEANT TO BE YOURS, ASGARDIAN. I WASN'T TRAINING YOU TO WIELD ANY WEAPON, THOR...
...OTHER THAN THE ONES YOU WERE BORN WITH.
THE WEAPONS THAT SPEAK LOUDER THAN THUNDER.
USE THEM WELL, OH MIGHTY THOR.

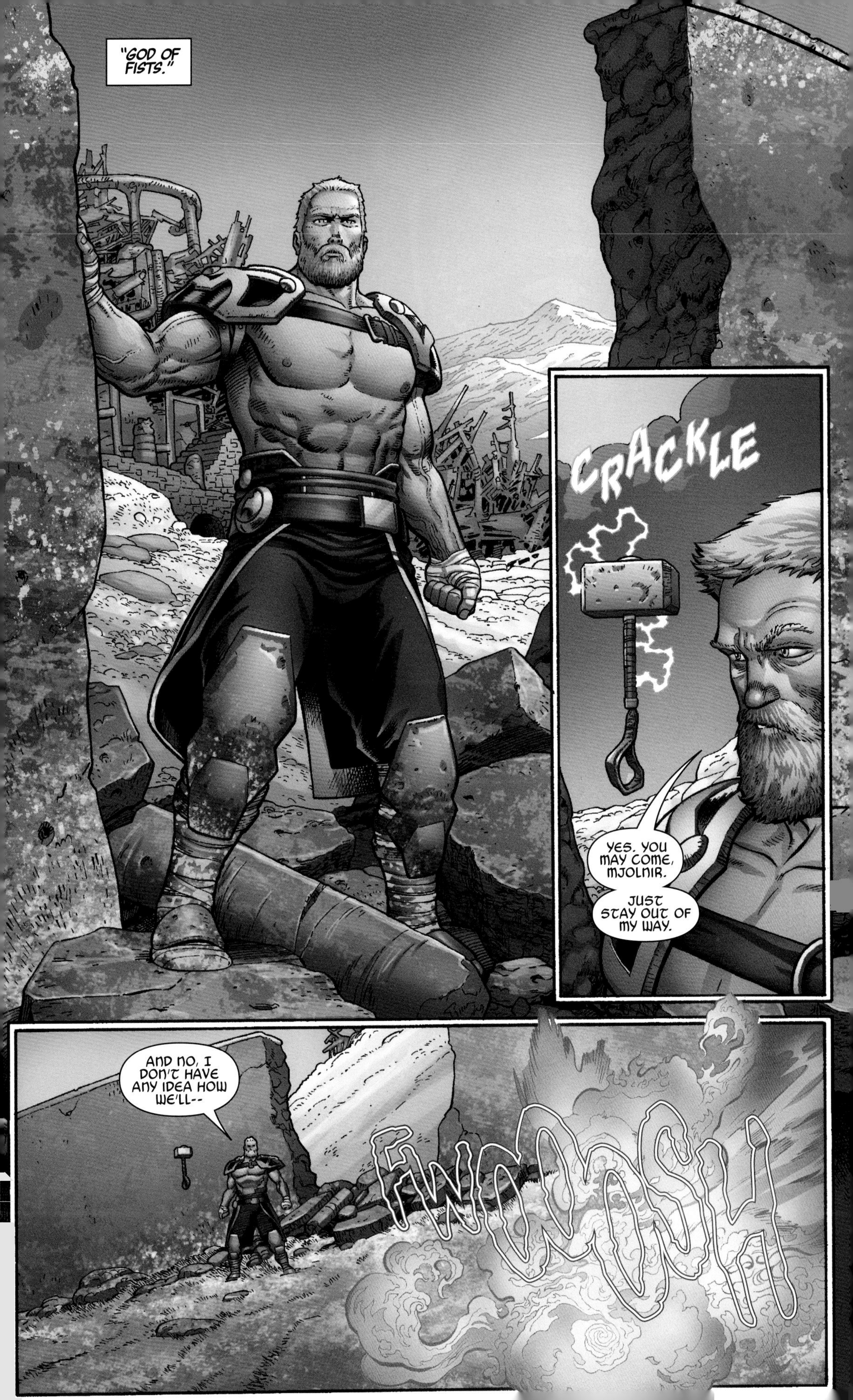
"GOD OF FISTS."
CRACKLE
YES. YOU MAY COME, MJOLNIR.
JUST STAY OUT OF MY WAY.
AND NO, I DON'T HAVE ANY IDEA HOW WE'LL--
FWOOOSH

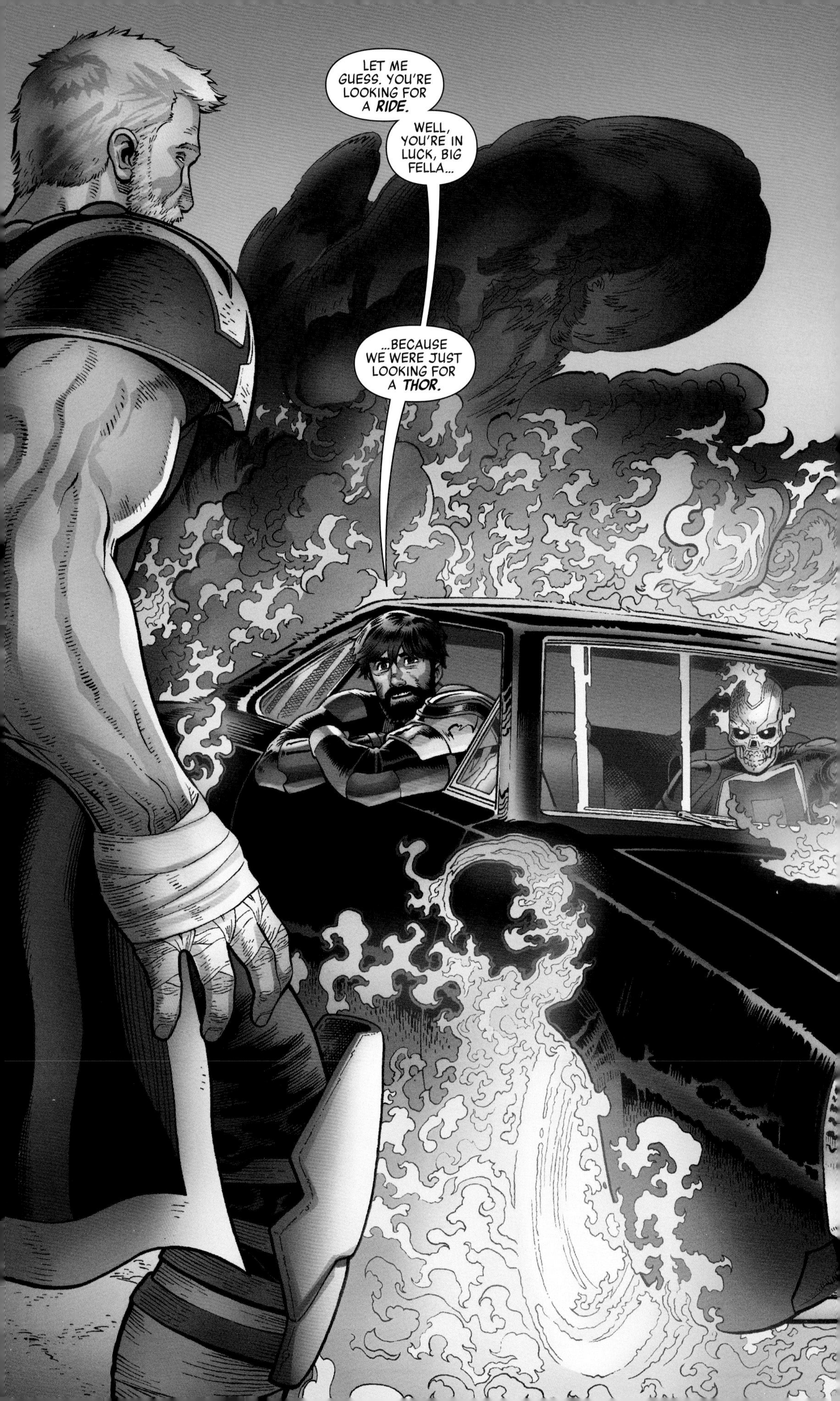

LET ME GUESS. YOU'RE LOOKING FOR A **RIDE.**
WELL, YOU'RE IN LUCK, BIG FELLA...
...BECAUSE WE WERE JUST LOOKING FOR A **THOR.**

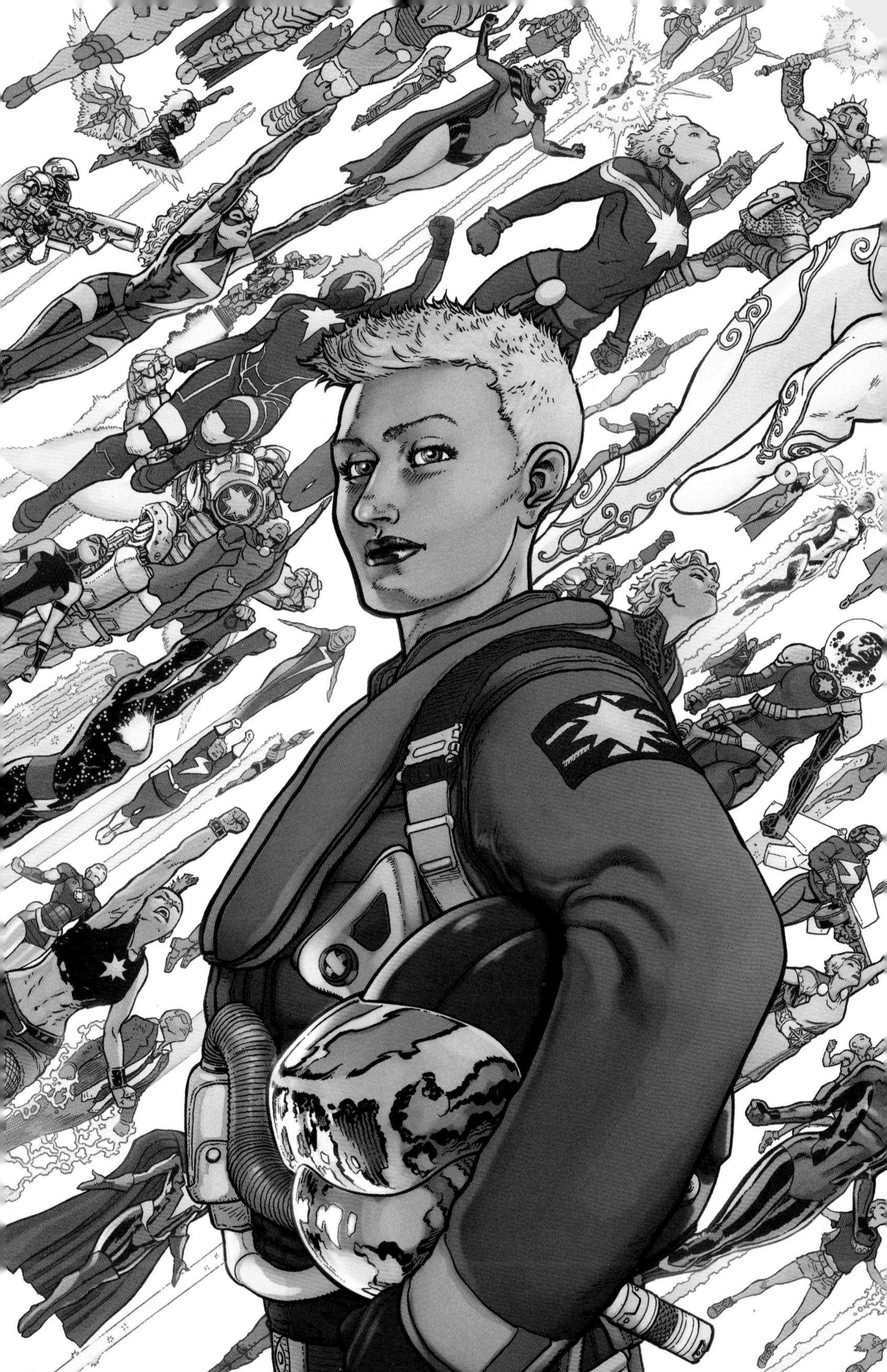

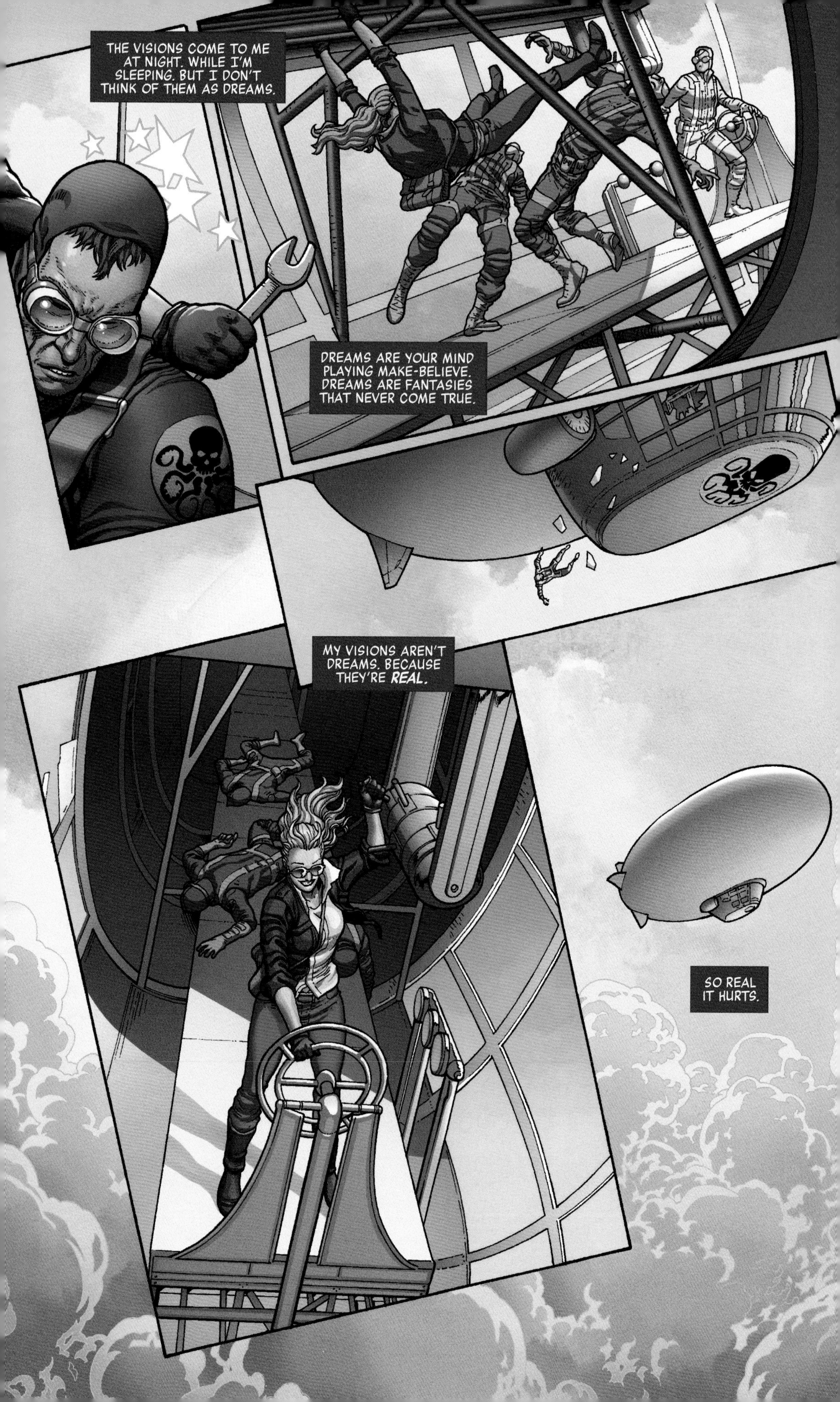
THE VISIONS COME TO ME AT NIGHT. WHILE I'M SLEEPING. BUT I DON'T THINK OF THEM AS DREAMS.
DREAMS ARE YOUR MIND PLAYING MAKE-BELIEVE. DREAMS ARE FANTASIES THAT NEVER COME TRUE.
MY VISIONS AREN'T DREAMS. BECAUSE THEY'RE *REAL.*
SO REAL IT HURTS.

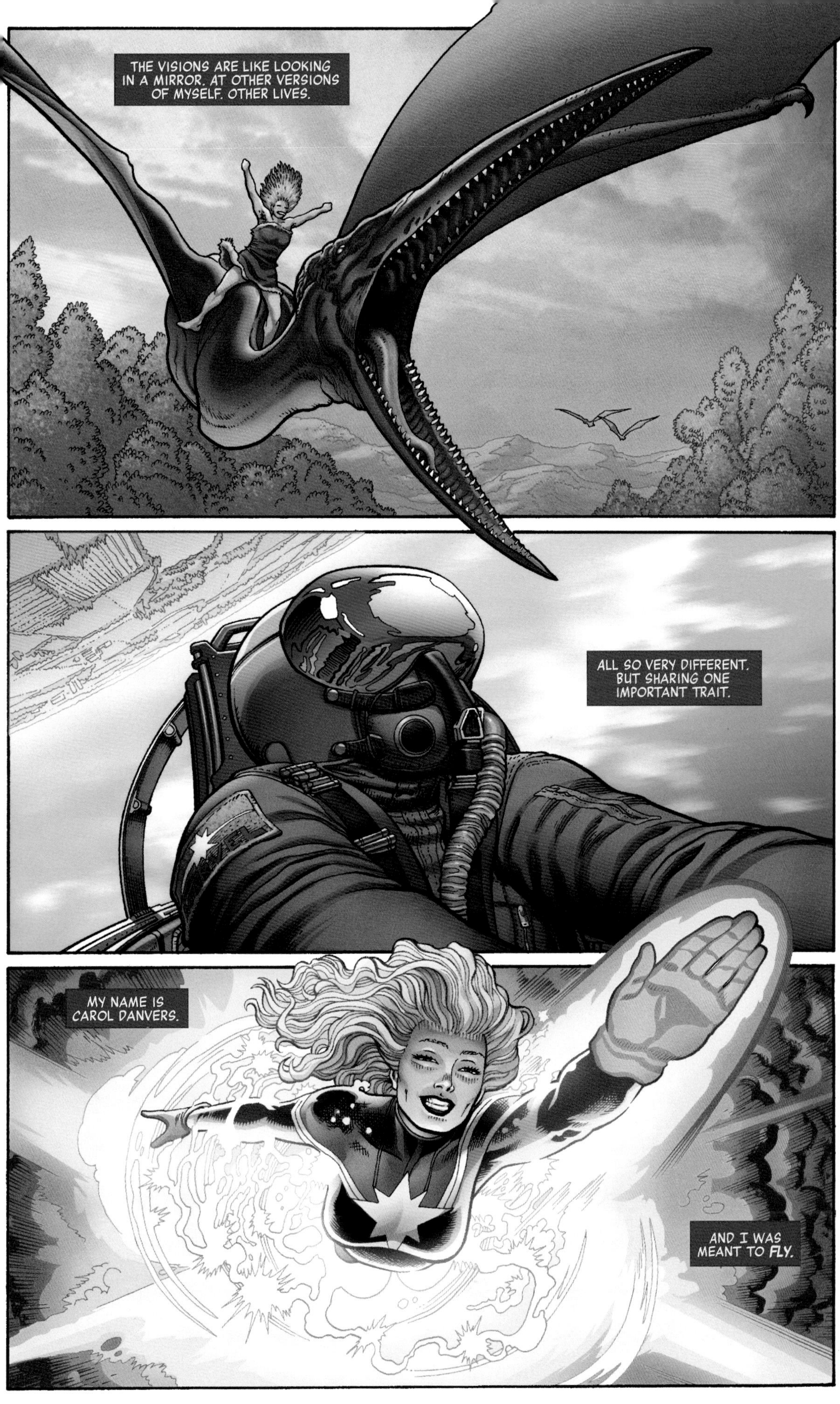
THE VISIONS ARE LIKE LOOKING IN A MIRROR. AT OTHER VERSIONS OF MYSELF. OTHER LIVES.
ALL SO VERY DIFFERENT. BUT SHARING ONE IMPORTANT TRAIT.
MY NAME IS CAROL DANVERS.
AND I WAS MEANT TO FLY.

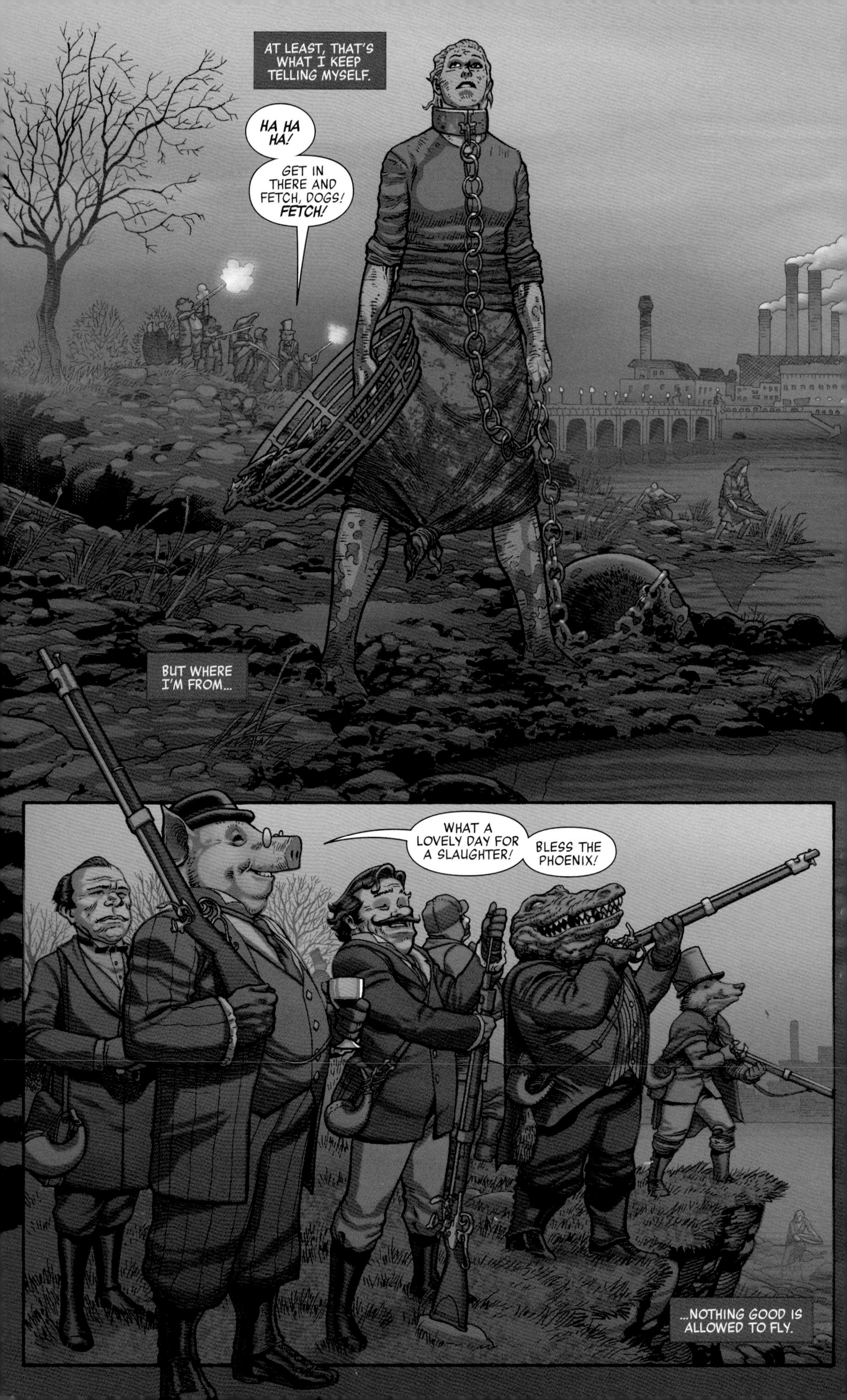
AT LEAST, THAT'S WHAT I KEEP TELLING MYSELF.
HA HA HA!
GET IN THERE AND FETCH, DOGS! FETCH!
BUT WHERE I'M FROM...
WHAT A LOVELY DAY FOR A SLAUGHTER!
BLESS THE PHOENIX!
...NOTHING GOOD IS ALLOWED TO FLY.

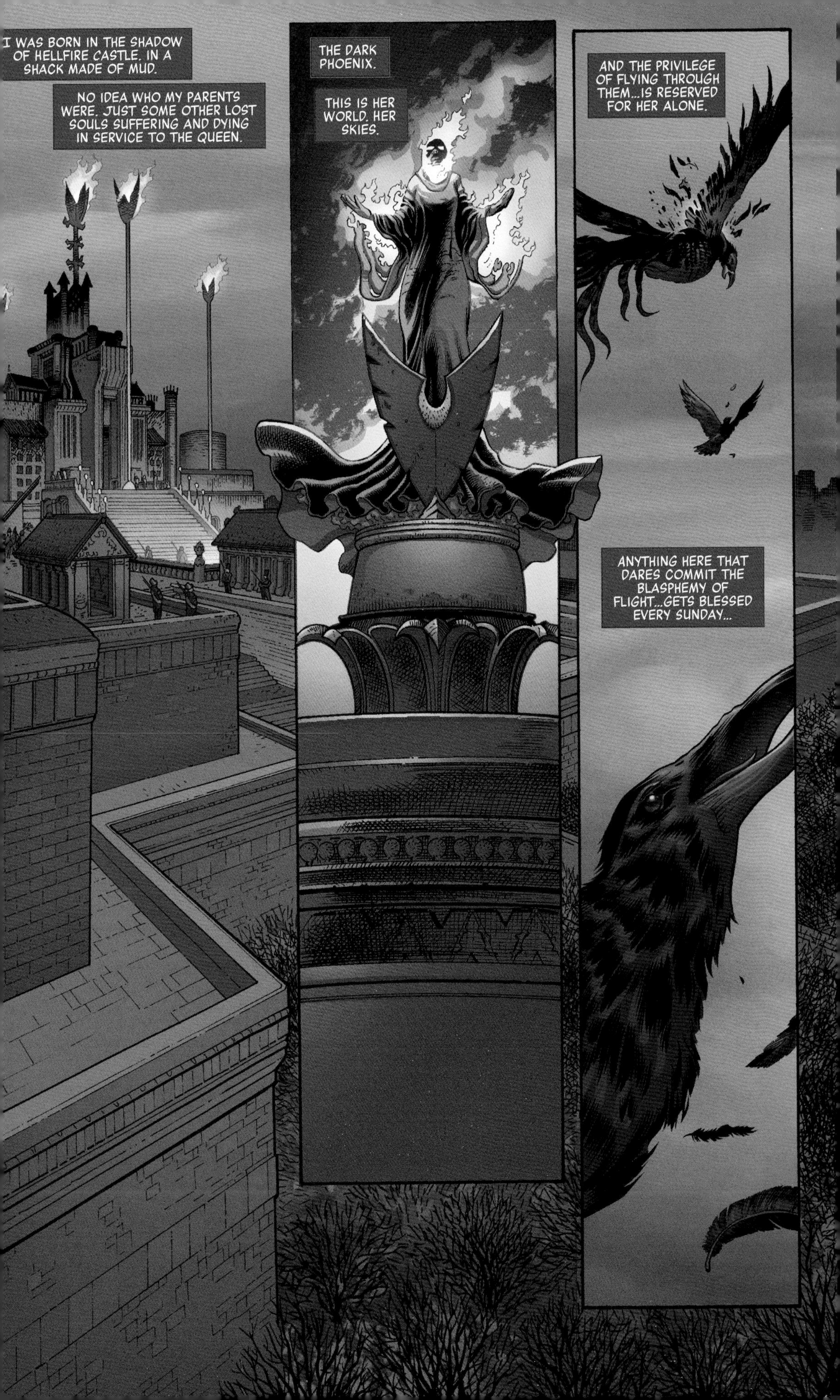
I WAS BORN IN THE SHADOW OF HELLFIRE CASTLE. IN A SHACK MADE OF MUD.
NO IDEA WHO MY PARENTS WERE. JUST SOME OTHER LOST SOULS SUFFERING AND DYING IN SERVICE TO THE QUEEN.
THE DARK PHOENIX.
THIS IS HER WORLD. HER SKIES.
AND THE PRIVILEGE OF FLYING THROUGH THEM...IS RESERVED FOR HER ALONE.
ANYTHING HERE THAT DARES COMMIT THE BLASPHEMY OF FLIGHT...GETS BLESSED EVERY SUNDAY...

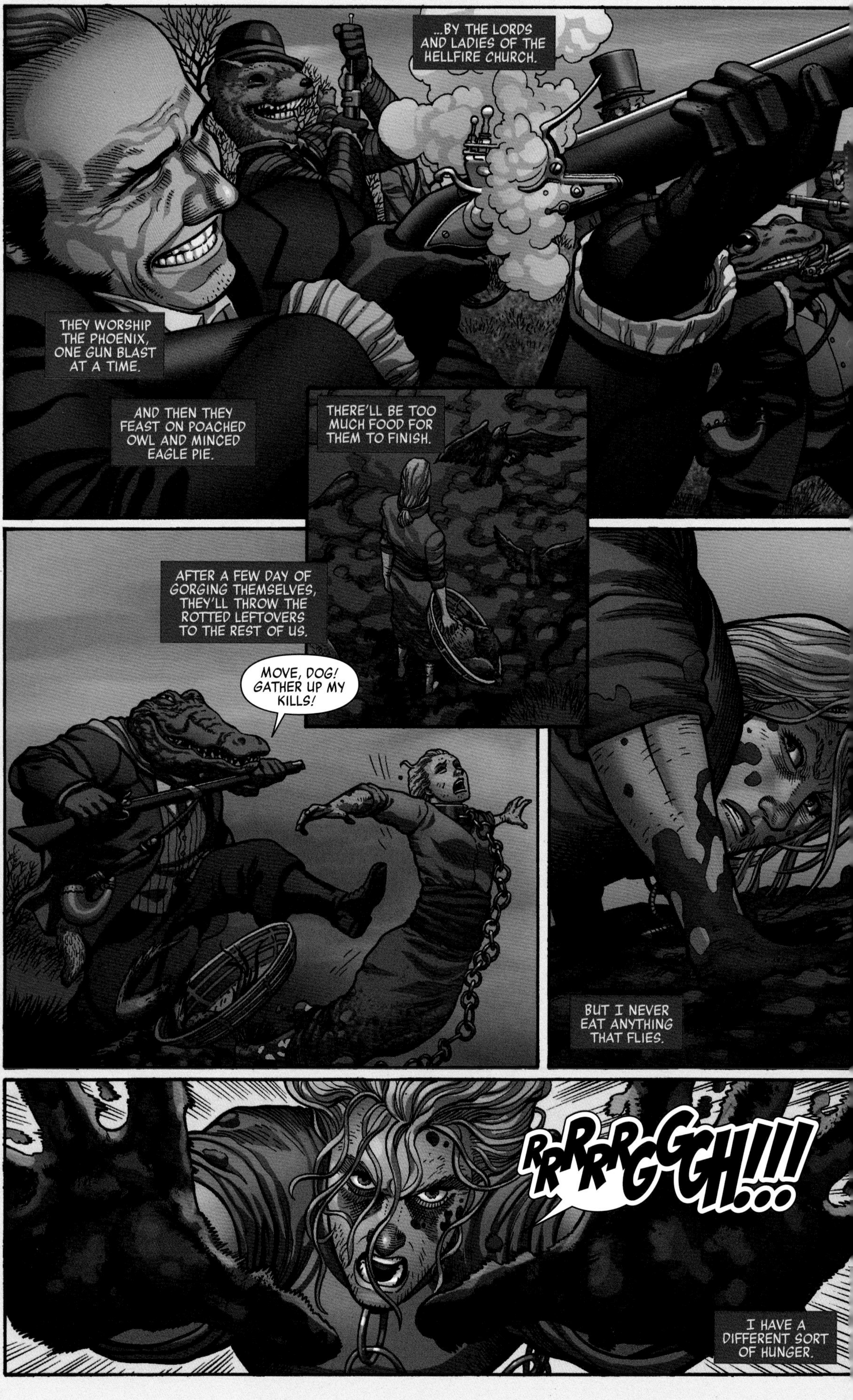
...BY THE LORDS AND LADIES OF THE HELLFIRE CHURCH.
THEY WORSHIP THE PHOENIX, ONE GUN BLAST AT A TIME.
AND THEN THEY FEAST ON POACHED OWL AND MINCED EAGLE PIE.
THERE'LL BE TOO MUCH FOOD FOR THEM TO FINISH.
AFTER A FEW DAY OF GORGING THEMSELVES, THEY'LL THROW THE ROTTED LEFTOVERS TO THE REST OF US.
MOVE, DOG! GATHER UP MY KILLS!
BUT I NEVER EAT ANYTHING THAT FLIES.
RRRRGGGH!!!...
I HAVE A DIFFERENT SORT OF HUNGER.

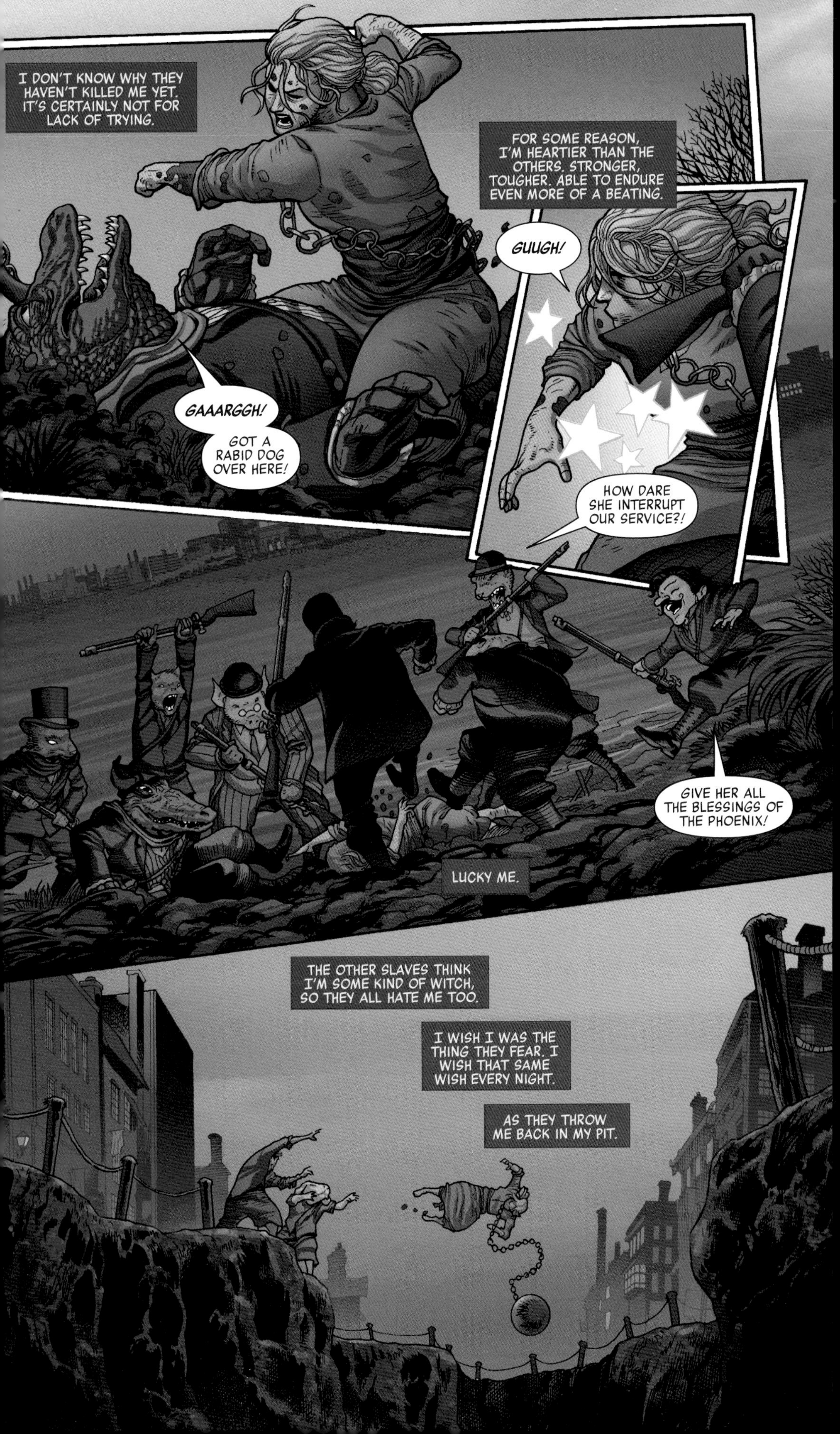
I DON'T KNOW WHY THEY HAVEN'T KILLED ME YET. IT'S CERTAINLY NOT FOR LACK OF TRYING.
GAAARGGH!
GOT A RABID DOG OVER HERE!
FOR SOME REASON, I'M HEARTIER THAN THE OTHERS. STRONGER, TOUGHER. ABLE TO ENDURE EVEN MORE OF A BEATING.
GUUGH!
HOW DARE SHE INTERRUPT OUR SERVICE?!
GIVE HER ALL THE BLESSINGS OF THE PHOENIX!
LUCKY ME.
THE OTHER SLAVES THINK I'M SOME KIND OF WITCH, SO THEY ALL HATE ME TOO.
I WISH I WAS THE THING THEY FEAR. I WISH THAT SAME WISH EVERY NIGHT.
AS THEY THROW ME BACK IN MY PIT.

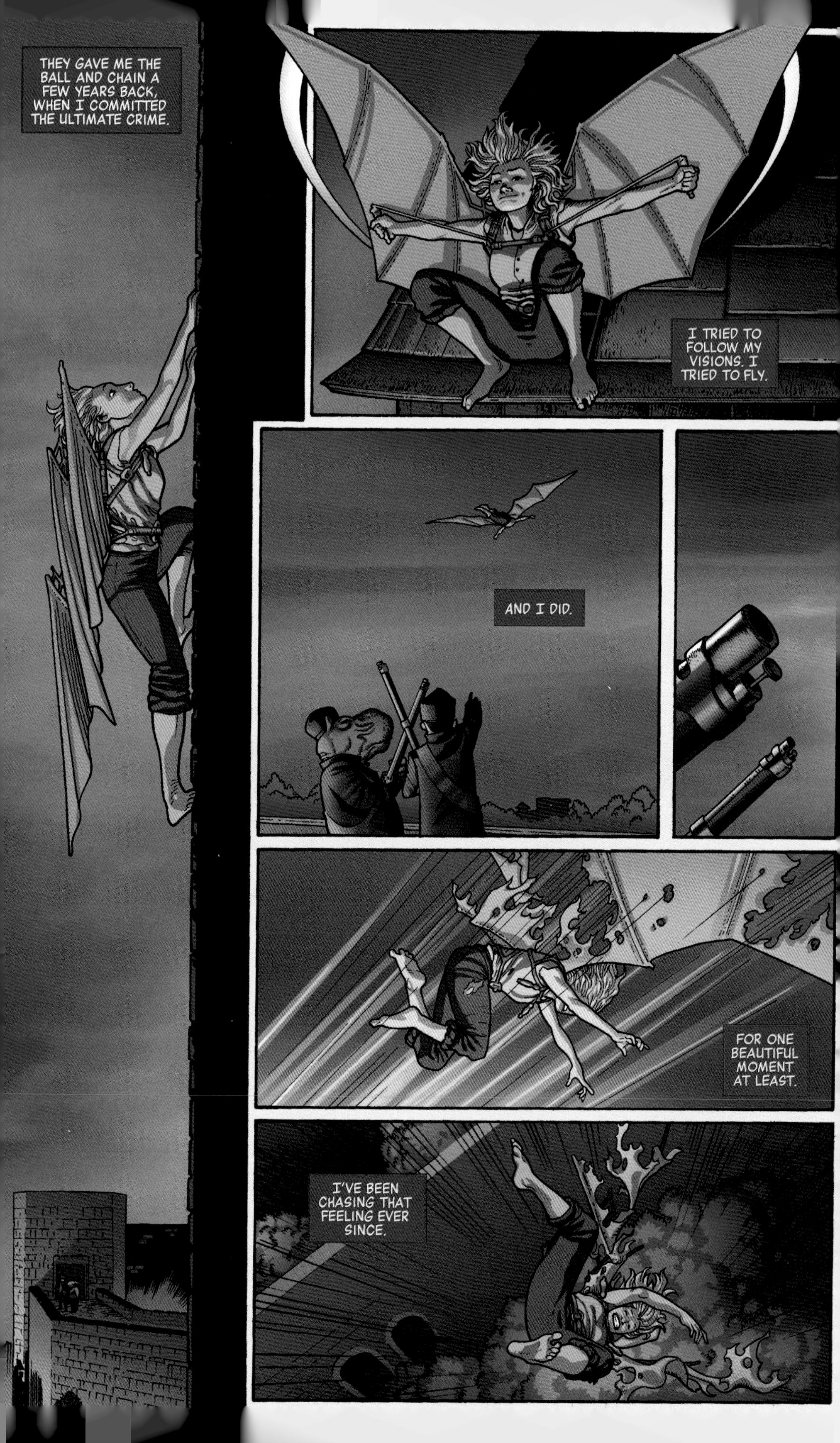
THEY GAVE ME THE BALL AND CHAIN A FEW YEARS BACK, WHEN I COMMITTED THE ULTIMATE CRIME.
I TRIED TO FOLLOW MY VISIONS. I TRIED TO FLY.
AND I DID.
FOR ONE BEAUTIFUL MOMENT AT LEAST.
I'VE BEEN CHASING THAT FEELING EVER SINCE.

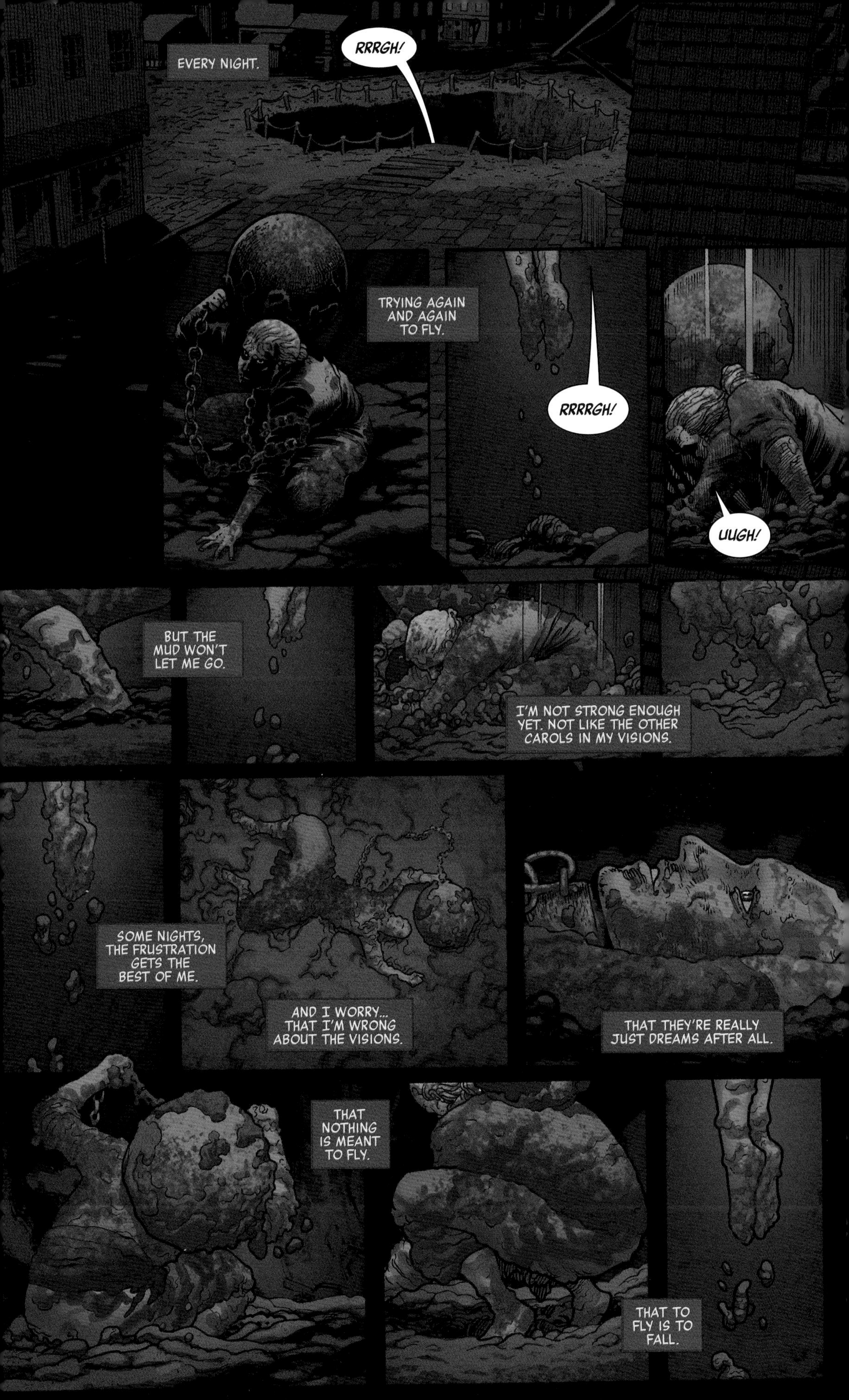
EVERY NIGHT.
RRRGH!
TRYING AGAIN AND AGAIN TO FLY.
RRRRGH!
UUGH!
BUT THE MUD WON'T LET ME GO.
I'M NOT STRONG ENOUGH YET. NOT LIKE THE OTHER CAROLS IN MY VISIONS.
SOME NIGHTS, THE FRUSTRATION GETS THE BEST OF ME.
AND I WORRY... THAT I'M WRONG ABOUT THE VISIONS.
THAT THEY'RE REALLY JUST DREAMS AFTER ALL.
THAT NOTHING IS MEANT TO FLY.
THAT TO FLY IS TO FALL.

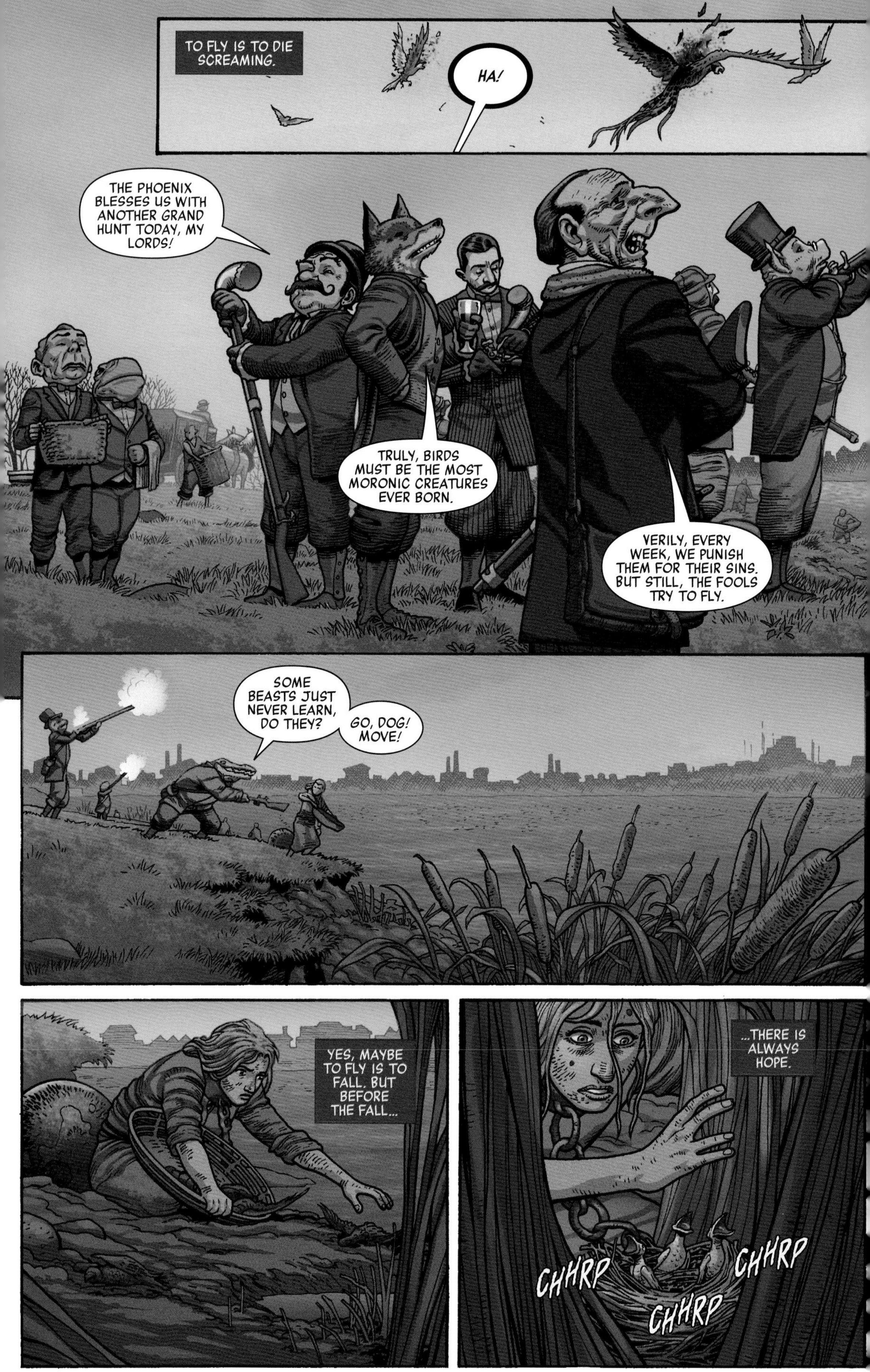

TO FLY IS TO DIE SCREAMING.
HA!
THE PHOENIX BLESSES US WITH ANOTHER GRAND HUNT TODAY, MY LORDS!
TRULY, BIRDS MUST BE THE MOST MORONIC CREATURES EVER BORN.
VERILY, EVERY WEEK, WE PUNISH THEM FOR THEIR SINS. BUT STILL, THE FOOLS TRY TO FLY.
SOME BEASTS JUST NEVER LEARN, DO THEY?
GO, DOG! MOVE!
YES, MAYBE TO FLY IS TO FALL. BUT BEFORE THE FALL...
...THERE IS ALWAYS HOPE.
CHHRP
CHHRP
CHHRP

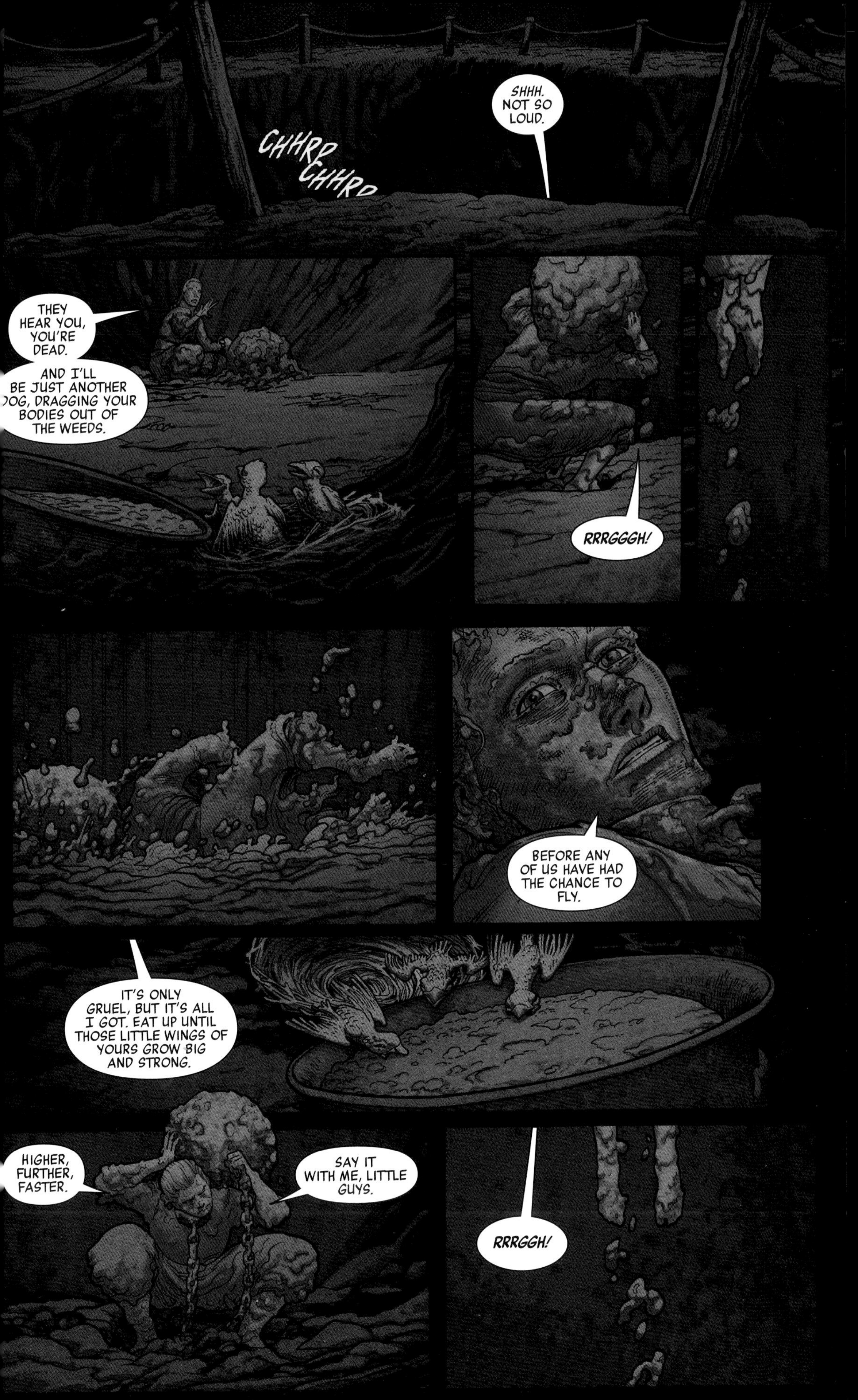
CHHRP CHHRP
SHHH. NOT SO LOUD.
THEY HEAR YOU, YOU'RE DEAD.
AND I'LL BE JUST ANOTHER DOG, DRAGGING YOUR BODIES OUT OF THE WEEDS.
RRRGGGH!
BEFORE ANY OF US HAVE HAD THE CHANCE TO FLY.
IT'S ONLY GRUEL, BUT IT'S ALL I GOT. EAT UP UNTIL THOSE LITTLE WINGS OF YOURS GROW BIG AND STRONG.
HIGHER, FURTHER, FASTER.
SAY IT WITH ME, LITTLE GUYS.
RRRGGH!

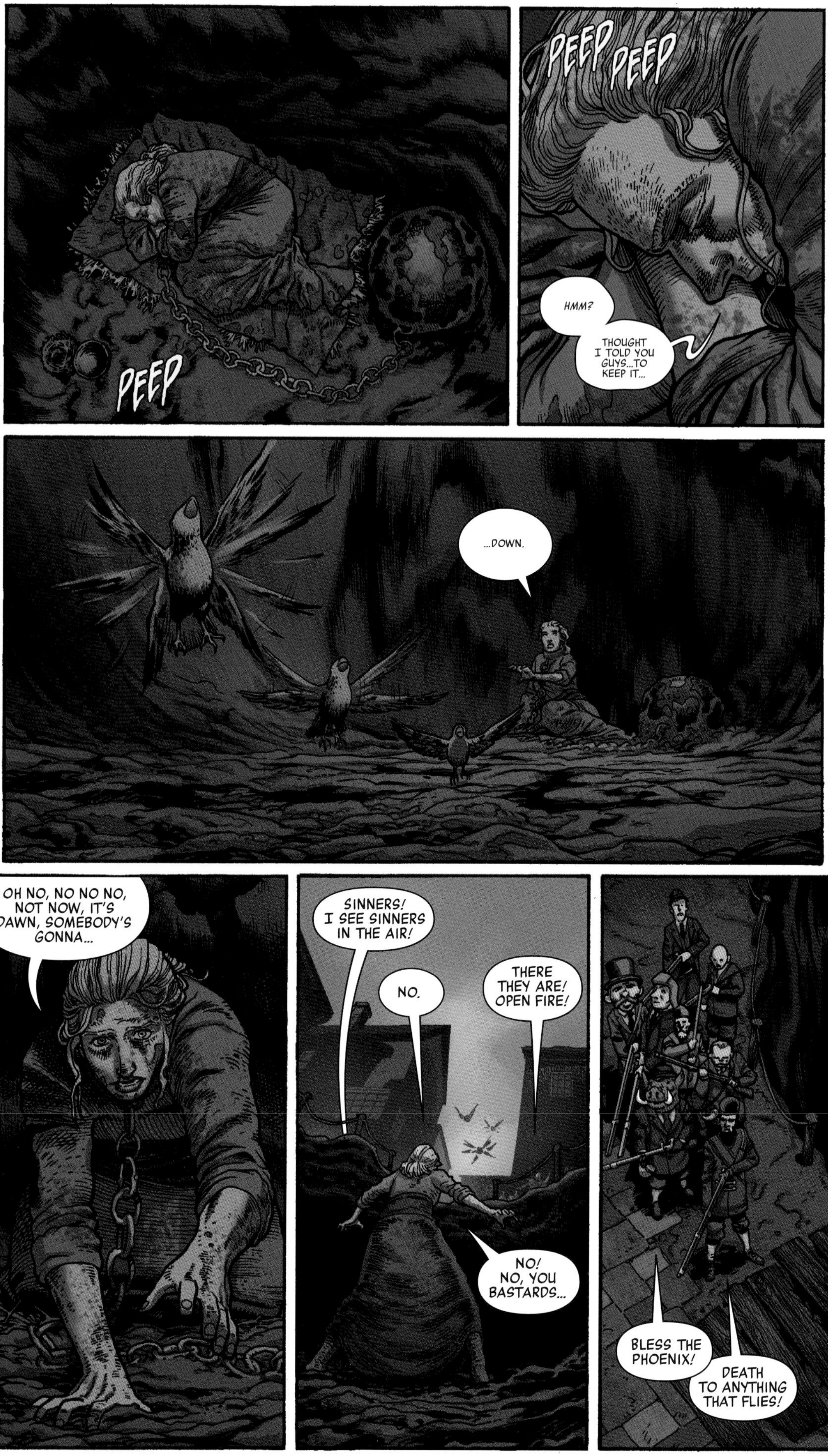
PEEP
PEEP PEEP
HMM?
THOUGHT I TOLD YOU GUYS...TO KEEP IT...
...DOWN.
OH NO, NO NO NO, NOT NOW, IT'S DAWN, SOMEBODY'S GONNA...
SINNERS! I SEE SINNERS IN THE AIR!
NO.
THERE THEY ARE! OPEN FIRE!
NO! NO, YOU BASTARDS...
BLESS THE PHOENIX!
DEATH TO ANYTHING THAT FLIES!

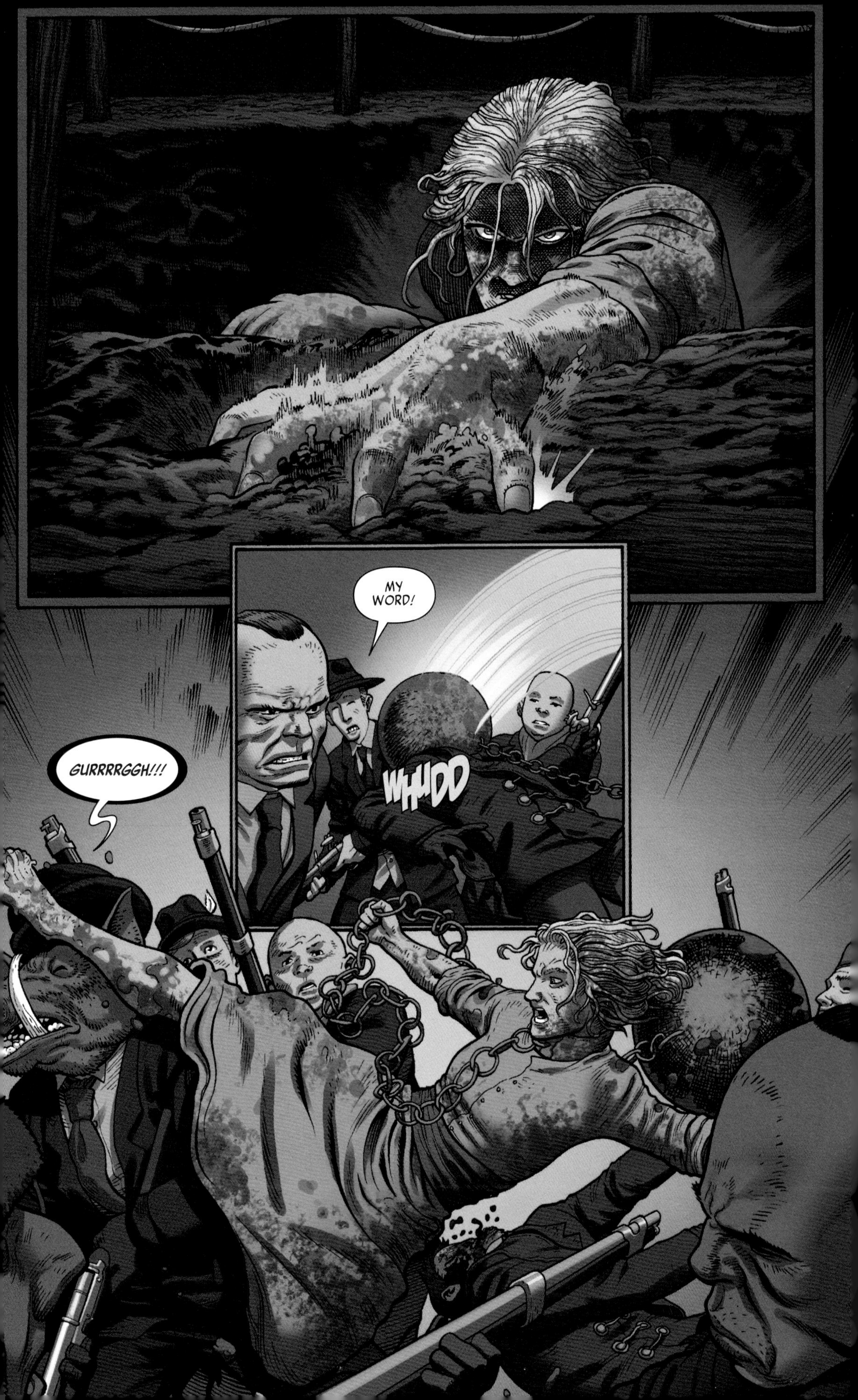
MY WORD!
WHUDD
GURRRRGGH!!!

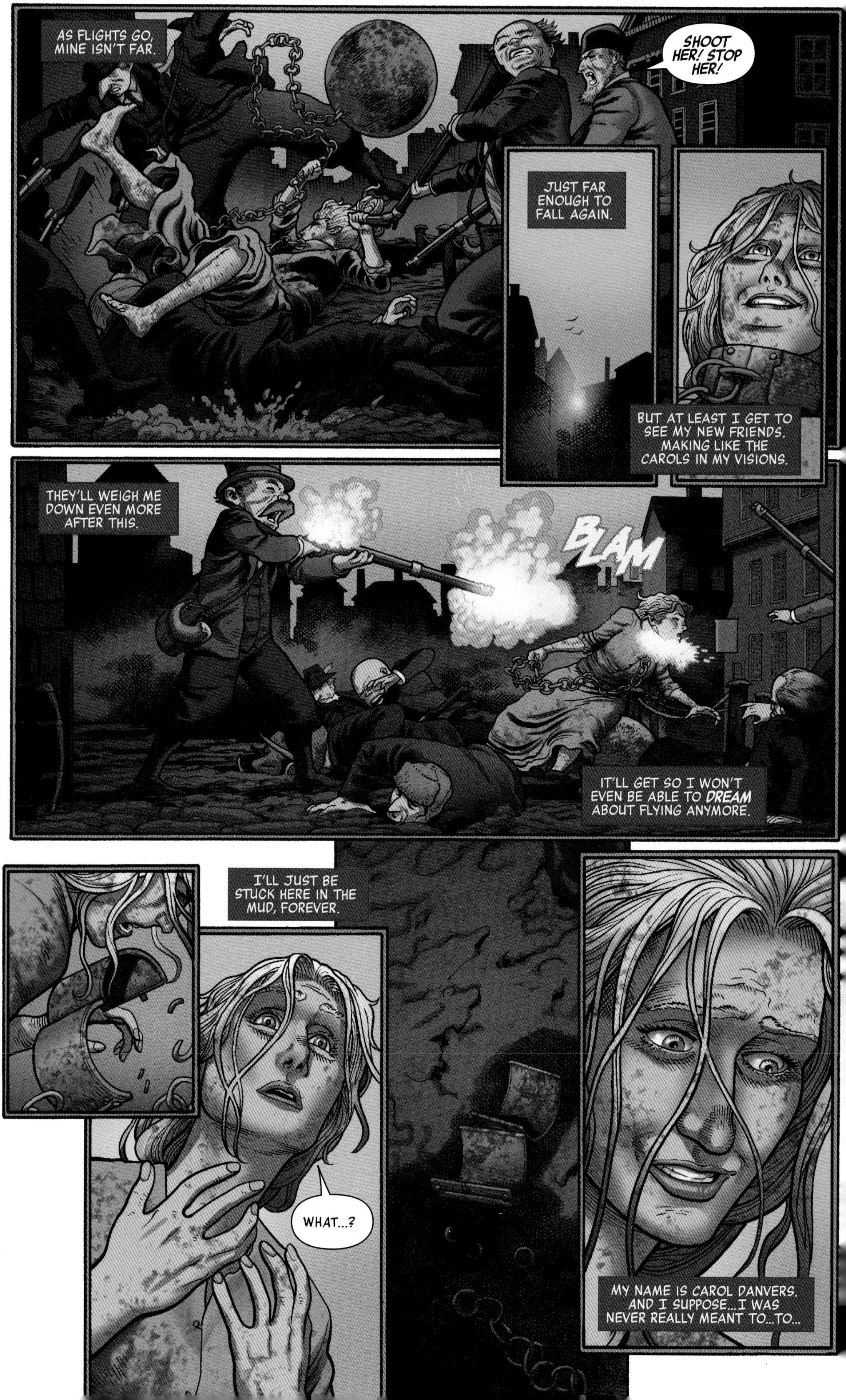
AS FLIGHTS GO, MINE ISN'T FAR.
SHOOT HER! STOP HER!
JUST FAR ENOUGH TO FALL AGAIN.
BUT AT LEAST I GET TO SEE MY NEW FRIENDS. MAKING LIKE THE CAROLS IN MY VISIONS.
THEY'LL WEIGH ME DOWN EVEN MORE AFTER THIS.
BLAM
IT'LL GET SO I WON'T EVEN BE ABLE TO DREAM ABOUT FLYING ANYMORE.
I'LL JUST BE STUCK HERE IN THE MUD, FOREVER.
WHAT...?
MY NAME IS CAROL DANVERS. AND I SUPPOSE...I WAS NEVER REALLY MEANT TO...TO...

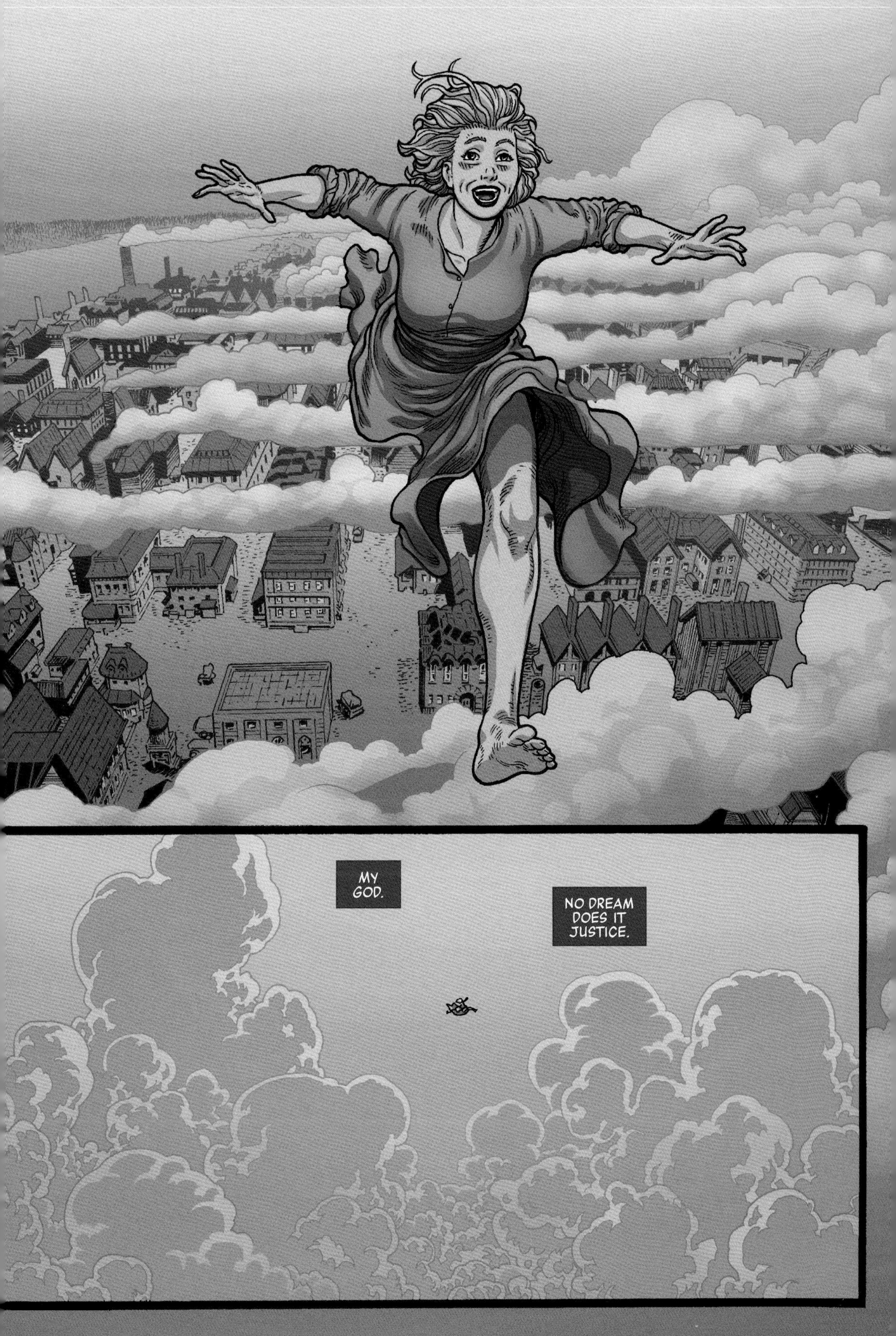
MY GOD.
NO DREAM DOES IT JUSTICE.

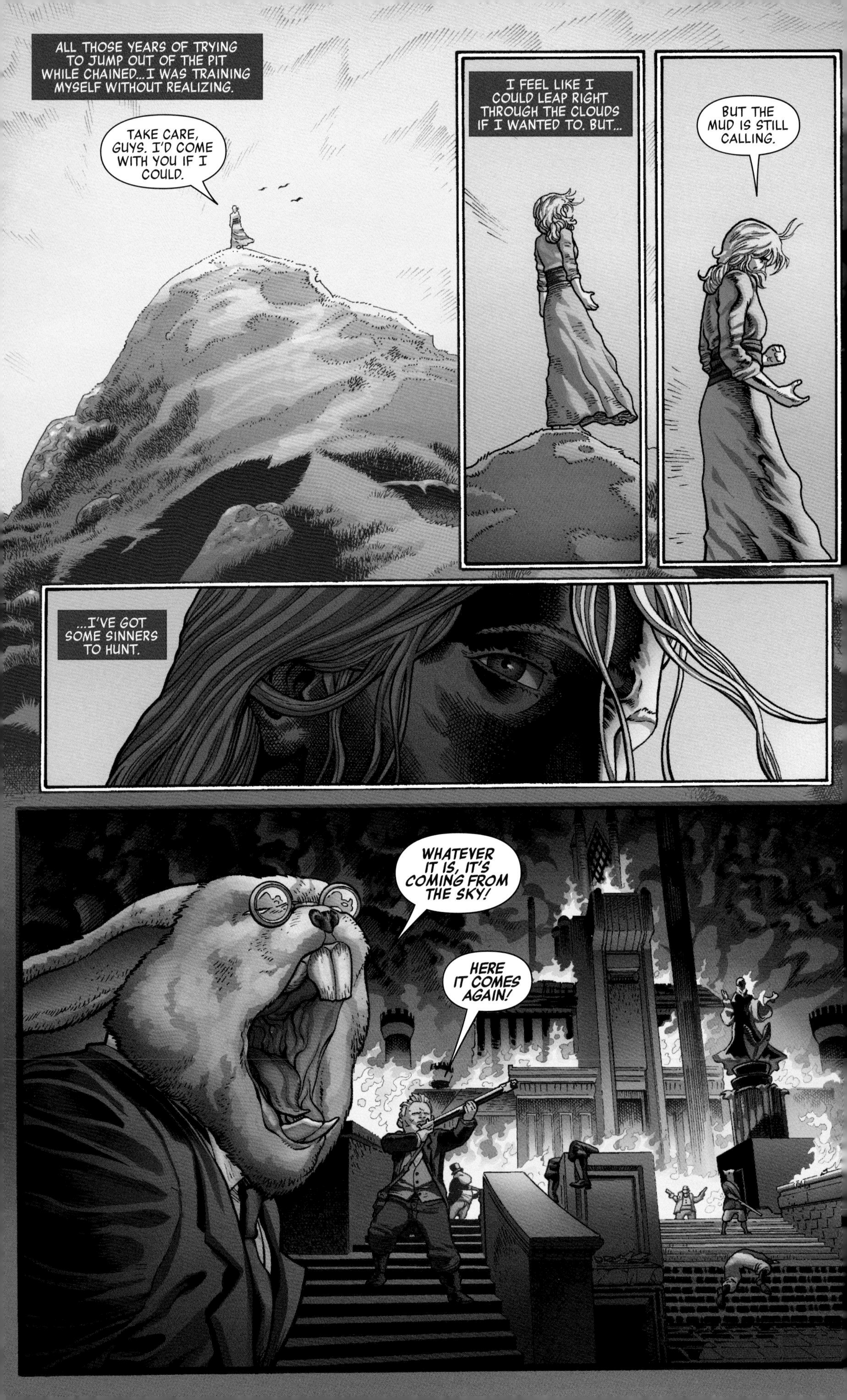
ALL THOSE YEARS OF TRYING TO JUMP OUT OF THE PIT WHILE CHAINED...I WAS TRAINING MYSELF WITHOUT REALIZING.
TAKE CARE, GUYS. I'D COME WITH YOU IF I COULD.
I FEEL LIKE I COULD LEAP RIGHT THROUGH THE CLOUDS IF I WANTED TO. BUT...
BUT THE MUD IS STILL CALLING.
...I'VE GOT SOME SINNERS TO HUNT.
WHATEVER IT IS, IT'S COMING FROM THE SKY!
HERE IT COMES AGAIN!

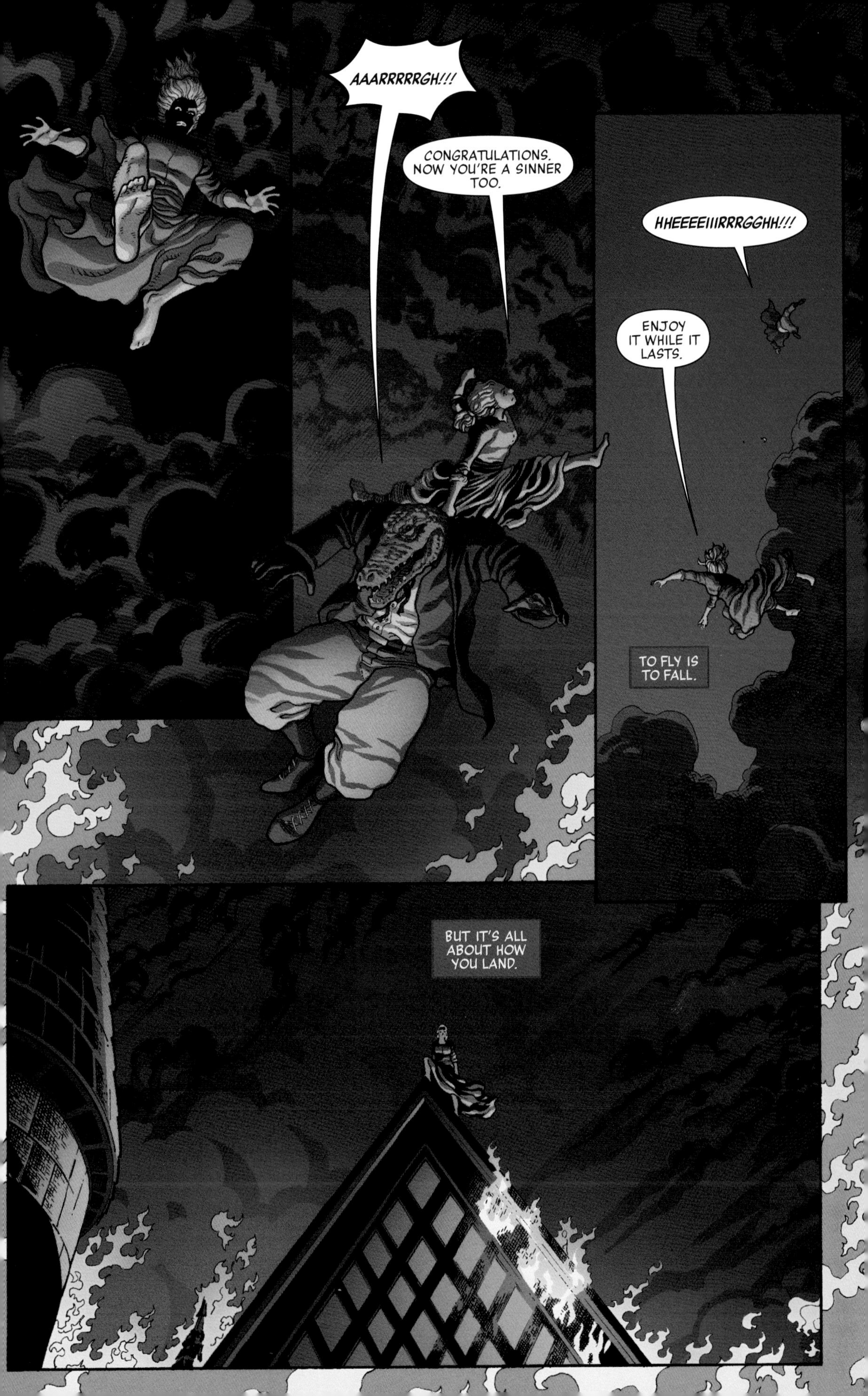
AAARRRRRGH!!!
CONGRATULATIONS. NOW YOU'RE A SINNER TOO.
HHEEEEIIIRRRGGHH!!!
ENJOY IT WHILE IT LASTS.
TO FLY IS TO FALL.
BUT IT'S ALL ABOUT HOW YOU LAND.

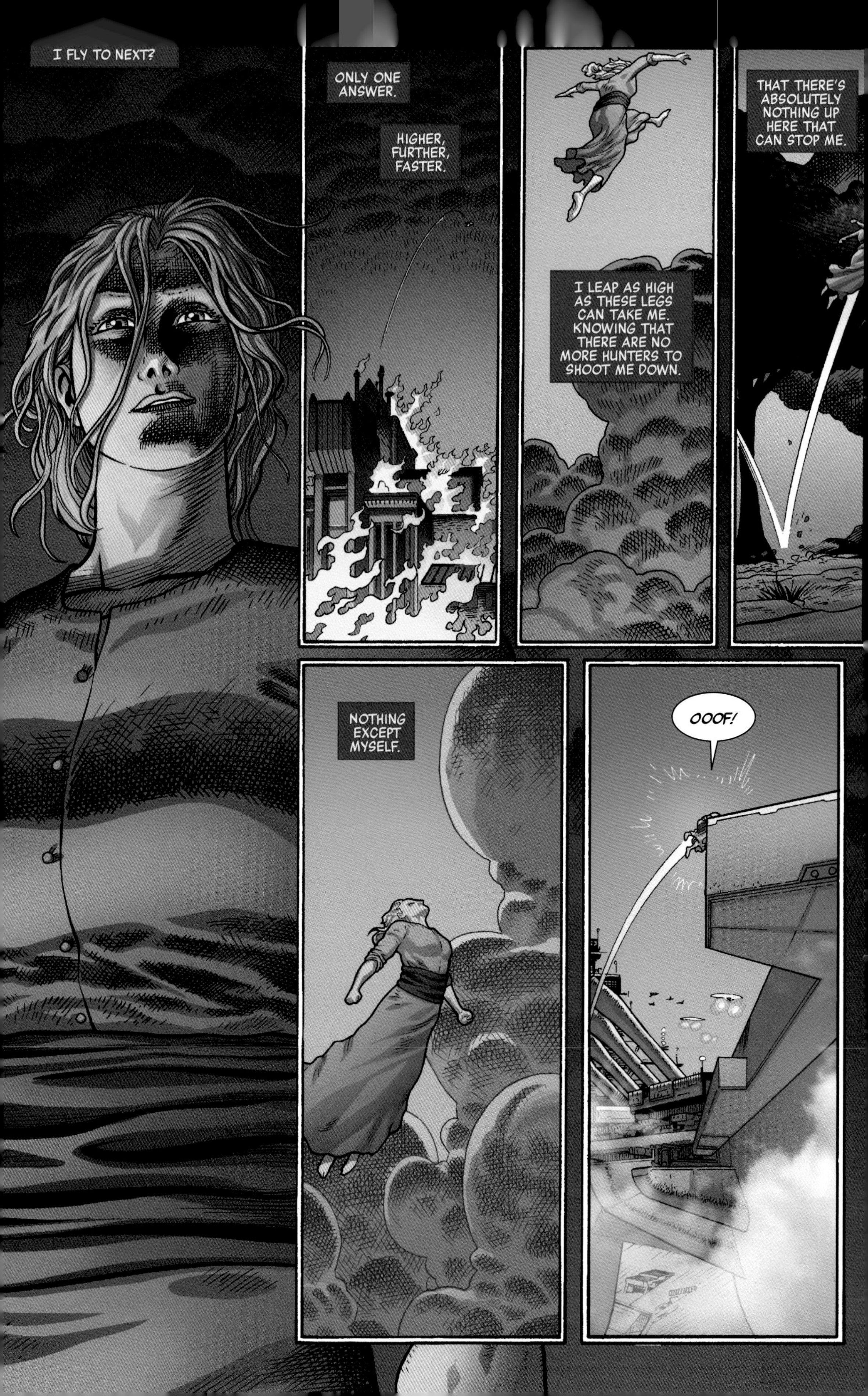
I FLY TO NEXT?
ONLY ONE ANSWER.
HIGHER, FURTHER, FASTER.
I LEAP AS HIGH AS THESE LEGS CAN TAKE ME. KNOWING THAT THERE ARE NO MORE HUNTERS TO SHOOT ME DOWN.
THAT THERE'S ABSOLUTELY NOTHING UP HERE THAT CAN STOP ME.
NOTHING EXCEPT MYSELF.
OOOF!

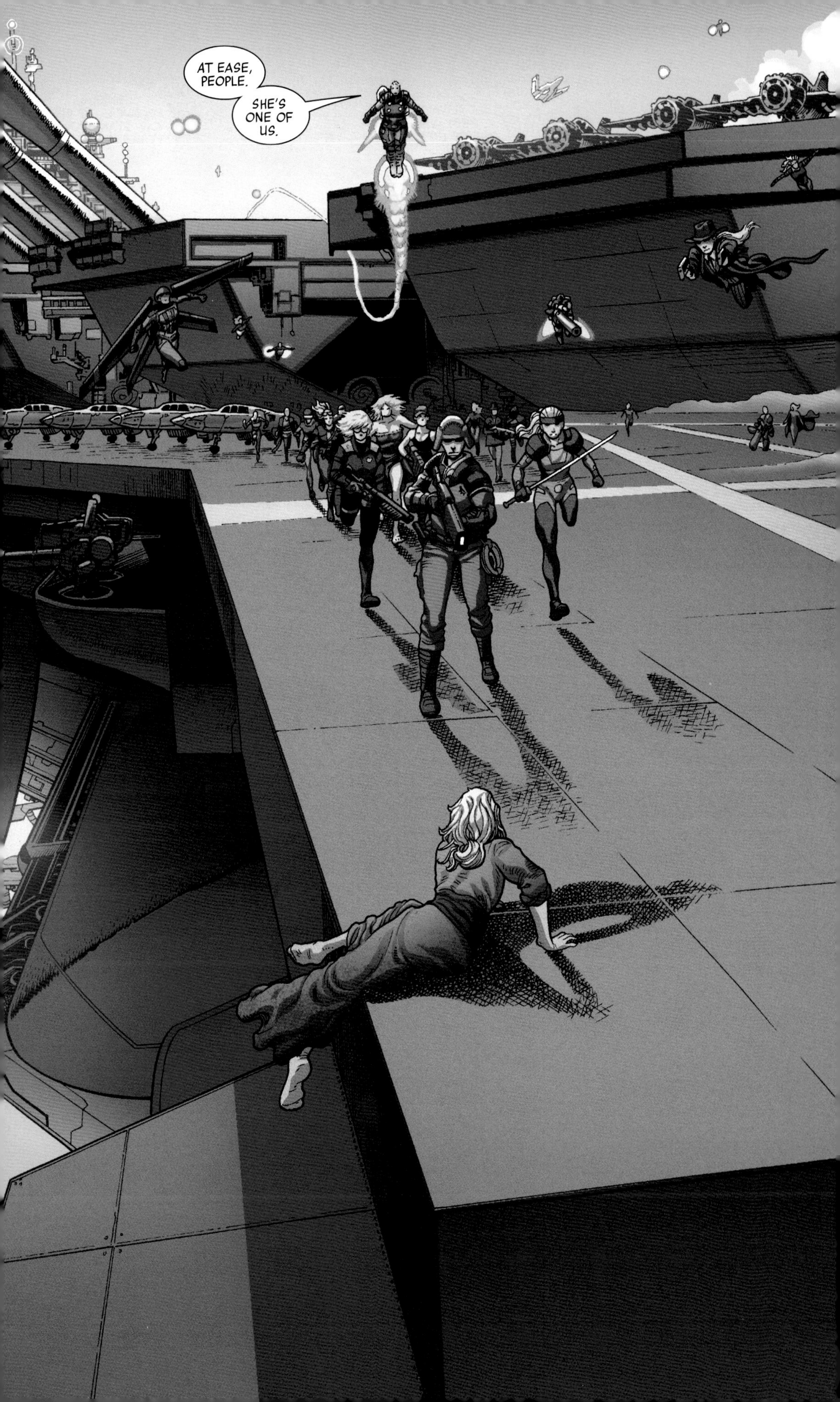
AT EASE, PEOPLE.
SHE'S ONE OF US.

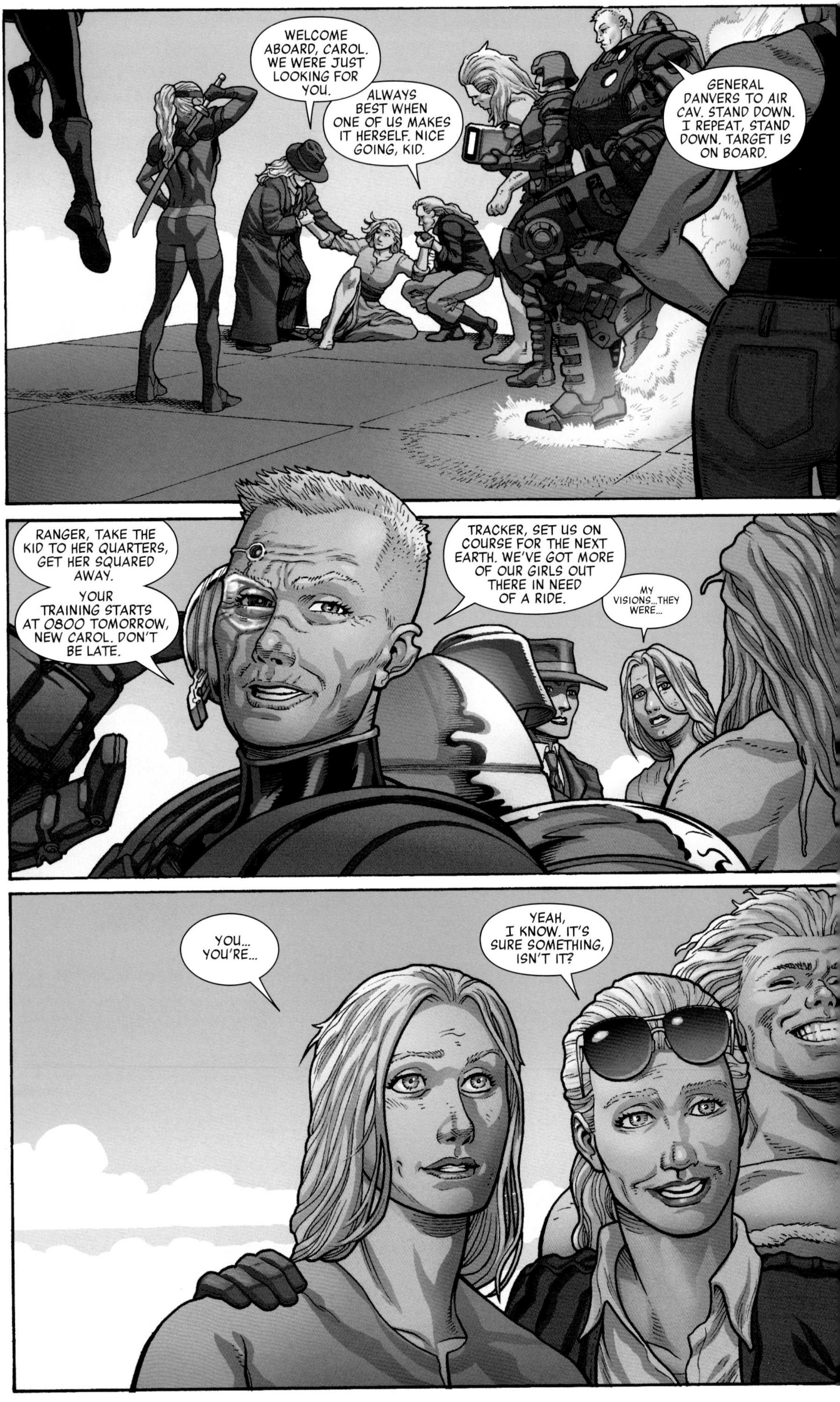
WELCOME ABOARD, CAROL. WE WERE JUST LOOKING FOR YOU.
ALWAYS BEST WHEN ONE OF US MAKES IT HERSELF. NICE GOING, KID.
GENERAL DANVERS TO AIR CAV. STAND DOWN. I REPEAT, STAND DOWN. TARGET IS ON BOARD.
RANGER, TAKE THE KID TO HER QUARTERS, GET HER SQUARED AWAY.
YOUR TRAINING STARTS AT 0800 TOMORROW, NEW CAROL. DON'T BE LATE.
TRACKER, SET US ON COURSE FOR THE NEXT EARTH. WE'VE GOT MORE OF OUR GIRLS OUT THERE IN NEED OF A RIDE.
MY VISIONS...THEY WERE...
YOU... YOU'RE...
YEAH, I KNOW. IT'S SURE SOMETHING, ISN'T IT?

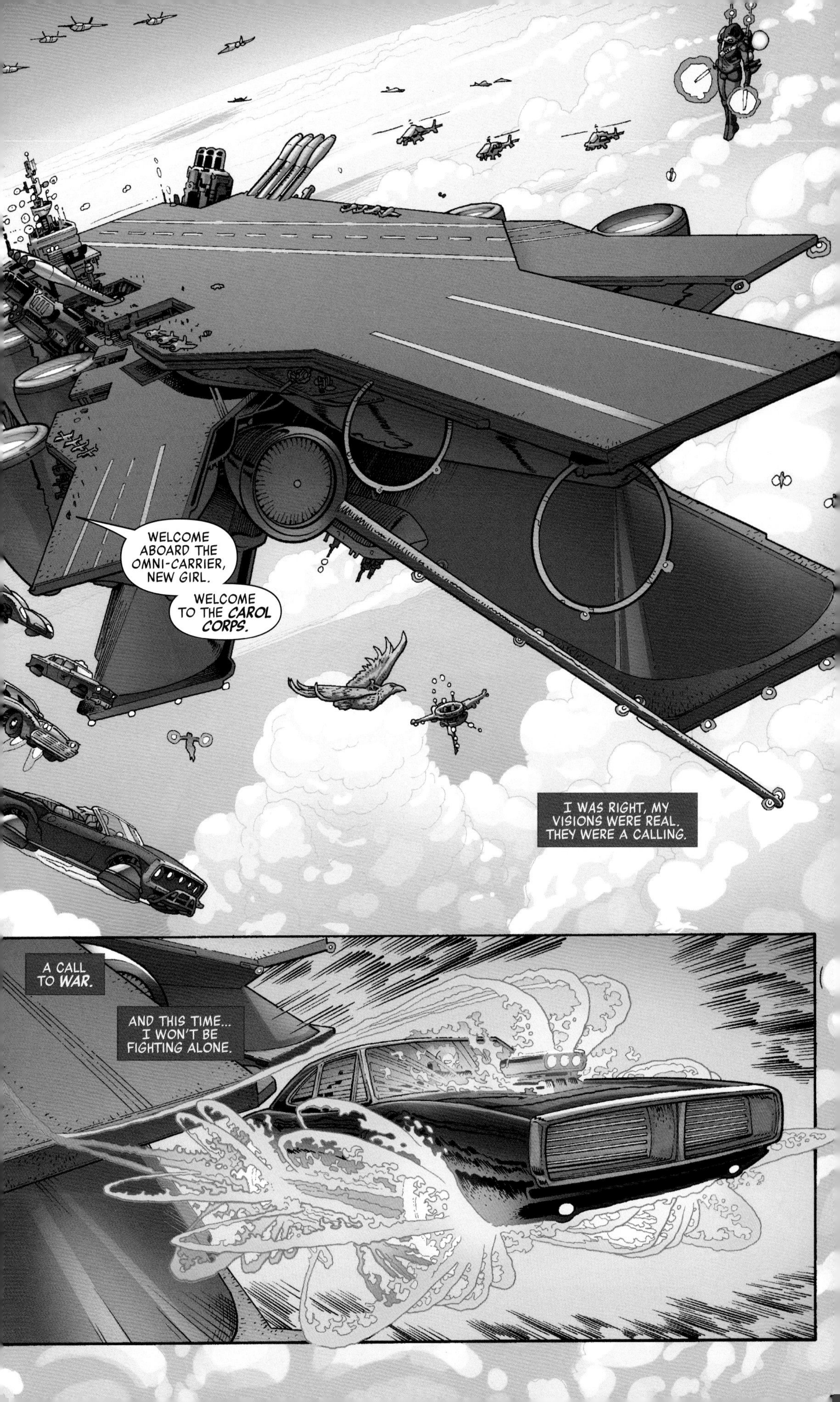

WELCOME ABOARD THE OMNI-CARRIER, NEW GIRL.
WELCOME TO THE CAROL CORPS.
I WAS RIGHT, MY VISIONS WERE REAL. THEY WERE A CALLING.
A CALL TO WAR.
AND THIS TIME... I WON'T BE FIGHTING ALONE.

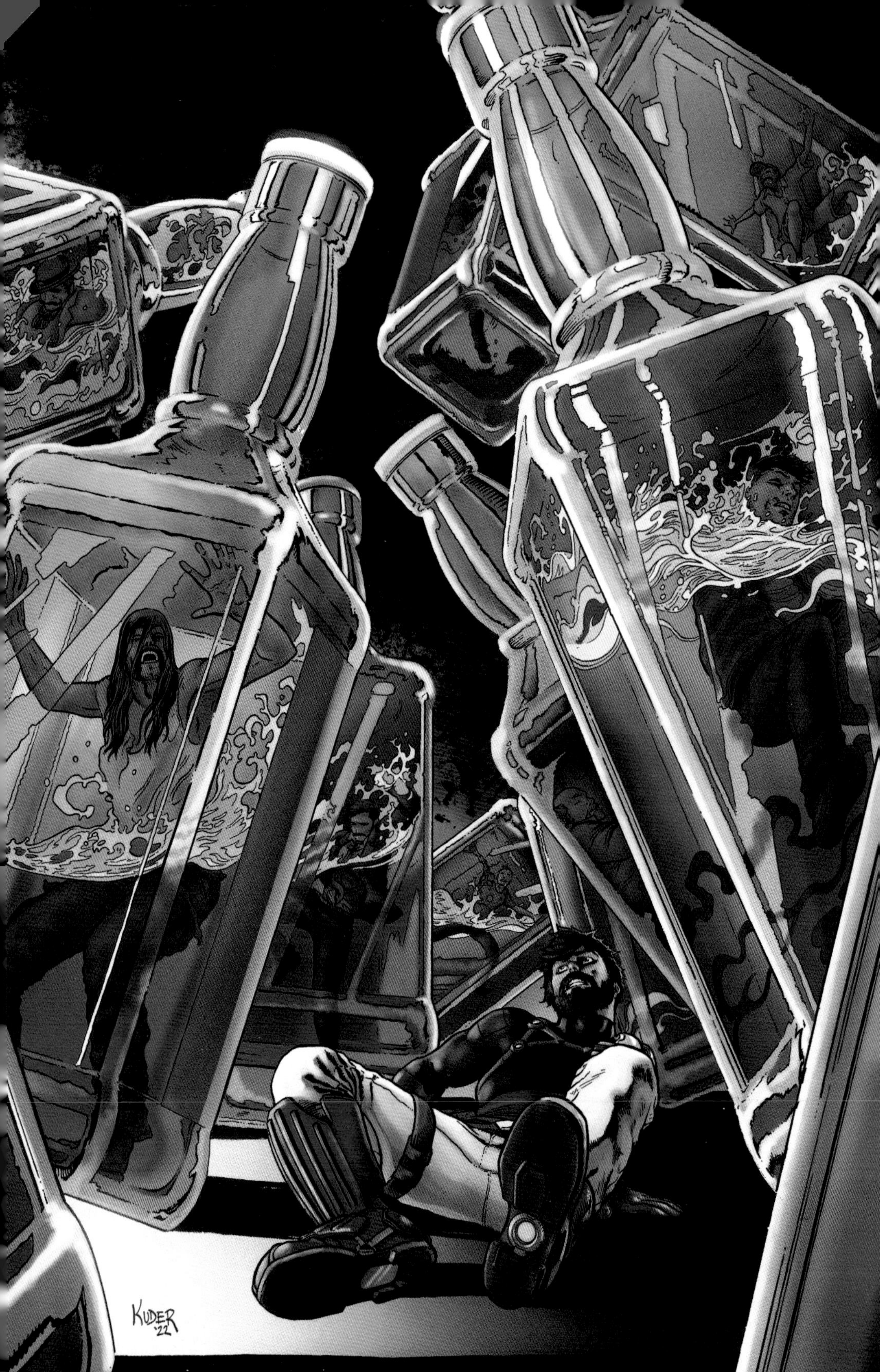
KUDER
'22

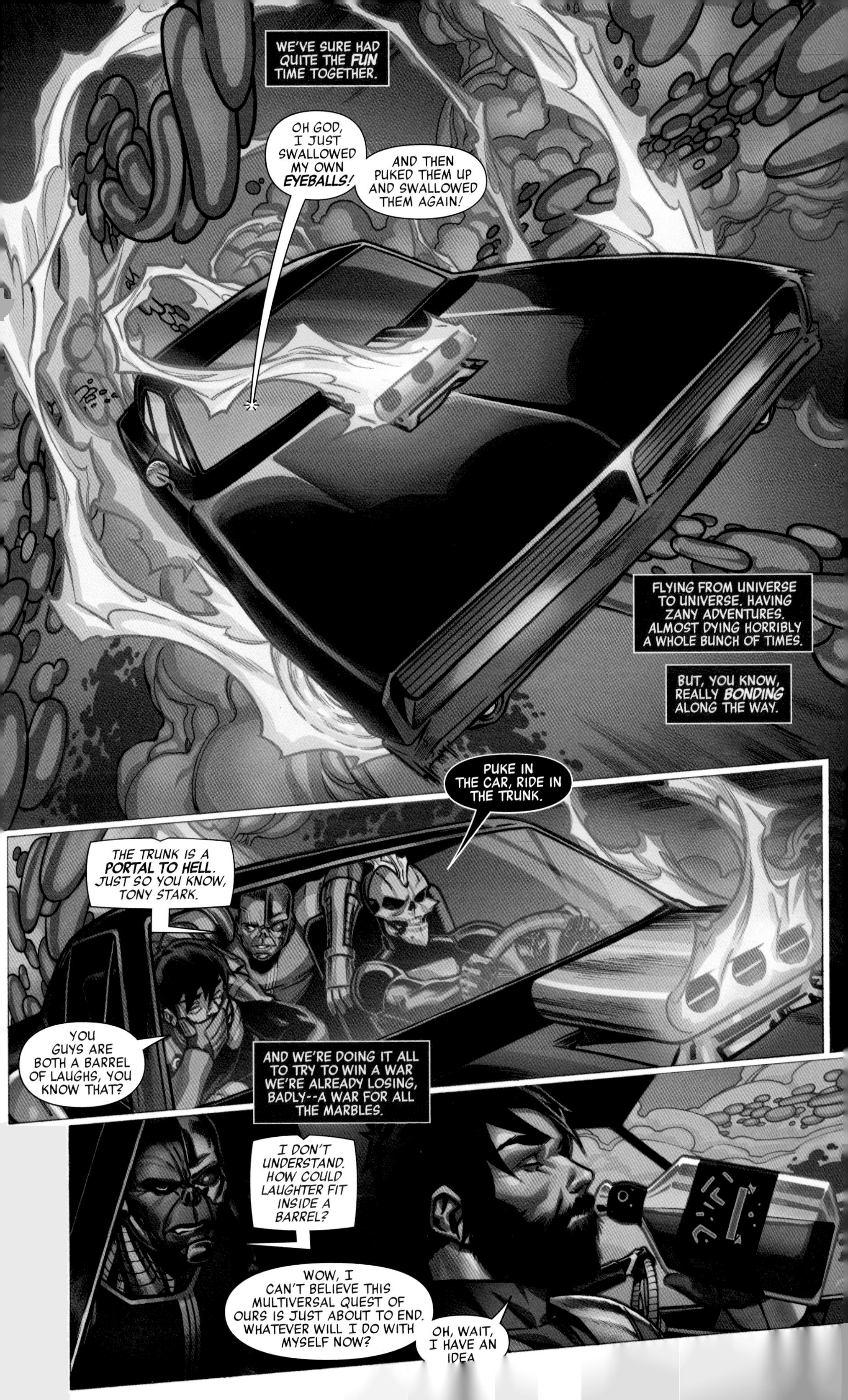
WE'VE SURE HAD QUITE THE FUN TIME TOGETHER.
OH GOD, I JUST SWALLOWED MY OWN EYEBALLS!
AND THEN PUKED THEM UP AND SWALLOWED THEM AGAIN!
FLYING FROM UNIVERSE TO UNIVERSE. HAVING ZANY ADVENTURES. ALMOST DYING HORRIBLY A WHOLE BUNCH OF TIMES.
BUT, YOU KNOW, REALLY BONDING ALONG THE WAY.
PUKE IN THE CAR, RIDE IN THE TRUNK.
THE TRUNK IS A PORTAL TO HELL. JUST SO YOU KNOW, TONY STARK.
YOU GUYS ARE BOTH A BARREL OF LAUGHS, YOU KNOW THAT?
AND WE'RE DOING IT ALL TO TRY TO WIN A WAR WE'RE ALREADY LOSING, BADLY--A WAR FOR ALL THE MARBLES.
I DON'T UNDERSTAND. HOW COULD LAUGHTER FIT INSIDE A BARREL?
WOW, I CAN'T BELIEVE THIS MULTIVERSAL QUEST OF OURS IS JUST ABOUT TO END. WHATEVER WILL I DO WITH MYSELF NOW?
OH, WAIT, I HAVE AN IDEA

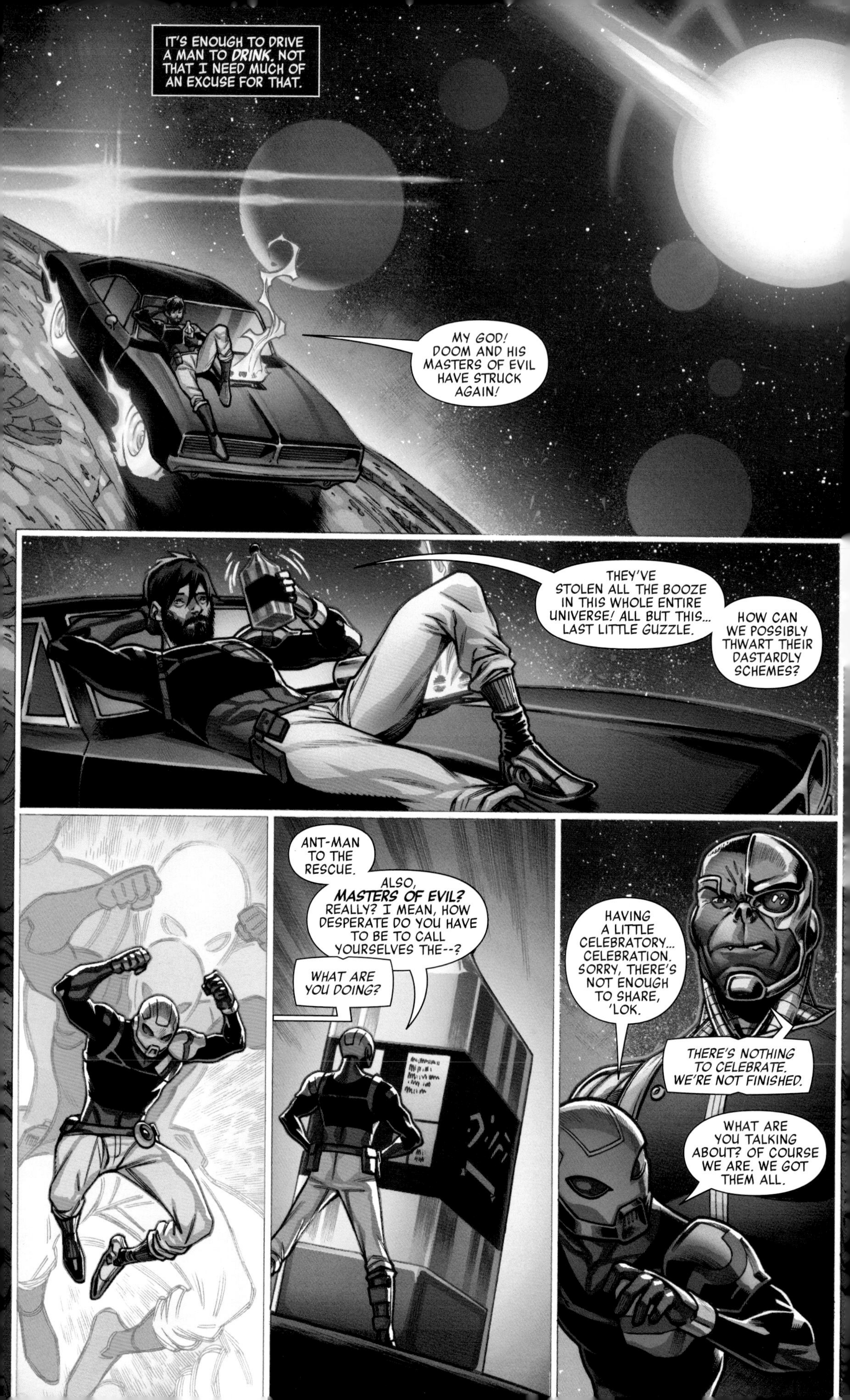
IT'S ENOUGH TO DRIVE A MAN TO DRINK. NOT THAT I NEED MUCH OF AN EXCUSE FOR THAT.
MY GOD! DOOM AND HIS MASTERS OF EVIL HAVE STRUCK AGAIN!
THEY'VE STOLEN ALL THE BOOZE IN THIS WHOLE ENTIRE UNIVERSE! ALL BUT THIS... LAST LITTLE GUZZLE.
HOW CAN WE POSSIBLY THWART THEIR DASTARDLY SCHEMES?
ANT-MAN TO THE RESCUE.
ALSO, MASTERS OF EVIL? REALLY? I MEAN, HOW DESPERATE DO YOU HAVE TO BE TO CALL YOURSELVES THE--?
WHAT ARE YOU DOING?
HAVING A LITTLE CELEBRATORY... CELEBRATION. SORRY, THERE'S NOT ENOUGH TO SHARE, 'LOK.
THERE'S NOTHING TO CELEBRATE. WE'RE NOT FINISHED.
WHAT ARE YOU TALKING ABOUT? OF COURSE WE ARE. WE GOT THEM ALL.

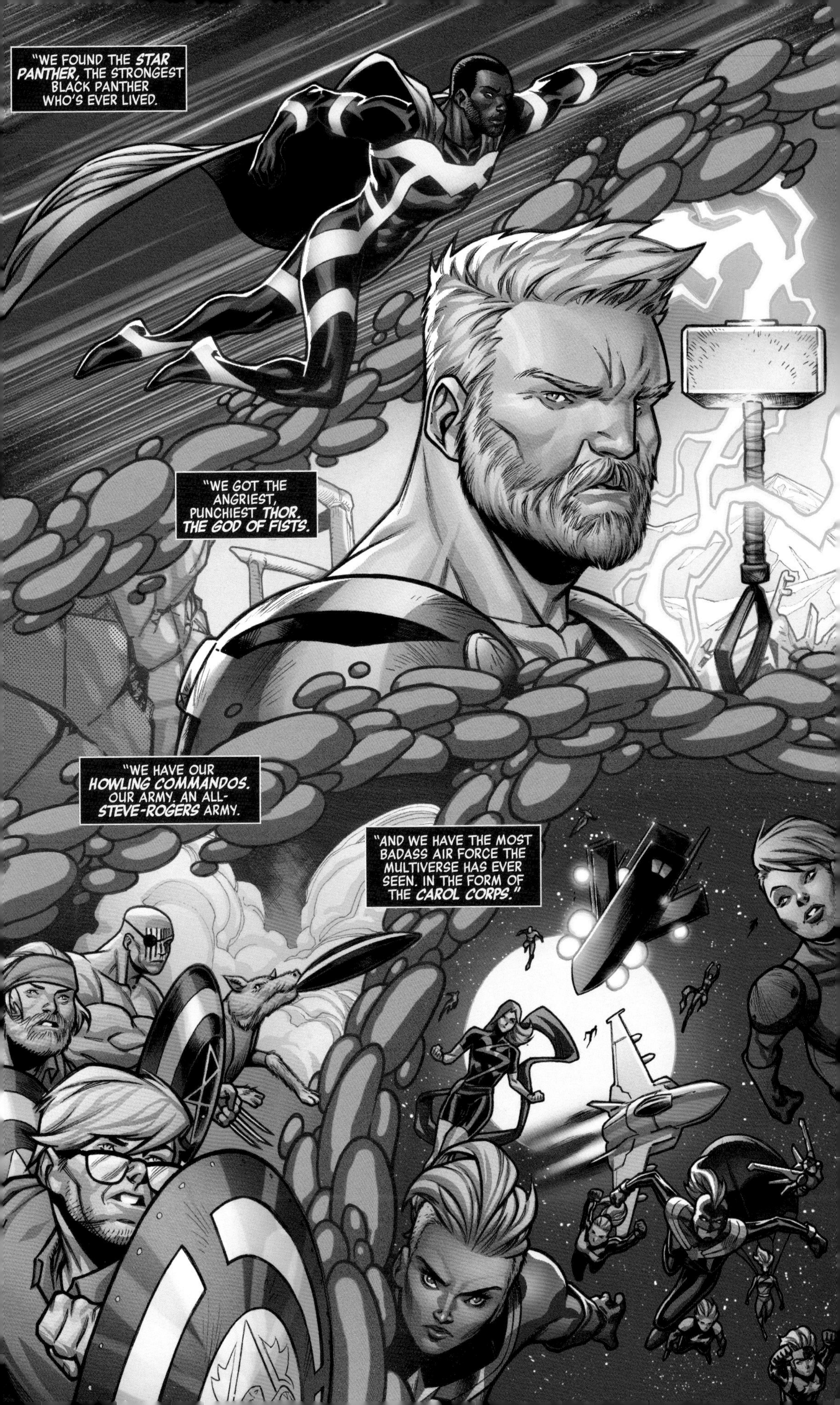
"WE FOUND THE STAR PANTHER, THE STRONGEST BLACK PANTHER WHO'S EVER LIVED.
"WE GOT THE ANGRIEST, PUNCHIEST THOR. THE GOD OF FISTS.
"WE HAVE OUR HOWLING COMMANDOS. OUR ARMY. AN ALL-STEVE-ROGERS ARMY.
"AND WE HAVE THE MOST BADASS AIR FORCE THE MULTIVERSE HAS EVER SEEN. IN THE FORM OF THE CAROL CORPS."

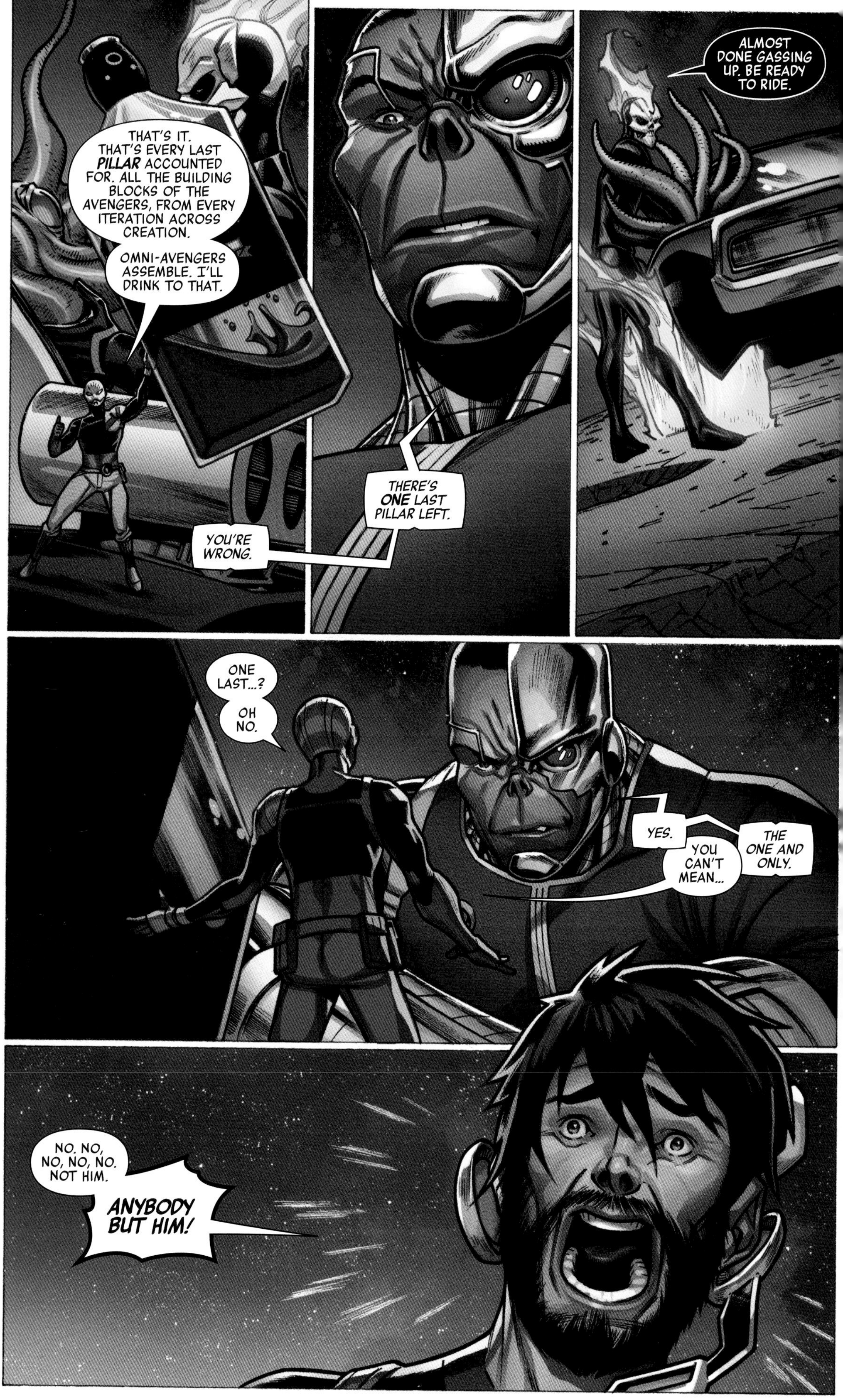
THAT'S IT. THAT'S EVERY LAST PILLAR ACCOUNTED FOR. ALL THE BUILDING BLOCKS OF THE AVENGERS, FROM EVERY ITERATION ACROSS CREATION.
OMNI-AVENGERS ASSEMBLE. I'LL DRINK TO THAT.
THERE'S ONE LAST PILLAR LEFT.
YOU'RE WRONG.
ALMOST DONE GASSING UP. BE READY TO RIDE.
ONE LAST...?
OH NO.
YES.
YOU CAN'T MEAN...
THE ONE AND ONLY.
NO. NO, NO, NO, NO. NOT HIM.
ANYBODY BUT HIM!

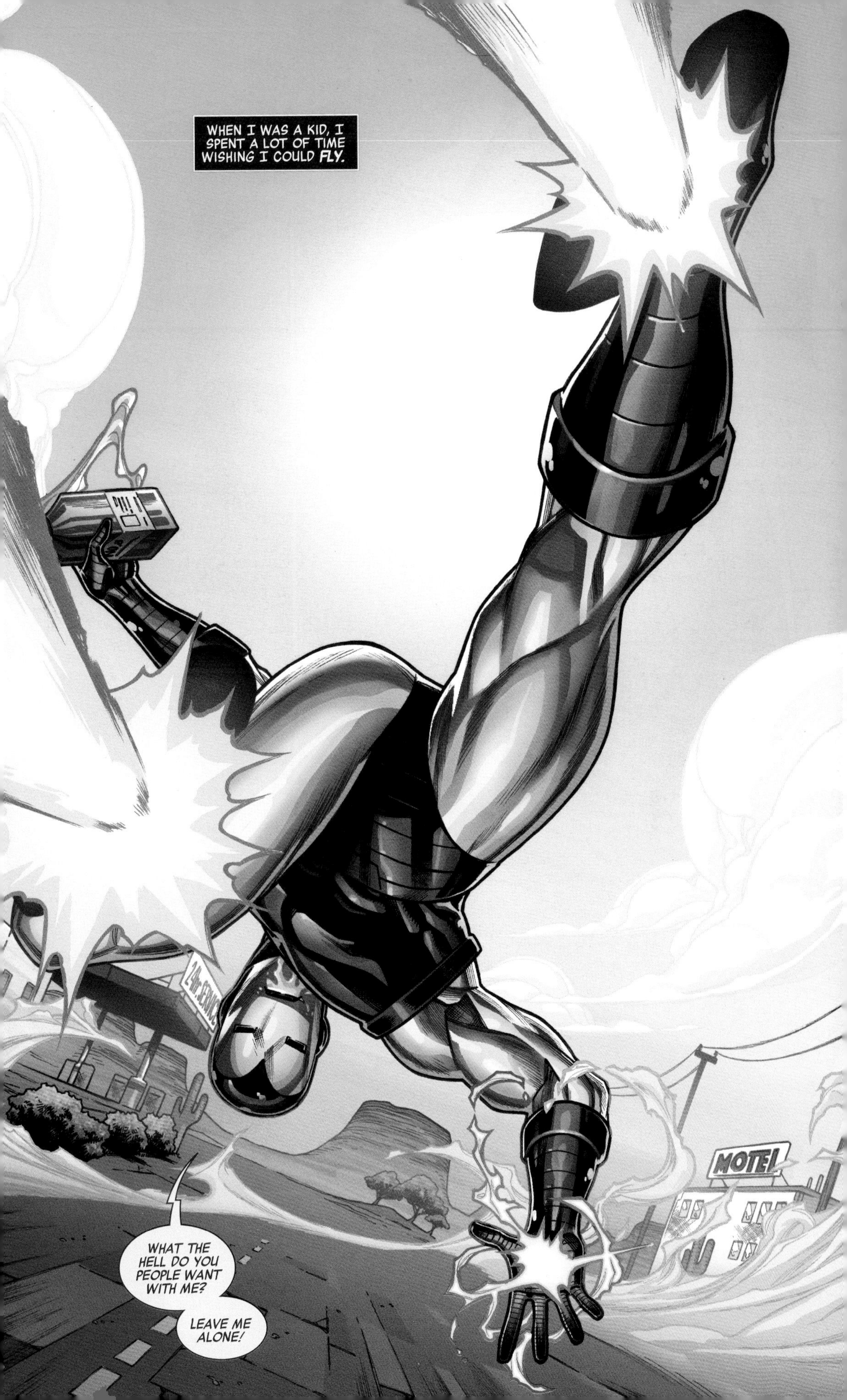
WHEN I WAS A KID, I SPENT A LOT OF TIME WISHING I COULD **FLY.**
WHAT THE HELL DO YOU PEOPLE WANT WITH ME?
LEAVE ME ALONE!
MOTEL

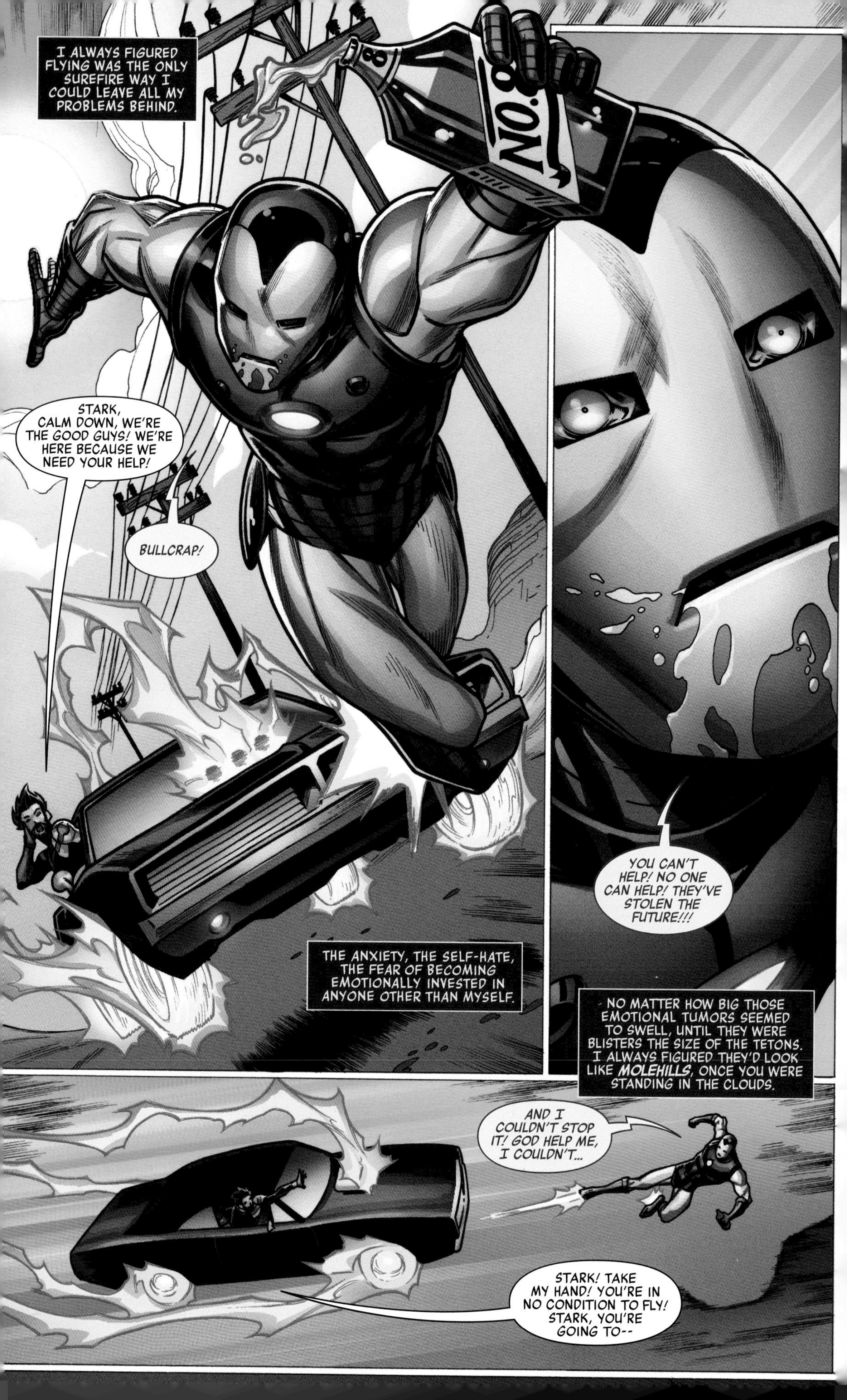
I ALWAYS FIGURED FLYING WAS THE ONLY SUREFIRE WAY I COULD LEAVE ALL MY PROBLEMS BEHIND.
NO.8
STARK, CALM DOWN, WE'RE THE GOOD GUYS! WE'RE HERE BECAUSE WE NEED YOUR HELP!
BULLCRAP!
YOU CAN'T HELP! NO ONE CAN HELP! THEY'VE STOLEN THE FUTURE!!!
THE ANXIETY, THE SELF-HATE, THE FEAR OF BECOMING EMOTIONALLY INVESTED IN ANYONE OTHER THAN MYSELF.
NO MATTER HOW BIG THOSE EMOTIONAL TUMORS SEEMED TO SWELL, UNTIL THEY WERE BLISTERS THE SIZE OF THE TETONS. I ALWAYS FIGURED THEY'D LOOK LIKE *MOLEHILLS*, ONCE YOU WERE STANDING IN THE CLOUDS.
AND I COULDN'T STOP IT! GOD HELP ME, I COULDN'T...
STARK! TAKE MY HAND! YOU'RE IN NO CONDITION TO FLY! STARK, YOU'RE GOING TO--

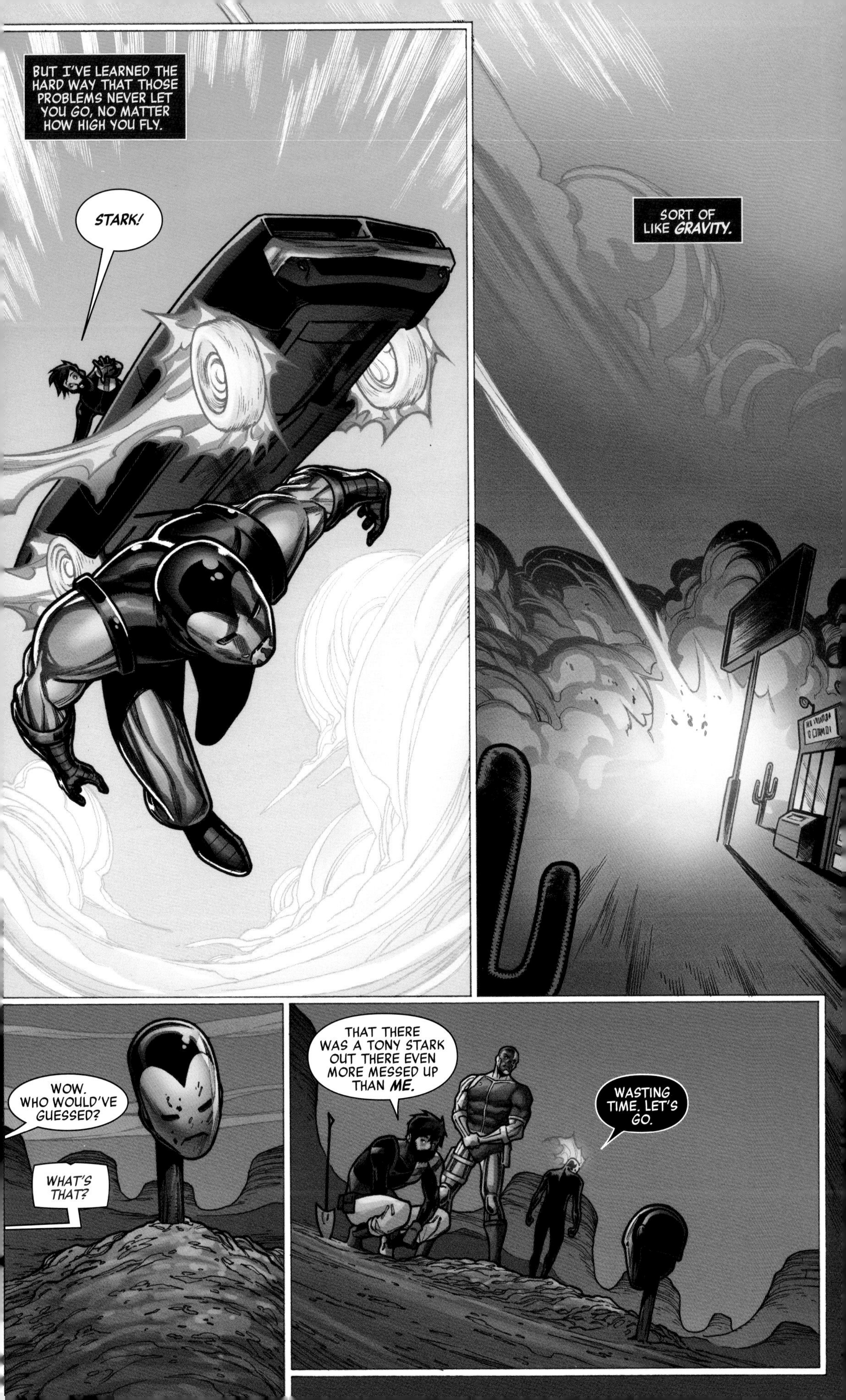
BUT I'VE LEARNED THE HARD WAY THAT THOSE PROBLEMS NEVER LET YOU GO, NO MATTER HOW HIGH YOU FLY.
STARK!
SORT OF LIKE GRAVITY.
WOW. WHO WOULD'VE GUESSED?
WHAT'S THAT?
THAT THERE WAS A TONY STARK OUT THERE EVEN MORE MESSED UP THAN ME.
WASTING TIME. LET'S GO.

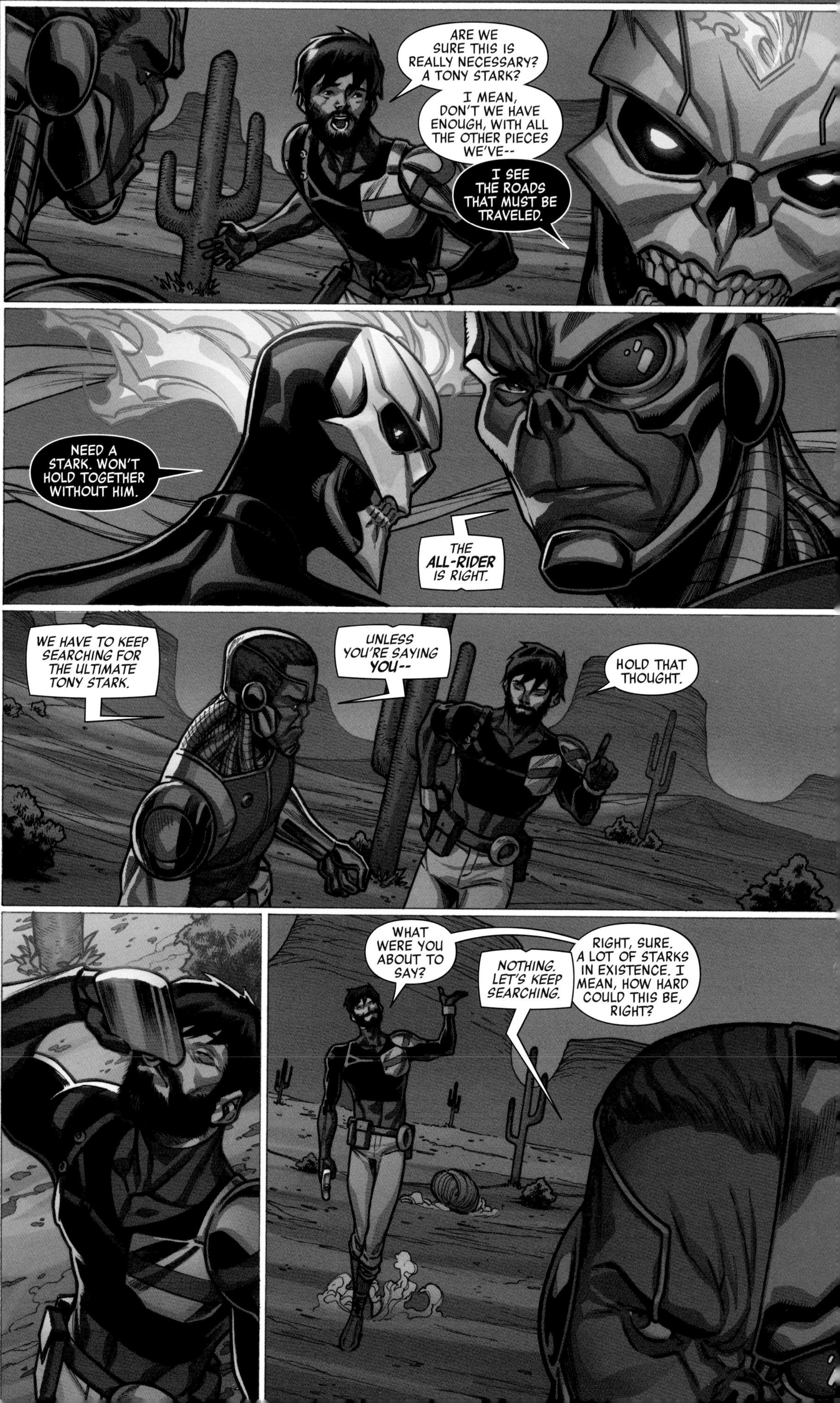
ARE WE SURE THIS IS REALLY NECESSARY? A TONY STARK?
I MEAN, DON'T WE HAVE ENOUGH, WITH ALL THE OTHER PIECES WE'VE--
I SEE THE ROADS THAT MUST BE TRAVELED.
NEED A STARK. WON'T HOLD TOGETHER WITHOUT HIM.
THE ALL-RIDER IS RIGHT.
WE HAVE TO KEEP SEARCHING FOR THE ULTIMATE TONY STARK.
UNLESS YOU'RE SAYING YOU--
HOLD THAT THOUGHT.
WHAT WERE YOU ABOUT TO SAY?
NOTHING. LET'S KEEP SEARCHING.
RIGHT, SURE. A LOT OF STARKS IN EXISTENCE. I MEAN, HOW HARD COULD THIS BE, RIGHT?

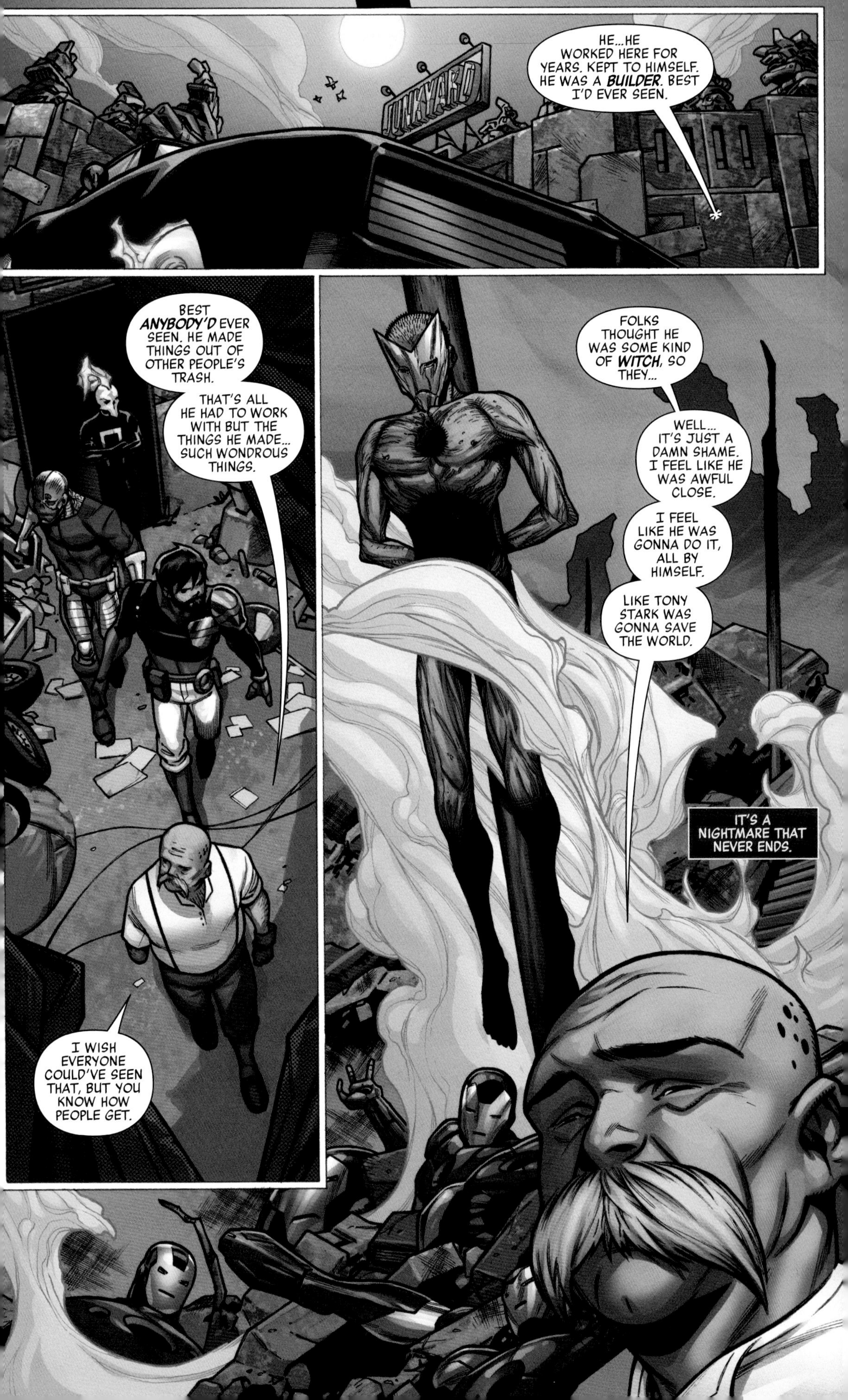
HE...HE WORKED HERE FOR YEARS. KEPT TO HIMSELF. HE WAS A BUILDER. BEST I'D EVER SEEN.
JUNKYARD
BEST ANYBODY'D EVER SEEN. HE MADE THINGS OUT OF OTHER PEOPLE'S TRASH.
THAT'S ALL HE HAD TO WORK WITH BUT THE THINGS HE MADE... SUCH WONDROUS THINGS.
I WISH EVERYONE COULD'VE SEEN THAT, BUT YOU KNOW HOW PEOPLE GET.
FOLKS THOUGHT HE WAS SOME KIND OF WITCH, SO THEY...
WELL... IT'S JUST A DAMN SHAME. I FEEL LIKE HE WAS AWFUL CLOSE.
I FEEL LIKE HE WAS GONNA DO IT, ALL BY HIMSELF.
LIKE TONY STARK WAS GONNA SAVE THE WORLD.
IT'S A NIGHTMARE THAT NEVER ENDS.

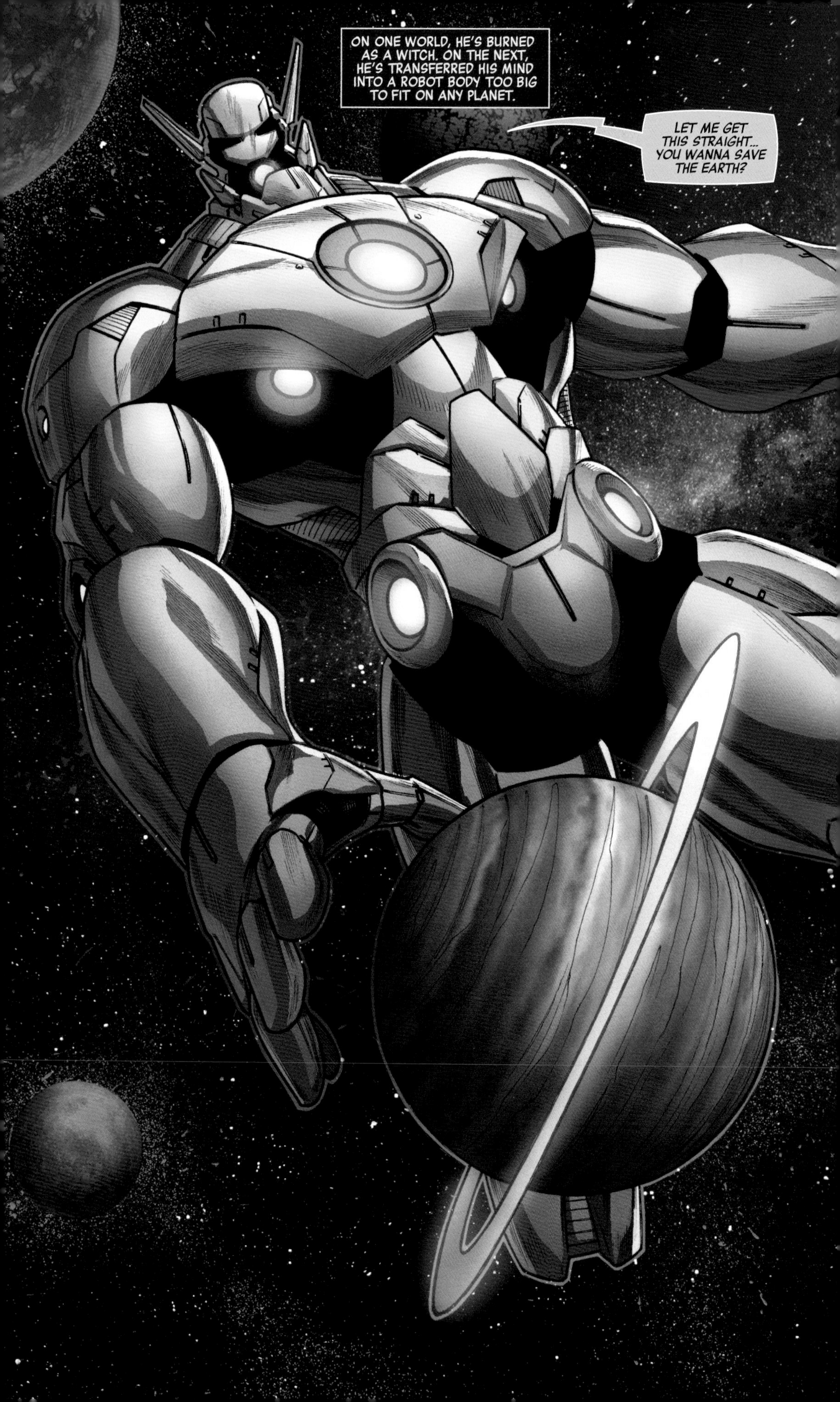
ON ONE WORLD, HE'S BURNED AS A WITCH. ON THE NEXT, HE'S TRANSFERRED HIS MIND INTO A ROBOT BODY TOO BIG TO FIT ON ANY PLANET.
LET ME GET THIS STRAIGHT... YOU WANNA SAVE THE EARTH?

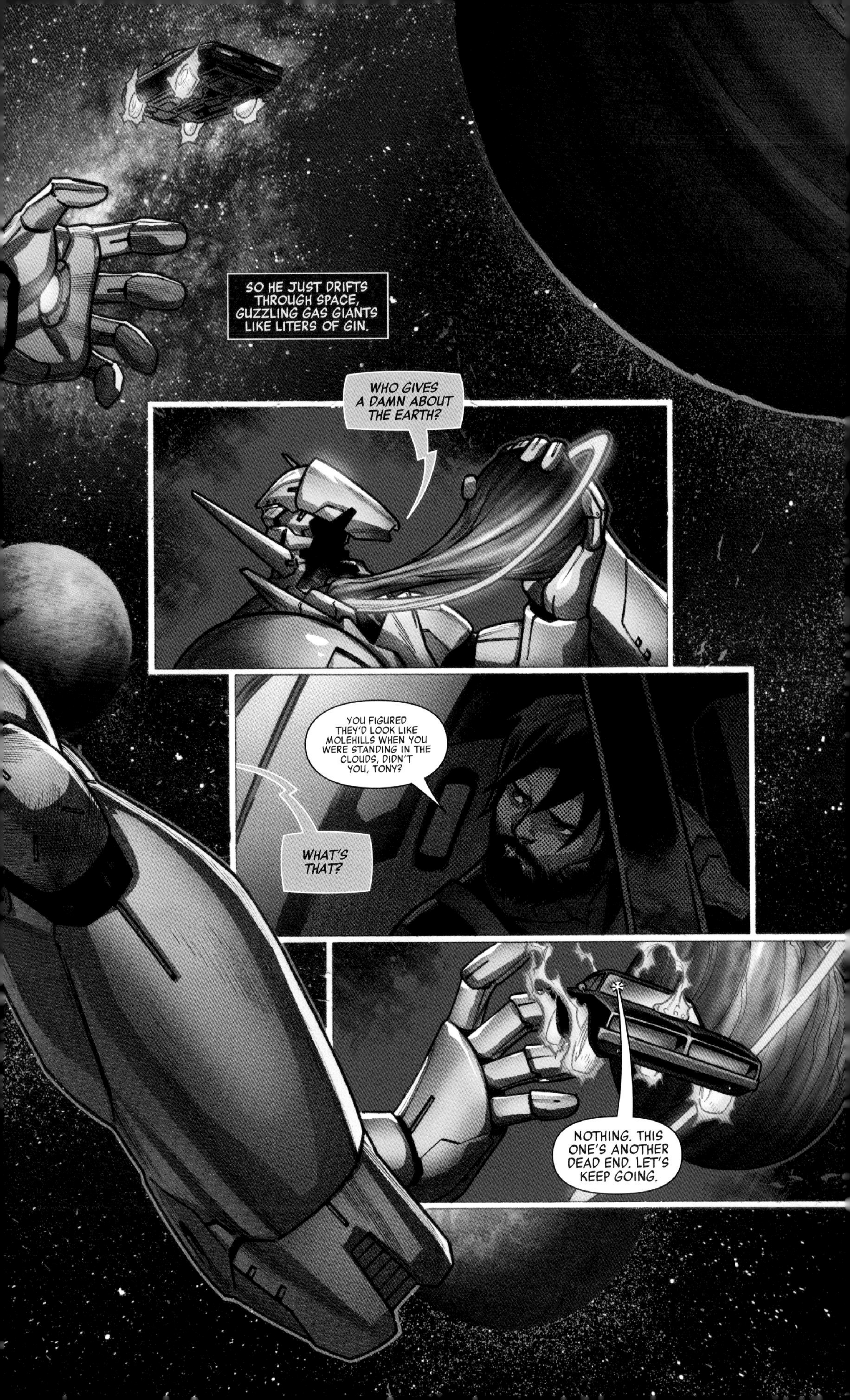
SO HE JUST DRIFTS THROUGH SPACE, GUZZLING GAS GIANTS LIKE LITERS OF GIN.
WHO GIVES A DAMN ABOUT THE EARTH?
YOU FIGURED THEY'D LOOK LIKE MOLEHILLS WHEN YOU WERE STANDING IN THE CLOUDS, DIDN'T YOU, TONY?
WHAT'S THAT?
NOTHING. THIS ONE'S ANOTHER DEAD END. LET'S KEEP GOING.

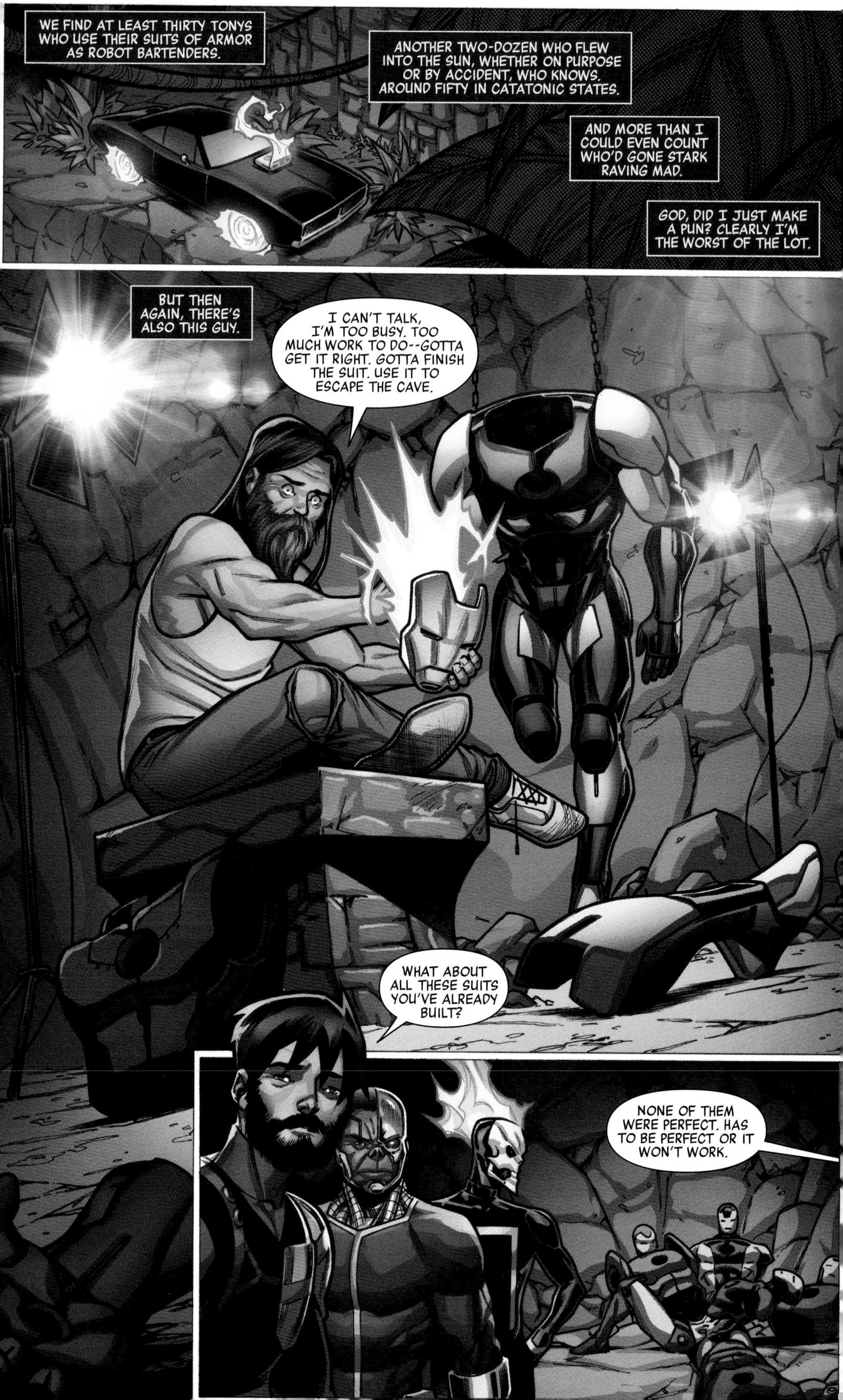
WE FIND AT LEAST THIRTY TONYS WHO USE THEIR SUITS OF ARMOR AS ROBOT BARTENDERS.
ANOTHER TWO-DOZEN WHO FLEW INTO THE SUN, WHETHER ON PURPOSE OR BY ACCIDENT, WHO KNOWS. AROUND FIFTY IN CATATONIC STATES.
AND MORE THAN I COULD EVEN COUNT WHO'D GONE STARK RAVING MAD.
GOD, DID I JUST MAKE A PUN? CLEARLY I'M THE WORST OF THE LOT.
BUT THEN AGAIN, THERE'S ALSO THIS GUY.
I CAN'T TALK, I'M TOO BUSY. TOO MUCH WORK TO DO--GOTTA GET IT RIGHT. GOTTA FINISH THE SUIT. USE IT TO ESCAPE THE CAVE.
WHAT ABOUT ALL THESE SUITS YOU'VE ALREADY BUILT?
NONE OF THEM WERE PERFECT. HAS TO BE PERFECT OR IT WON'T WORK.

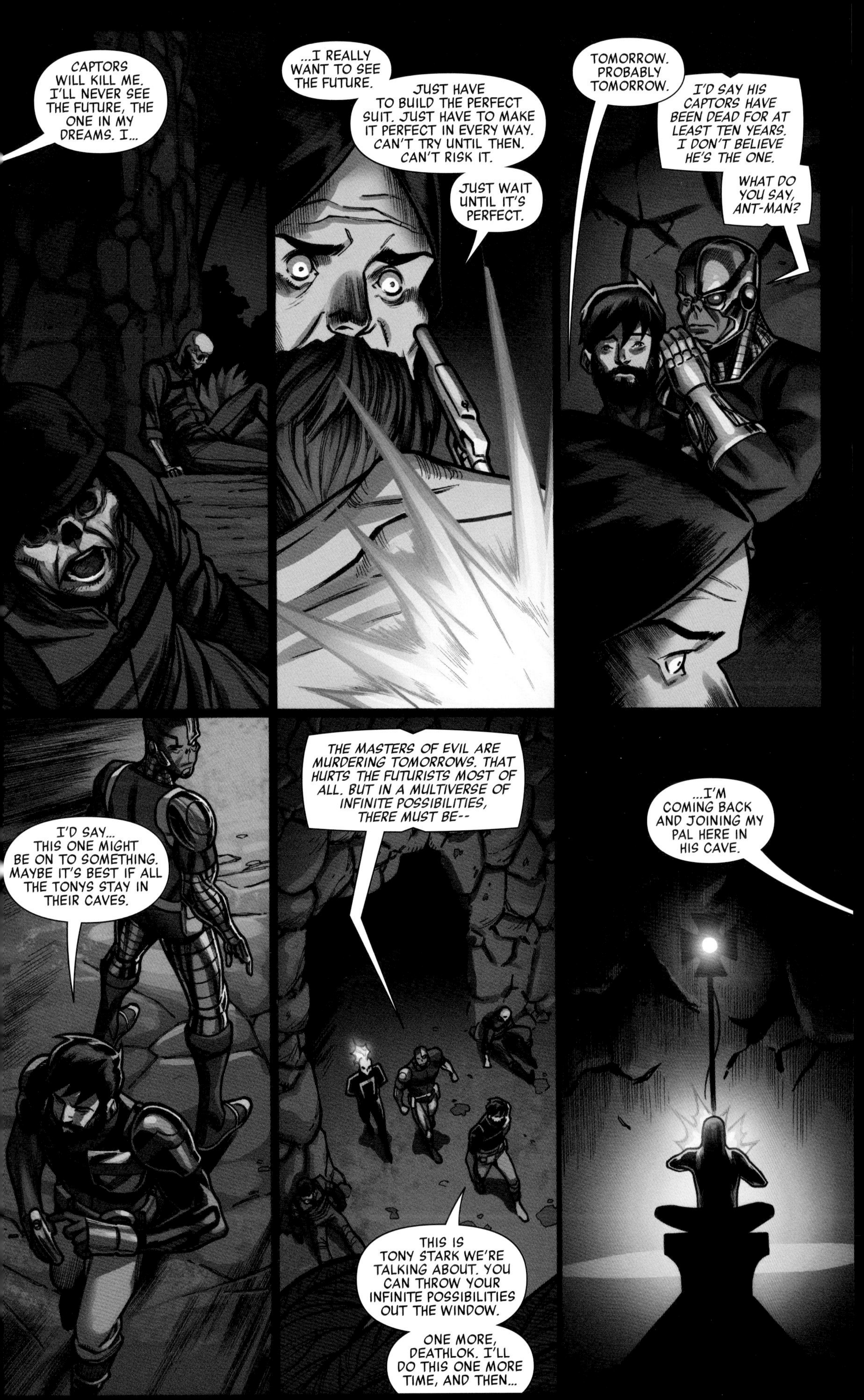
CAPTORS WILL KILL ME. I'LL NEVER SEE THE FUTURE, THE ONE IN MY DREAMS. I...
...I REALLY WANT TO SEE THE FUTURE.
JUST HAVE TO BUILD THE PERFECT SUIT. JUST HAVE TO MAKE IT PERFECT IN EVERY WAY. CAN'T TRY UNTIL THEN. CAN'T RISK IT.
JUST WAIT UNTIL IT'S PERFECT.
TOMORROW. PROBABLY TOMORROW.
I'D SAY HIS CAPTORS HAVE BEEN DEAD FOR AT LEAST TEN YEARS. I DON'T BELIEVE HE'S THE ONE.
WHAT DO YOU SAY, ANT-MAN?
I'D SAY... THIS ONE MIGHT BE ON TO SOMETHING. MAYBE IT'S BEST IF ALL THE TONYS STAY IN THEIR CAVES.
THE MASTERS OF EVIL ARE MURDERING TOMORROWS. THAT HURTS THE FUTURISTS MOST OF ALL. BUT IN A MULTIVERSE OF INFINITE POSSIBILITIES, THERE MUST BE--
THIS IS TONY STARK WE'RE TALKING ABOUT. YOU CAN THROW YOUR INFINITE POSSIBILITIES OUT THE WINDOW.
ONE MORE, DEATHLOK. I'LL DO THIS ONE MORE TIME, AND THEN...
...I'M COMING BACK AND JOINING MY PAL HERE IN HIS CAVE.

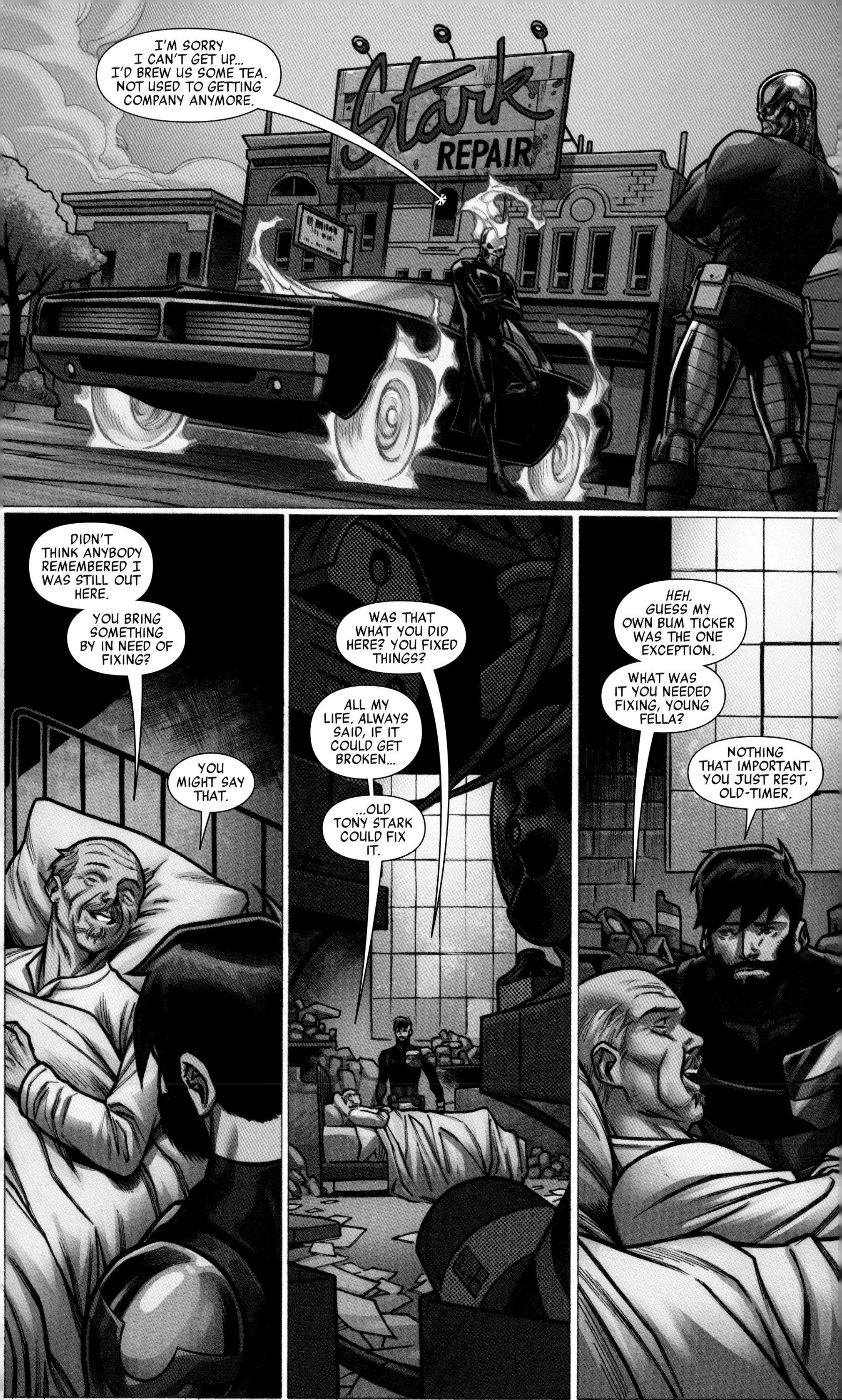
Stark
REPAIR
I'M SORRY I CAN'T GET UP... I'D BREW US SOME TEA. NOT USED TO GETTING COMPANY ANYMORE.
DIDN'T THINK ANYBODY REMEMBERED I WAS STILL OUT HERE.
YOU BRING SOMETHING BY IN NEED OF FIXING?
YOU MIGHT SAY THAT.
WAS THAT WHAT YOU DID HERE? YOU FIXED THINGS?
ALL MY LIFE. ALWAYS SAID, IF IT COULD GET BROKEN...
...OLD TONY STARK COULD FIX IT.
HEH. GUESS MY OWN BUM TICKER WAS THE ONE EXCEPTION.
WHAT WAS IT YOU NEEDED FIXING, YOUNG FELLA?
NOTHING THAT IMPORTANT. YOU JUST REST, OLD-TIMER.

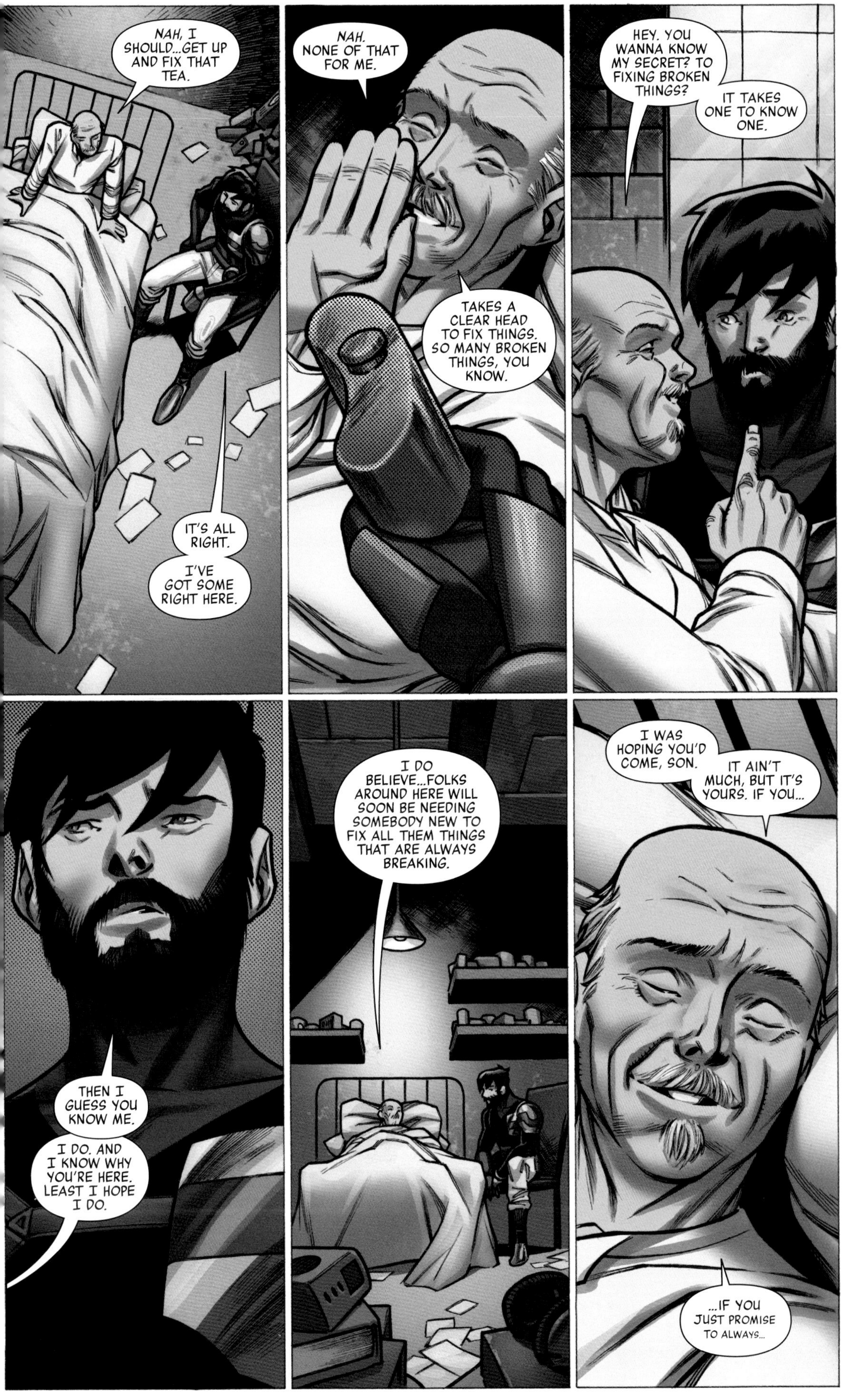
NAH, I SHOULD...GET UP AND FIX THAT TEA.
IT'S ALL RIGHT.
I'VE GOT SOME RIGHT HERE.
NAH. NONE OF THAT FOR ME.
TAKES A CLEAR HEAD TO FIX THINGS. SO MANY BROKEN THINGS, YOU KNOW.
HEY. YOU WANNA KNOW MY SECRET? TO FIXING BROKEN THINGS?
IT TAKES ONE TO KNOW ONE.
THEN I GUESS YOU KNOW ME.
I DO. AND I KNOW WHY YOU'RE HERE. LEAST I HOPE I DO.
I DO BELIEVE...FOLKS AROUND HERE WILL SOON BE NEEDING SOMEBODY NEW TO FIX ALL THEM THINGS THAT ARE ALWAYS BREAKING.
I WAS HOPING YOU'D COME, SON.
IT AIN'T MUCH, BUT IT'S YOURS. IF YOU...
...IF YOU JUST PROMISE TO ALWAYS...

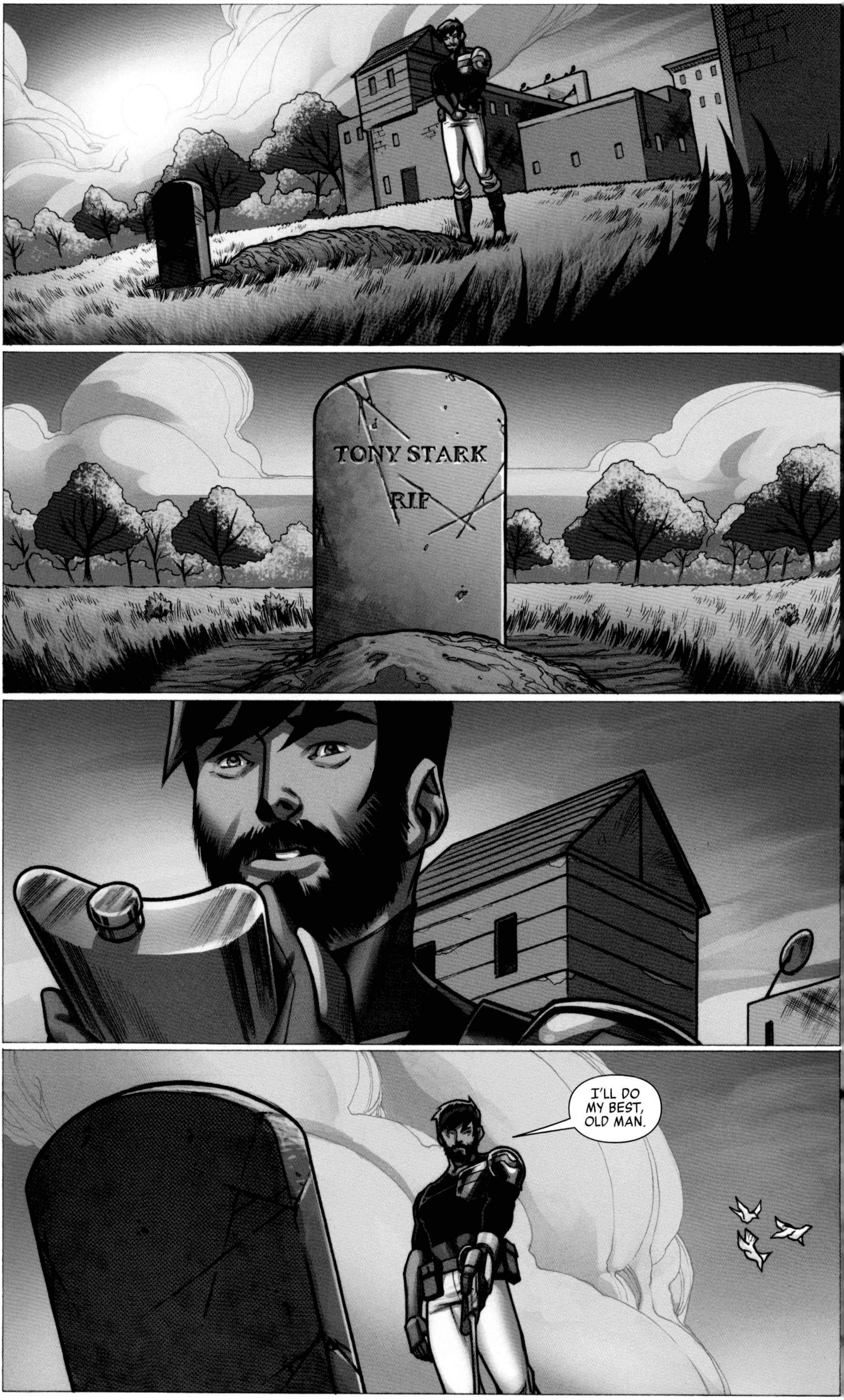
TONY STARK
R.I.P.
I'LL DO MY BEST, OLD MAN.

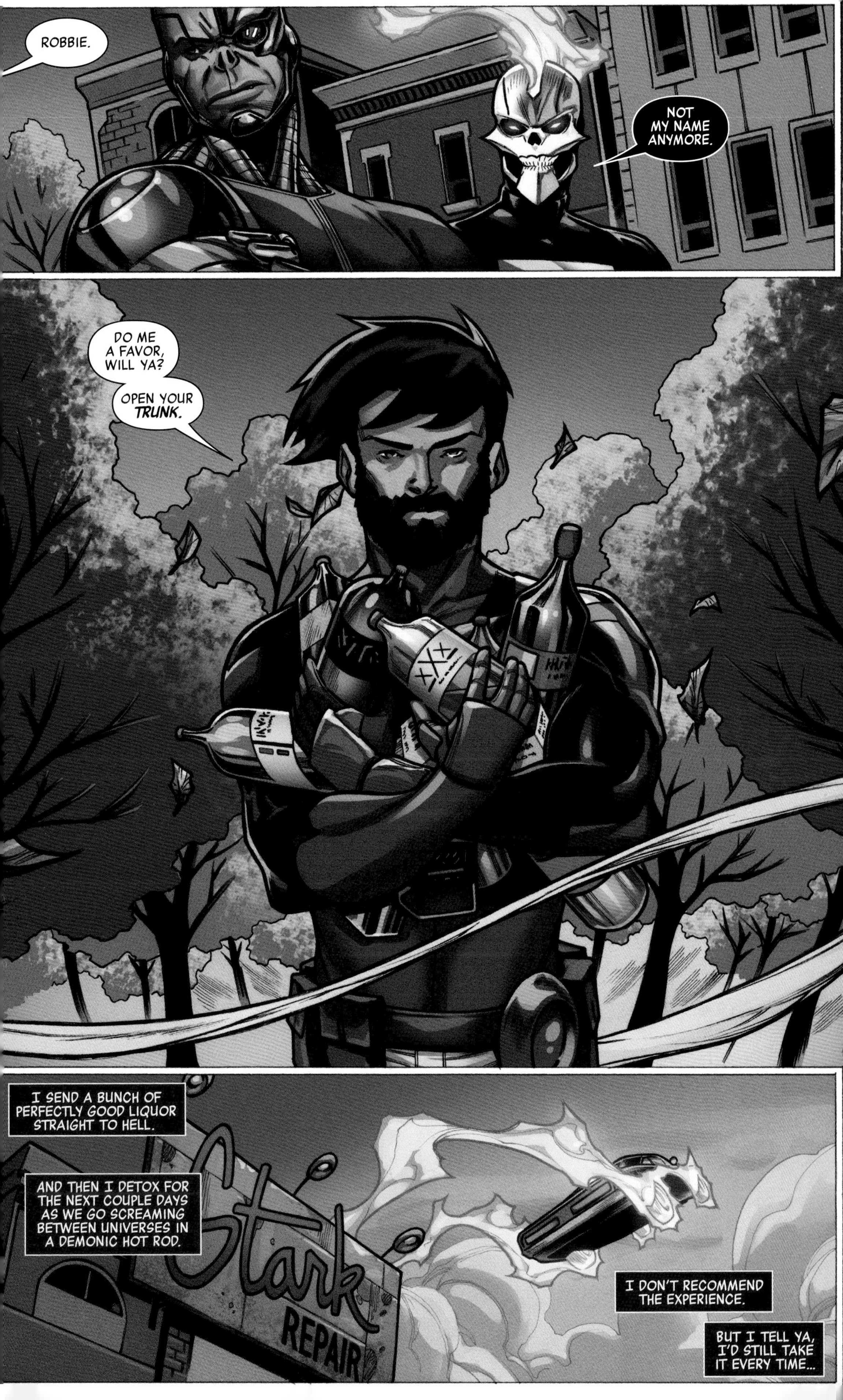
ROBBIE.
NOT MY NAME ANYMORE.
DO ME A FAVOR, WILL YA?
OPEN YOUR *TRUNK.*
I SEND A BUNCH OF PERFECTLY GOOD LIQUOR STRAIGHT TO HELL.
AND THEN I DETOX FOR THE NEXT COUPLE DAYS AS WE GO SCREAMING BETWEEN UNIVERSES IN A DEMONIC HOT ROD.
Stark
REPAIR
I DON'T RECOMMEND THE EXPERIENCE.
BUT I TELL YA, I'D STILL TAKE IT EVERY TIME...

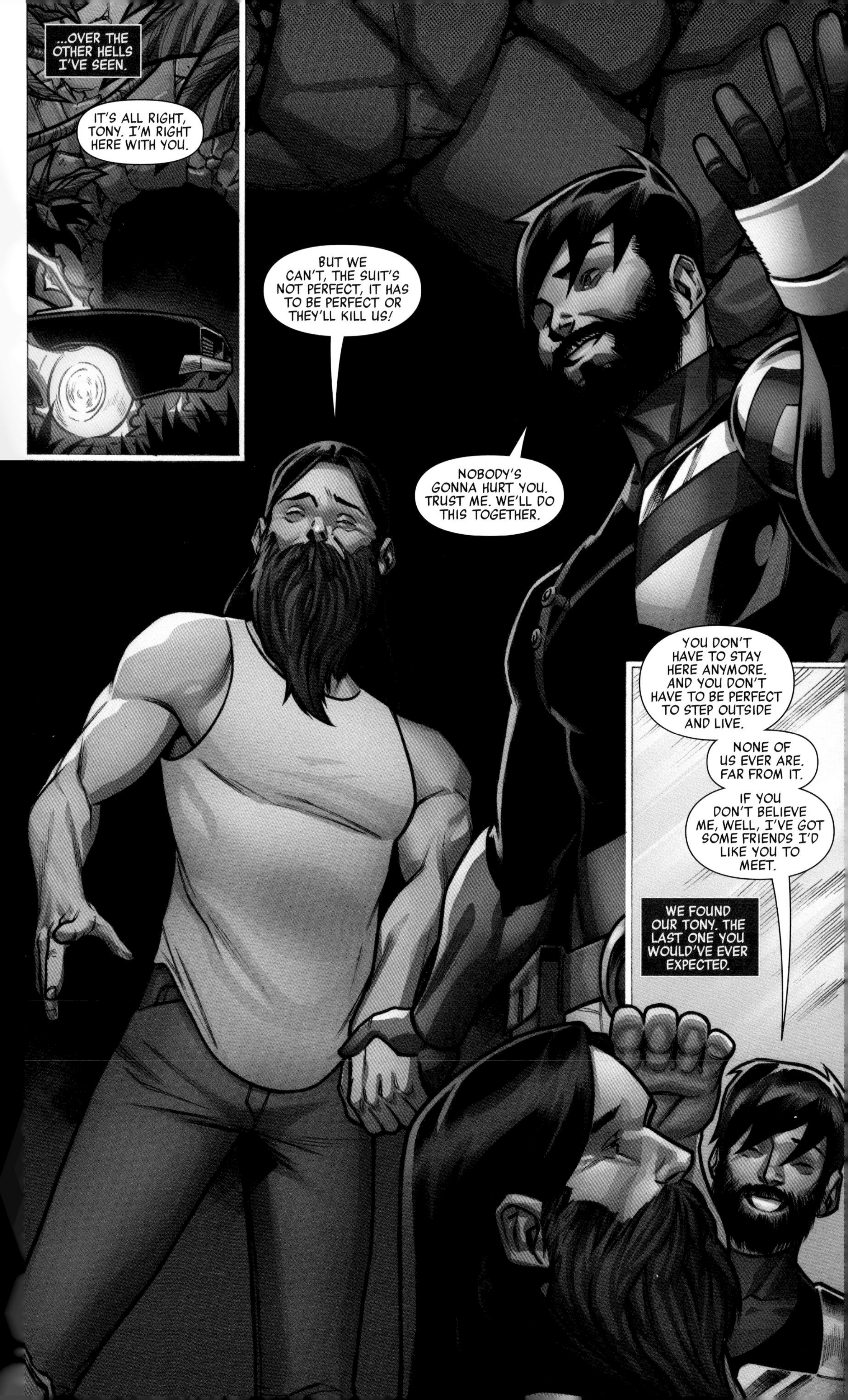
...OVER THE OTHER HELLS I'VE SEEN.
IT'S ALL RIGHT, TONY. I'M RIGHT HERE WITH YOU.
BUT WE CAN'T, THE SUIT'S NOT PERFECT, IT HAS TO BE PERFECT OR THEY'LL KILL US!
NOBODY'S GONNA HURT YOU. TRUST ME. WE'LL DO THIS TOGETHER.
YOU DON'T HAVE TO STAY HERE ANYMORE. AND YOU DON'T HAVE TO BE PERFECT TO STEP OUTSIDE AND LIVE.
NONE OF US EVER ARE. FAR FROM IT.
IF YOU DON'T BELIEVE ME, WELL, I'VE GOT SOME FRIENDS I'D LIKE YOU TO MEET.
WE FOUND OUR TONY. THE LAST ONE YOU WOULD'VE EVER EXPECTED.

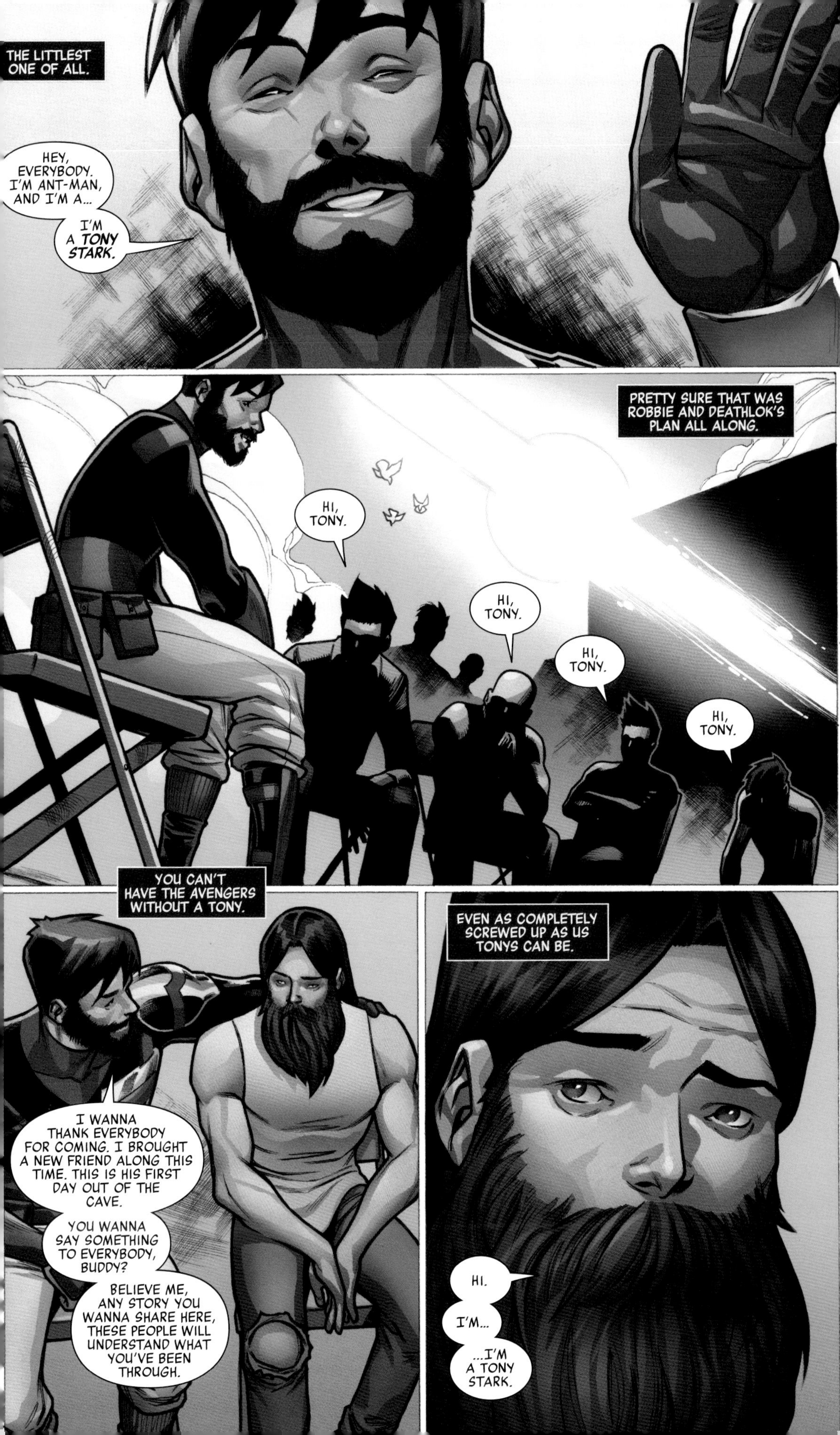
THE LITTLEST ONE OF ALL.
HEY, EVERYBODY. I'M ANT-MAN, AND I'M A...
I'M A TONY STARK.
PRETTY SURE THAT WAS ROBBIE AND DEATHLOK'S PLAN ALL ALONG.
HI, TONY.
HI, TONY.
HI, TONY.
HI, TONY.
YOU CAN'T HAVE THE AVENGERS WITHOUT A TONY.
I WANNA THANK EVERYBODY FOR COMING. I BROUGHT A NEW FRIEND ALONG THIS TIME. THIS IS HIS FIRST DAY OUT OF THE CAVE.
YOU WANNA SAY SOMETHING TO EVERYBODY, BUDDY?
BELIEVE ME, ANY STORY YOU WANNA SHARE HERE, THESE PEOPLE WILL UNDERSTAND WHAT YOU'VE BEEN THROUGH.
EVEN AS COMPLETELY SCREWED UP AS US TONYS CAN BE.
HI.
I'M...
...I'M A TONY STARK.

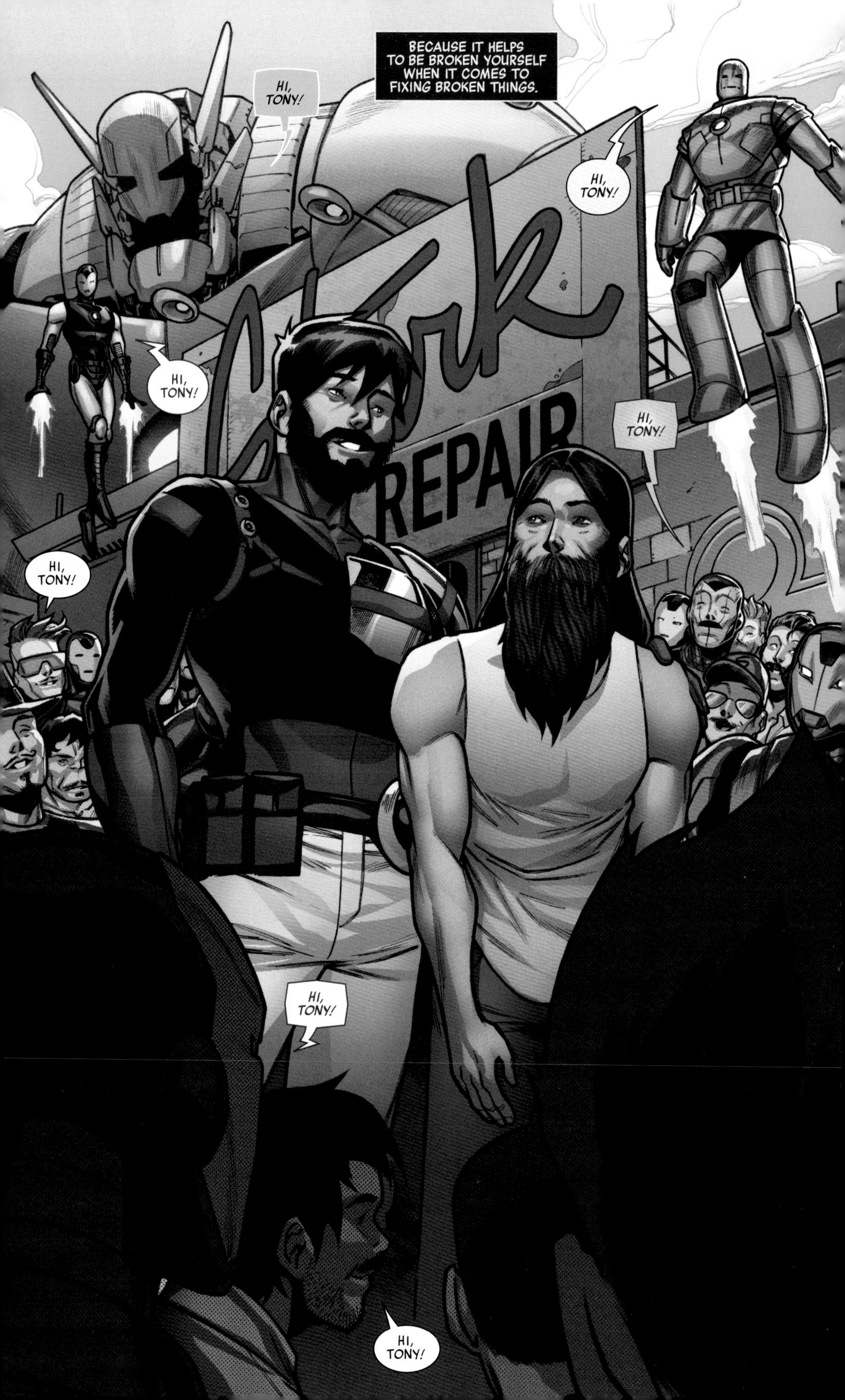

BECAUSE IT HELPS TO BE BROKEN YOURSELF WHEN IT COMES TO FIXING BROKEN THINGS.
HI, TONY!
HI, TONY!
HI, TONY!
HI, TONY!
HI, TONY!
REPAIR
HI, TONY!
HI, TONY!

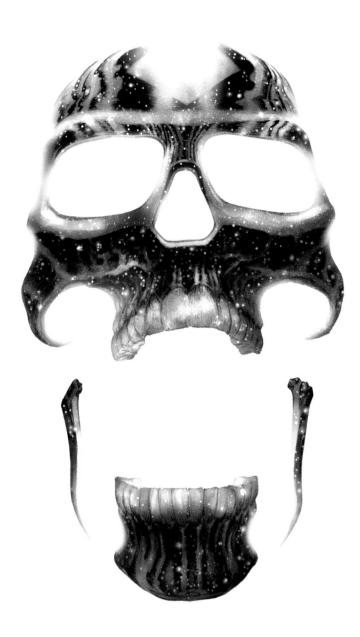

KUDER '22
SINC

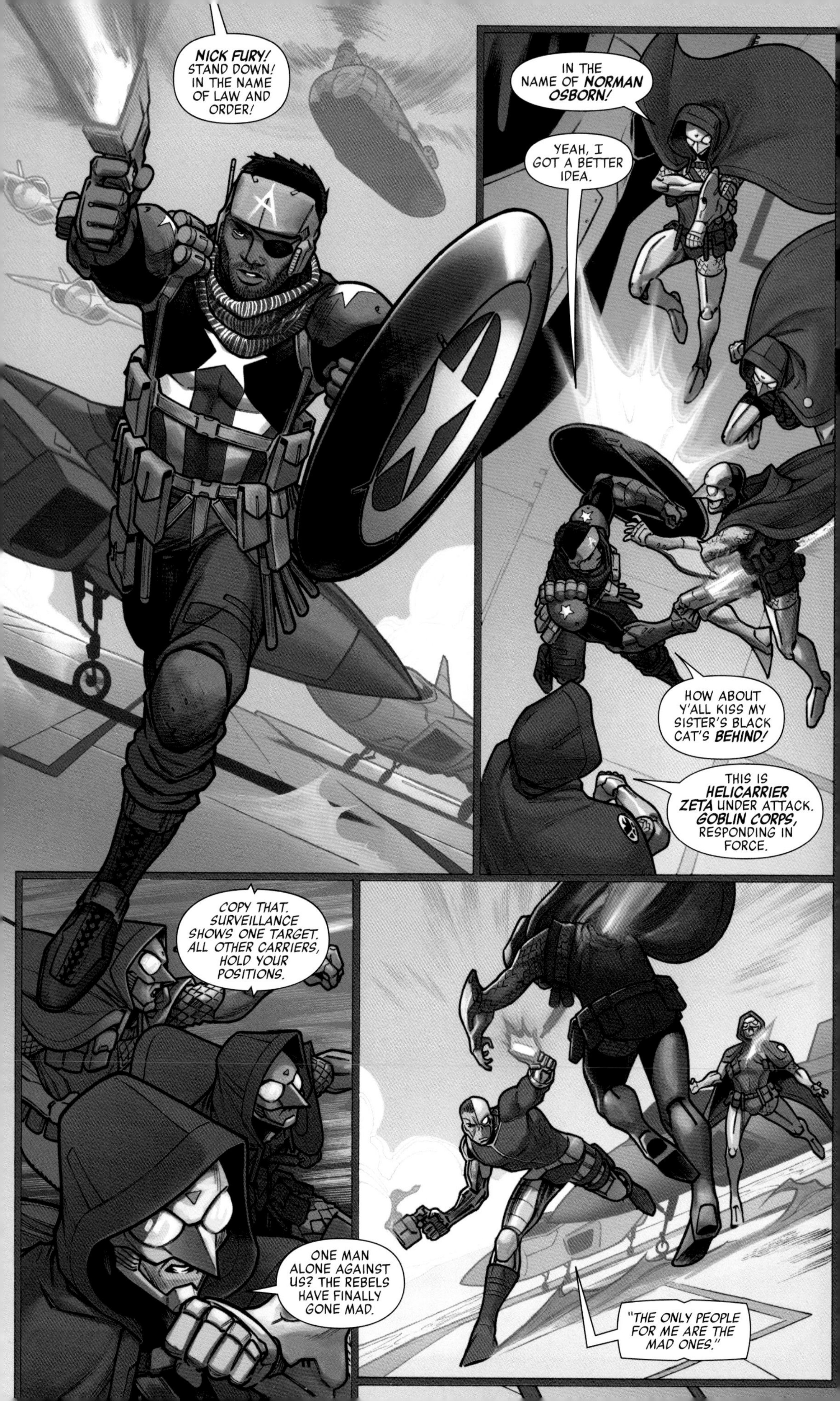
NICK FURY! STAND DOWN! IN THE NAME OF LAW AND ORDER!
IN THE NAME OF NORMAN OSBORN!
YEAH, I GOT A BETTER IDEA.
HOW ABOUT Y'ALL KISS MY SISTER'S BLACK CAT'S BEHIND!
THIS IS HELICARRIER ZETA UNDER ATTACK. GOBLIN CORPS, RESPONDING IN FORCE.
COPY THAT. SURVEILLANCE SHOWS ONE TARGET. ALL OTHER CARRIERS, HOLD YOUR POSITIONS.
ONE MAN ALONE AGAINST US? THE REBELS HAVE FINALLY GONE MAD.
"THE ONLY PEOPLE FOR ME ARE THE MAD ONES."

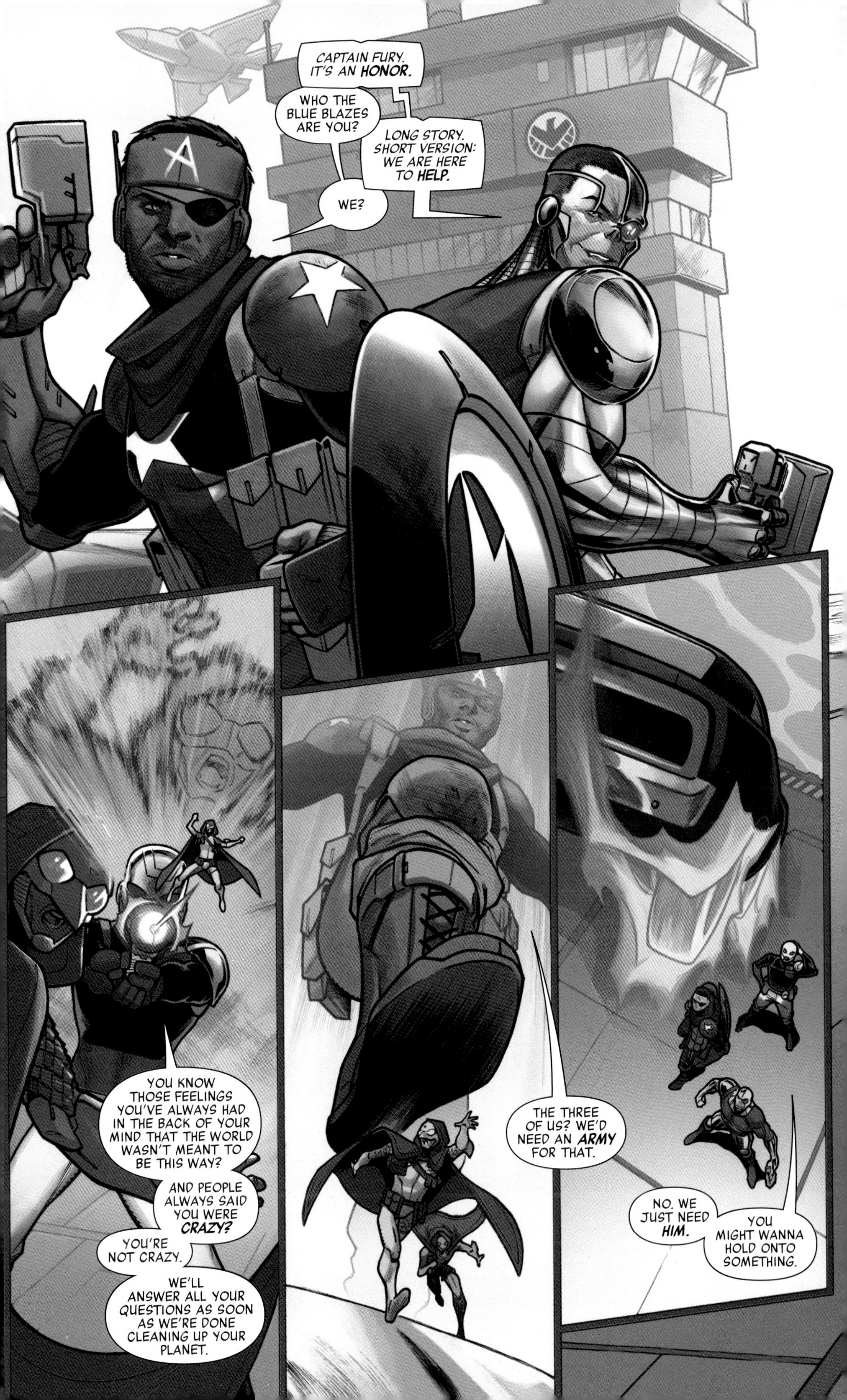
CAPTAIN FURY. IT'S AN HONOR.
WHO THE BLUE BLAZES ARE YOU?
LONG STORY. SHORT VERSION: WE ARE HERE TO HELP.
WE?
YOU KNOW THOSE FEELINGS YOU'VE ALWAYS HAD IN THE BACK OF YOUR MIND THAT THE WORLD WASN'T MEANT TO BE THIS WAY?
AND PEOPLE ALWAYS SAID YOU WERE CRAZY?
YOU'RE NOT CRAZY.
WE'LL ANSWER ALL YOUR QUESTIONS AS SOON AS WE'RE DONE CLEANING UP YOUR PLANET.
THE THREE OF US? WE'D NEED AN ARMY FOR THAT.
NO. WE JUST NEED HIM.
YOU MIGHT WANNA HOLD ONTO SOMETHING.

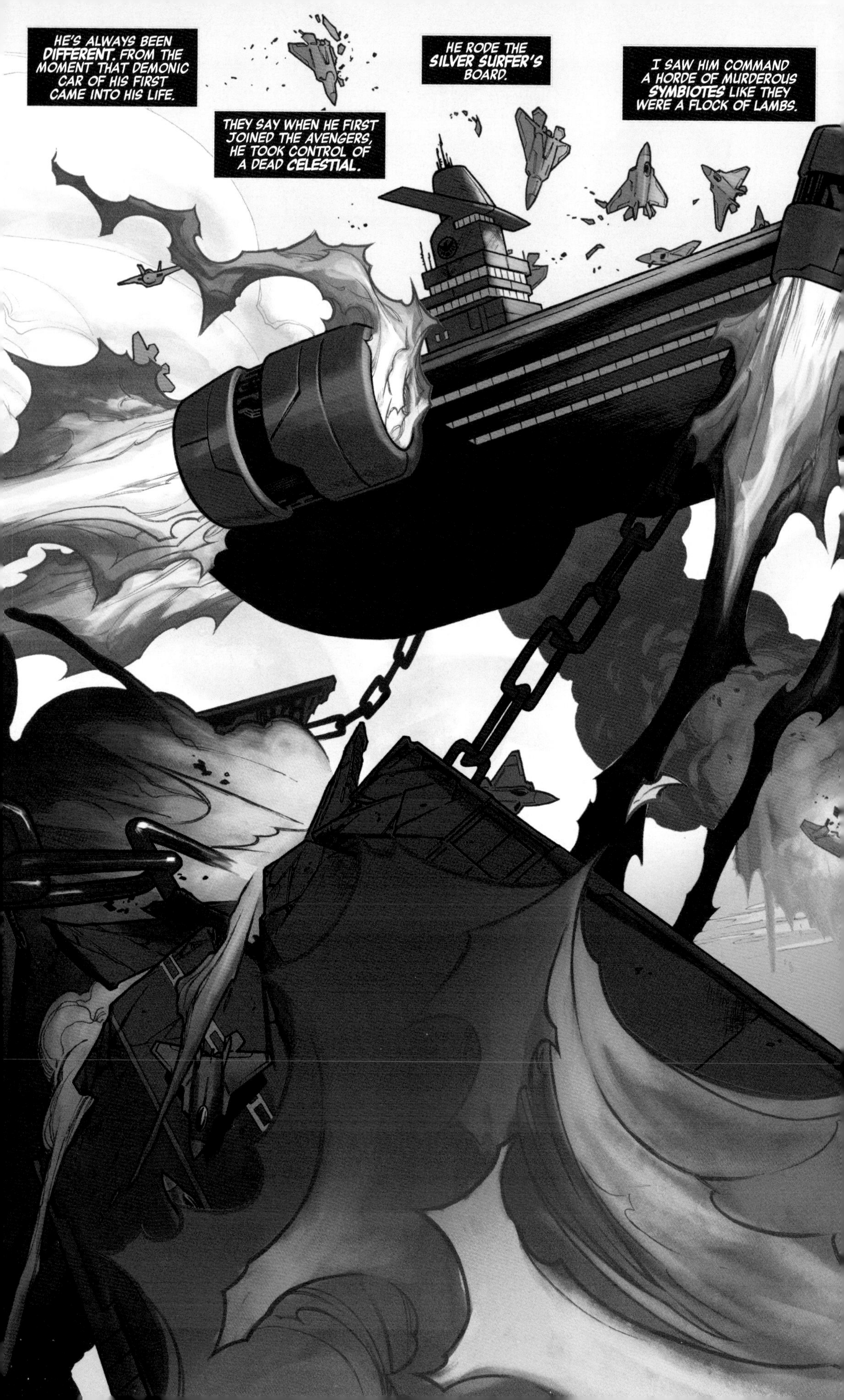
HE'S ALWAYS BEEN DIFFERENT. FROM THE MOMENT THAT DEMONIC CAR OF HIS FIRST CAME INTO HIS LIFE.
THEY SAY WHEN HE FIRST JOINED THE AVENGERS, HE TOOK CONTROL OF A DEAD CELESTIAL.
HE RODE THE SILVER SURFER'S BOARD.
I SAW HIM COMMAND A HORDE OF MURDEROUS SYMBIOTES LIKE THEY WERE A FLOCK OF LAMBS.

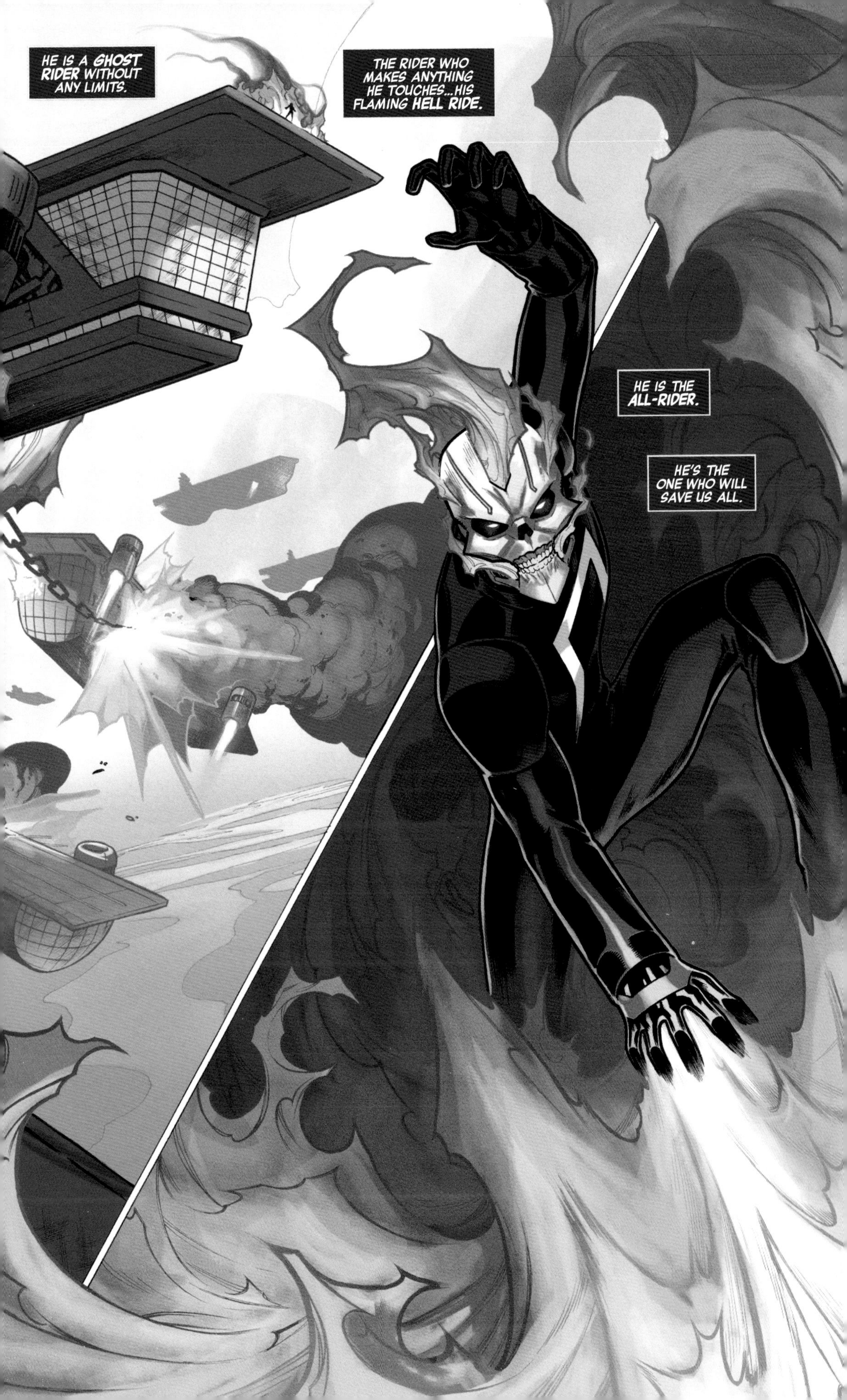
HE IS A GHOST RIDER WITHOUT ANY LIMITS.
THE RIDER WHO MAKES ANYTHING HE TOUCHES...HIS FLAMING HELL RIDE.
HE IS THE ALL-RIDER.
HE'S THE ONE WHO WILL SAVE US ALL.

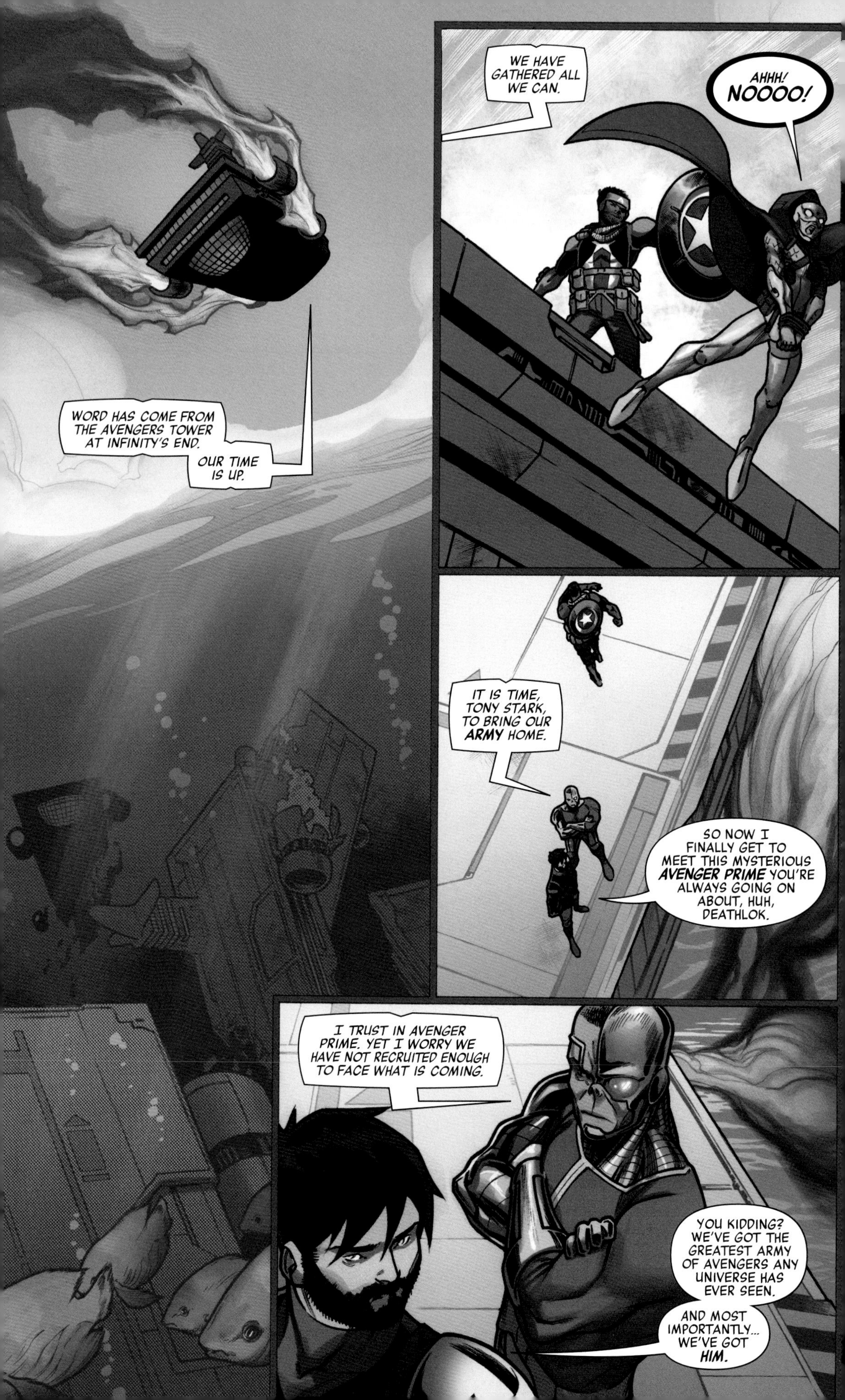

WORD HAS COME FROM THE AVENGERS TOWER AT INFINITY'S END.
OUR TIME IS UP.
WE HAVE GATHERED ALL WE CAN.
AHHH! NOOOO!
IT IS TIME, TONY STARK, TO BRING OUR ARMY HOME.
SO NOW I FINALLY GET TO MEET THIS MYSTERIOUS AVENGER PRIME YOU'RE ALWAYS GOING ON ABOUT, HUH, DEATHLOK.
I TRUST IN AVENGER PRIME. YET I WORRY WE HAVE NOT RECRUITED ENOUGH TO FACE WHAT IS COMING.
YOU KIDDING? WE'VE GOT THE GREATEST ARMY OF AVENGERS ANY UNIVERSE HAS EVER SEEN.
AND MOST IMPORTANTLY... WE'VE GOT HIM.

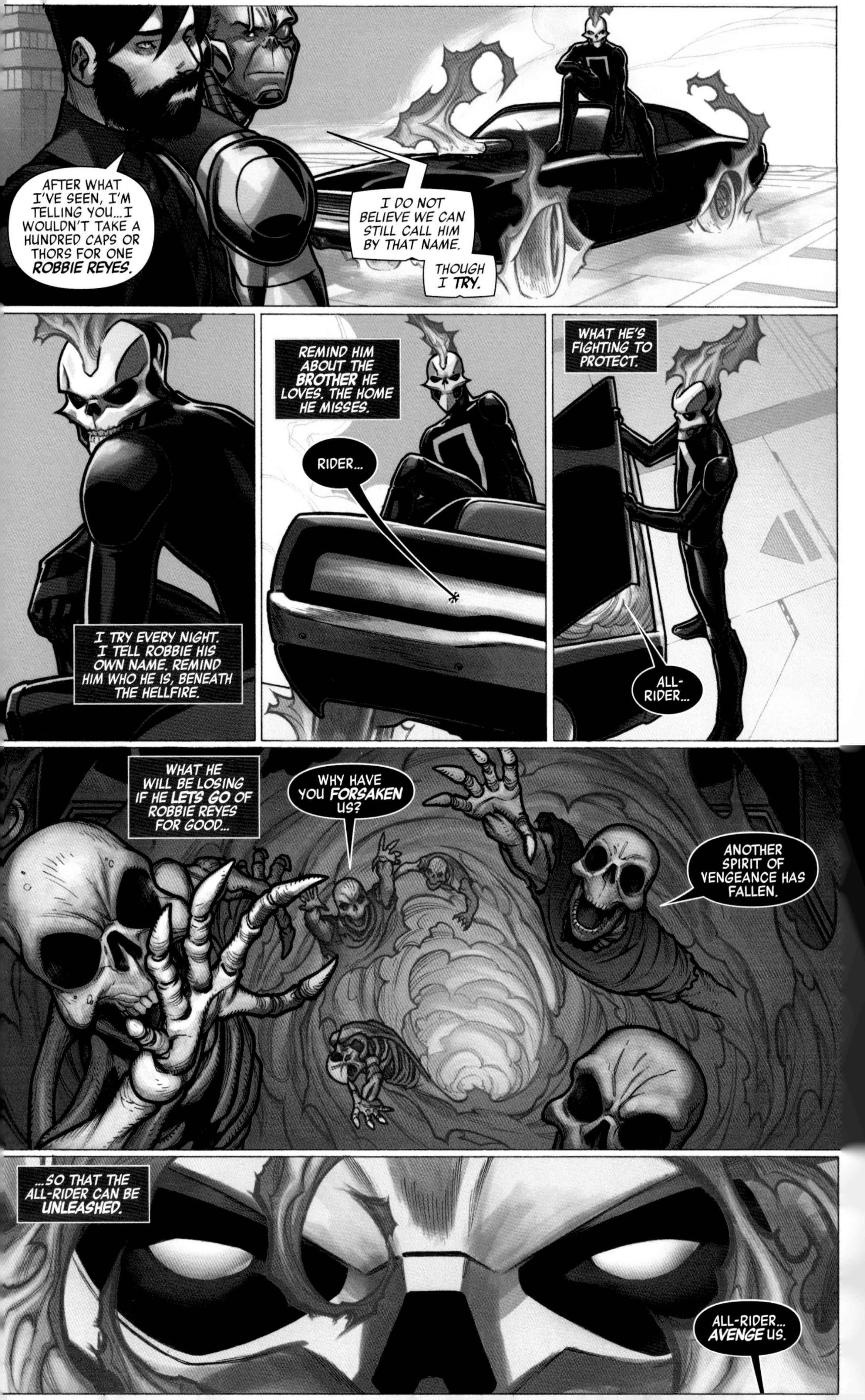
AFTER WHAT I'VE SEEN, I'M TELLING YOU...I WOULDN'T TAKE A HUNDRED CAPS OR THORS FOR ONE ROBBIE REYES.
I DO NOT BELIEVE WE CAN STILL CALL HIM BY THAT NAME.
THOUGH I TRY.
I TRY EVERY NIGHT. I TELL ROBBIE HIS OWN NAME. REMIND HIM WHO HE IS, BENEATH THE HELLFIRE.
REMIND HIM ABOUT THE BROTHER HE LOVES. THE HOME HE MISSES.
RIDER...
WHAT HE'S FIGHTING TO PROTECT.
ALL-RIDER...
WHAT HE WILL BE LOSING IF HE LETS GO OF ROBBIE REYES FOR GOOD...
WHY HAVE YOU FORSAKEN US?
ANOTHER SPIRIT OF VENGEANCE HAS FALLEN.
...SO THAT THE ALL-RIDER CAN BE UNLEASHED.
ALL-RIDER... AVENGE US.

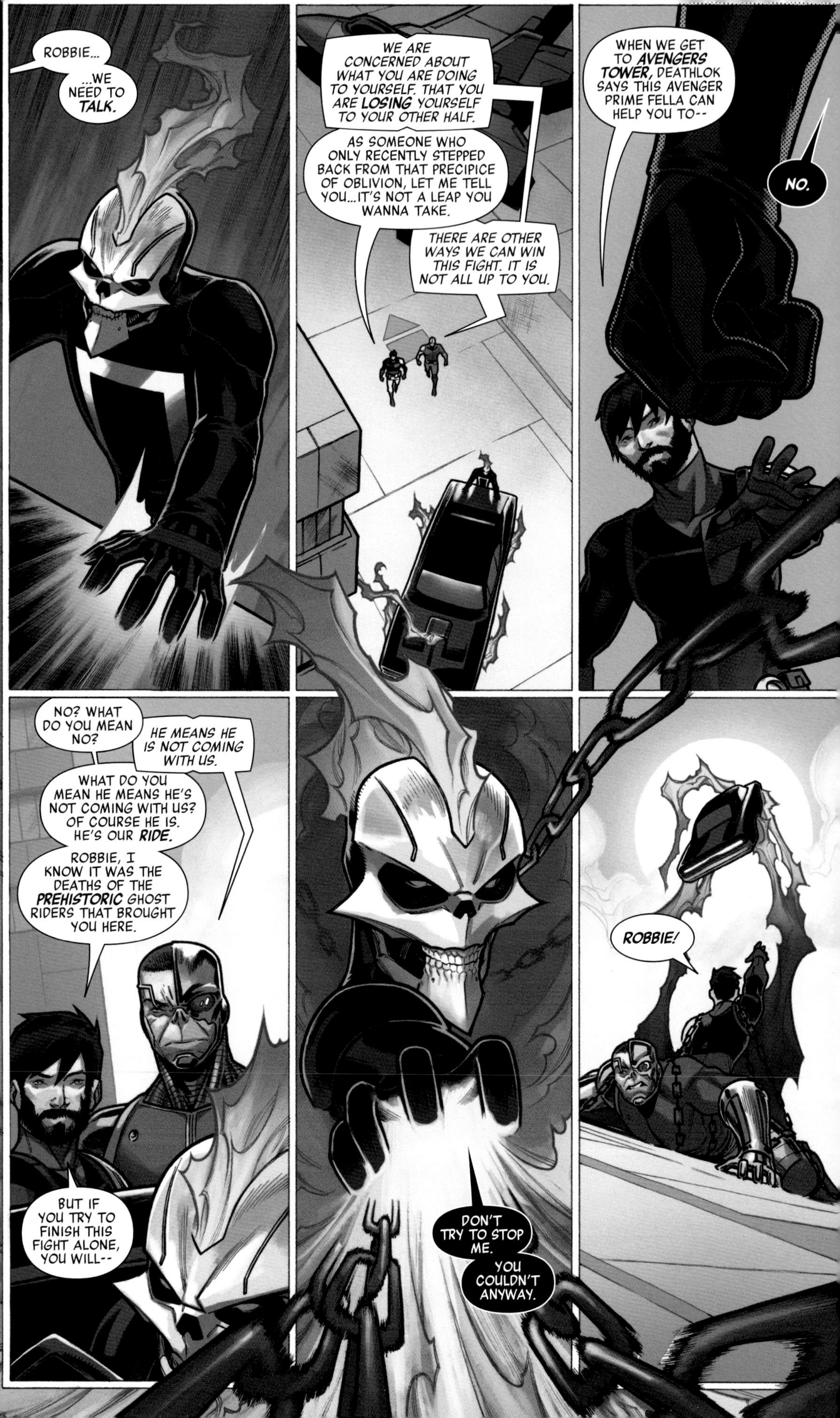
ROBBIE...
...WE NEED TO TALK.
WE ARE CONCERNED ABOUT WHAT YOU ARE DOING TO YOURSELF. THAT YOU ARE LOSING YOURSELF TO YOUR OTHER HALF.
AS SOMEONE WHO ONLY RECENTLY STEPPED BACK FROM THAT PRECIPICE OF OBLIVION, LET ME TELL YOU...IT'S NOT A LEAP YOU WANNA TAKE.
THERE ARE OTHER WAYS WE CAN WIN THIS FIGHT. IT IS NOT ALL UP TO YOU.
WHEN WE GET TO AVENGERS TOWER, DEATHLOK SAYS THIS AVENGER PRIME FELLA CAN HELP YOU TO--
NO.
NO? WHAT DO YOU MEAN NO?
HE MEANS HE IS NOT COMING WITH US.
WHAT DO YOU MEAN HE MEANS HE'S NOT COMING WITH US? OF COURSE HE IS. HE'S OUR RIDE.
ROBBIE, I KNOW IT WAS THE DEATHS OF THE PREHISTORIC GHOST RIDERS THAT BROUGHT YOU HERE.
BUT IF YOU TRY TO FINISH THIS FIGHT ALONE, YOU WILL--
DON'T TRY TO STOP ME.
YOU COULDN'T ANYWAY.
ROBBIE!

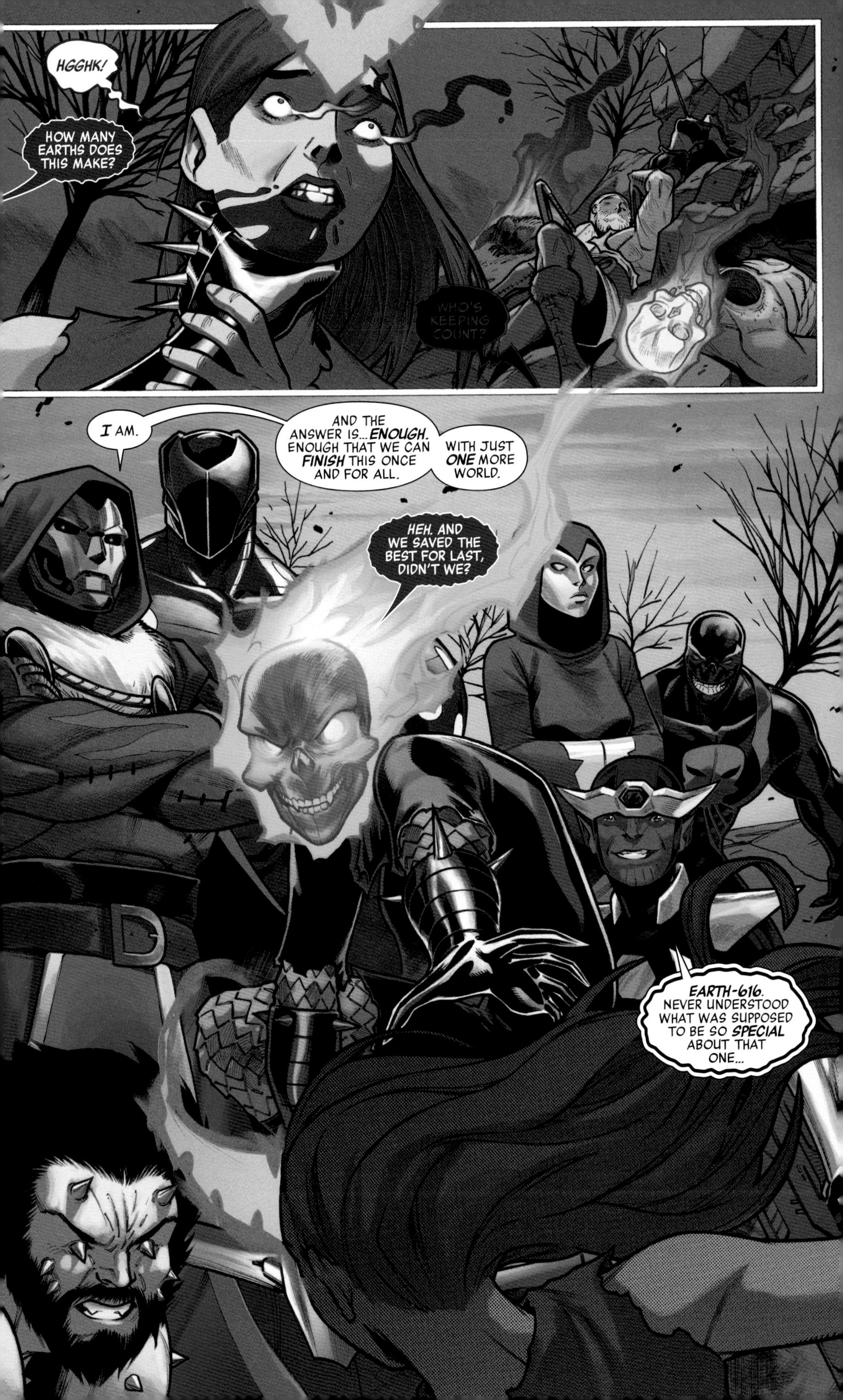
HGGHK!
HOW MANY EARTHS DOES THIS MAKE?
WHO'S KEEPING COUNT?
I AM.
AND THE ANSWER IS...ENOUGH. ENOUGH THAT WE CAN FINISH THIS ONCE AND FOR ALL.
WITH JUST ONE MORE WORLD.
HEH. AND WE SAVED THE BEST FOR LAST, DIDN'T WE?
EARTH-616. NEVER UNDERSTOOD WHAT WAS SUPPOSED TO BE SO SPECIAL ABOUT THAT ONE...

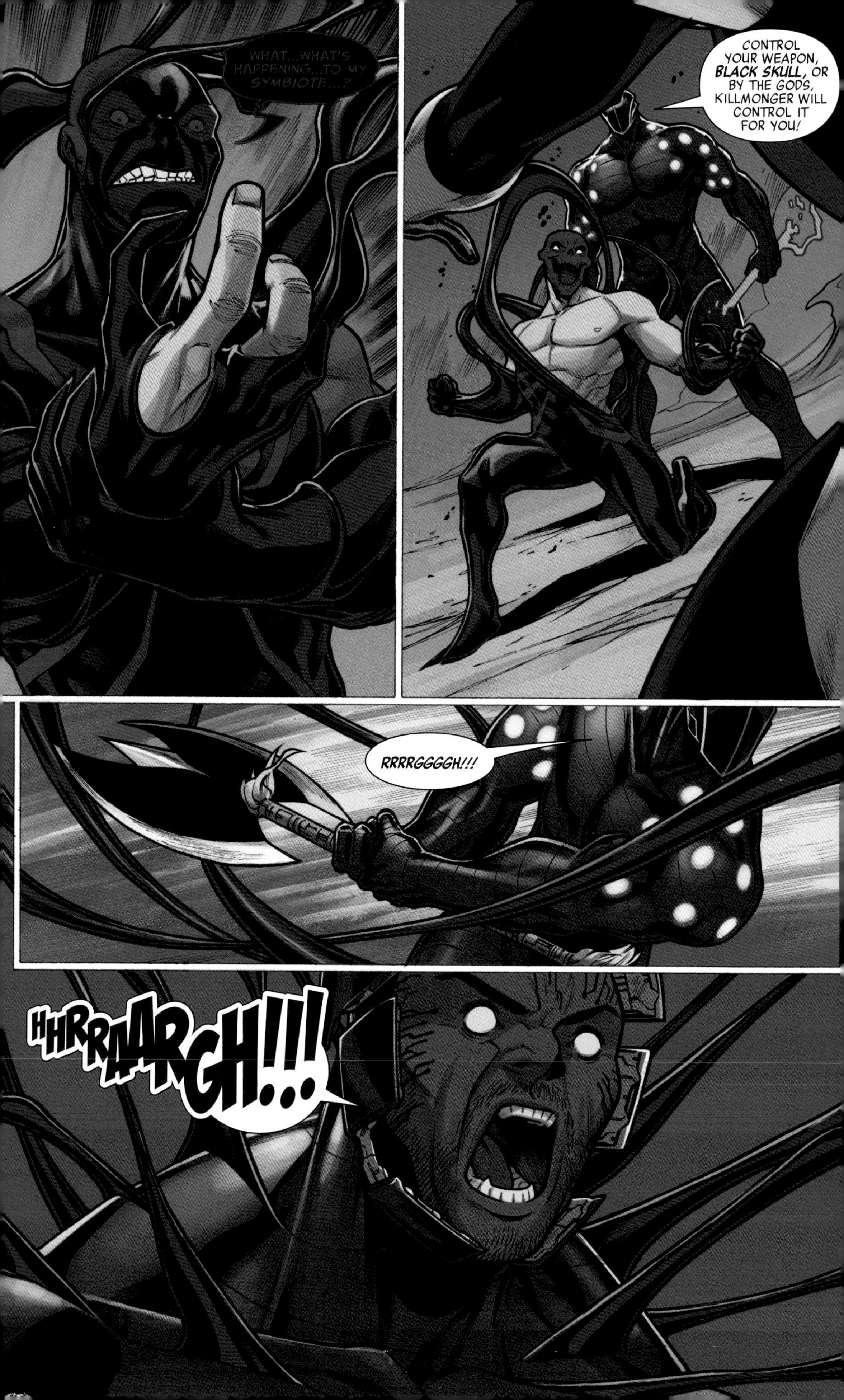
WHAT...WHAT'S HAPPENING...TO MY SYMBIOTE...?
CONTROL YOUR WEAPON, BLACK SKULL, OR BY THE GODS, KILLMONGER WILL CONTROL IT FOR YOU!
RRRRGGGGH!!!
HHRRAARGH!!!

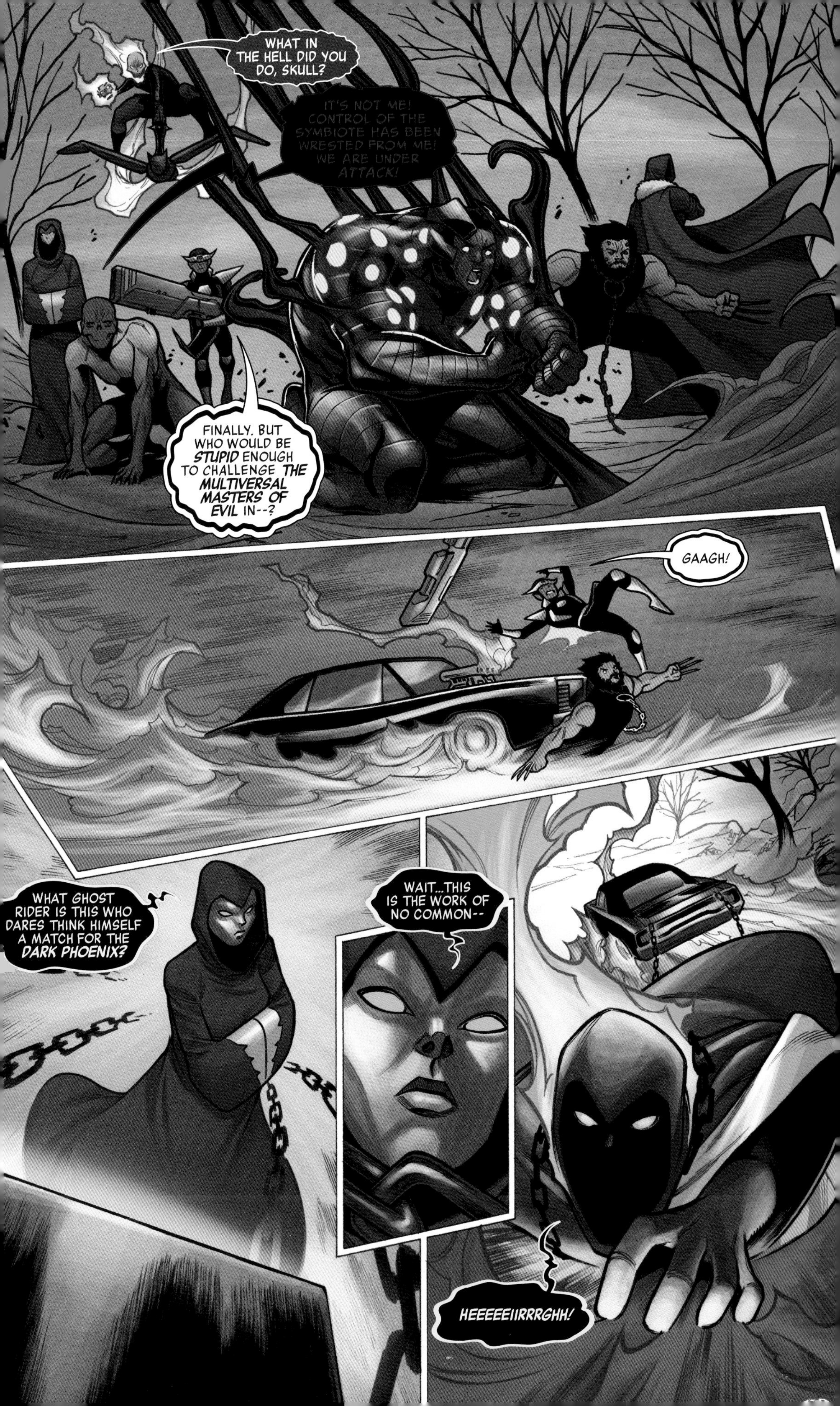

WHAT IN THE HELL DID YOU DO, SKULL?
IT'S NOT ME! CONTROL OF THE SYMBIOTE HAS BEEN WRESTED FROM ME! WE ARE UNDER ATTACK!
FINALLY. BUT WHO WOULD BE STUPID ENOUGH TO CHALLENGE THE MULTIVERSAL MASTERS OF EVIL IN--?
GAAGH!
WHAT GHOST RIDER IS THIS WHO DARES THINK HIMSELF A MATCH FOR THE DARK PHOENIX?
WAIT...THIS IS THE WORK OF NO COMMON--
HEEEEEIIRRRGHH!

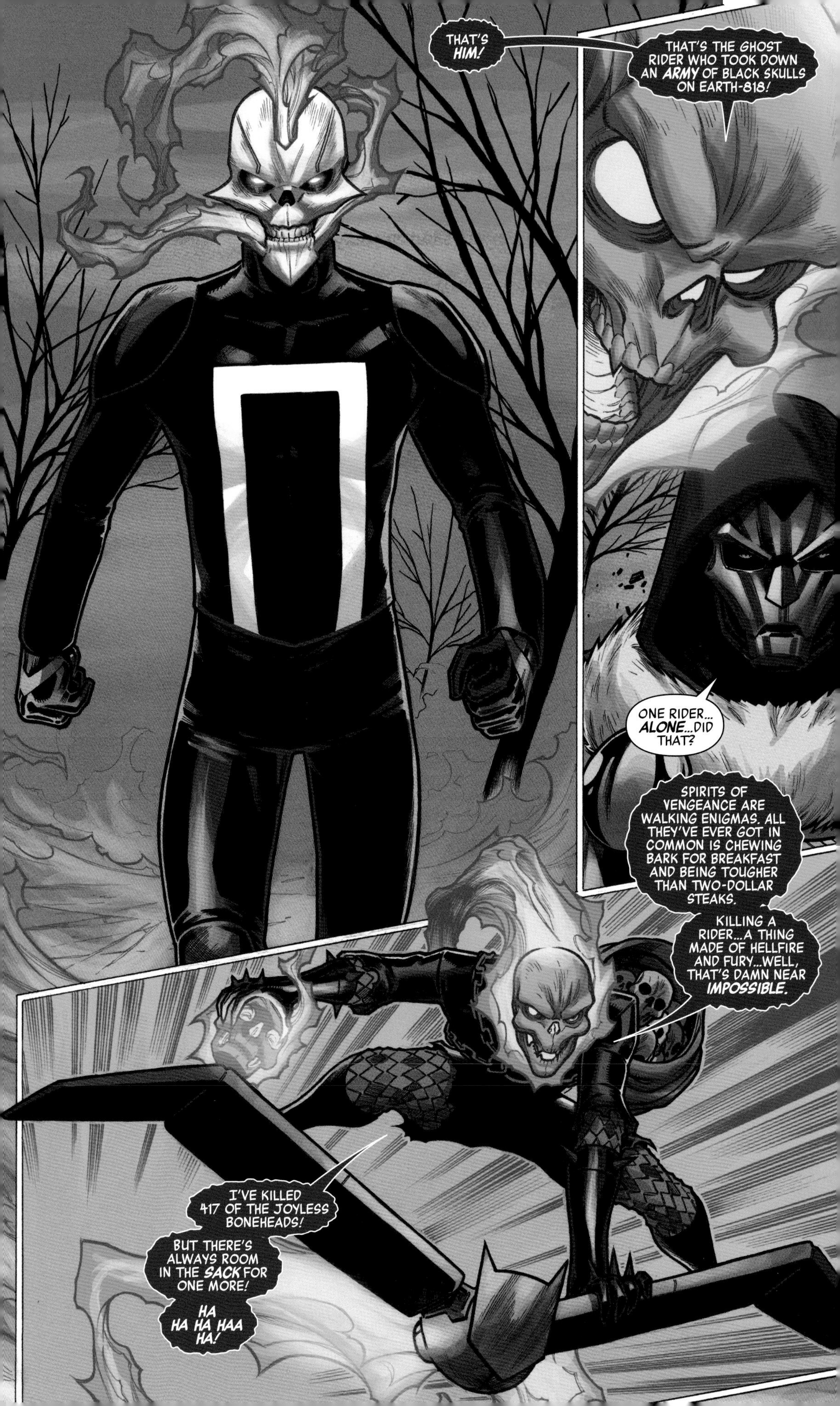

THAT'S HIM!
THAT'S THE GHOST RIDER WHO TOOK DOWN AN ARMY OF BLACK SKULLS ON EARTH-818!
ONE RIDER... ALONE...DID THAT?
SPIRITS OF VENGEANCE ARE WALKING ENIGMAS. ALL THEY'VE EVER GOT IN COMMON IS CHEWING BARK FOR BREAKFAST AND BEING TOUGHER THAN TWO-DOLLAR STEAKS.
KILLING A RIDER...A THING MADE OF HELLFIRE AND FURY...WELL, THAT'S DAMN NEAR IMPOSSIBLE.
I'VE KILLED 417 OF THE JOYLESS BONEHEADS!
BUT THERE'S ALWAYS ROOM IN THE SACK FOR ONE MORE!
HA HA HA HAA HA!

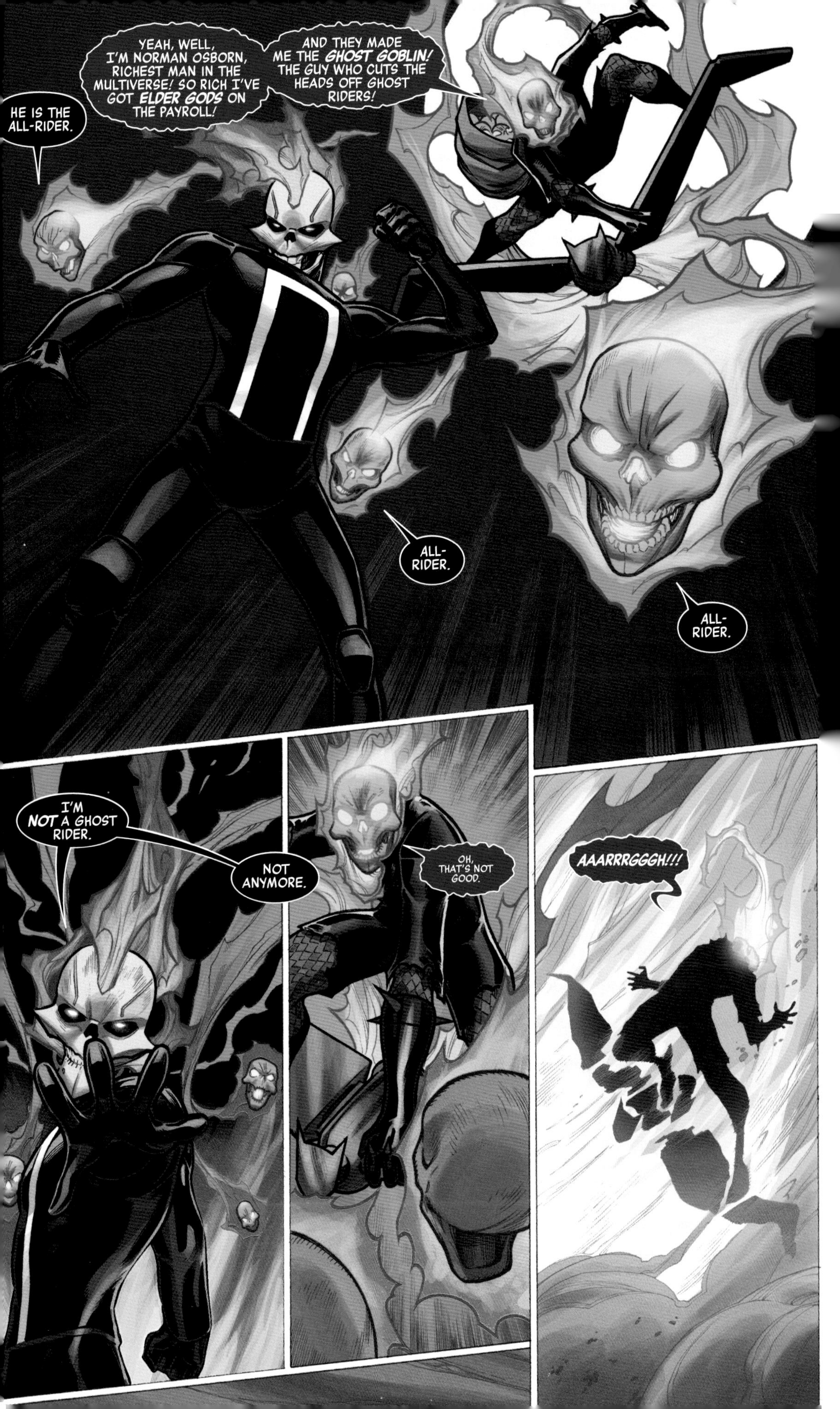

HE IS THE ALL-RIDER.
YEAH, WELL, I'M NORMAN OSBORN, RICHEST MAN IN THE MULTIVERSE! SO RICH I'VE GOT ELDER GODS ON THE PAYROLL!
AND THEY MADE ME THE GHOST GOBLIN! THE GUY WHO CUTS THE HEADS OFF GHOST RIDERS!
ALL-RIDER.
ALL-RIDER.
I'M NOT A GHOST RIDER.
NOT ANYMORE.
OH, THAT'S NOT GOOD.
AAARRRGGGH!!!

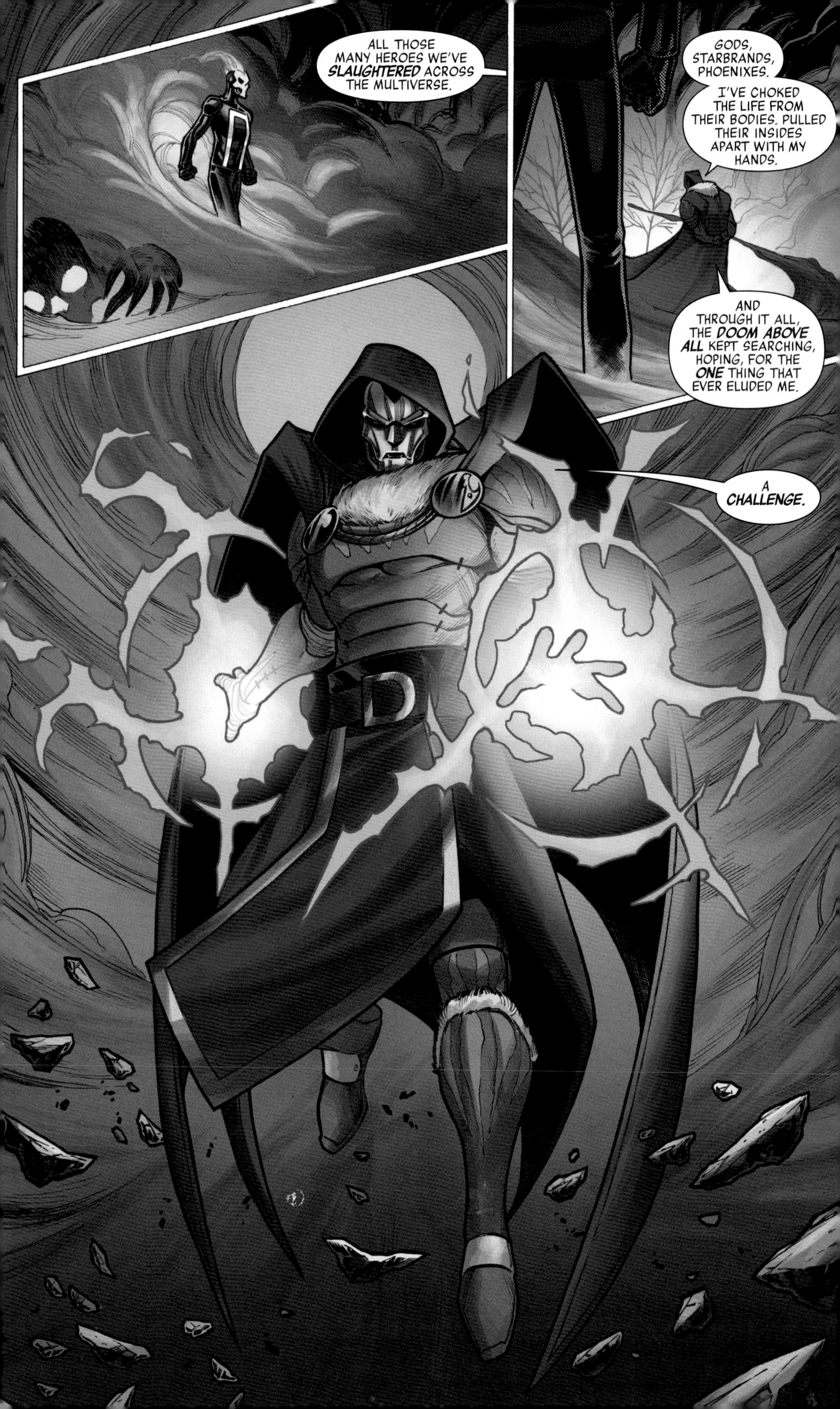
ALL THOSE MANY HEROES WE'VE SLAUGHTERED ACROSS THE MULTIVERSE.
GODS, STARBRANDS, PHOENIXES.
I'VE CHOKED THE LIFE FROM THEIR BODIES. PULLED THEIR INSIDES APART WITH MY HANDS.
AND THROUGH IT ALL, THE DOOM ABOVE ALL KEPT SEARCHING, HOPING, FOR THE ONE THING THAT EVER ELUDED ME.
A CHALLENGE.

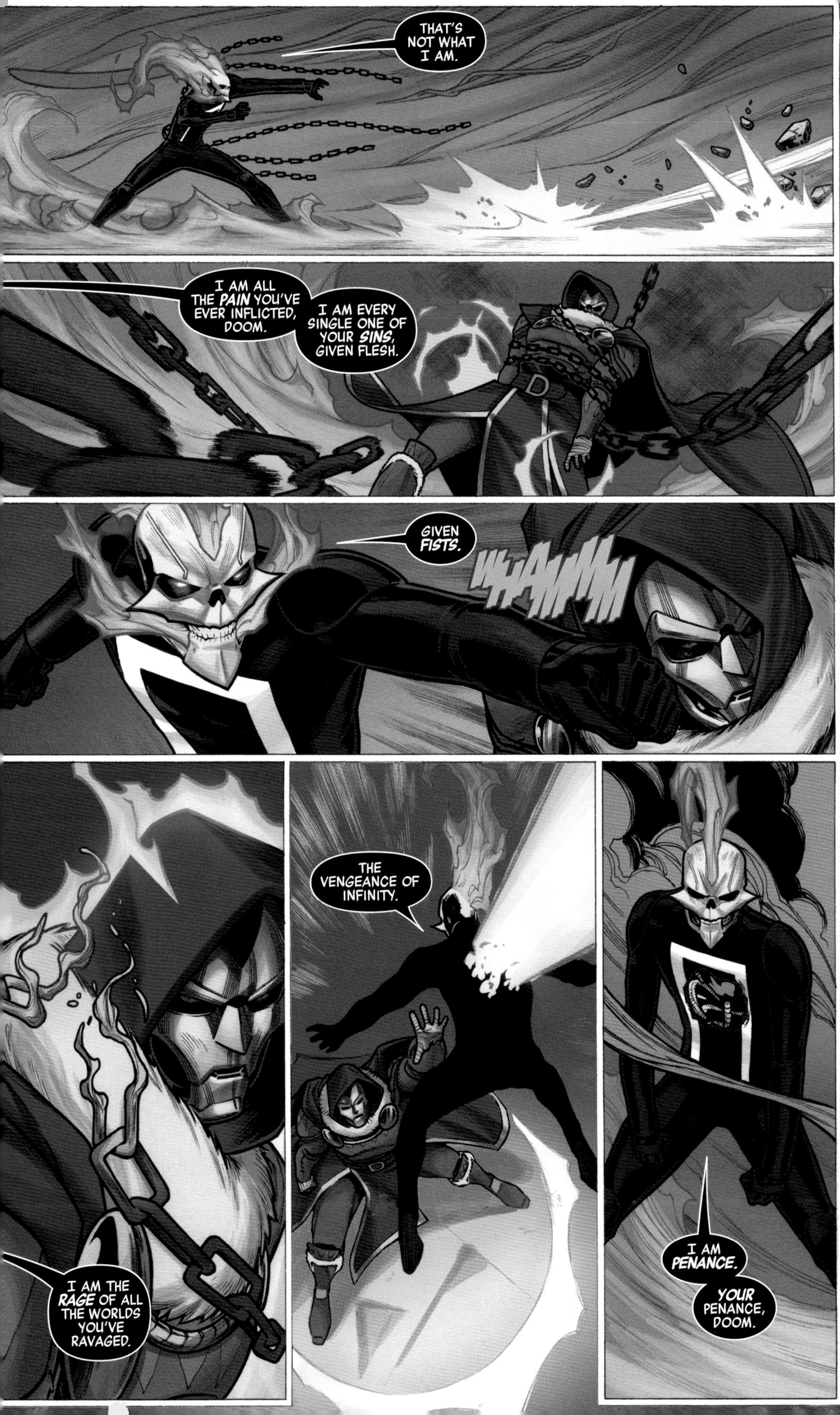
THAT'S NOT WHAT I AM.
I AM ALL THE PAIN YOU'VE EVER INFLICTED, DOOM.
I AM EVERY SINGLE ONE OF YOUR SINS, GIVEN FLESH.
GIVEN FISTS.
WHAMM
I AM THE RAGE OF ALL THE WORLDS YOU'VE RAVAGED.
THE VENGEANCE OF INFINITY.
I AM PENANCE.
YOUR PENANCE, DOOM.

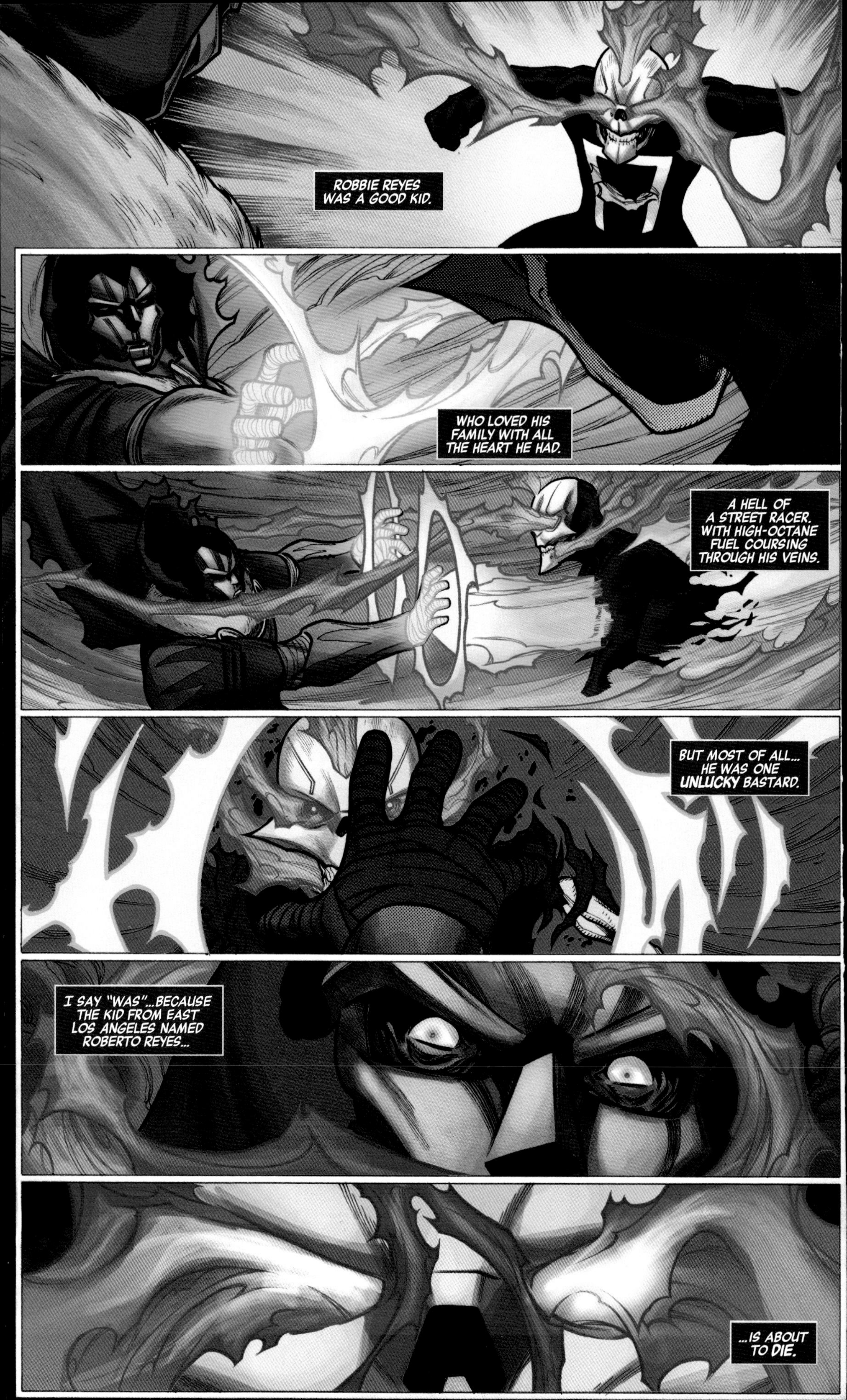
ROBBIE REYES WAS A GOOD KID.
WHO LOVED HIS FAMILY WITH ALL THE HEART HE HAD.
A HELL OF A STREET RACER. WITH HIGH-OCTANE FUEL COURSING THROUGH HIS VEINS.
BUT MOST OF ALL... HE WAS ONE UNLUCKY BASTARD.
I SAY "WAS"...BECAUSE THE KID FROM EAST LOS ANGELES NAMED ROBERTO REYES...
...IS ABOUT TO DIE.

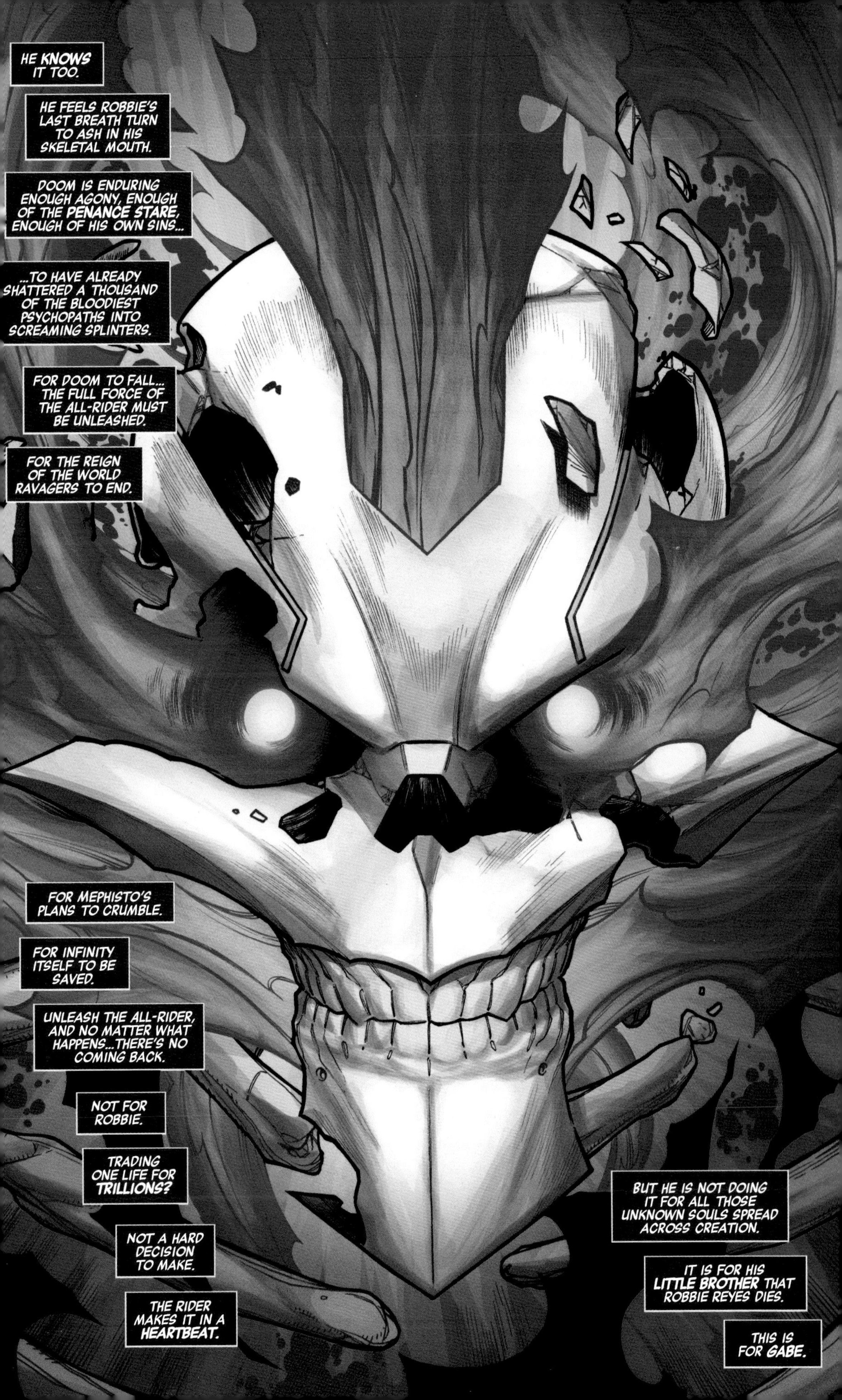

HE KNOWS IT TOO.
HE FEELS ROBBIE'S LAST BREATH TURN TO ASH IN HIS SKELETAL MOUTH.
DOOM IS ENDURING ENOUGH AGONY, ENOUGH OF THE PENANCE STARE, ENOUGH OF HIS OWN SINS...
...TO HAVE ALREADY SHATTERED A THOUSAND OF THE BLOODIEST PSYCHOPATHS INTO SCREAMING SPLINTERS.
FOR DOOM TO FALL... THE FULL FORCE OF THE ALL-RIDER MUST BE UNLEASHED.
FOR THE REIGN OF THE WORLD RAVAGERS TO END.
FOR MEPHISTO'S PLANS TO CRUMBLE.
FOR INFINITY ITSELF TO BE SAVED.
UNLEASH THE ALL-RIDER, AND NO MATTER WHAT HAPPENS...THERE'S NO COMING BACK.
NOT FOR ROBBIE.
TRADING ONE LIFE FOR TRILLIONS?
NOT A HARD DECISION TO MAKE.
THE RIDER MAKES IT IN A HEARTBEAT.
BUT HE IS NOT DOING IT FOR ALL THOSE UNKNOWN SOULS SPREAD ACROSS CREATION.
IT IS FOR HIS LITTLE BROTHER THAT ROBBIE REYES DIES.
THIS IS FOR GABE.

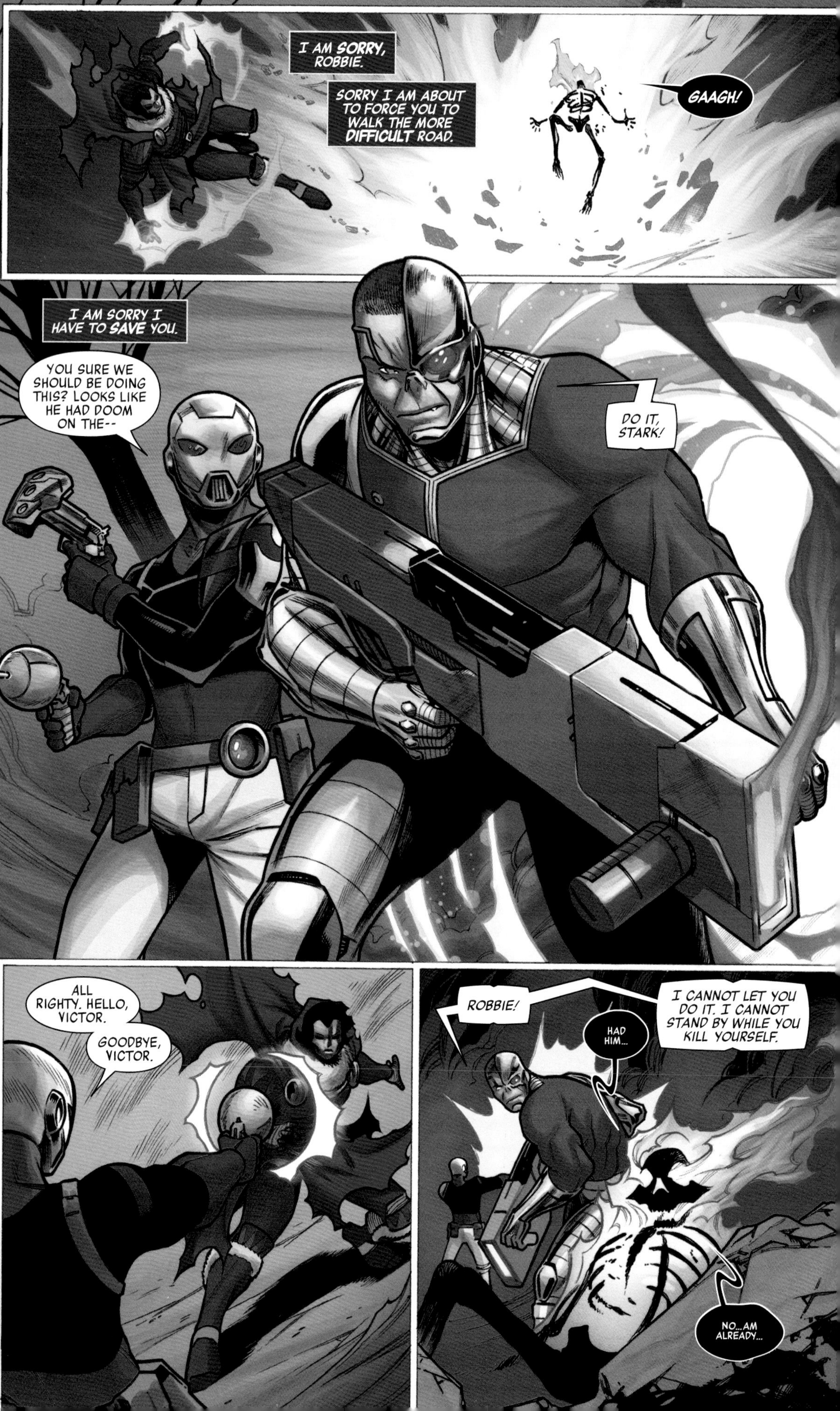

I AM SORRY, ROBBIE.
SORRY I AM ABOUT TO FORCE YOU TO WALK THE MORE DIFFICULT ROAD.
GAAGH!
I AM SORRY I HAVE TO SAVE YOU.
YOU SURE WE SHOULD BE DOING THIS? LOOKS LIKE HE HAD DOOM ON THE--
DO IT, STARK!
ALL RIGHTY. HELLO, VICTOR.
GOODBYE, VICTOR.
ROBBIE!
I CANNOT LET YOU DO IT. I CANNOT STAND BY WHILE YOU KILL YOURSELF.
HAD HIM...
NO...AM ALREADY...

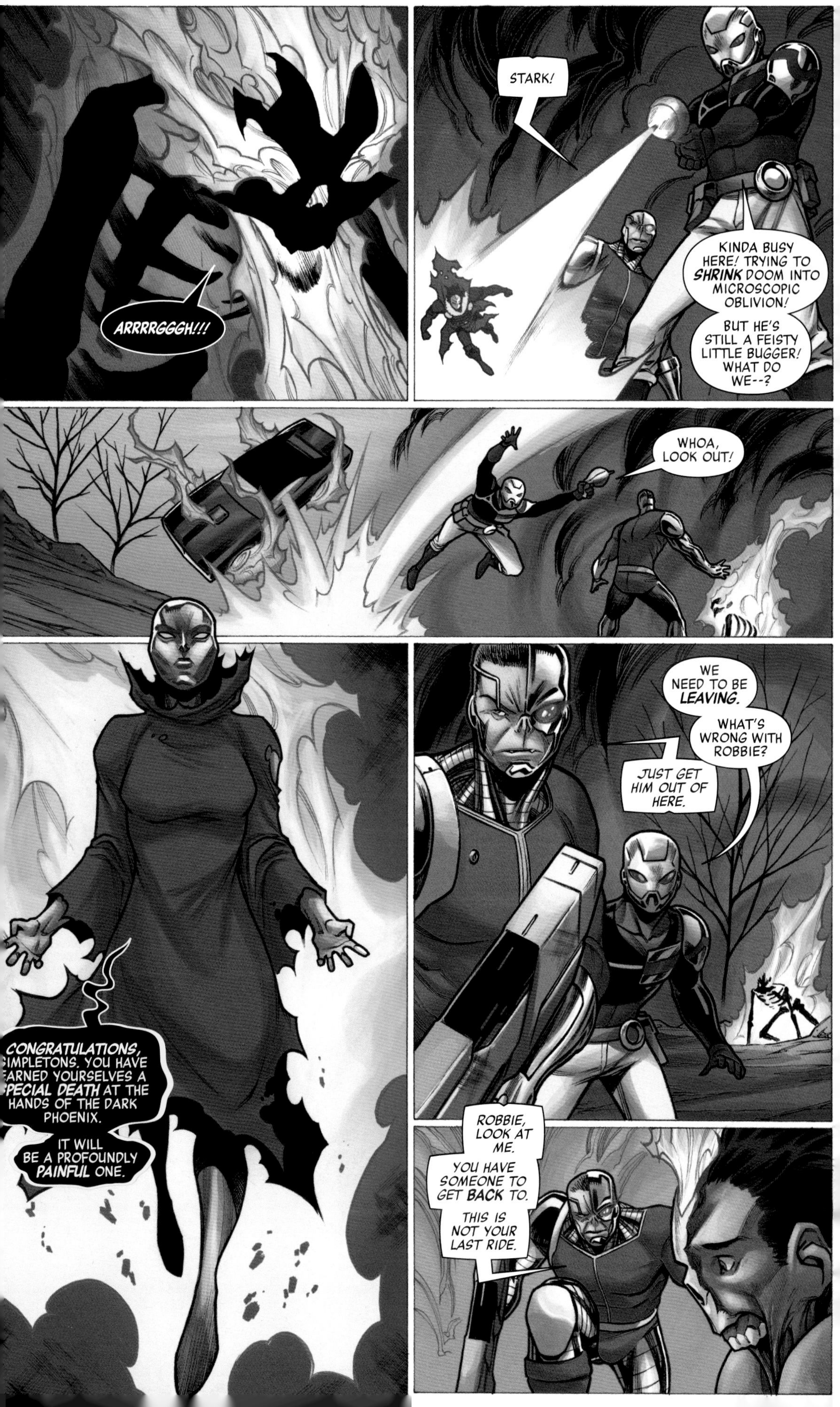

ARRRRGGGH!!!
STARK!
KINDA BUSY HERE! TRYING TO SHRINK DOOM INTO MICROSCOPIC OBLIVION!
BUT HE'S STILL A FEISTY LITTLE BUGGER! WHAT DO WE--?
WHOA, LOOK OUT!
CONGRATULATIONS, SIMPLETONS. YOU HAVE EARNED YOURSELVES A SPECIAL DEATH AT THE HANDS OF THE DARK PHOENIX.
IT WILL BE A PROFOUNDLY PAINFUL ONE.
WE NEED TO BE LEAVING.
WHAT'S WRONG WITH ROBBIE?
JUST GET HIM OUT OF HERE.
ROBBIE, LOOK AT ME.
YOU HAVE SOMEONE TO GET BACK TO.
THIS IS NOT YOUR LAST RIDE.

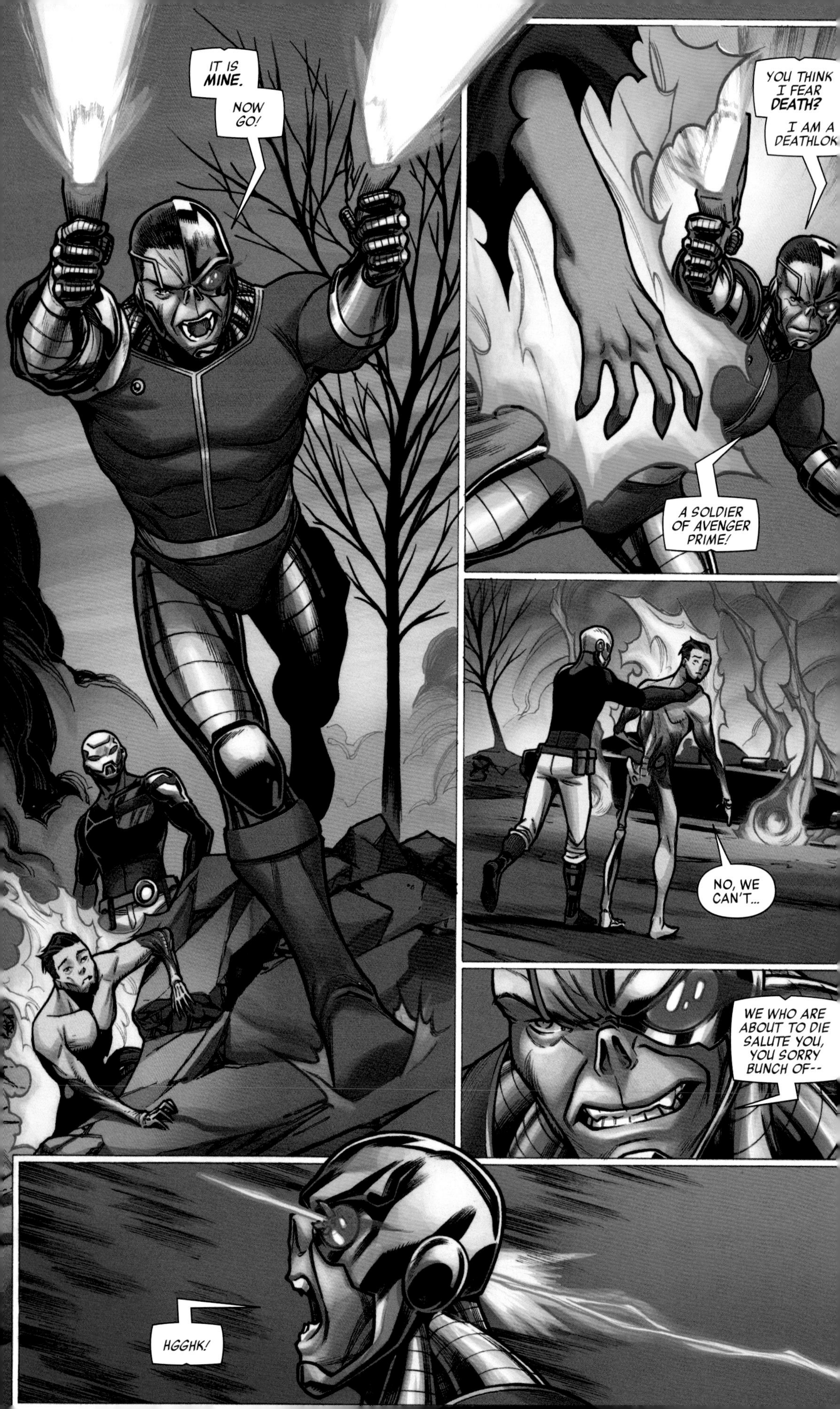
IT IS MINE.
NOW GO!
YOU THINK I FEAR DEATH?
I AM A DEATHLOK
A SOLDIER OF AVENGER PRIME!
NO, WE CAN'T...
WE WHO ARE ABOUT TO DIE SALUTE YOU, YOU SORRY BUNCH OF--
HGGHK!

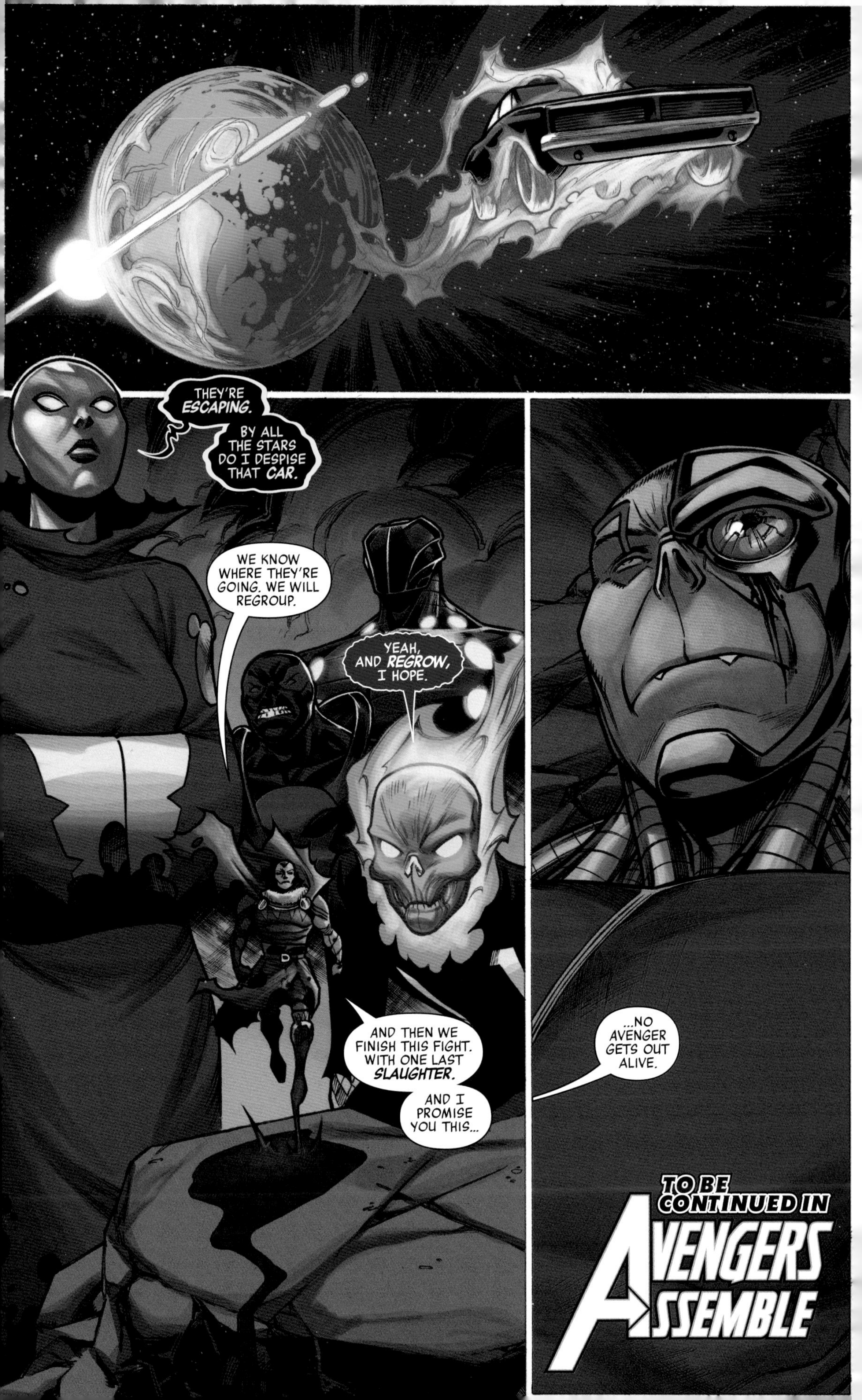
THEY'RE ESCAPING.
BY ALL THE STARS DO I DESPISE THAT CAR.
WE KNOW WHERE THEY'RE GOING. WE WILL REGROUP.
YEAH, AND REGROW, I HOPE.
AND THEN WE FINISH THIS FIGHT. WITH ONE LAST SLAUGHTER.
AND I PROMISE YOU THIS...
...NO AVENGER GETS OUT ALIVE.
TO BE CONTINUED IN AVENGERS ASSEMBLE

AVENGERS FOREVER

MARVEL INFINITY COMICS

"THE AVENGING"

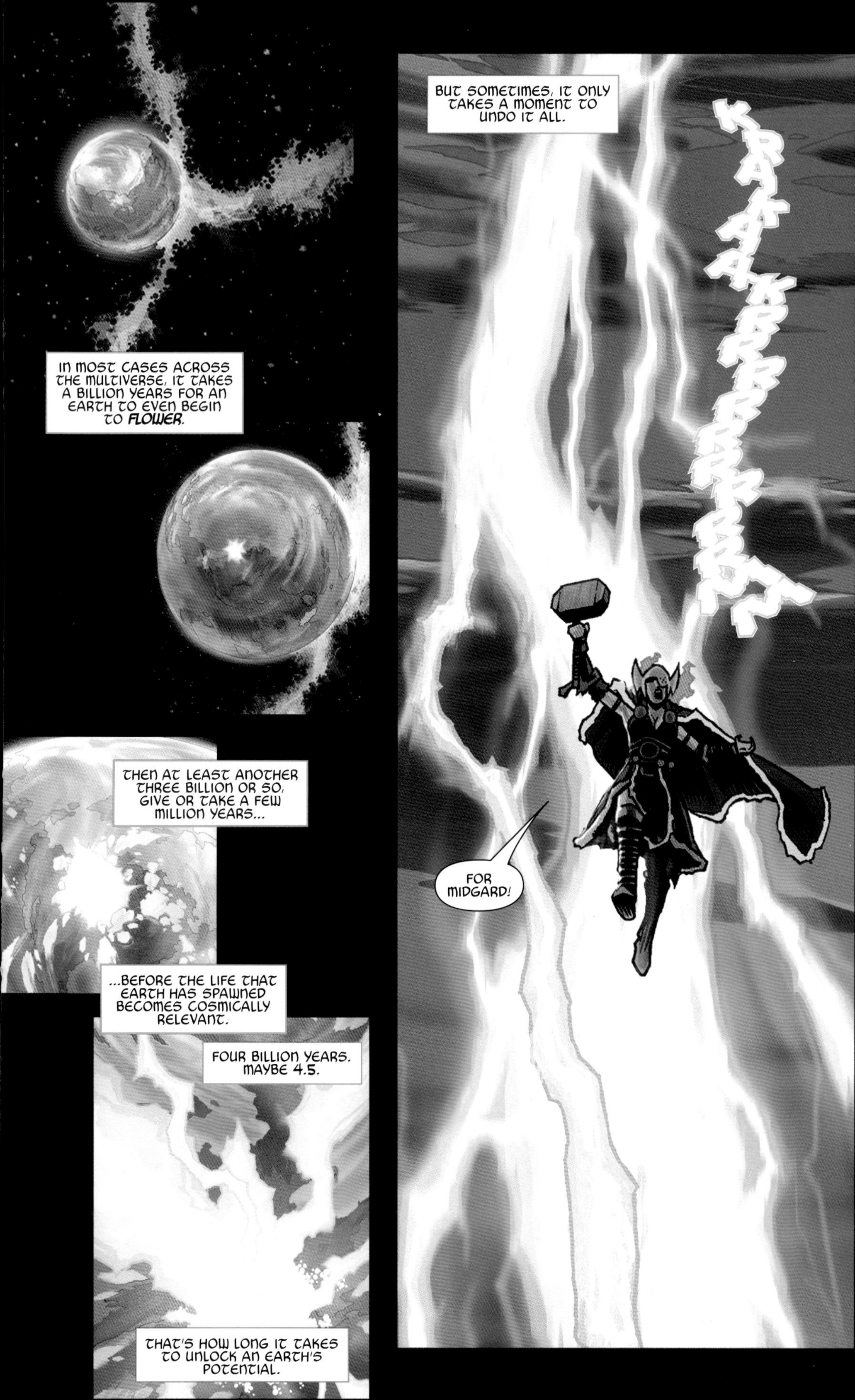
IN MOST CASES ACROSS THE MULTIVERSE, IT TAKES A BILLION YEARS FOR AN EARTH TO EVEN BEGIN TO FLOWER.
THEN AT LEAST ANOTHER THREE BILLION OR SO, GIVE OR TAKE A FEW MILLION YEARS...
...BEFORE THE LIFE THAT EARTH HAS SPAWNED BECOMES COSMICALLY RELEVANT.
FOUR BILLION YEARS. MAYBE 4.5.
THAT'S HOW LONG IT TAKES TO UNLOCK AN EARTH'S POTENTIAL.
BUT SOMETIMES, IT ONLY TAKES A MOMENT TO UNDO IT ALL.
KRAKAKABRRRRRRBOOM
FOR MIDGARD!

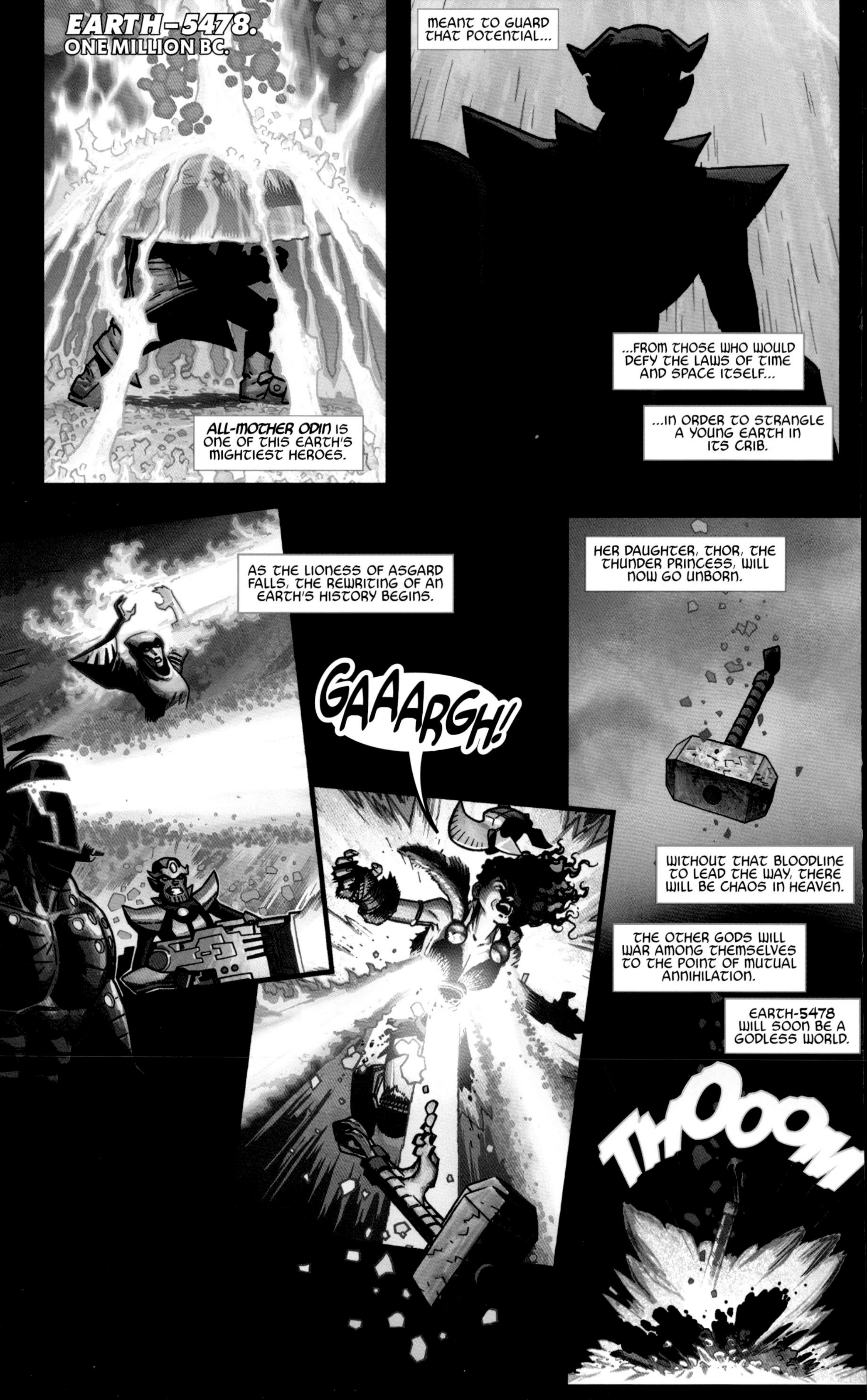
EARTH-5478.
ONE MILLION BC.
ALL-MOTHER ODIN IS ONE OF THIS EARTH'S MIGHTIEST HEROES.
MEANT TO GUARD THAT POTENTIAL...
...FROM THOSE WHO WOULD DEFY THE LAWS OF TIME AND SPACE ITSELF...
...IN ORDER TO STRANGLE A YOUNG EARTH IN ITS CRIB.
AS THE LIONESS OF ASGARD FALLS, THE REWRITING OF AN EARTH'S HISTORY BEGINS.
GAAARGH!
HER DAUGHTER, THOR, THE THUNDER PRINCESS, WILL NOW GO UNBORN.
WITHOUT THAT BLOODLINE TO LEAD THE WAY, THERE WILL BE CHAOS IN HEAVEN.
THE OTHER GODS WILL WAR AMONG THEMSELVES TO THE POINT OF MUTUAL ANNIHILATION.
EARTH-5478 WILL SOON BE A GODLESS WORLD.
THOOOM

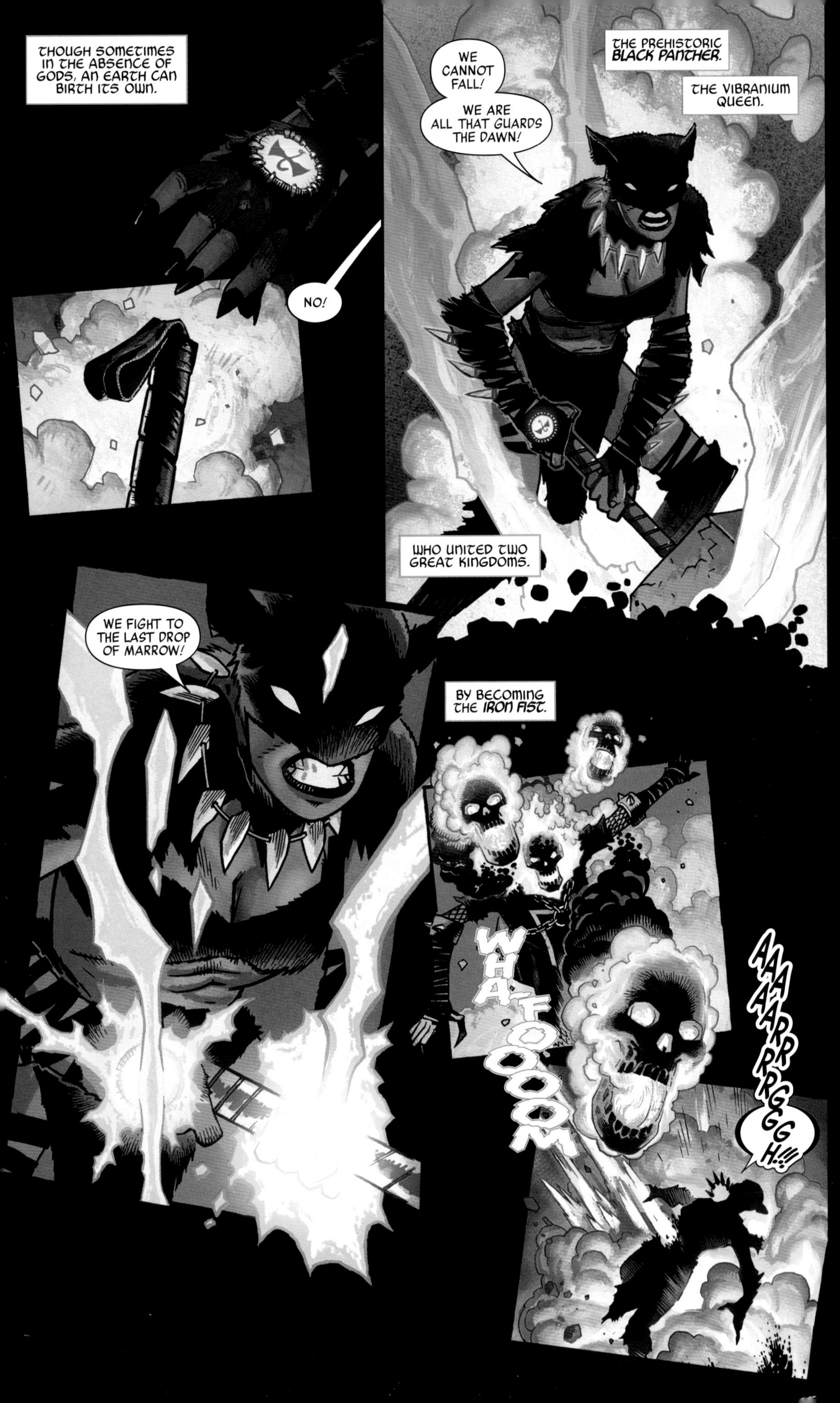
THOUGH SOMETIMES IN THE ABSENCE OF GODS, AN EARTH CAN BIRTH ITS OWN.
NO!
WE CANNOT FALL!
WE ARE ALL THAT GUARDS THE DAWN!
THE PREHISTORIC BLACK PANTHER.
THE VIBRANIUM QUEEN.
WHO UNITED TWO GREAT KINGDOMS.
WE FIGHT TO THE LAST DROP OF MARROW!
BY BECOMING THE IRON FIST.
WHA-FOOOOOM
AAAAARRRGGH!!!

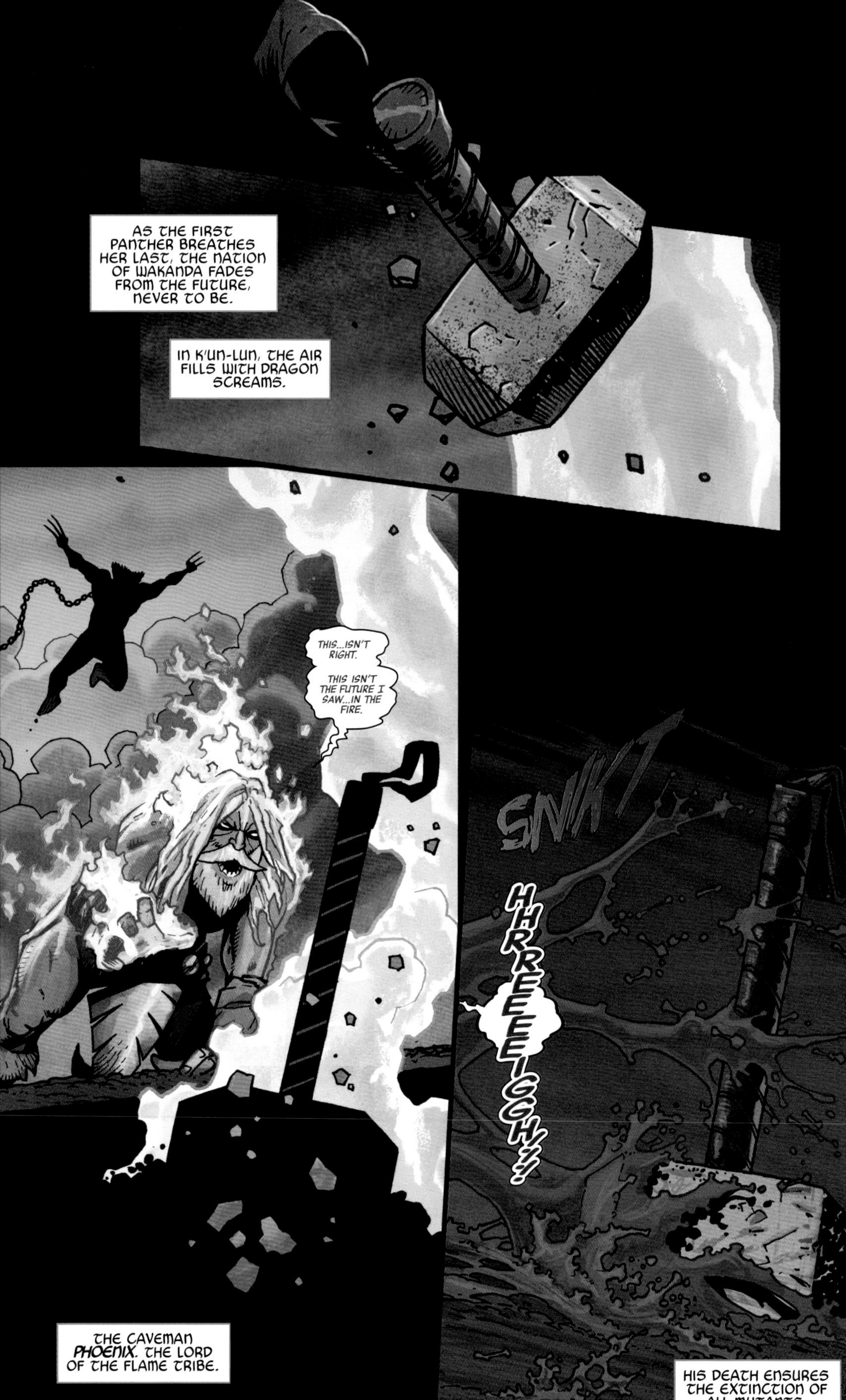
AS THE FIRST PANTHER BREATHES HER LAST, THE NATION OF WAKANDA FADES FROM THE FUTURE, NEVER TO BE.
IN K'UN-LUN, THE AIR FILLS WITH DRAGON SCREAMS.
THIS...ISN'T RIGHT.
THIS ISN'T THE FUTURE I SAW...IN THE FIRE.
SNIKT
HHRREEEEIGGH!!
THE CAVEMAN *PHOENIX*. THE LORD OF THE FLAME TRIBE.
HIS DEATH ENSURES THE EXTINCTION OF

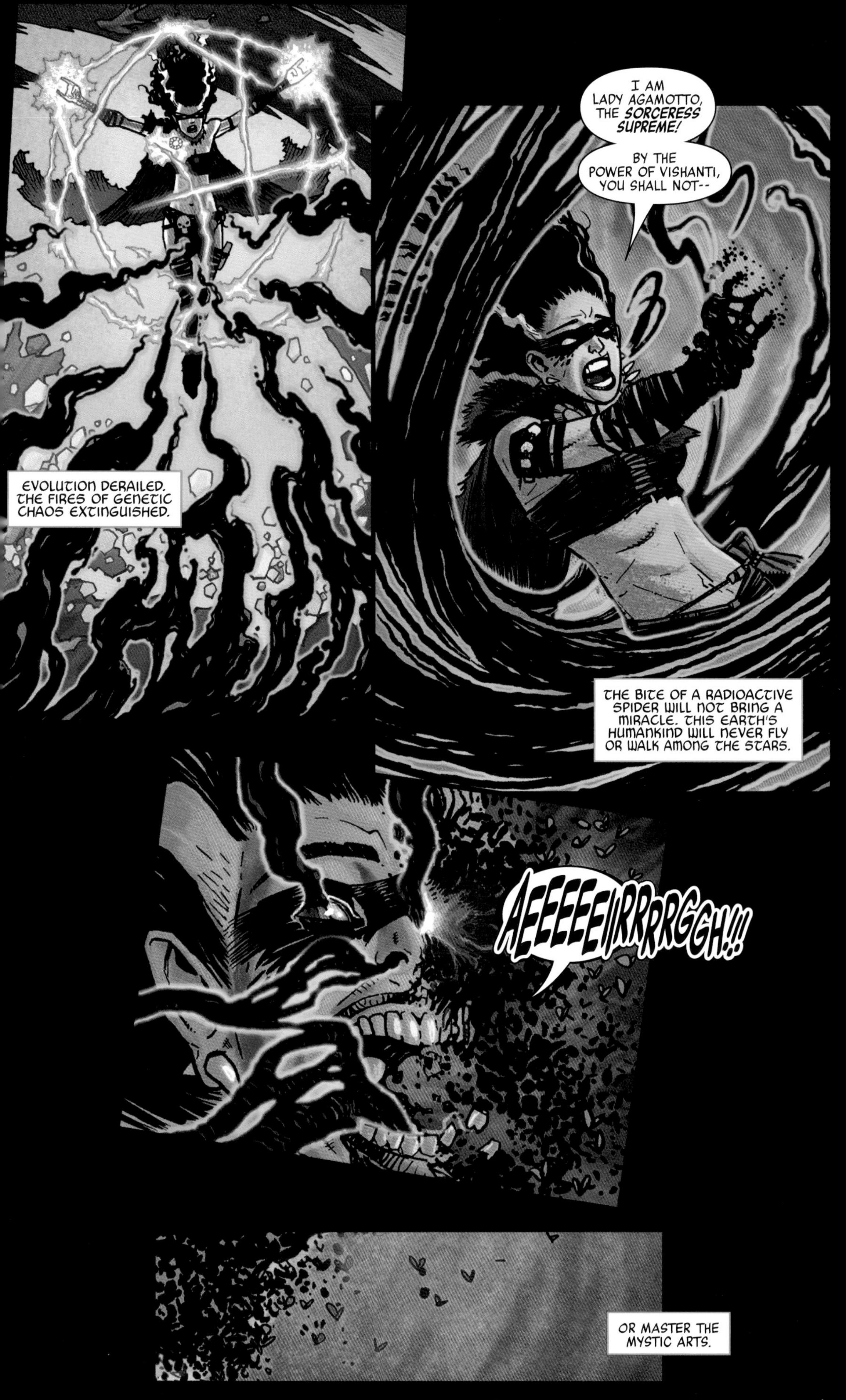
EVOLUTION DERAILED. THE FIRES OF GENETIC CHAOS EXTINGUISHED.
I AM LADY AGAMOTTO, THE SORCERESS SUPREME!
BY THE POWER OF VISHANTI, YOU SHALL NOT--
THE BITE OF A RADIOACTIVE SPIDER WILL NOT BRING A MIRACLE. THIS EARTH'S HUMANKIND WILL NEVER FLY OR WALK AMONG THE STARS.
AEEEEEIIRRRRGGH!!!
OR MASTER THE MYSTIC ARTS.

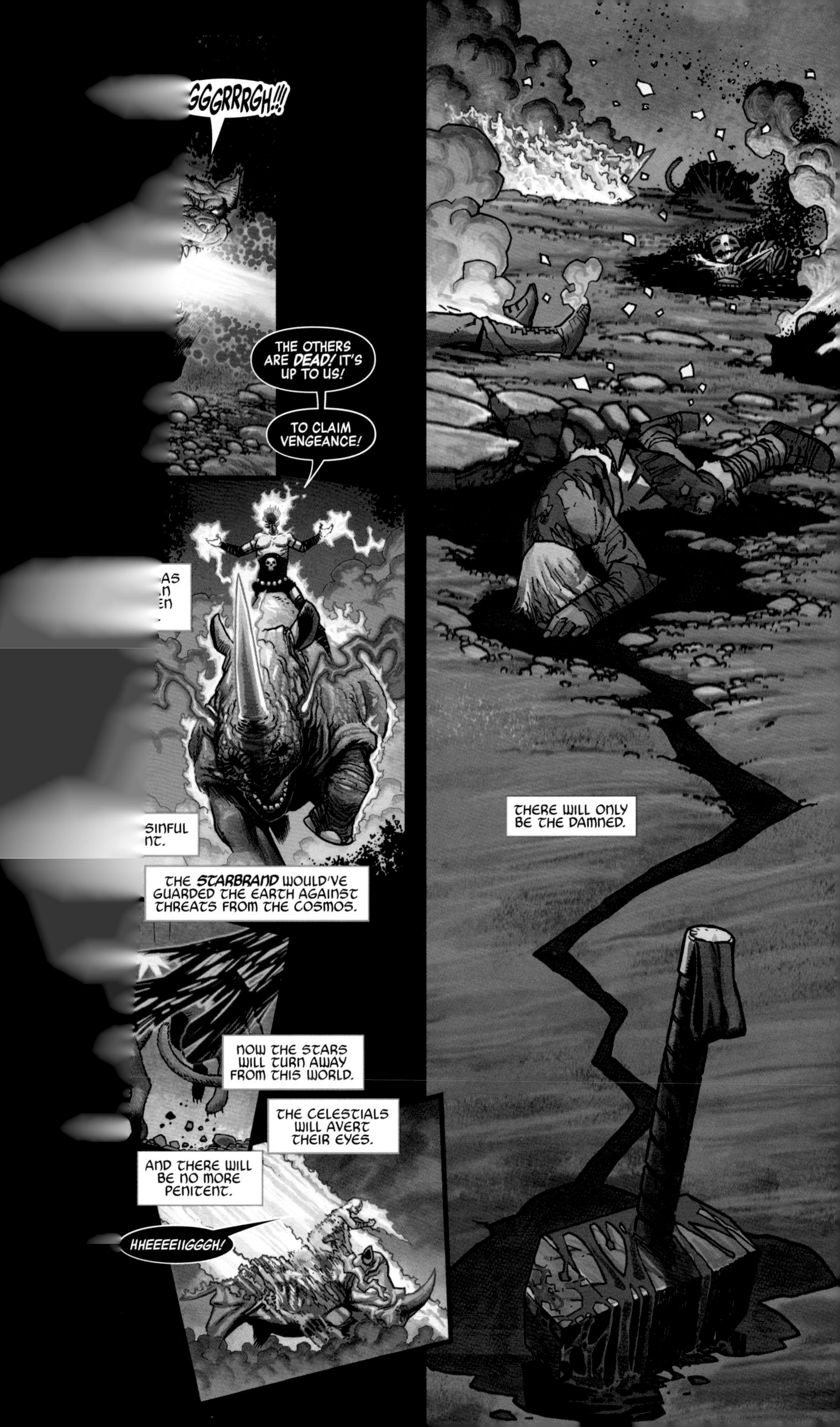
GGGRRRGH!!!
THE OTHERS ARE DEAD! IT'S UP TO US!
TO CLAIM VENGEANCE!
SINFUL
THE STARBRAND WOULD'VE GUARDED THE EARTH AGAINST THREATS FROM THE COSMOS.
NOW THE STARS WILL TURN AWAY FROM THIS WORLD.
THE CELESTIALS WILL AVERT THEIR EYES.
AND THERE WILL BE NO MORE PENITENT.
HHEEEEIIGGGH!
THERE WILL ONLY BE THE DAMNED.

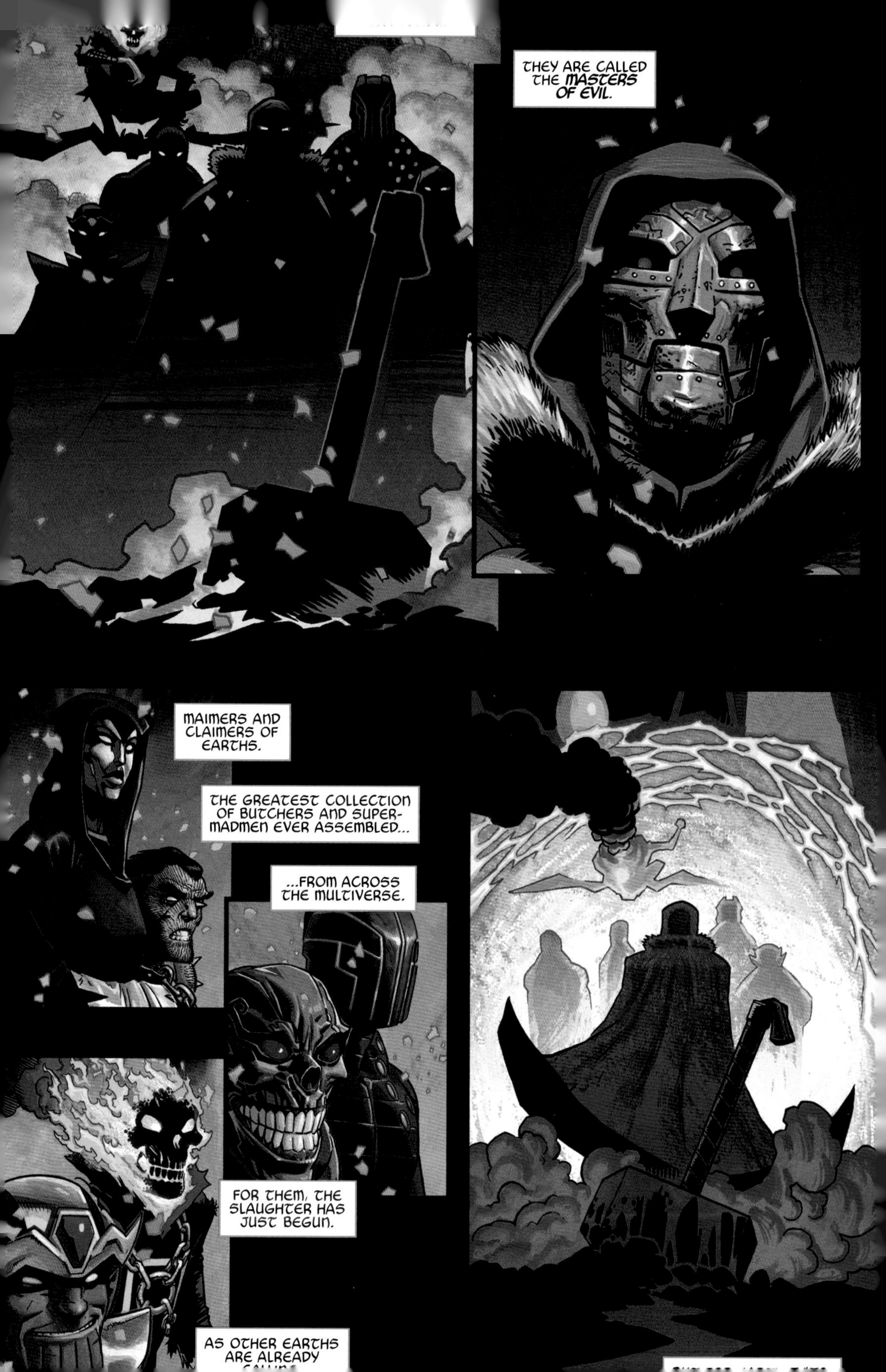
THEY ARE CALLED THE MASTERS OF EVIL.
MAIMERS AND CLAIMERS OF EARTHS.
THE GREATEST COLLECTION OF BUTCHERS AND SUPER-MADMEN EVER ASSEMBLED...
...FROM ACROSS THE MULTIVERSE.
FOR THEM, THE SLAUGHTER HAS JUST BEGUN.
AS OTHER EARTHS ARE ALREADY

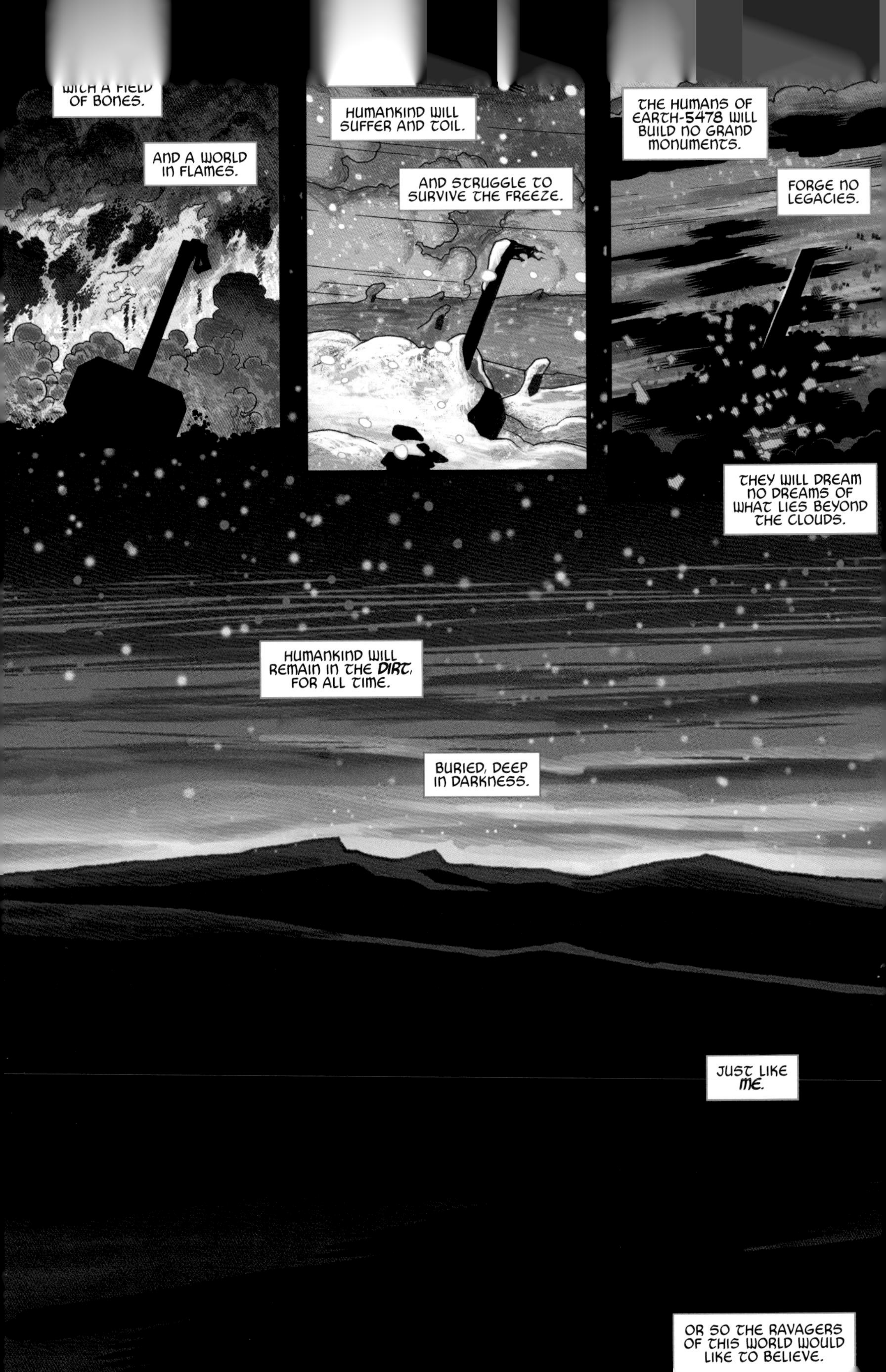
WITH A FIELD OF BONES.
AND A WORLD IN FLAMES.
HUMANKIND WILL SUFFER AND TOIL.
AND STRUGGLE TO SURVIVE THE FREEZE.
THE HUMANS OF EARTH-5478 WILL BUILD NO GRAND MONUMENTS.
FORGE NO LEGACIES.
THEY WILL DREAM NO DREAMS OF WHAT LIES BEYOND THE CLOUDS.
HUMANKIND WILL REMAIN IN THE DIRT, FOR ALL TIME.
BURIED, DEEP IN DARKNESS.
JUST LIKE ME.
OR SO THE RAVAGERS OF THIS WORLD WOULD LIKE TO BELIEVE.

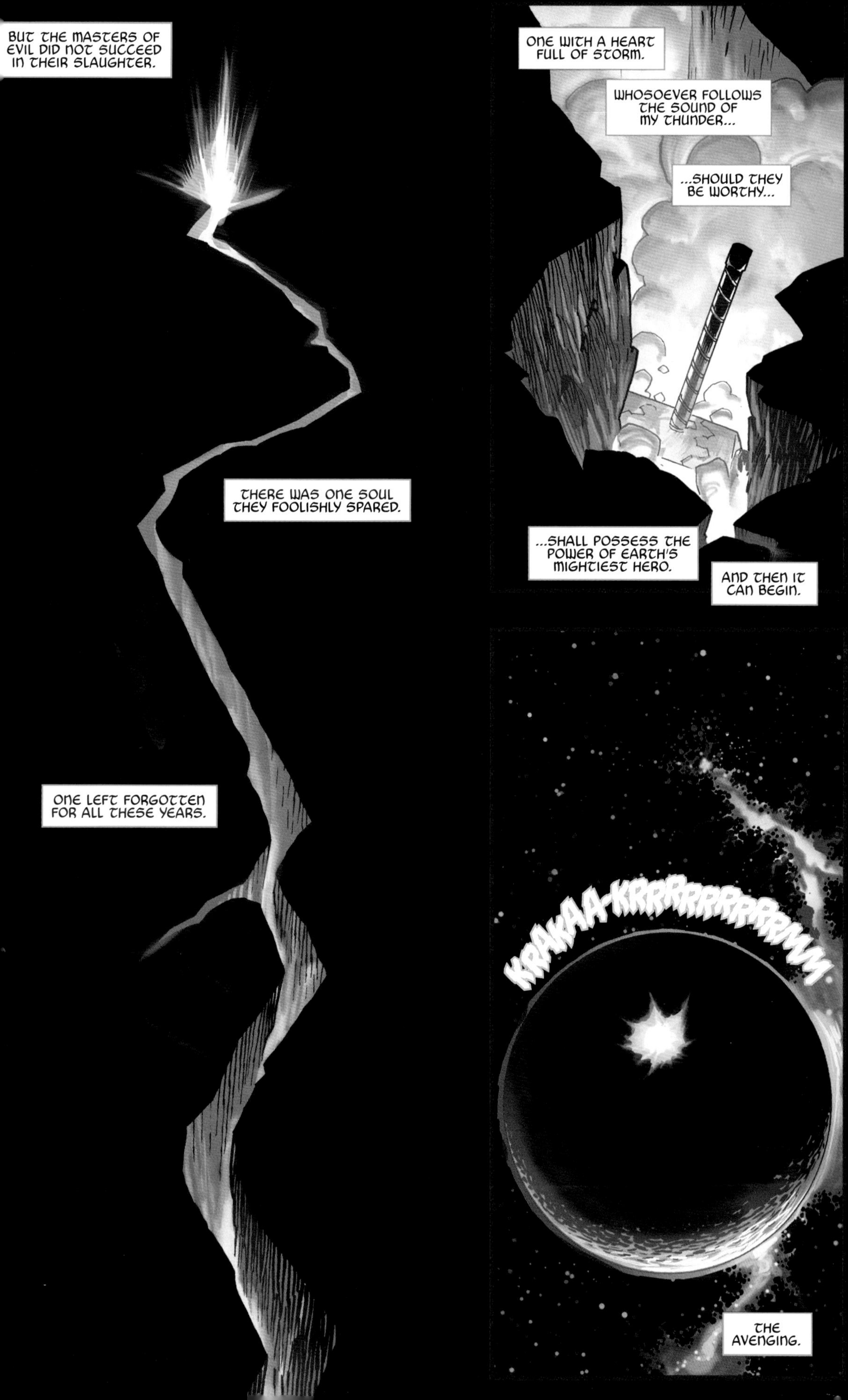
BUT THE MASTERS OF EVIL DID NOT SUCCEED IN THEIR SLAUGHTER.
THERE WAS ONE SOUL THEY FOOLISHLY SPARED.
ONE LEFT FORGOTTEN FOR ALL THESE YEARS.
ONE WITH A HEART FULL OF STORM.
WHOSOEVER FOLLOWS THE SOUND OF MY THUNDER...
...SHOULD THEY BE WORTHY...
...SHALL POSSESS THE POWER OF EARTH'S MIGHTIEST HERO.
AND THEN IT CAN BEGIN.
KRAKAA-KRRRRRRRRRMM
THE AVENGING.

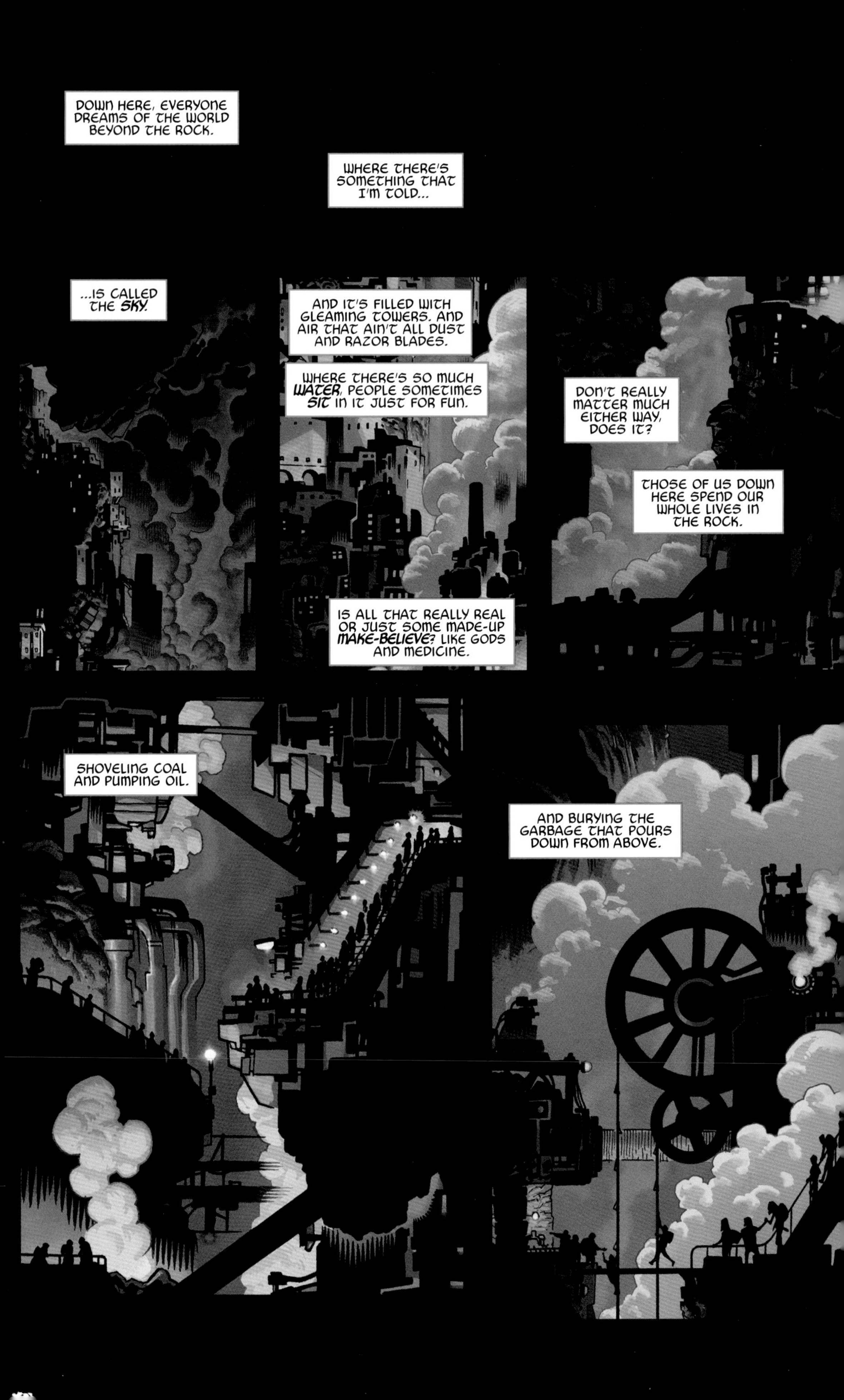
DOWN HERE, EVERYONE DREAMS OF THE WORLD BEYOND THE ROCK.
WHERE THERE'S SOMETHING THAT I'M TOLD...
...IS CALLED THE SKY.
AND IT'S FILLED WITH GLEAMING TOWERS. AND AIR THAT AIN'T ALL DUST AND RAZOR BLADES.
WHERE THERE'S SO MUCH WATER, PEOPLE SOMETIMES SIT IN IT JUST FOR FUN.
IS ALL THAT REALLY REAL OR JUST SOME MADE-UP MAKE-BELIEVE? LIKE GODS AND MEDICINE.
DON'T REALLY MATTER MUCH EITHER WAY, DOES IT?
THOSE OF US DOWN HERE SPEND OUR WHOLE LIVES IN THE ROCK.
SHOVELING COAL AND PUMPING OIL.
AND BURYING THE GARBAGE THAT POURS DOWN FROM ABOVE.

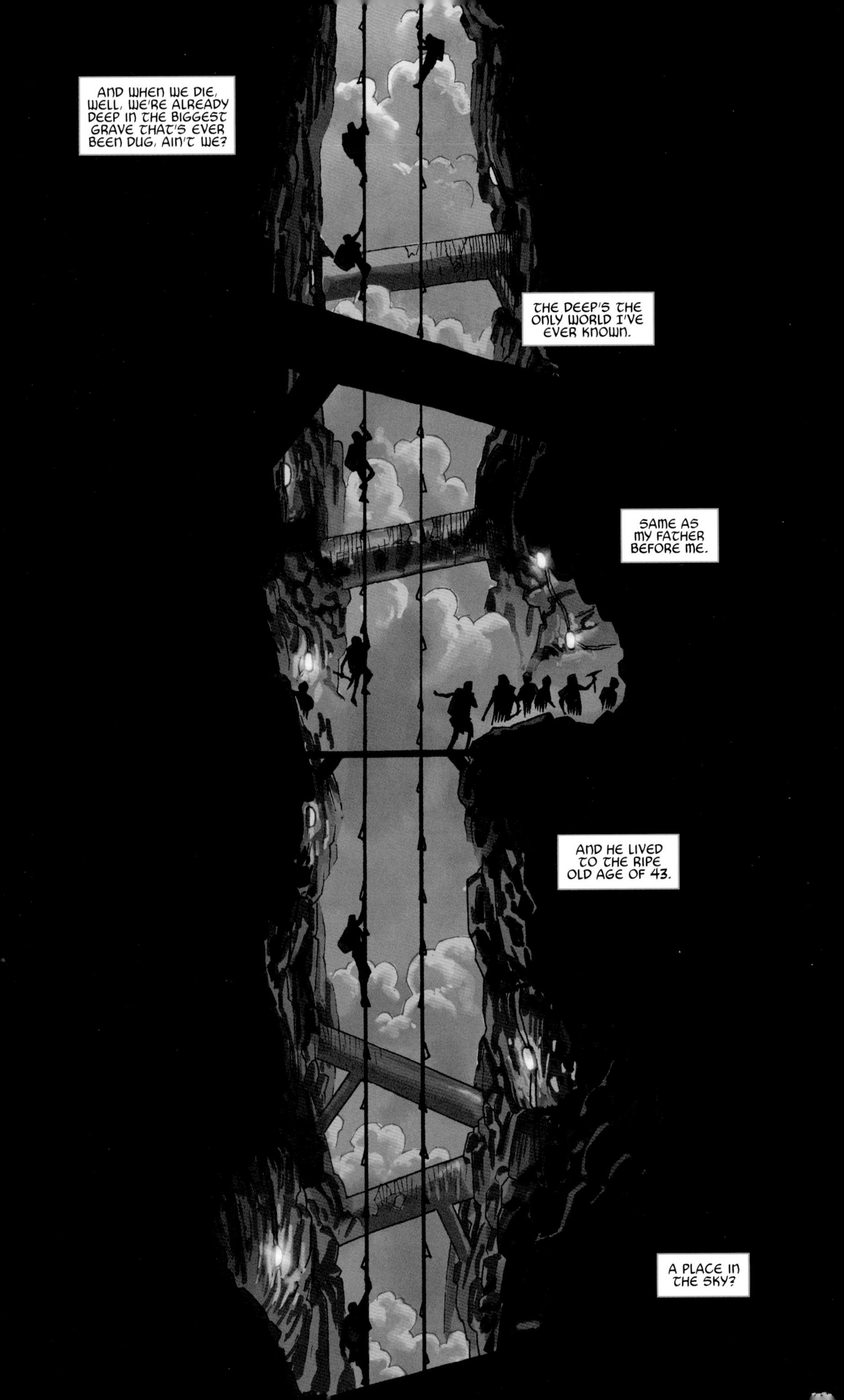
AND WHEN WE DIE, WELL, WE'RE ALREADY DEEP IN THE BIGGEST GRAVE THAT'S EVER BEEN DUG, AIN'T WE?
THE DEEP'S THE ONLY WORLD I'VE EVER KNOWN.
SAME AS MY FATHER BEFORE ME.
AND HE LIVED TO THE RIPE OLD AGE OF 43.
A PLACE IN THE SKY?

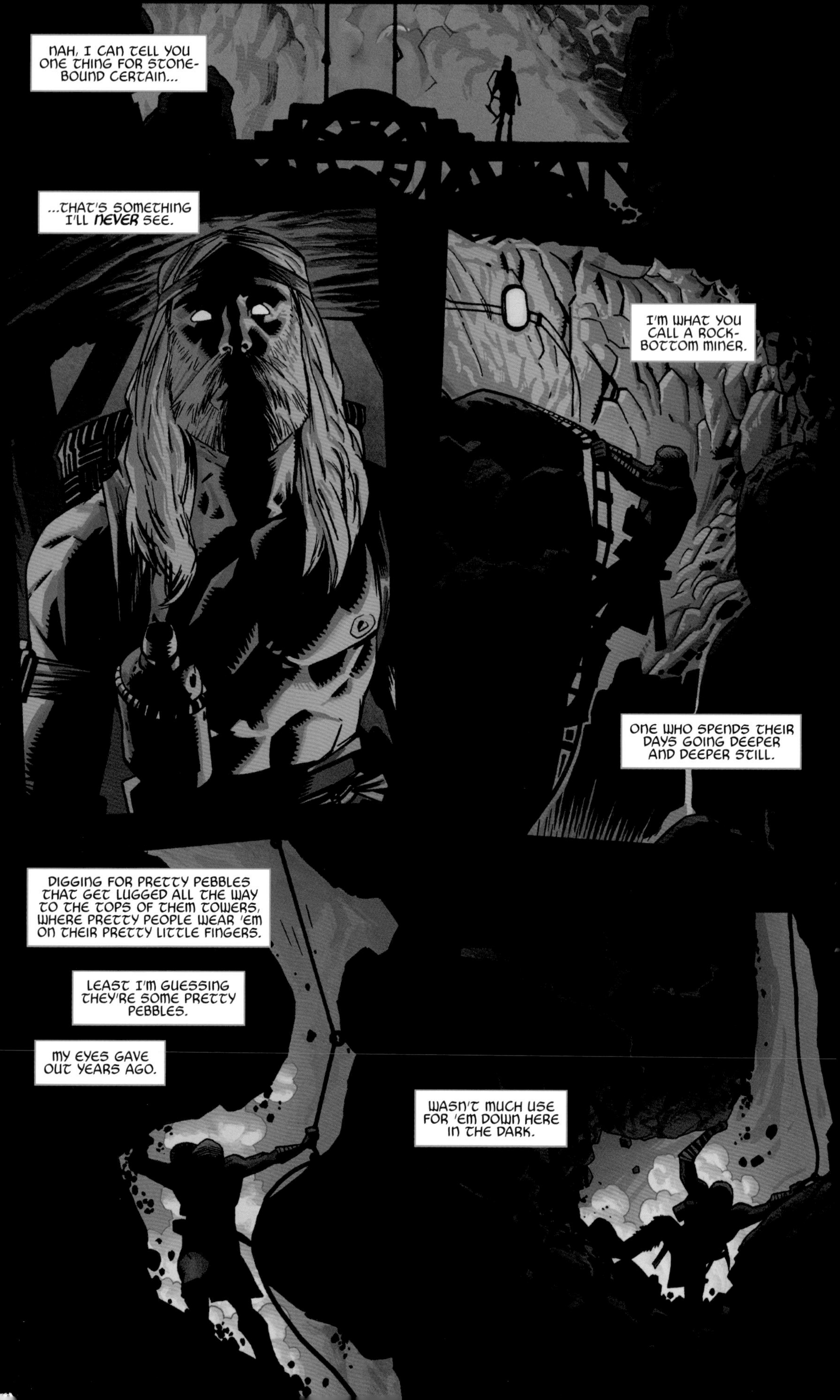
NAH, I CAN TELL YOU ONE THING FOR STONE-BOUND CERTAIN...
...THAT'S SOMETHING I'LL NEVER SEE.
I'M WHAT YOU CALL A ROCK-BOTTOM MINER.
ONE WHO SPENDS THEIR DAYS GOING DEEPER AND DEEPER STILL.
DIGGING FOR PRETTY PEBBLES THAT GET LUGGED ALL THE WAY TO THE TOPS OF THEM TOWERS, WHERE PRETTY PEOPLE WEAR 'EM ON THEIR PRETTY LITTLE FINGERS.
LEAST I'M GUESSING THEY'RE SOME PRETTY PEBBLES.
MY EYES GAVE OUT YEARS AGO.
WASN'T MUCH USE FOR 'EM DOWN HERE IN THE DARK.

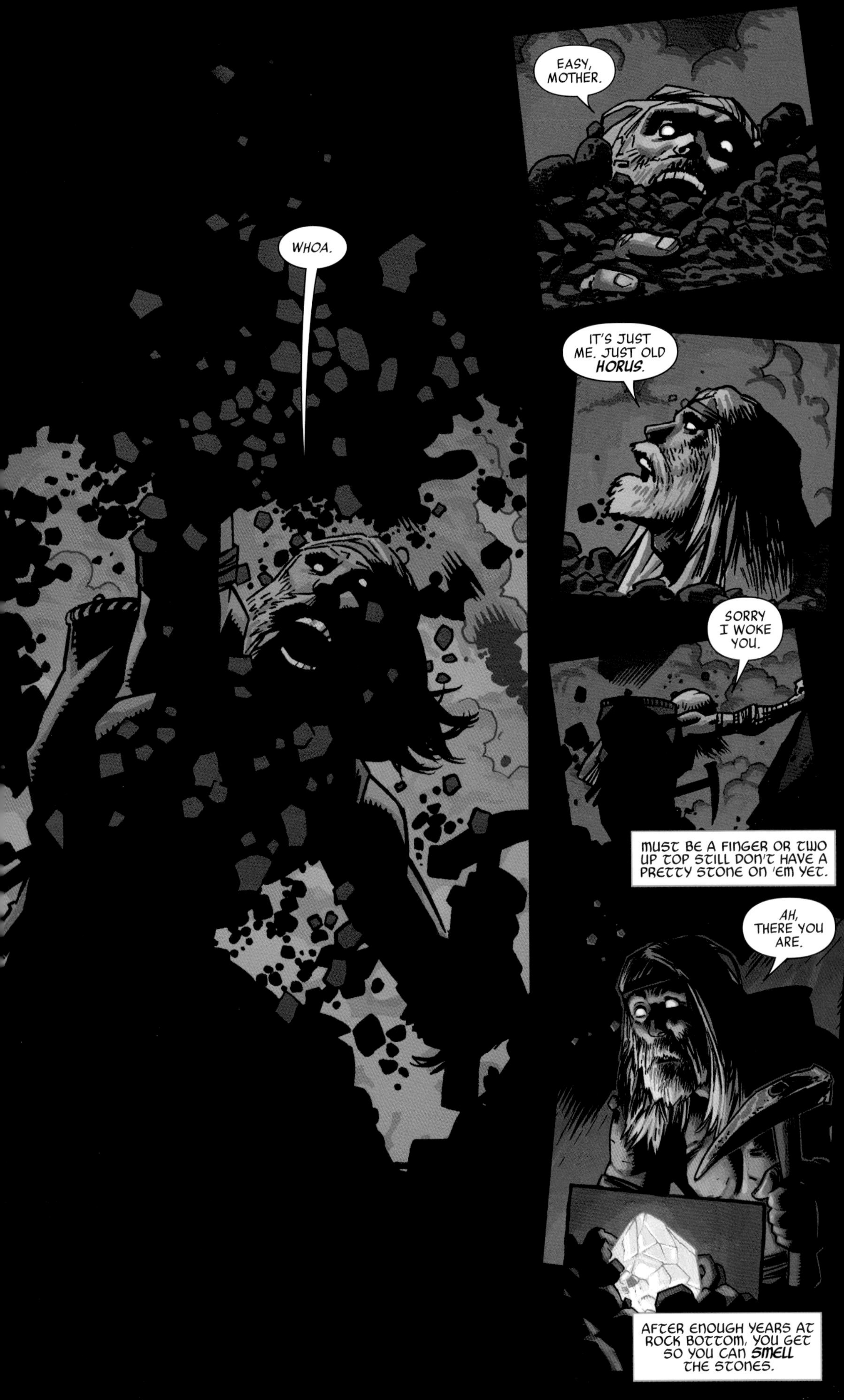
EASY, MOTHER.
WHOA.
IT'S JUST ME. JUST OLD HORUS.
SORRY I WOKE YOU.
MUST BE A FINGER OR TWO UP TOP STILL DON'T HAVE A PRETTY STONE ON 'EM YET.
AH, THERE YOU ARE.
AFTER ENOUGH YEARS AT ROCK BOTTOM, YOU GET SO YOU CAN SMELL THE STONES.

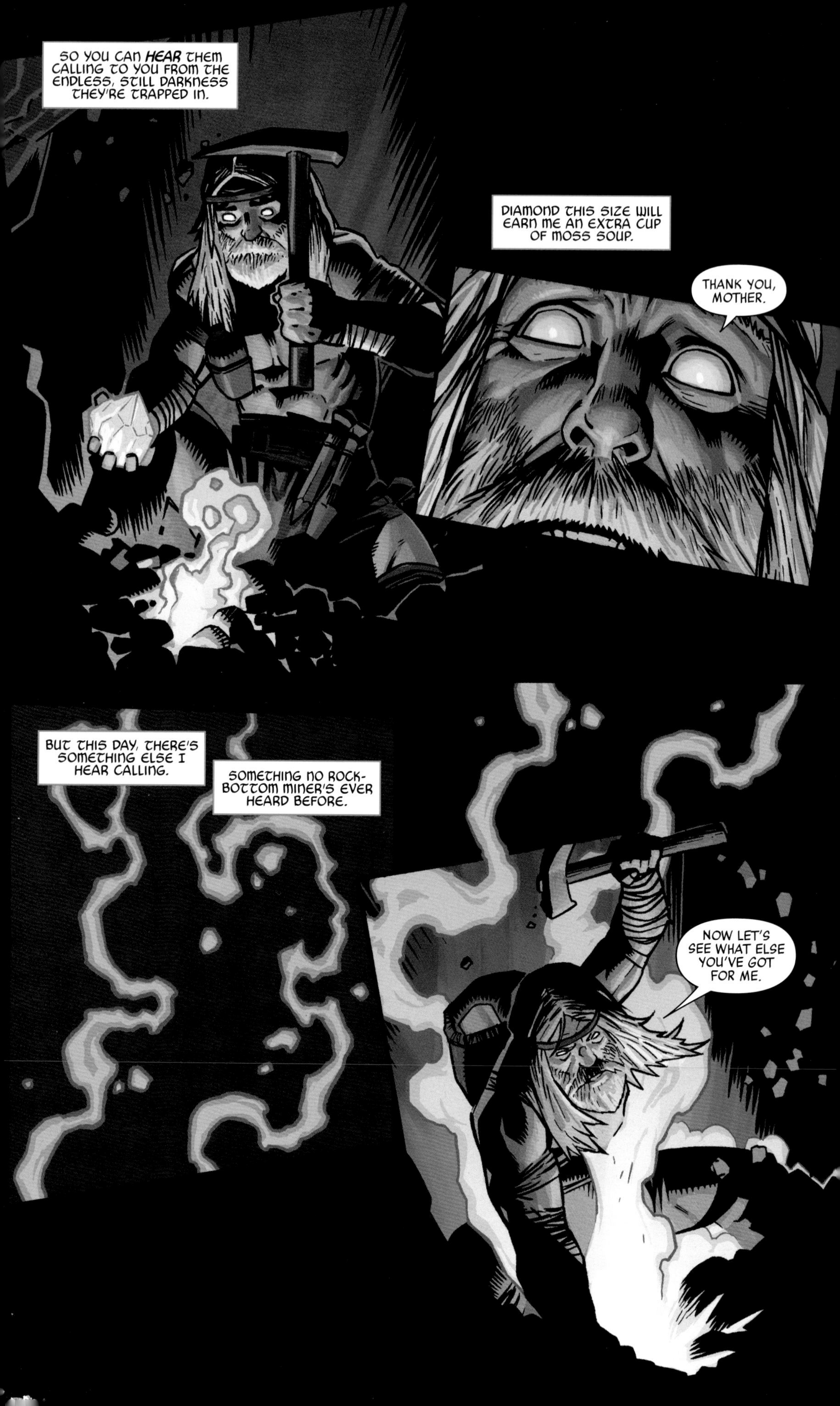

SO YOU CAN HEAR THEM CALLING TO YOU FROM THE ENDLESS, STILL DARKNESS THEY'RE TRAPPED IN.
DIAMOND THIS SIZE WILL EARN ME AN EXTRA CUP OF MOSS SOUP.
THANK YOU, MOTHER.
BUT THIS DAY, THERE'S SOMETHING ELSE I HEAR CALLING.
SOMETHING NO ROCK-BOTTOM MINER'S EVER HEARD BEFORE.
NOW LET'S SEE WHAT ELSE YOU'VE GOT FOR ME.

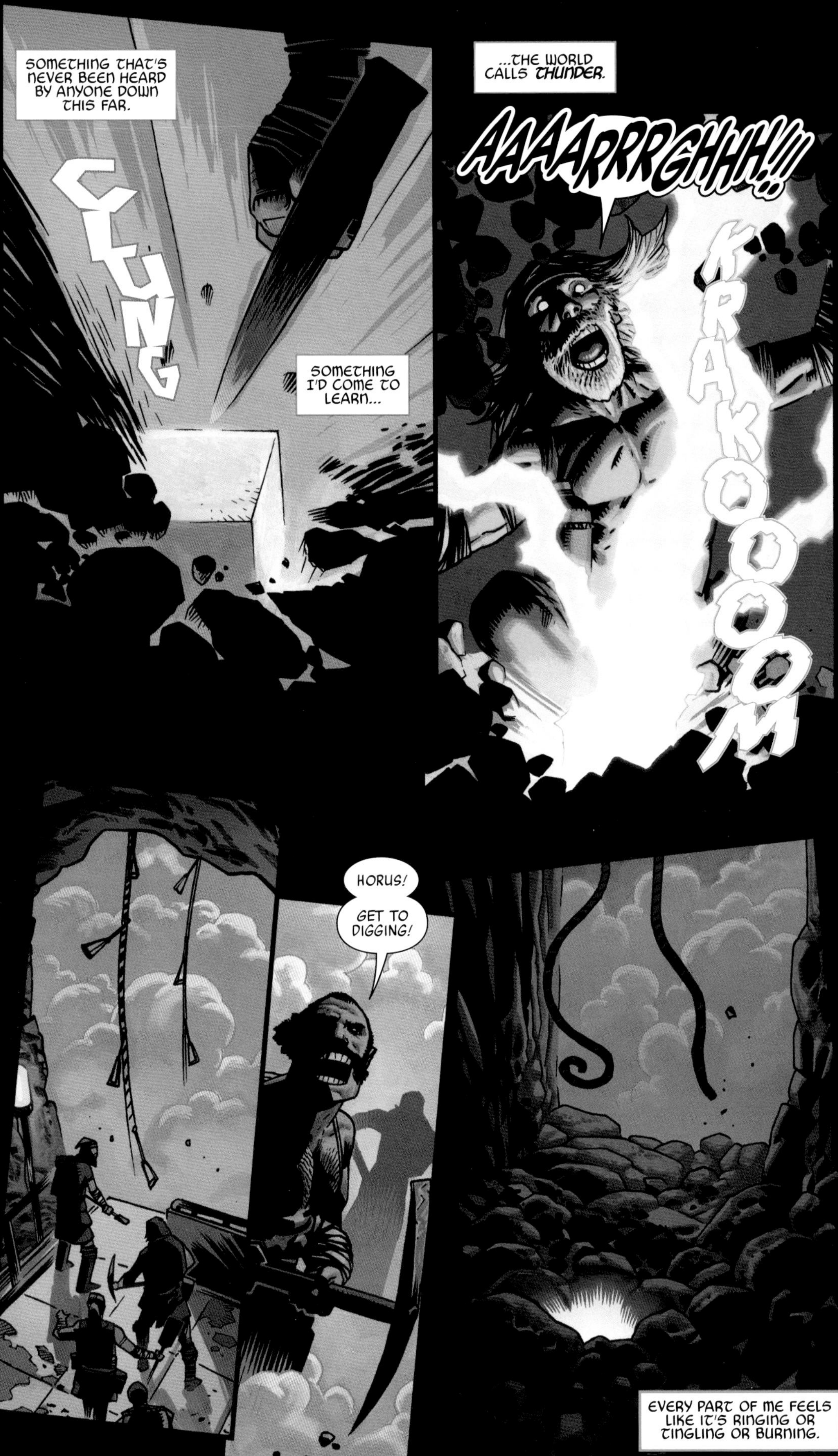
SOMETHING THAT'S NEVER BEEN HEARD BY ANYONE DOWN THIS FAR.
CLUNG
SOMETHING I'D COME TO LEARN...
...THE WORLD CALLS THUNDER.
AAAARRRGHHH!!
KRAKOOOOM
HORUS!
GET TO DIGGING!
EVERY PART OF ME FEELS LIKE IT'S RINGING OR TINGLING OR BURNING.

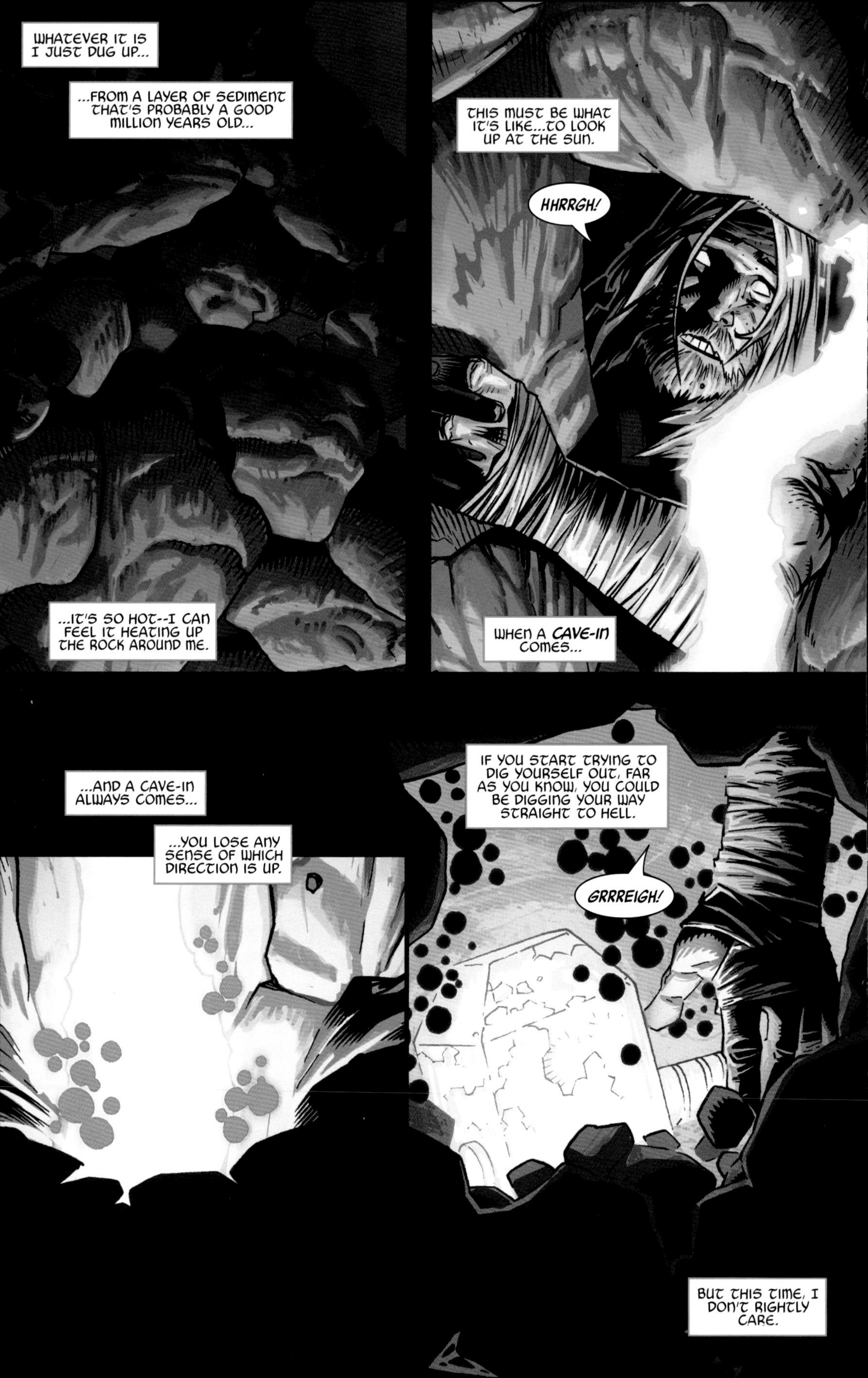
WHATEVER IT IS I JUST DUG UP...
...FROM A LAYER OF SEDIMENT THAT'S PROBABLY A GOOD MILLION YEARS OLD...
...IT'S SO HOT--I CAN FEEL IT HEATING UP THE ROCK AROUND ME.
THIS MUST BE WHAT IT'S LIKE...TO LOOK UP AT THE SUN.
HHRRGH!
WHEN A CAVE-IN COMES...
...AND A CAVE-IN ALWAYS COMES...
...YOU LOSE ANY SENSE OF WHICH DIRECTION IS UP.
IF YOU START TRYING TO DIG YOURSELF OUT, FAR AS YOU KNOW, YOU COULD BE DIGGING YOUR WAY STRAIGHT TO HELL.
GRRREIGH!
BUT THIS TIME, I DON'T RIGHTLY CARE.

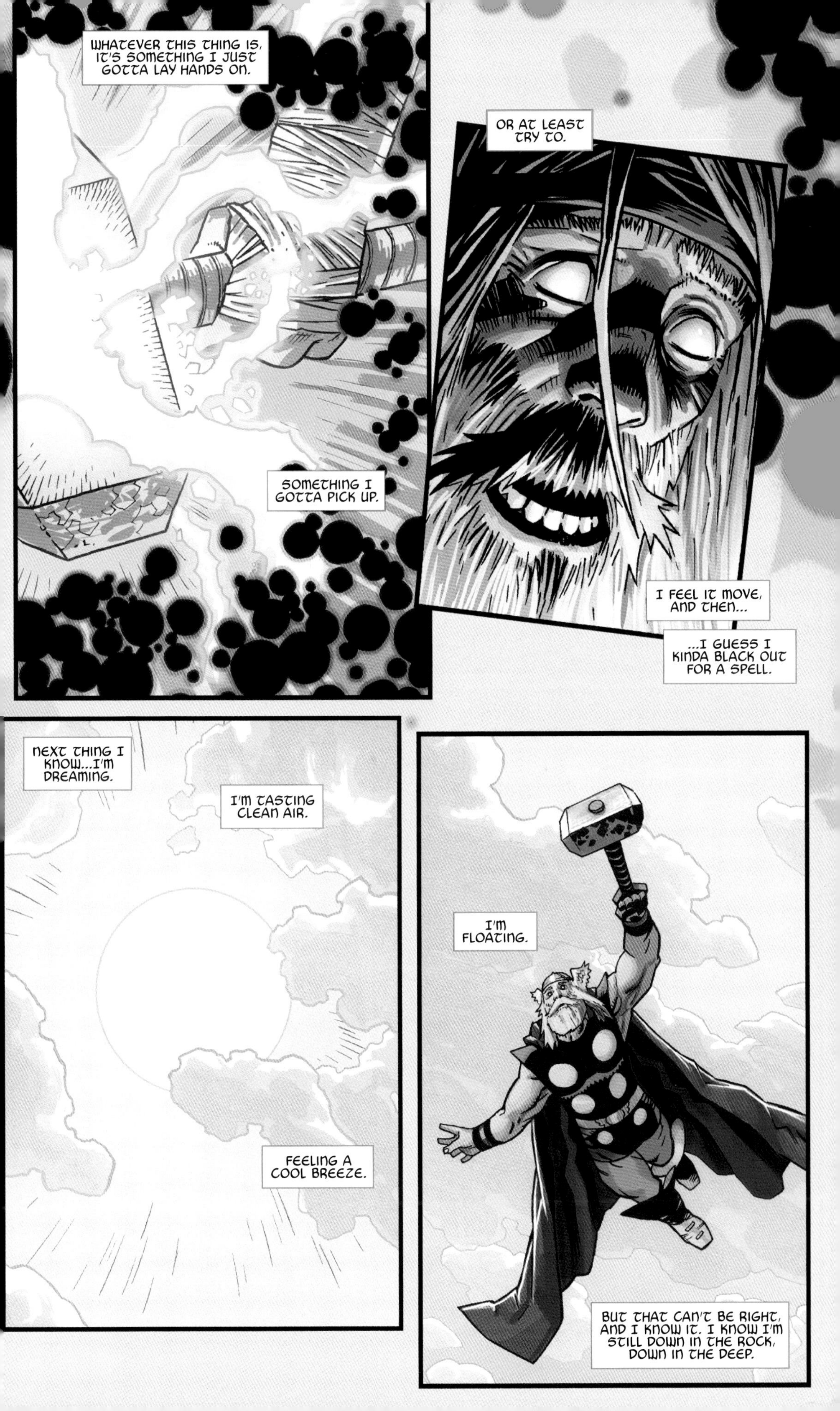
WHATEVER THIS THING IS, IT'S SOMETHING I JUST GOTTA LAY HANDS ON.
SOMETHING I GOTTA PICK UP.
OR AT LEAST TRY TO.
I FEEL IT MOVE, AND THEN...
...I GUESS I KINDA BLACK OUT FOR A SPELL.
NEXT THING I KNOW...I'M DREAMING.
I'M TASTING CLEAN AIR.
FEELING A COOL BREEZE.
I'M FLOATING.
BUT THAT CAN'T BE RIGHT, AND I KNOW IT. I KNOW I'M STILL DOWN IN THE ROCK, DOWN IN THE DEEP.

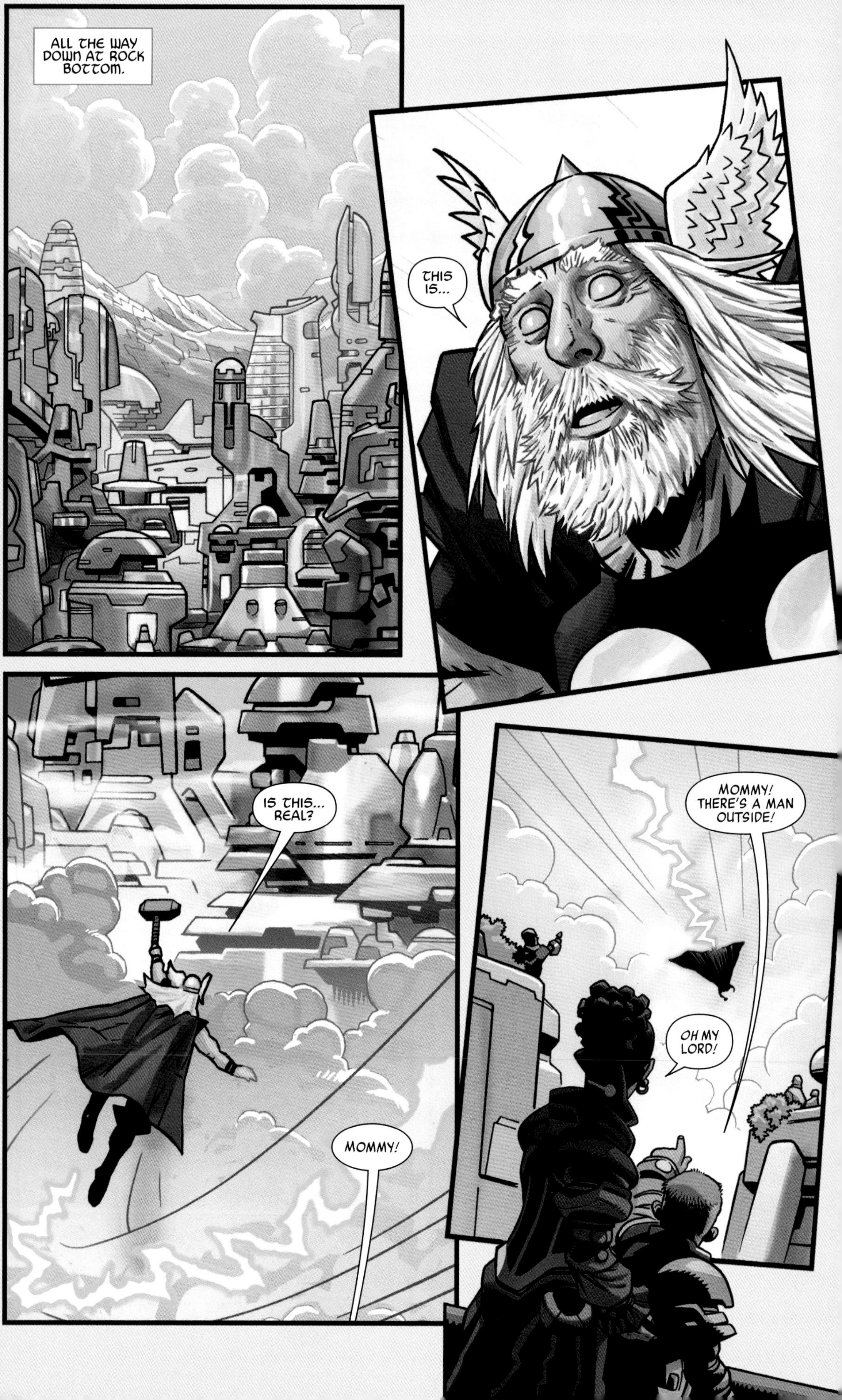
ALL THE WAY DOWN AT ROCK BOTTOM.
THIS IS...
IS THIS... REAL?
MOMMY!
MOMMY! THERE'S A MAN OUTSIDE!
OH MY LORD!

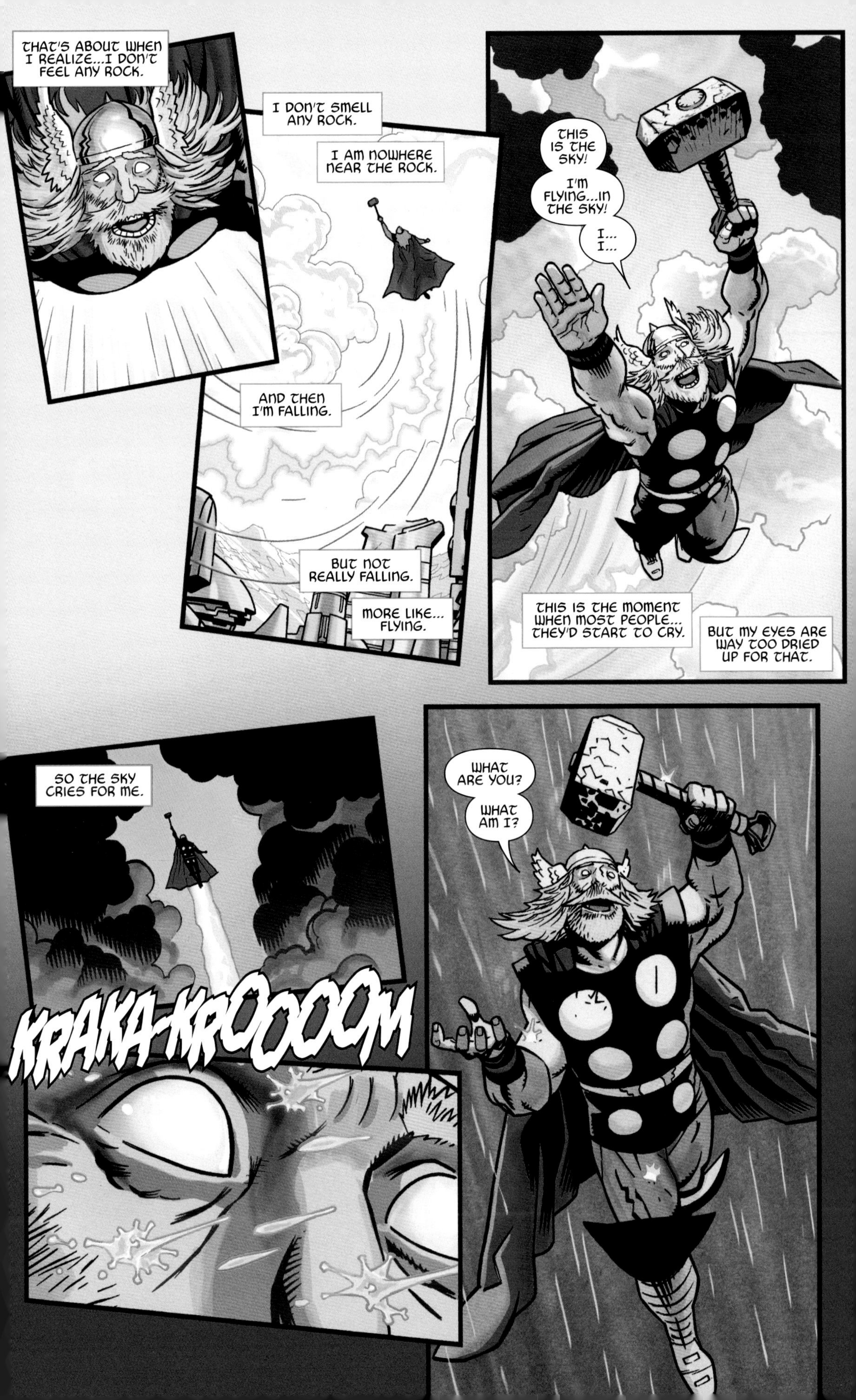
THAT'S ABOUT WHEN I REALIZE...I DON'T FEEL ANY ROCK.
I DON'T SMELL ANY ROCK.
I AM NOWHERE NEAR THE ROCK.
AND THEN I'M FALLING.
BUT NOT REALLY FALLING.
MORE LIKE... FLYING.
THIS IS THE SKY!
I'M FLYING...IN THE SKY!
I... I...
THIS IS THE MOMENT WHEN MOST PEOPLE... THEY'D START TO CRY.
BUT MY EYES ARE WAY TOO DRIED UP FOR THAT.
SO THE SKY CRIES FOR ME.
KRAKA-KROOOOM
WHAT ARE YOU?
WHAT AM I?

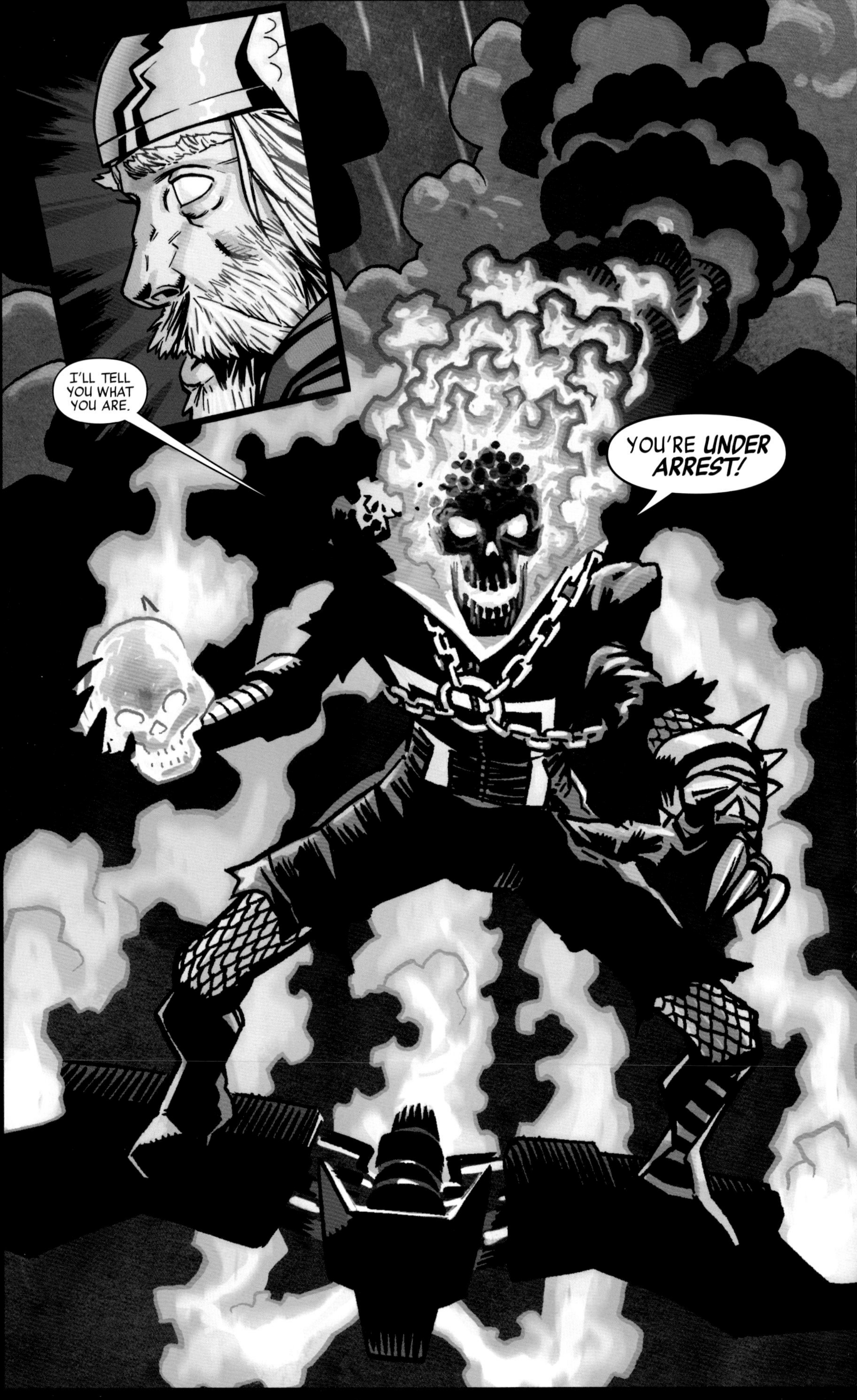
I'LL TELL YOU WHAT YOU ARE.
YOU'RE UNDER ARREST!

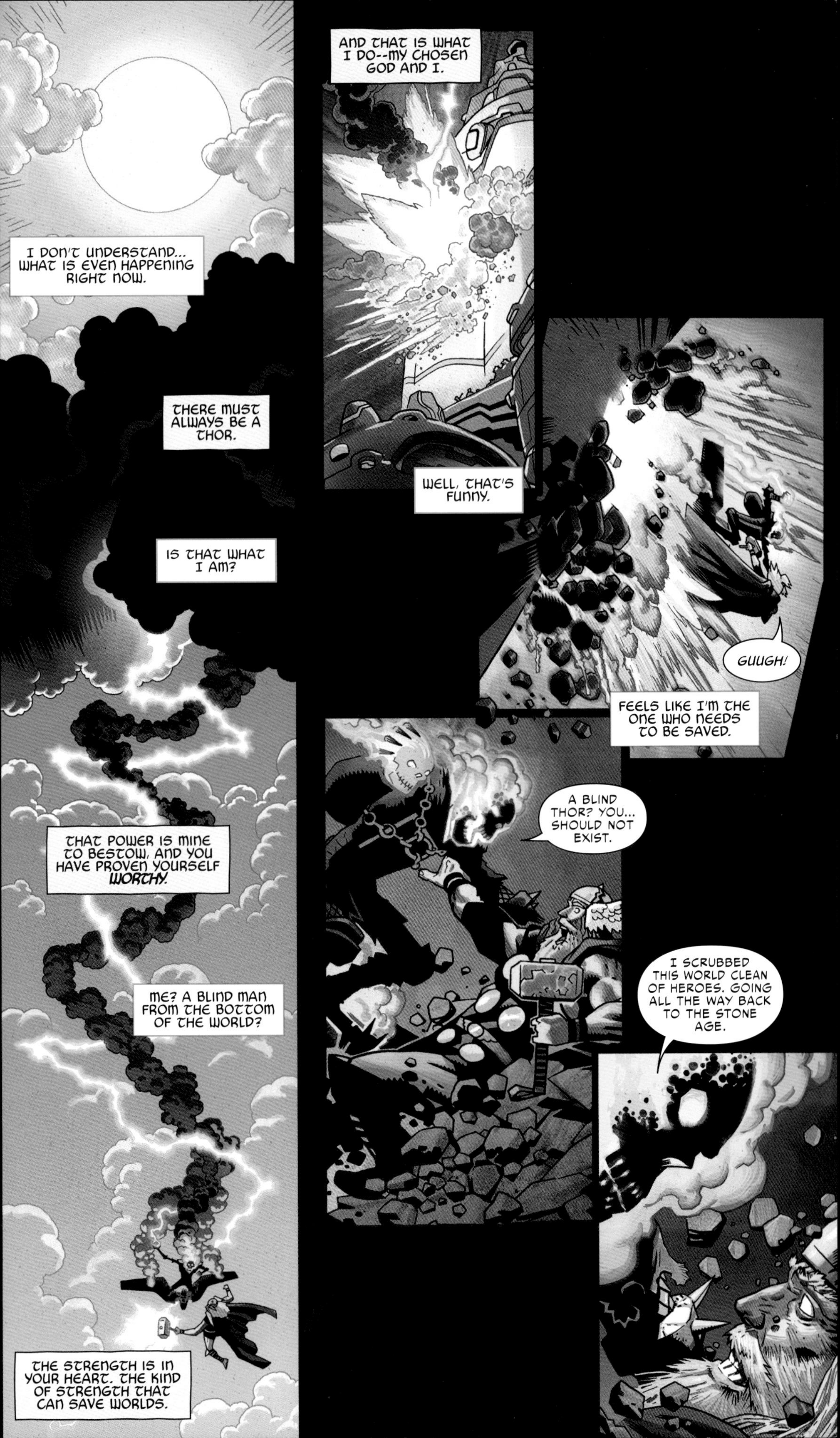
I DON'T UNDERSTAND... WHAT IS EVEN HAPPENING RIGHT NOW.
THERE MUST ALWAYS BE A THOR.
IS THAT WHAT I AM?
THAT POWER IS MINE TO BESTOW, AND YOU HAVE PROVEN YOURSELF WORTHY.
ME? A BLIND MAN FROM THE BOTTOM OF THE WORLD?
THE STRENGTH IS IN YOUR HEART. THE KIND OF STRENGTH THAT CAN SAVE WORLDS.
AND THAT IS WHAT I DO--MY CHOSEN GOD AND I.
WELL, THAT'S FUNNY.
GUUGH!
FEELS LIKE I'M THE ONE WHO NEEDS TO BE SAVED.
A BLIND THOR? YOU... SHOULD NOT EXIST.
I SCRUBBED THIS WORLD CLEAN OF HEROES. GOING ALL THE WAY BACK TO THE STONE AGE.

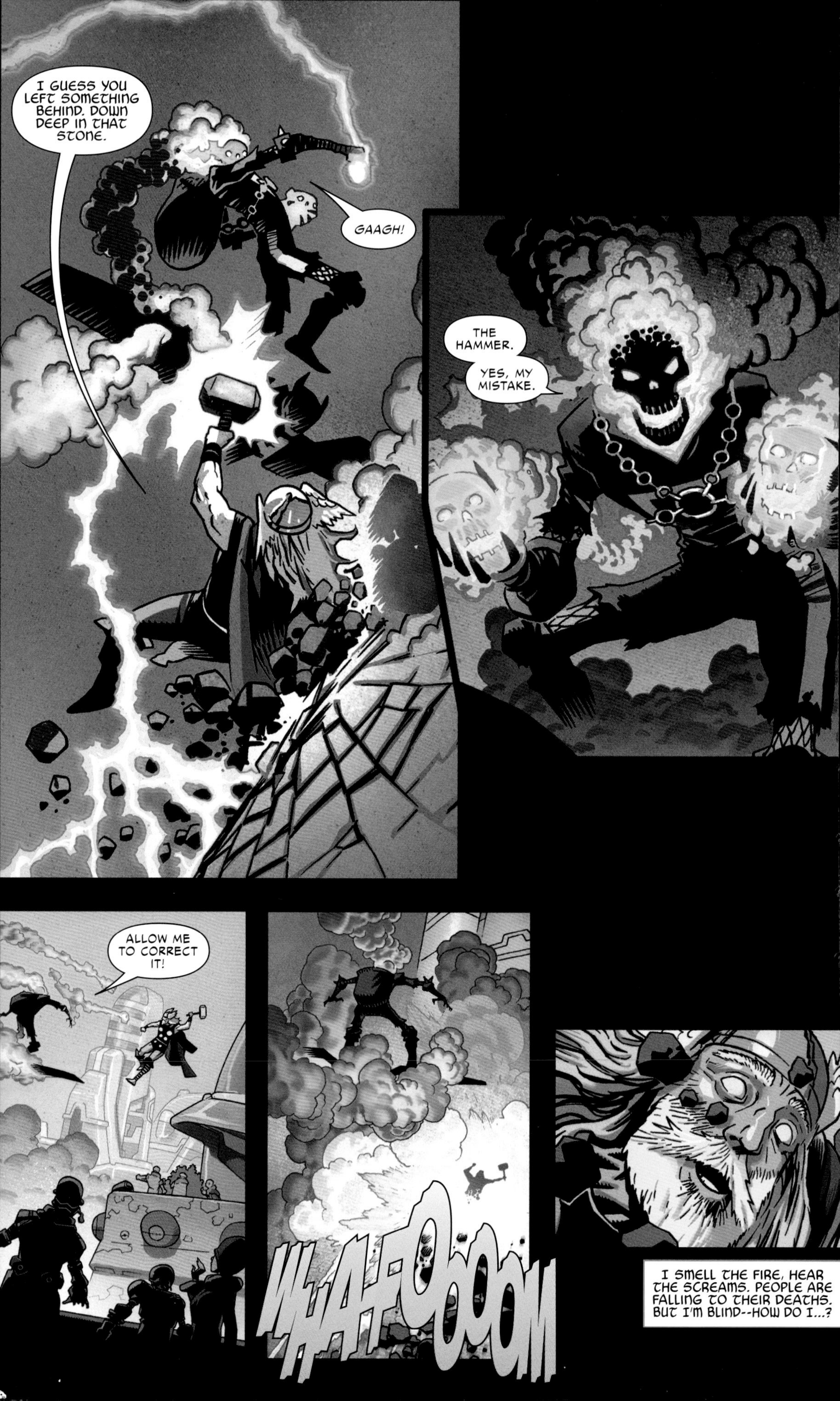

I GUESS YOU LEFT SOMETHING BEHIND. DOWN DEEP IN THAT STONE.
GAAGH!
THE HAMMER.
YES, MY MISTAKE.
ALLOW ME TO CORRECT IT!
WHAFOOOOM
I SMELL THE FIRE, HEAR THE SCREAMS. PEOPLE ARE FALLING TO THEIR DEATHS. BUT I'M BLIND--HOW DO I...?

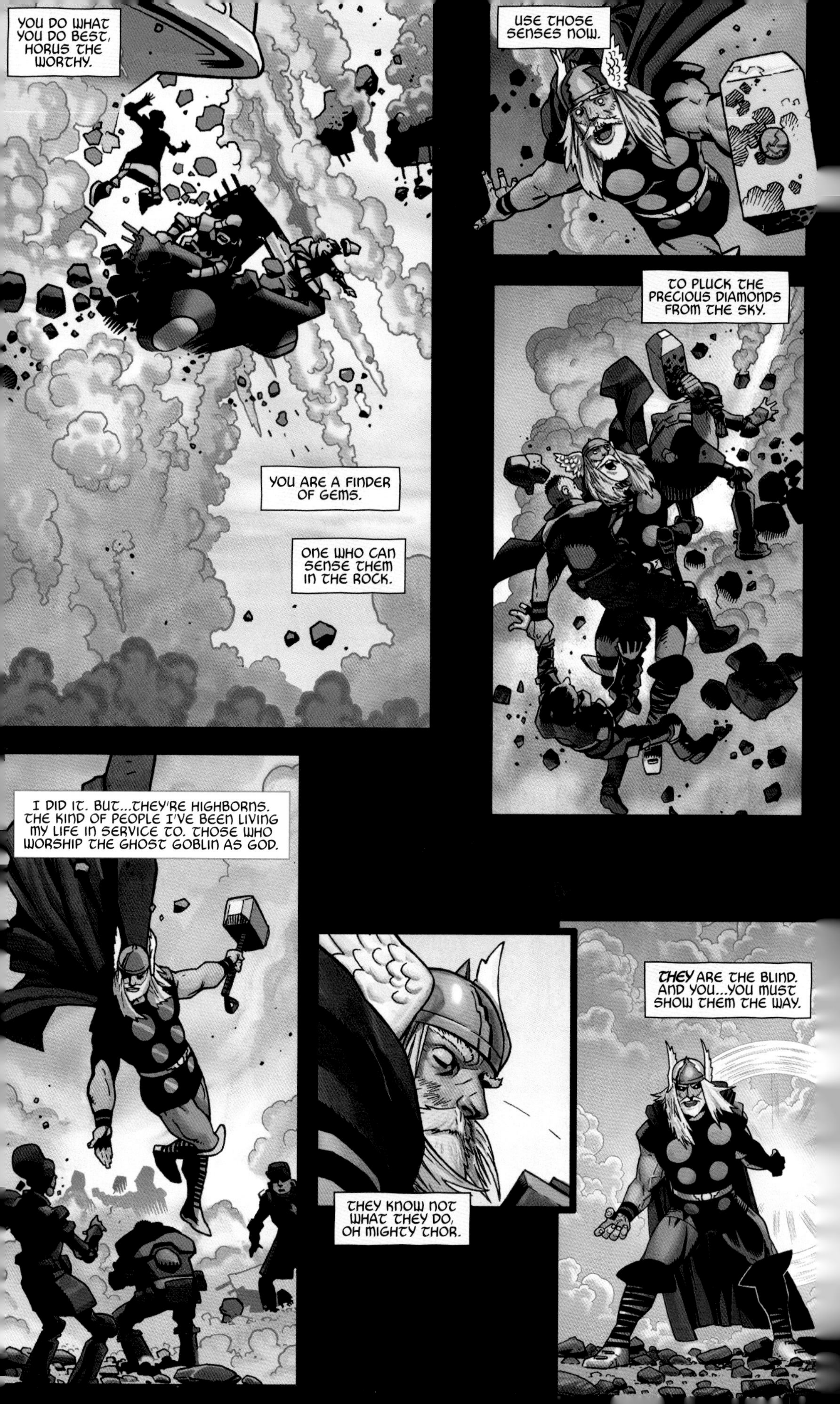
YOU DO WHAT YOU DO BEST, HORUS THE WORTHY.
USE THOSE SENSES NOW.
YOU ARE A FINDER OF GEMS.
ONE WHO CAN SENSE THEM IN THE ROCK.
TO PLUCK THE PRECIOUS DIAMONDS FROM THE SKY.
I DID IT. BUT...THEY'RE HIGHBORNS. THE KIND OF PEOPLE I'VE BEEN LIVING MY LIFE IN SERVICE TO. THOSE WHO WORSHIP THE GHOST GOBLIN AS GOD.
THEY KNOW NOT WHAT THEY DO, OH MIGHTY THOR.
THEY ARE THE BLIND. AND YOU...YOU MUST SHOW THEM THE WAY.

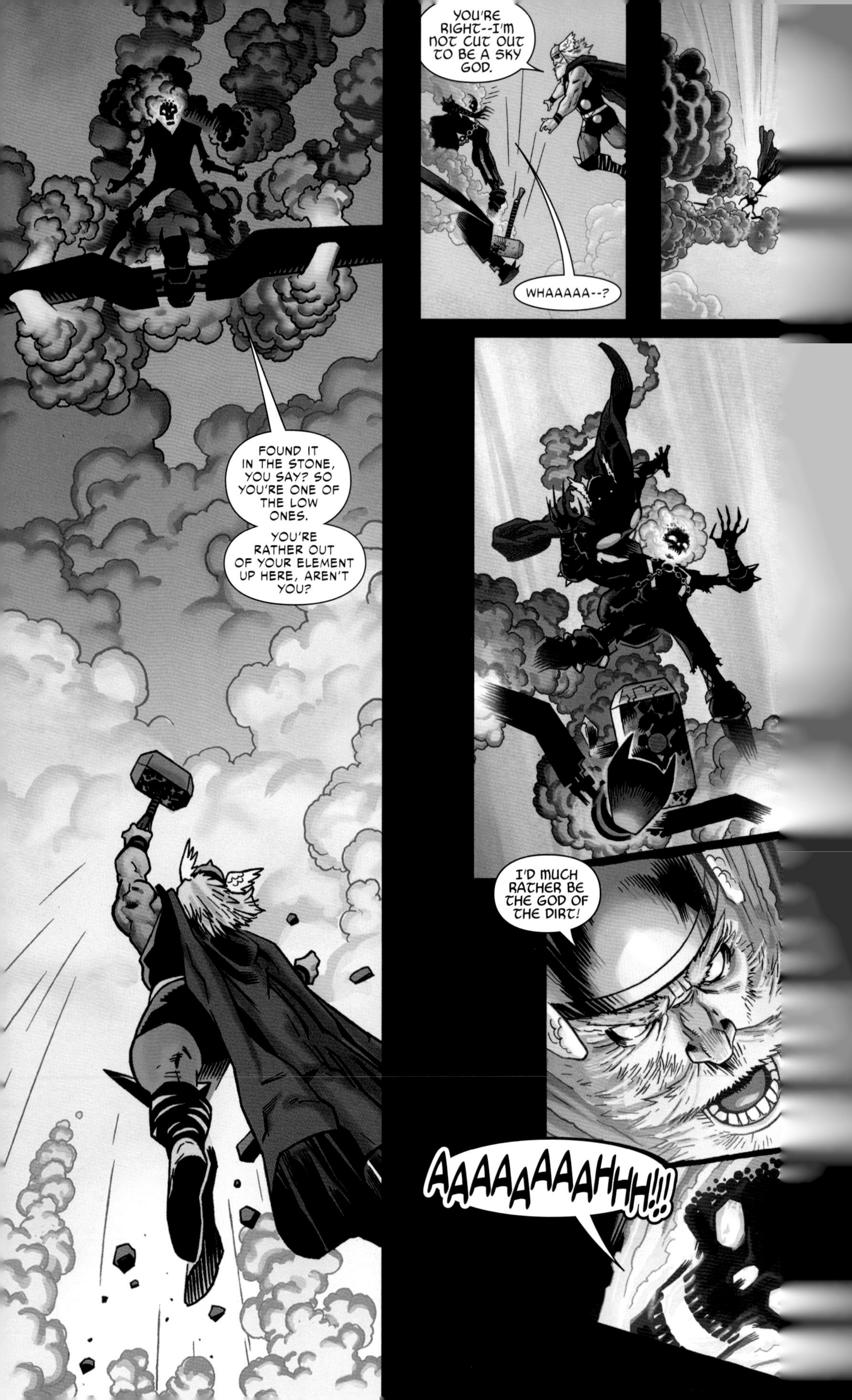
FOUND IT IN THE STONE, YOU SAY? SO YOU'RE ONE OF THE LOW ONES.
YOU'RE RATHER OUT OF YOUR ELEMENT UP HERE, AREN'T YOU?
YOU'RE RIGHT--I'M NOT CUT OUT TO BE A SKY GOD.
WHAAAAA--?
I'D MUCH RATHER BE THE GOD OF THE DIRT!
AAAAAAAAHHH!!!

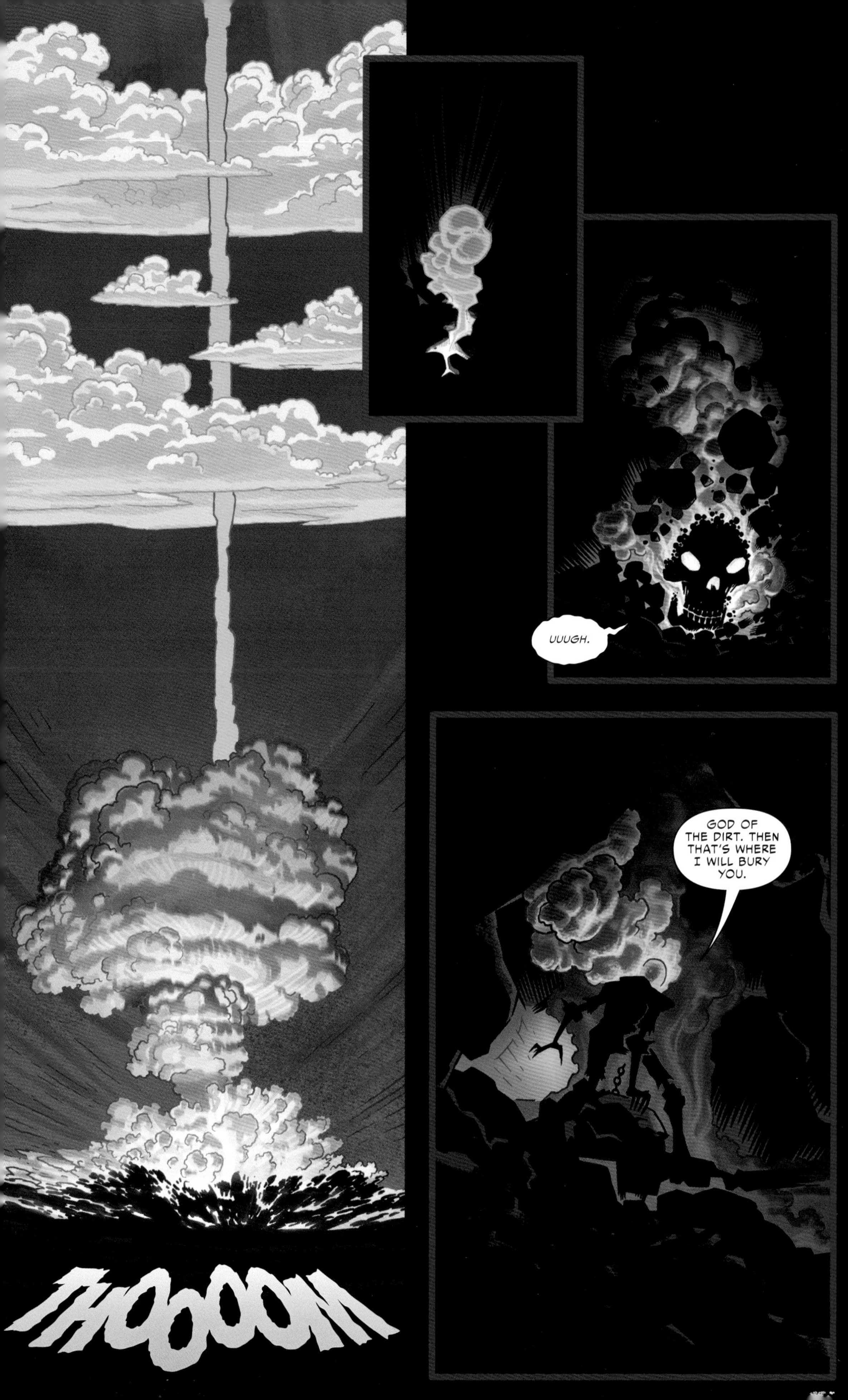
THOOOOM
UUUGH.
GOD OF THE DIRT. THEN THAT'S WHERE I WILL BURY YOU.

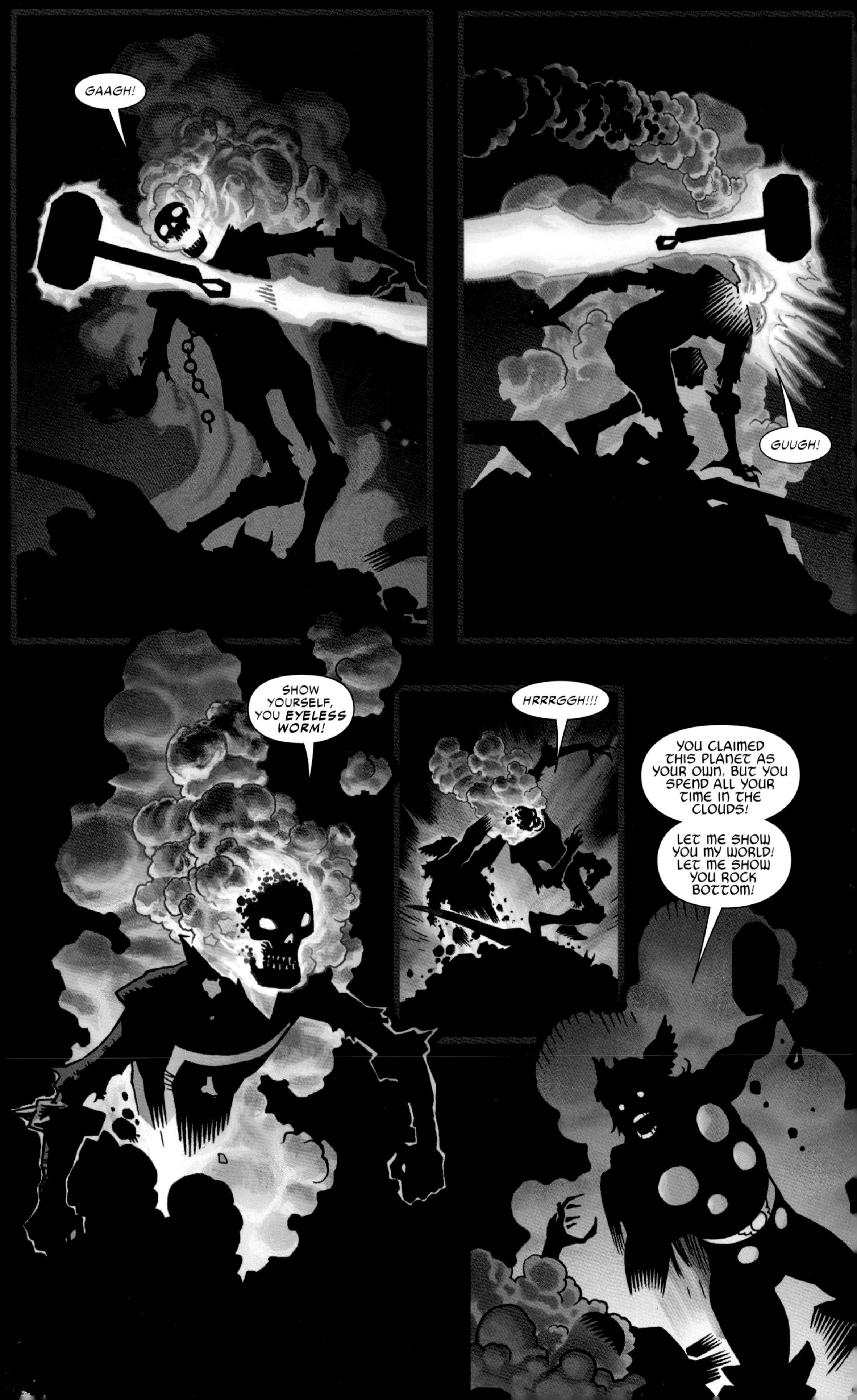
GAAGH!
GUUGH!
SHOW YOURSELF, YOU EYELESS WORM!
HRRRGGH!!!
YOU CLAIMED THIS PLANET AS YOUR OWN, BUT YOU SPEND ALL YOUR TIME IN THE CLOUDS!
LET ME SHOW YOU MY WORLD! LET ME SHOW YOU ROCK BOTTOM!

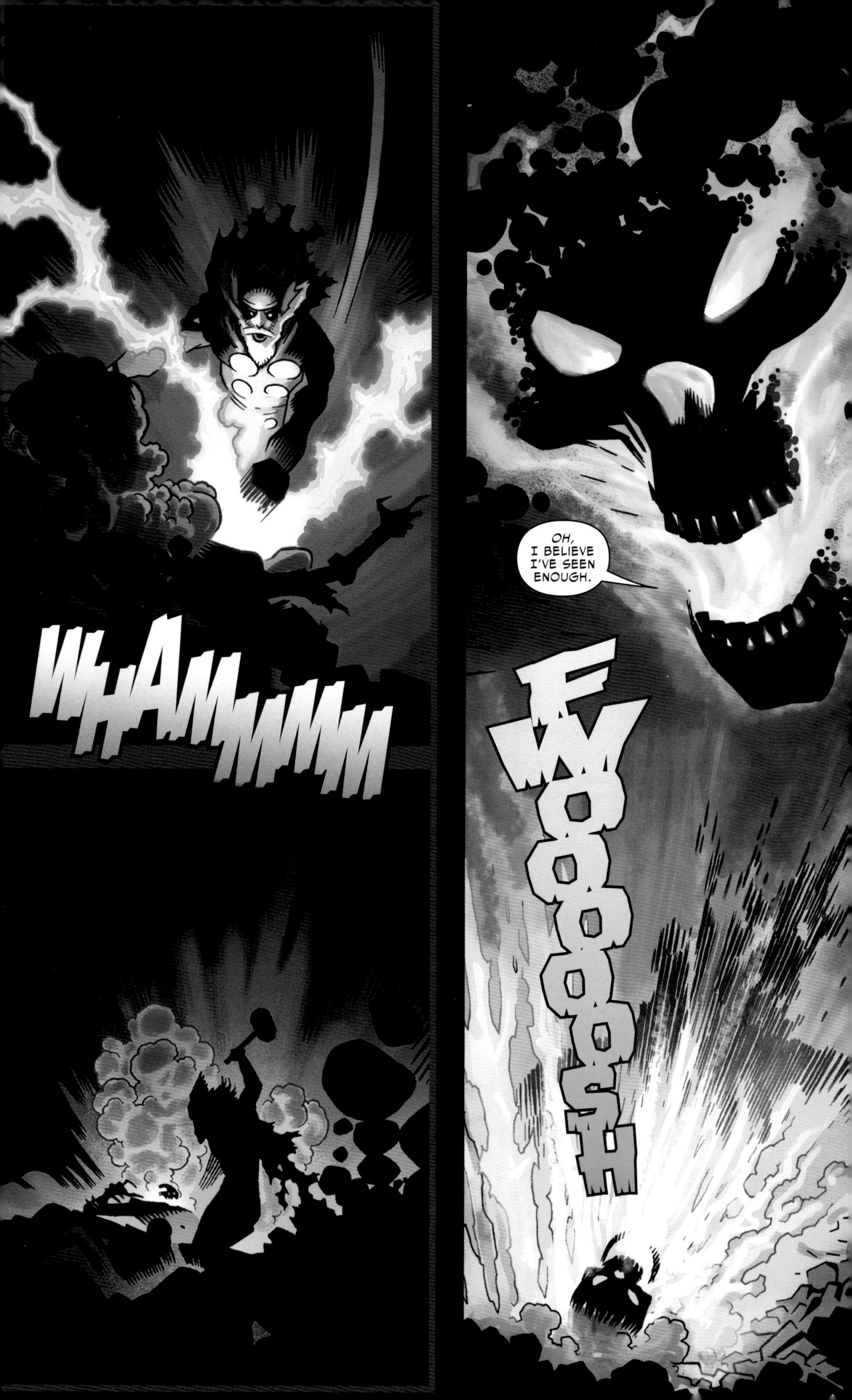
WHAMMMMMM
OH, I BELIEVE I'VE SEEN ENOUGH.
FWOOOOOOSH

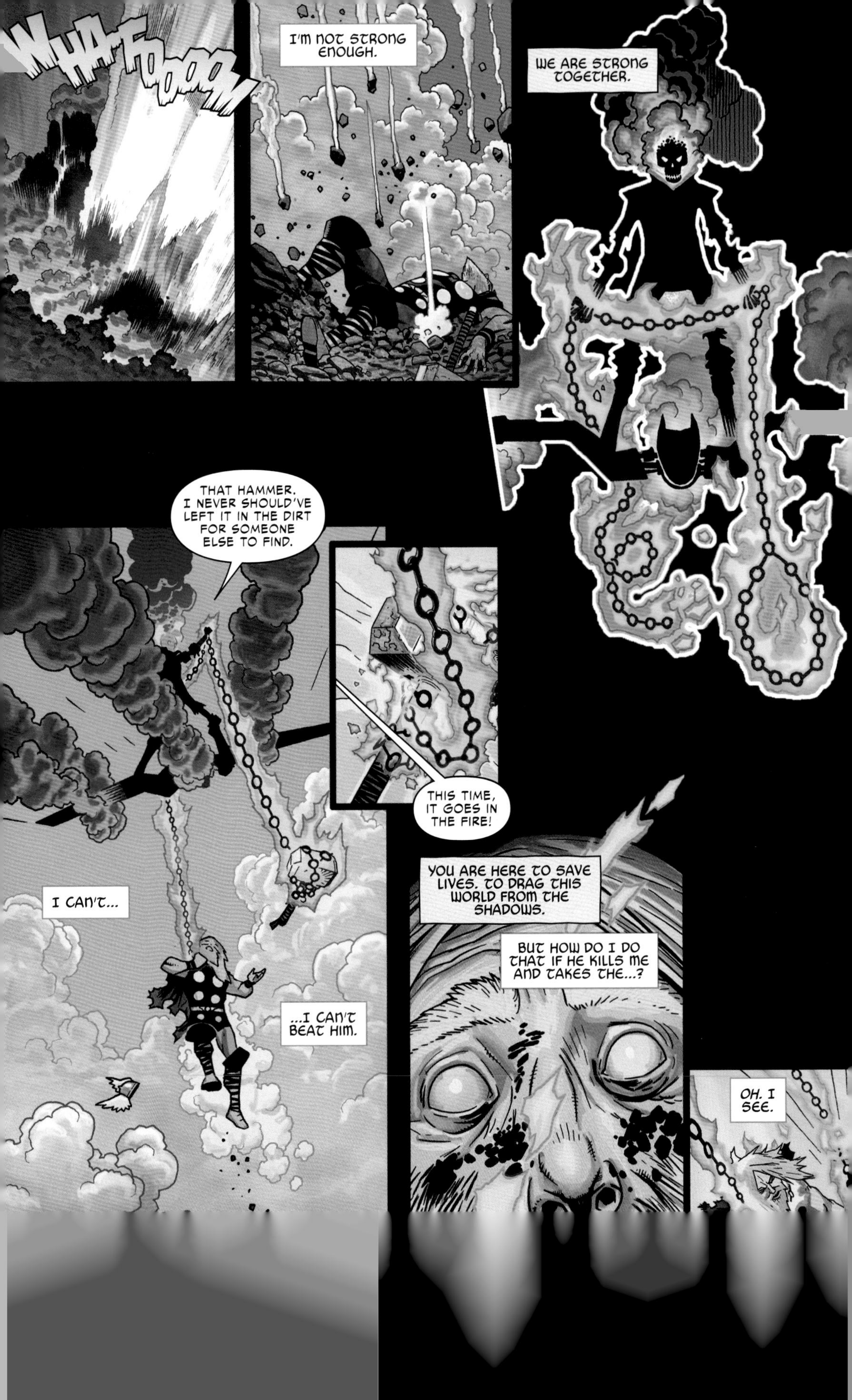
WHA-TOOOOM
I'M NOT STRONG ENOUGH.
WE ARE STRONG TOGETHER.
THAT HAMMER. I NEVER SHOULD'VE LEFT IT IN THE DIRT FOR SOMEONE ELSE TO FIND.
THIS TIME, IT GOES IN THE FIRE!
I CAN'T...
...I CAN'T BEAT HIM.
YOU ARE HERE TO SAVE LIVES. TO DRAG THIS WORLD FROM THE SHADOWS.
BUT HOW DO I DO THAT IF HE KILLS ME AND TAKES THE...?
OH. I SEE.

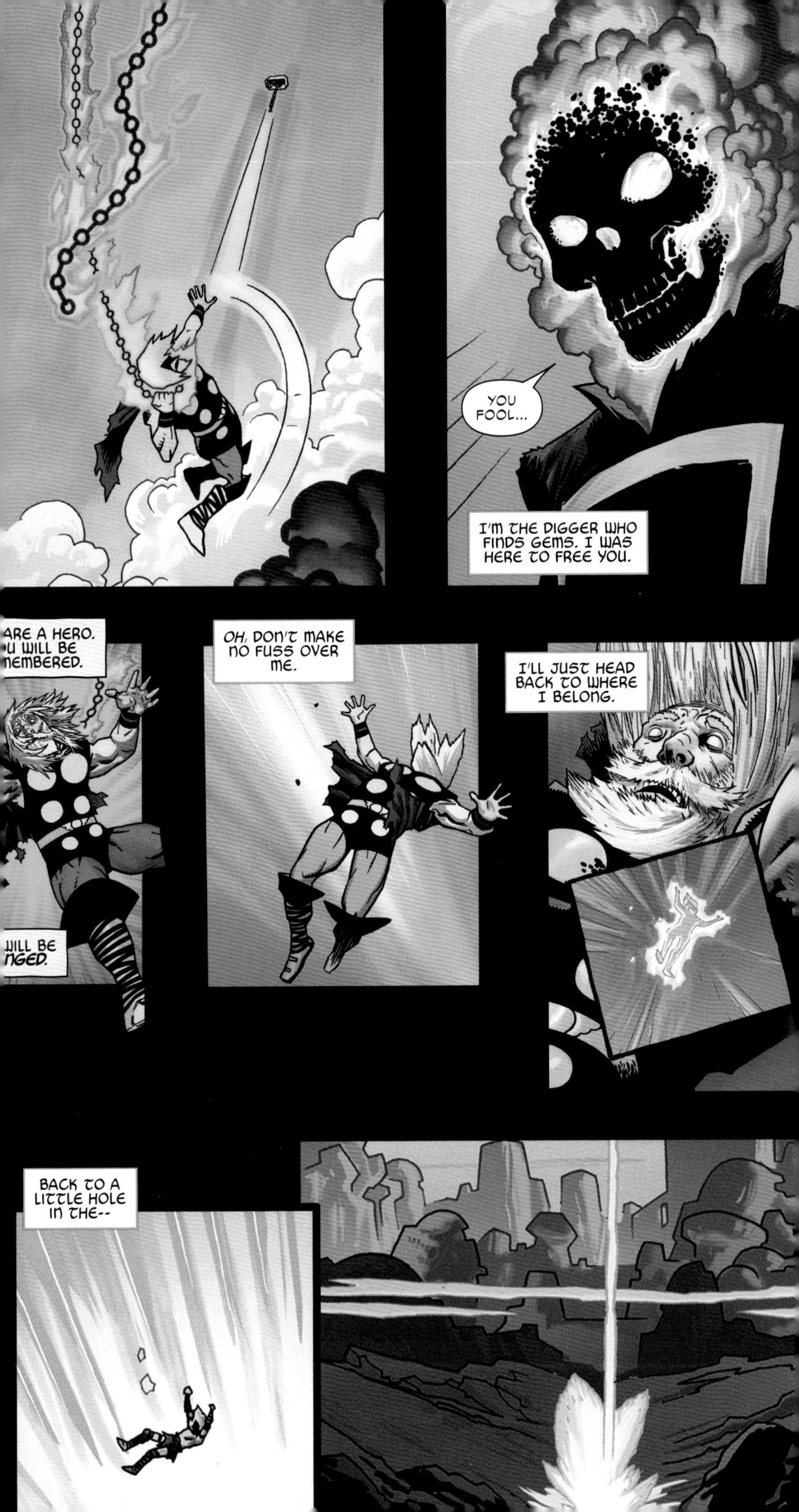
YOU FOOL...
I'M THE DIGGER WHO FINDS GEMS. I WAS HERE TO FREE YOU.
ARE A HERO. WILL BE
WILL BE
OH, DON'T MAKE NO FUSS OVER ME.
I'LL JUST HEAD BACK TO WHERE I BELONG.
BACK TO A LITTLE HOLE IN THE--

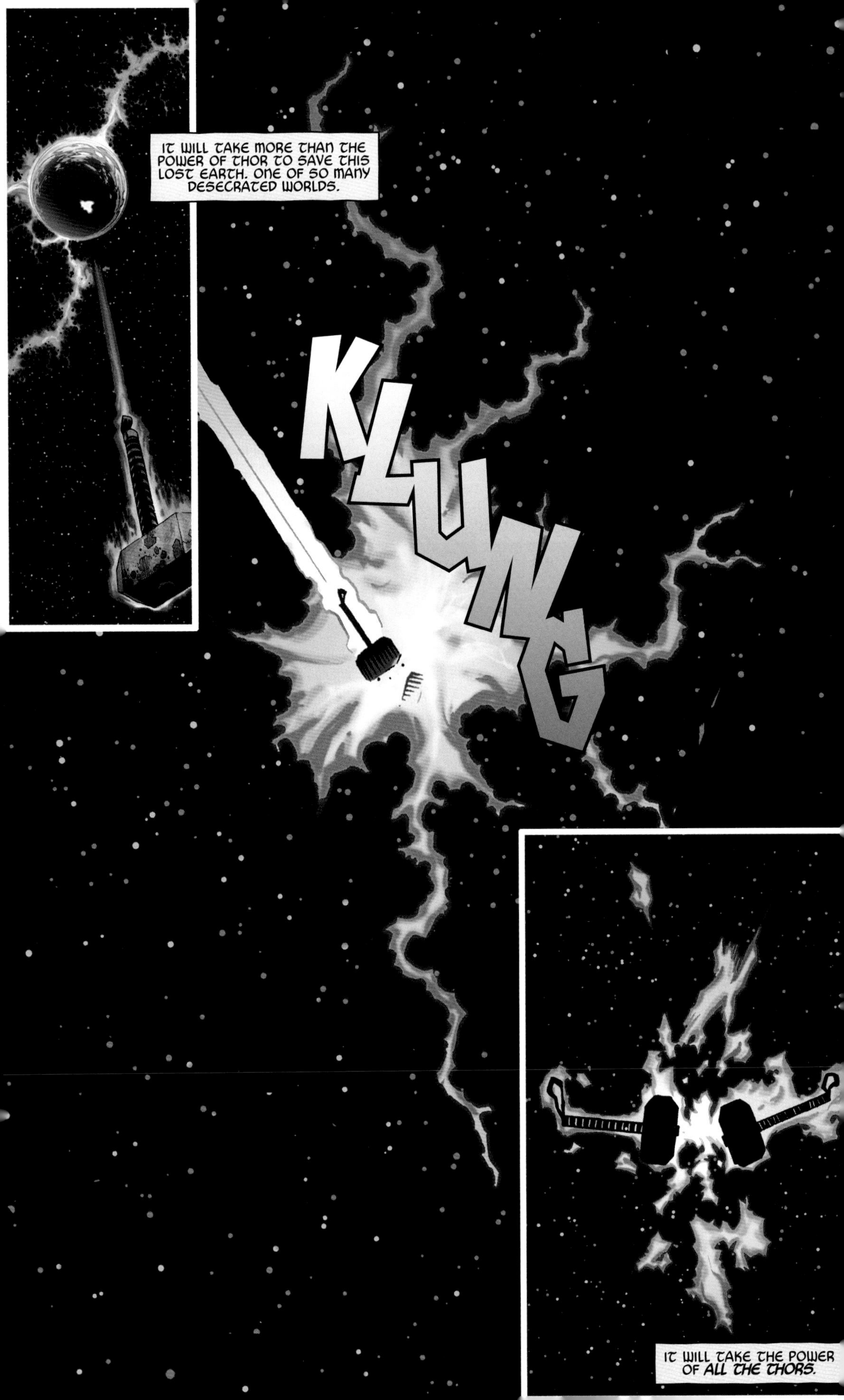

IT WILL TAKE MORE THAN THE POWER OF THOR TO SAVE THIS LOST EARTH. ONE OF SO MANY DESECRATED WORLDS.
KLUNNG
IT WILL TAKE THE POWER OF ALL THE THORS.

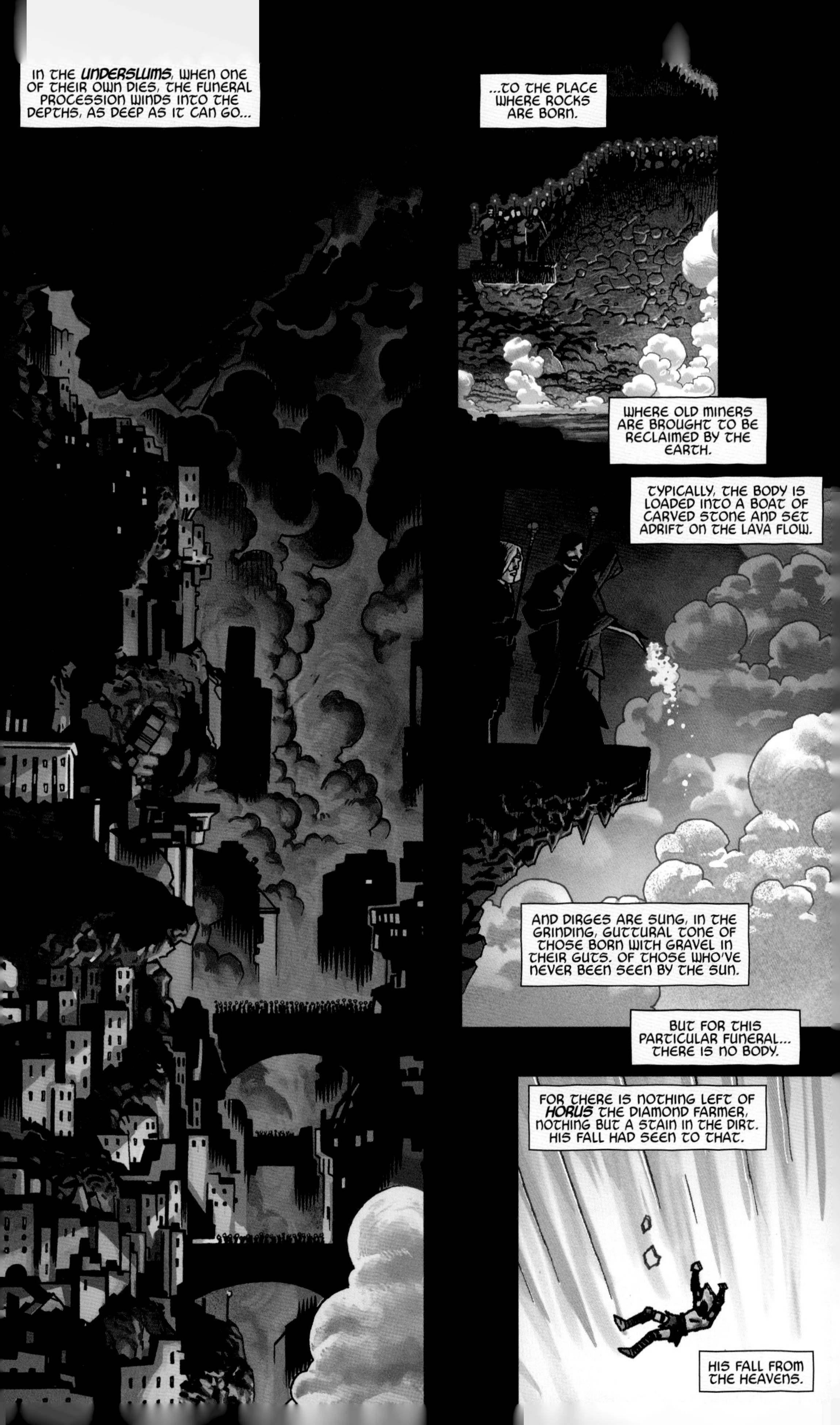
IN THE UNDERSLUMS, WHEN ONE OF THEIR OWN DIES, THE FUNERAL PROCESSION WINDS INTO THE DEPTHS, AS DEEP AS IT CAN GO...
...TO THE PLACE WHERE ROCKS ARE BORN.
WHERE OLD MINERS ARE BROUGHT TO BE RECLAIMED BY THE EARTH.
TYPICALLY, THE BODY IS LOADED INTO A BOAT OF CARVED STONE AND SET ADRIFT ON THE LAVA FLOW.
AND DIRGES ARE SUNG, IN THE GRINDING, GUTTURAL TONE OF THOSE BORN WITH GRAVEL IN THEIR GUTS. OF THOSE WHO'VE NEVER BEEN SEEN BY THE SUN.
BUT FOR THIS PARTICULAR FUNERAL... THERE IS NO BODY.
FOR THERE IS NOTHING LEFT OF HORUS THE DIAMOND FARMER, NOTHING BUT A STAIN IN THE DIRT. HIS FALL HAD SEEN TO THAT.
HIS FALL FROM THE HEAVENS.

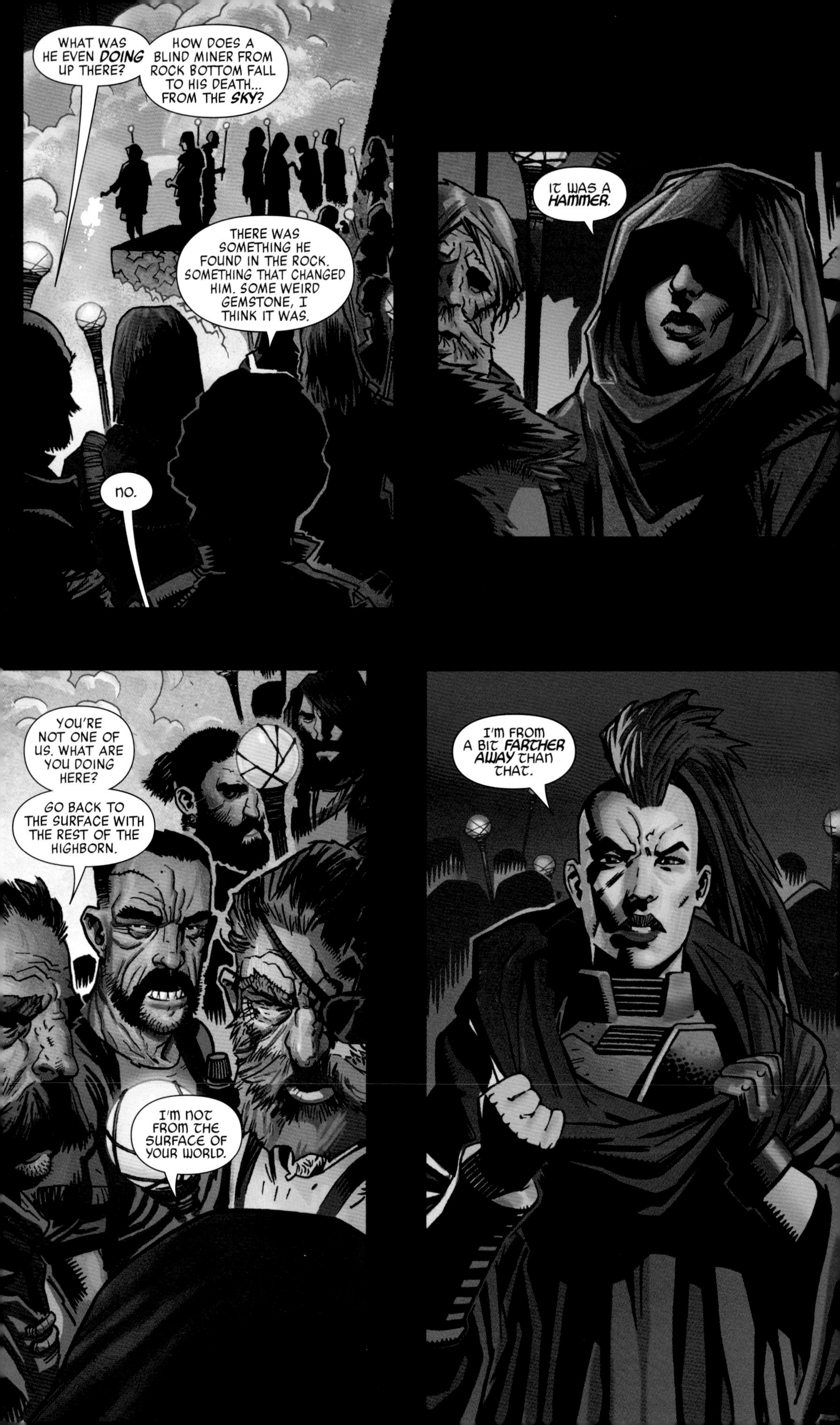
WHAT WAS HE EVEN DOING UP THERE?
HOW DOES A BLIND MINER FROM ROCK BOTTOM FALL TO HIS DEATH... FROM THE SKY?
THERE WAS SOMETHING HE FOUND IN THE ROCK. SOMETHING THAT CHANGED HIM. SOME WEIRD GEMSTONE, I THINK IT WAS.
no.
IT WAS A HAMMER.
YOU'RE NOT ONE OF US. WHAT ARE YOU DOING HERE?
GO BACK TO THE SURFACE WITH THE REST OF THE HIGHBORN.
I'M NOT FROM THE SURFACE OF YOUR WORLD.
I'M FROM A BIT FARTHER AWAY THAN THAT.

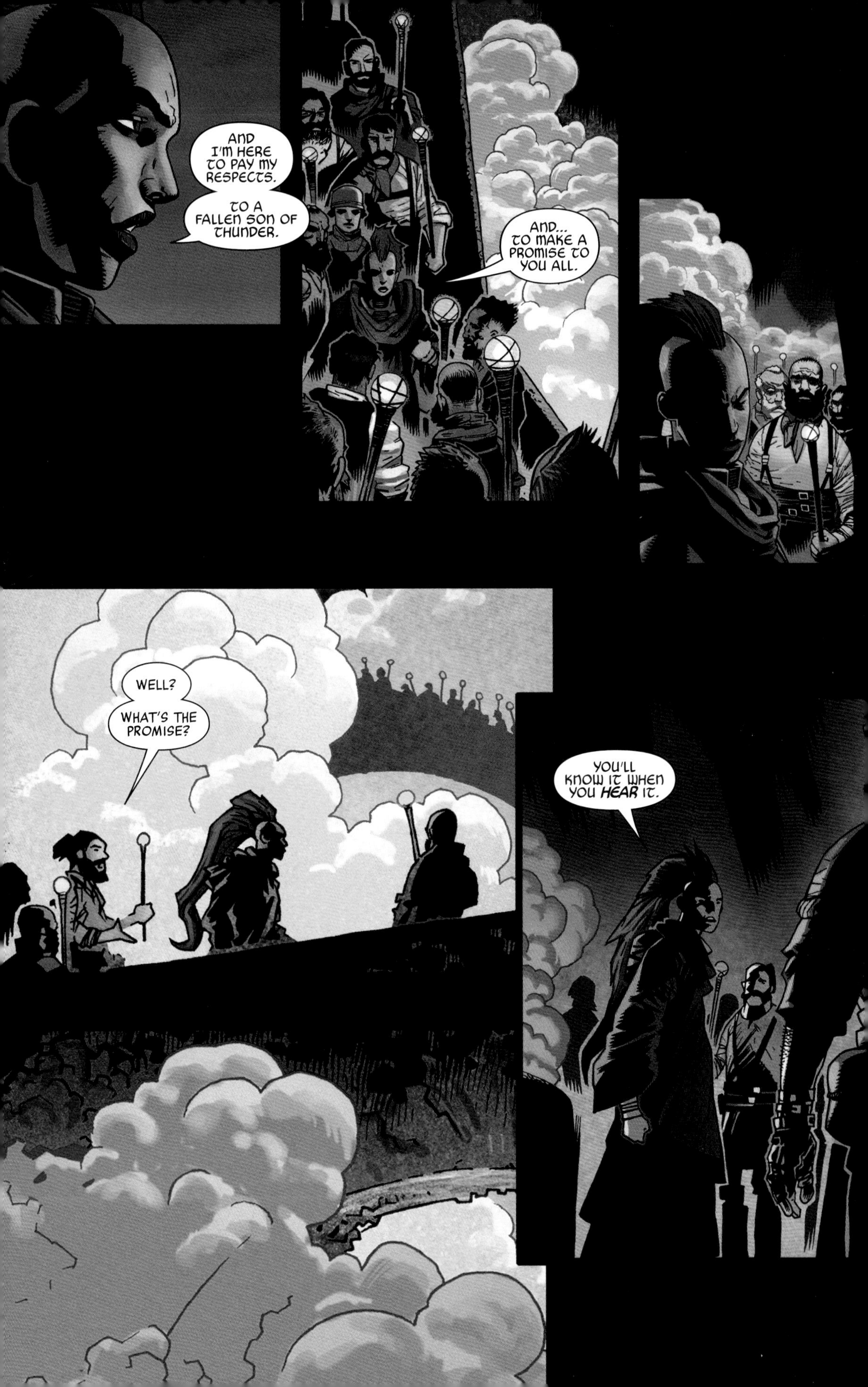
AND I'M HERE TO PAY MY RESPECTS.
TO A FALLEN SON OF THUNDER.
AND... TO MAKE A PROMISE TO YOU ALL.
WELL?
WHAT'S THE PROMISE?
YOU'LL KNOW IT WHEN YOU HEAR IT.

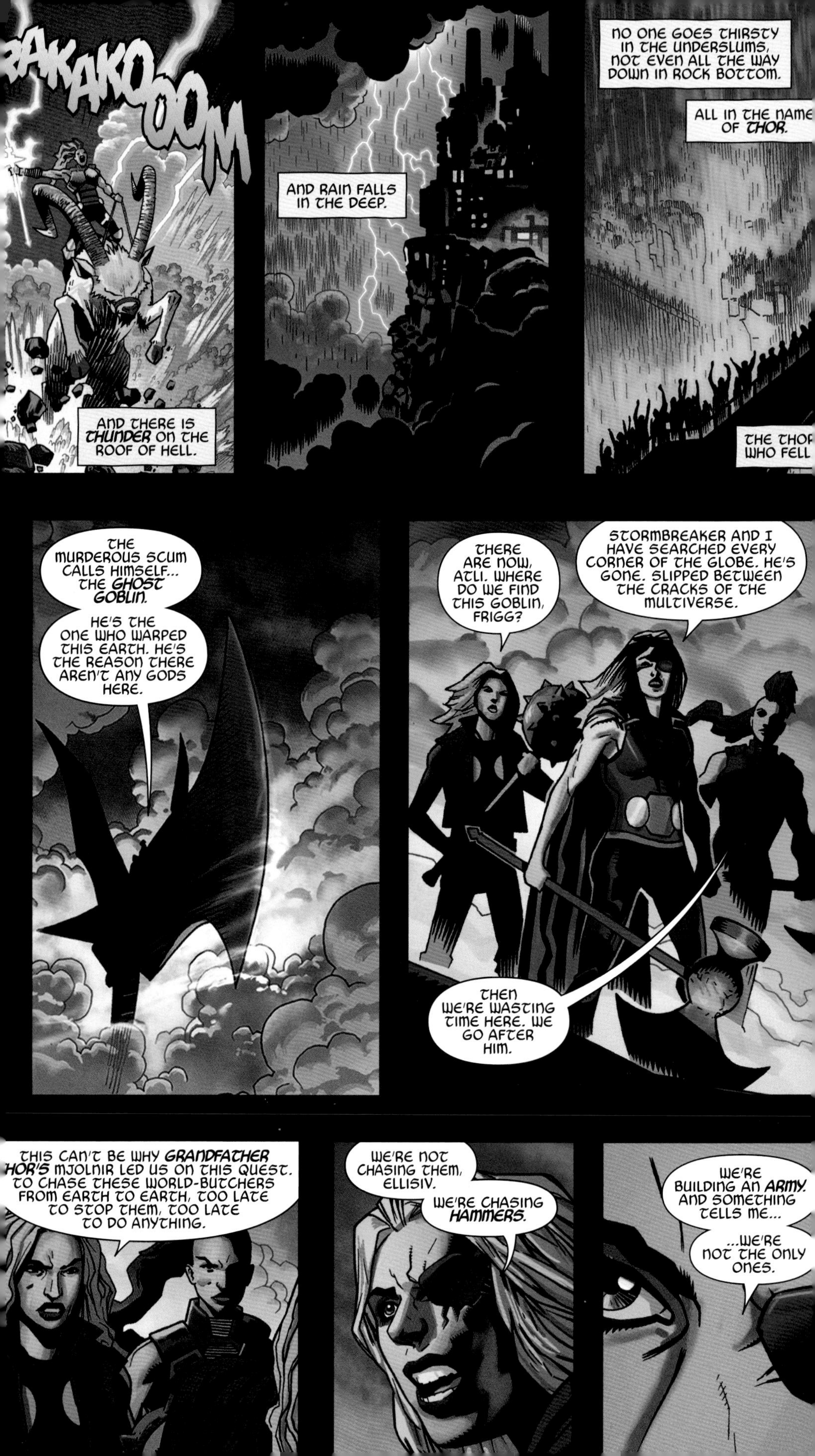
AKAKOOOM
AND THERE IS THUNDER ON THE ROOF OF HELL.
AND RAIN FALLS IN THE DEEP.
NO ONE GOES THIRSTY IN THE UNDERSLUMS, NOT EVEN ALL THE WAY DOWN IN ROCK BOTTOM.
ALL IN THE NAME OF THOR.
THE THOR WHO FELL
THE MURDEROUS SCUM CALLS HIMSELF... THE GHOST GOBLIN.
HE'S THE ONE WHO WARPED THIS EARTH. HE'S THE REASON THERE AREN'T ANY GODS HERE.
THERE ARE NOW, ATLI. WHERE DO WE FIND THIS GOBLIN, FRIGG?
STORMBREAKER AND I HAVE SEARCHED EVERY CORNER OF THE GLOBE. HE'S GONE. SLIPPED BETWEEN THE CRACKS OF THE MULTIVERSE.
THEN WE'RE WASTING TIME HERE. WE GO AFTER HIM.
THIS CAN'T BE WHY GRANDFATHER THOR'S MJOLNIR LED US ON THIS QUEST. TO CHASE THESE WORLD-BUTCHERS FROM EARTH TO EARTH, TOO LATE TO STOP THEM, TOO LATE TO DO ANYTHING.
WE'RE NOT CHASING THEM, ELLISIV.
WE'RE CHASING HAMMERS.
WE'RE BUILDING AN ARMY. AND SOMETHING TELLS ME...
...WE'RE NOT THE ONLY ONES.

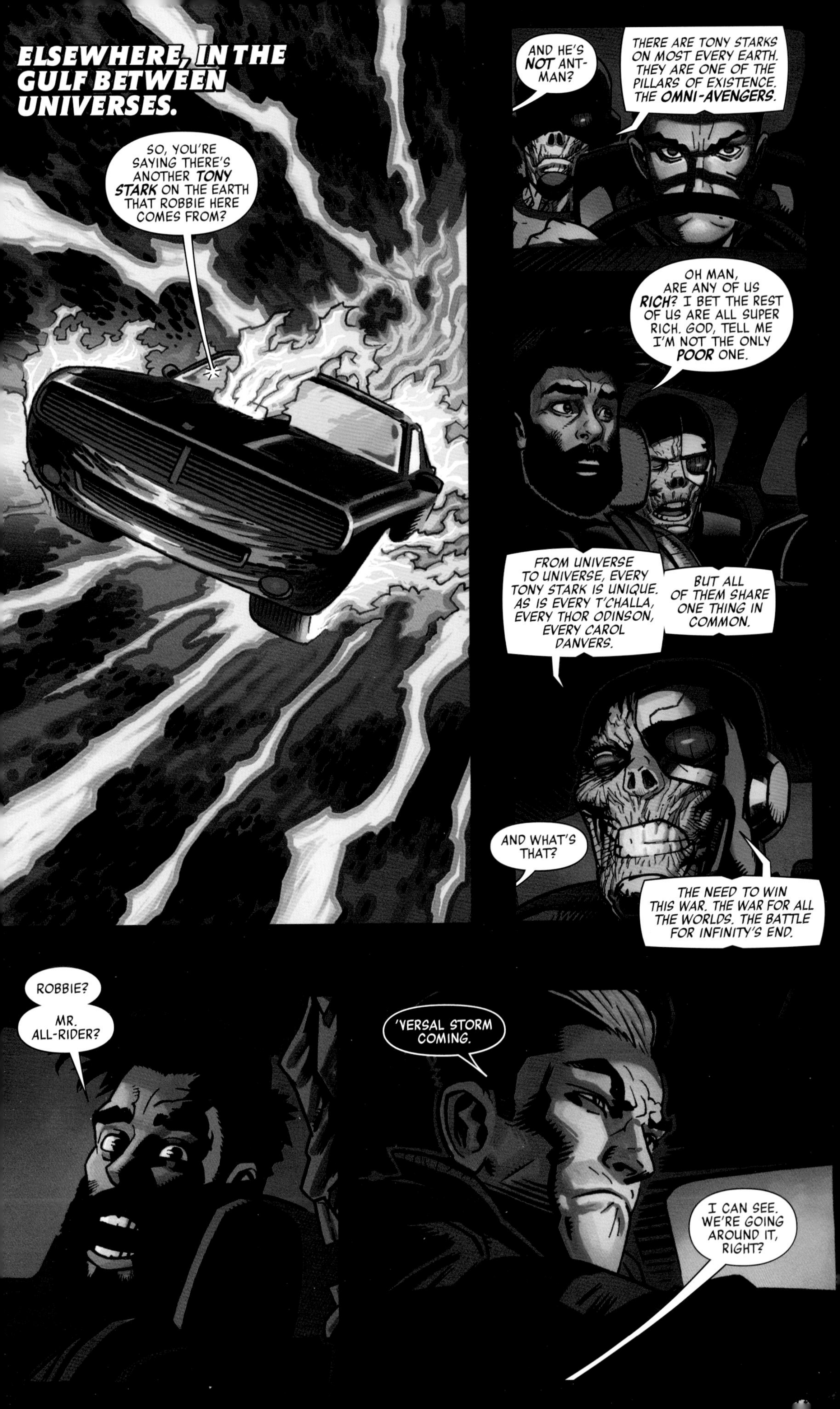
ELSEWHERE, IN THE GULF BETWEEN UNIVERSES.
SO, YOU'RE SAYING THERE'S ANOTHER TONY STARK ON THE EARTH THAT ROBBIE HERE COMES FROM?
AND HE'S NOT ANT-MAN?
THERE ARE TONY STARKS ON MOST EVERY EARTH. THEY ARE ONE OF THE PILLARS OF EXISTENCE. THE OMNI-AVENGERS.
OH MAN, ARE ANY OF US RICH? I BET THE REST OF US ARE ALL SUPER RICH. GOD, TELL ME I'M NOT THE ONLY POOR ONE.
FROM UNIVERSE TO UNIVERSE, EVERY TONY STARK IS UNIQUE. AS IS EVERY T'CHALLA, EVERY THOR ODINSON, EVERY CAROL DANVERS.
BUT ALL OF THEM SHARE ONE THING IN COMMON.
AND WHAT'S THAT?
THE NEED TO WIN THIS WAR. THE WAR FOR ALL THE WORLDS. THE BATTLE FOR INFINITY'S END.
ROBBIE?
MR. ALL-RIDER?
'VERSAL STORM COMING.
I CAN SEE. WE'RE GOING AROUND IT, RIGHT?

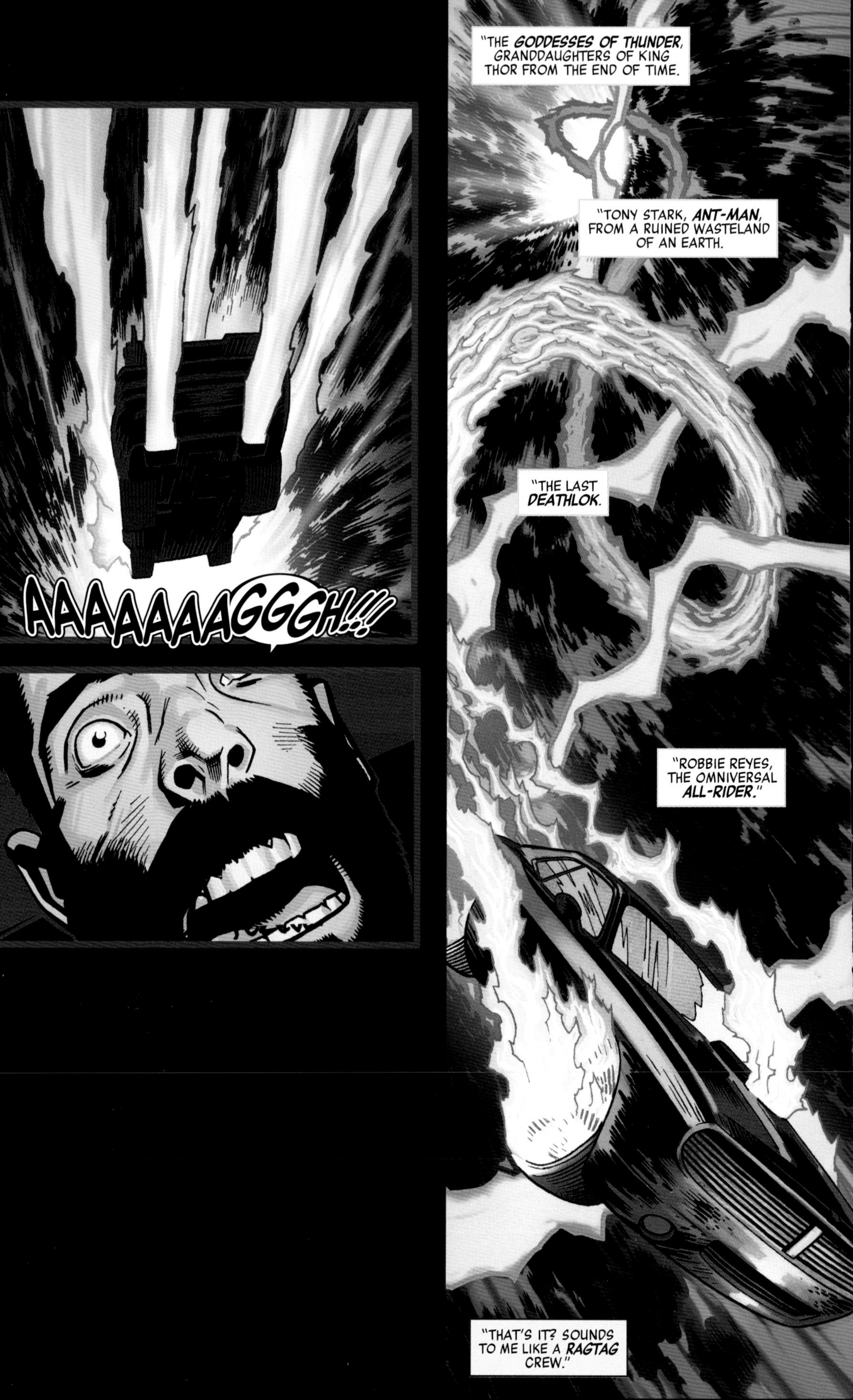
AAAAAAAAGGGH!!!
"THE GODDESSES OF THUNDER, GRANDDAUGHTERS OF KING THOR FROM THE END OF TIME.
"TONY STARK, ANT-MAN, FROM A RUINED WASTELAND OF AN EARTH.
"THE LAST DEATHLOK.
"ROBBIE REYES, THE OMNIVERSAL ALL-RIDER."
"THAT'S IT? SOUNDS TO ME LIKE A RAGTAG CREW."

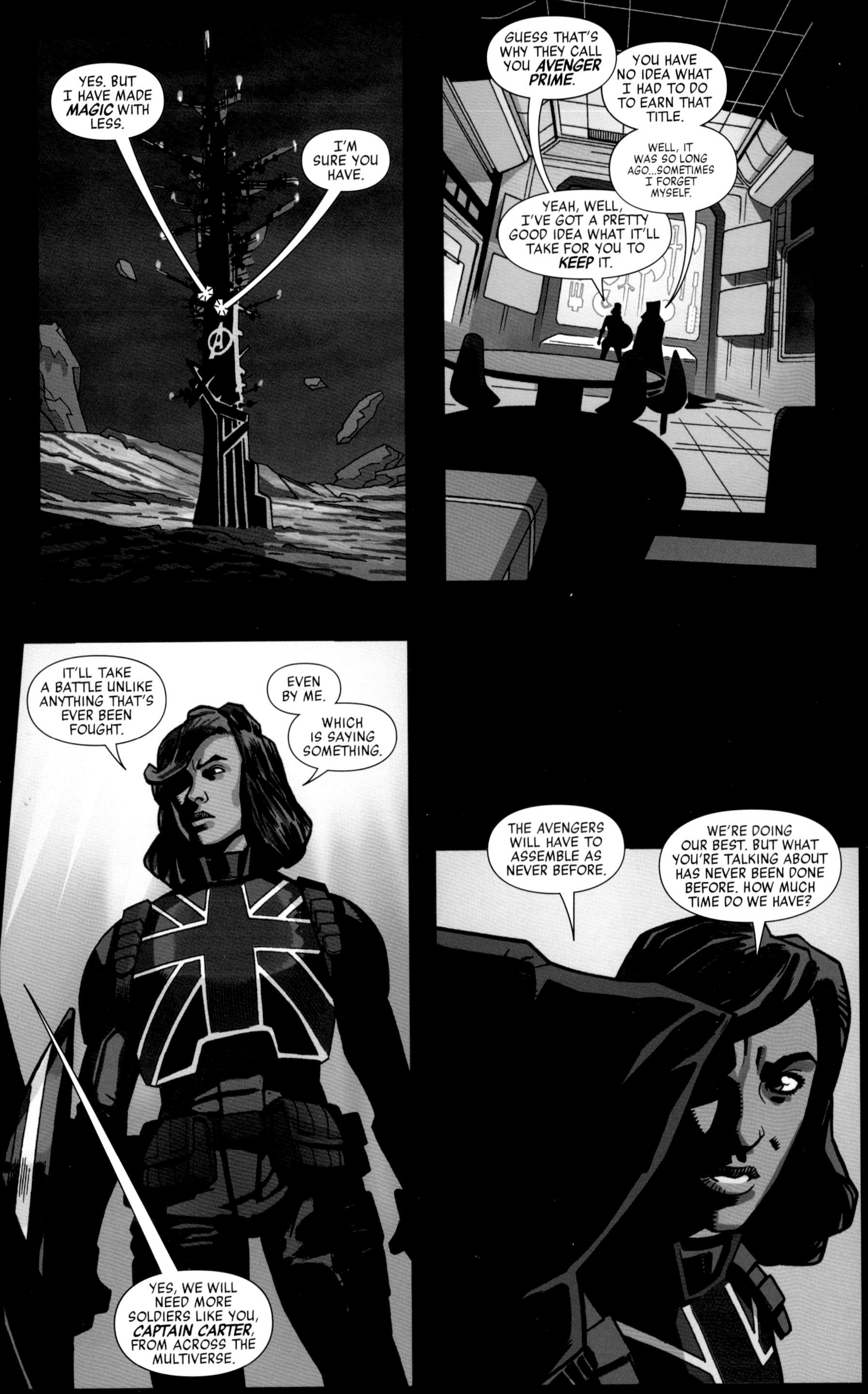
YES. BUT I HAVE MADE MAGIC WITH LESS.
I'M SURE YOU HAVE.
GUESS THAT'S WHY THEY CALL YOU AVENGER PRIME.
YOU HAVE NO IDEA WHAT I HAD TO DO TO EARN THAT TITLE.
WELL, IT WAS SO LONG AGO...SOMETIMES I FORGET MYSELF.
YEAH, WELL, I'VE GOT A PRETTY GOOD IDEA WHAT IT'LL TAKE FOR YOU TO KEEP IT.
IT'LL TAKE A BATTLE UNLIKE ANYTHING THAT'S EVER BEEN FOUGHT.
EVEN BY ME.
WHICH IS SAYING SOMETHING.
YES, WE WILL NEED MORE SOLDIERS LIKE YOU, CAPTAIN CARTER, FROM ACROSS THE MULTIVERSE.
THE AVENGERS WILL HAVE TO ASSEMBLE AS NEVER BEFORE.
WE'RE DOING OUR BEST. BUT WHAT YOU'RE TALKING ABOUT HAS NEVER BEEN DONE BEFORE. HOW MUCH TIME DO WE HAVE?

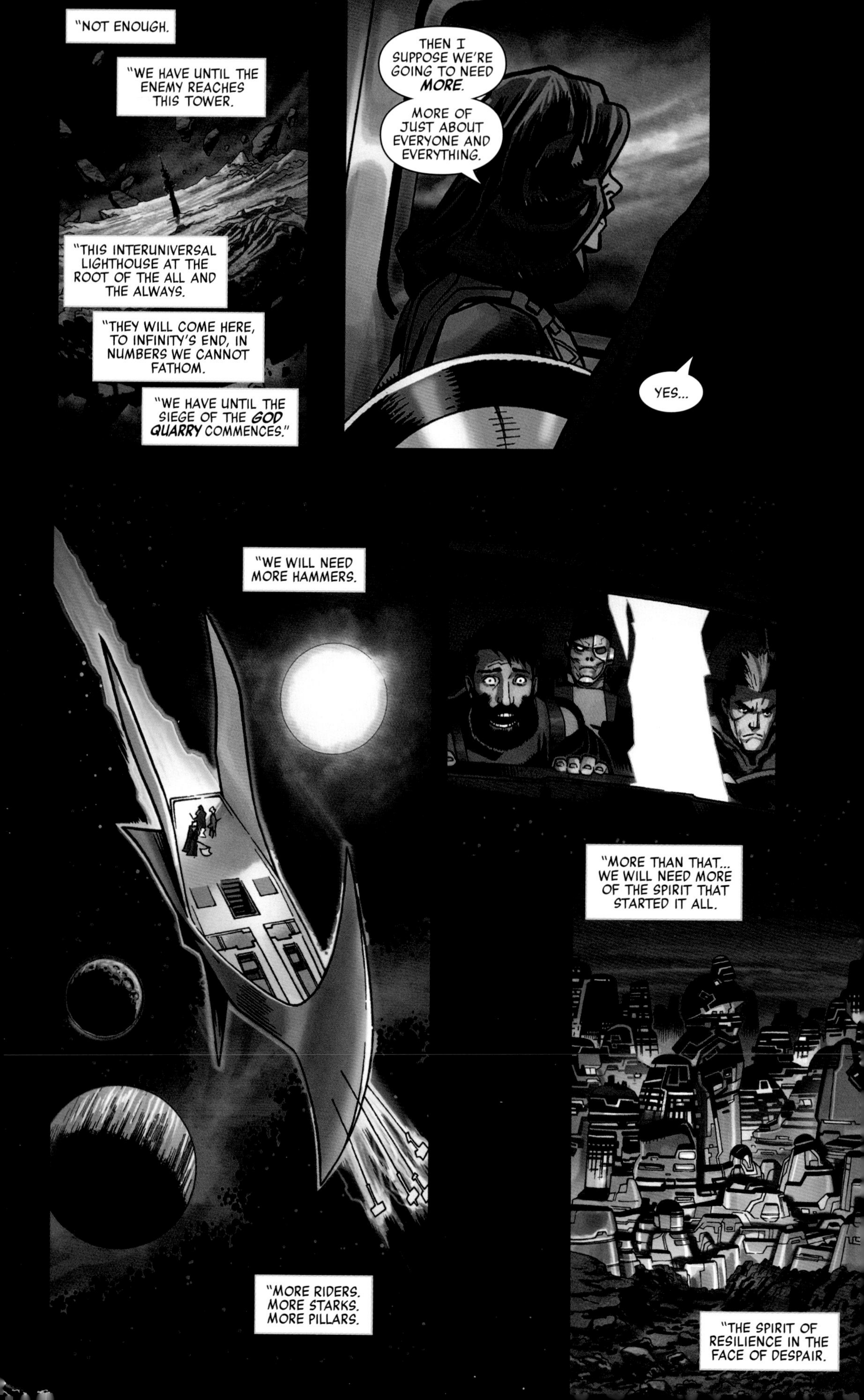
"NOT ENOUGH.
"WE HAVE UNTIL THE ENEMY REACHES THIS TOWER.
"THIS INTERUNIVERSAL LIGHTHOUSE AT THE ROOT OF THE ALL AND THE ALWAYS.
"THEY WILL COME HERE, TO INFINITY'S END, IN NUMBERS WE CANNOT FATHOM.
"WE HAVE UNTIL THE SIEGE OF THE **GOD QUARRY** COMMENCES."
THEN I SUPPOSE WE'RE GOING TO NEED **MORE**.
MORE OF JUST ABOUT EVERYONE AND EVERYTHING.
YES...
"WE WILL NEED MORE HAMMERS.
"MORE RIDERS. MORE STARKS. MORE PILLARS.
"MORE THAN THAT... WE WILL NEED MORE OF THE SPIRIT THAT STARTED IT ALL.
"THE SPIRIT OF RESILIENCE IN THE FACE OF DESPAIR.

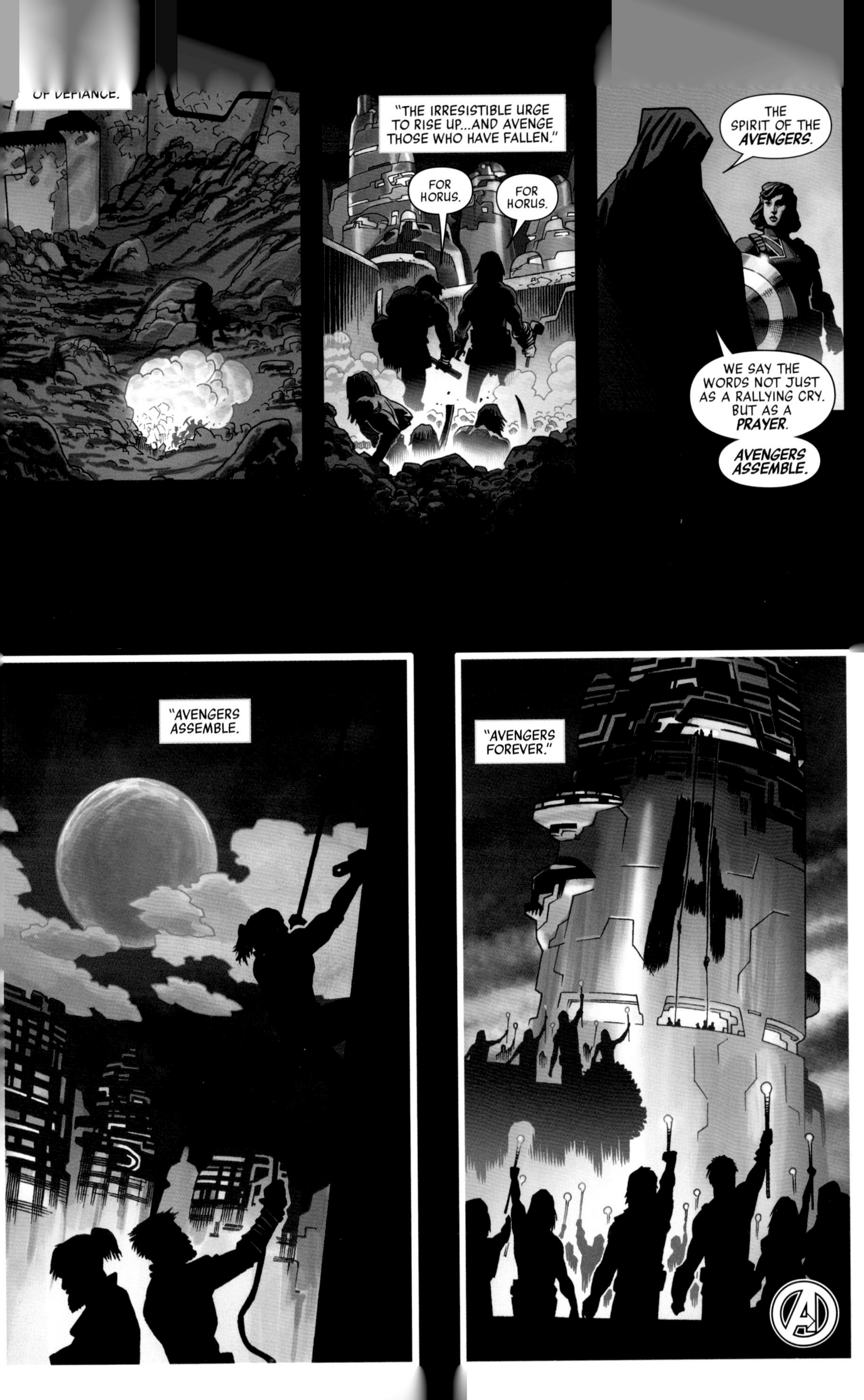
OF DEFIANCE."
"THE IRRESISTIBLE URGE TO RISE UP...AND AVENGE THOSE WHO HAVE FALLEN."
FOR HORUS.
FOR HORUS.
THE SPIRIT OF THE AVENGERS.
WE SAY THE WORDS NOT JUST AS A RALLYING CRY. BUT AS A PRAYER.
AVENGERS ASSEMBLE.
"AVENGERS ASSEMBLE.
"AVENGERS FOREVER."

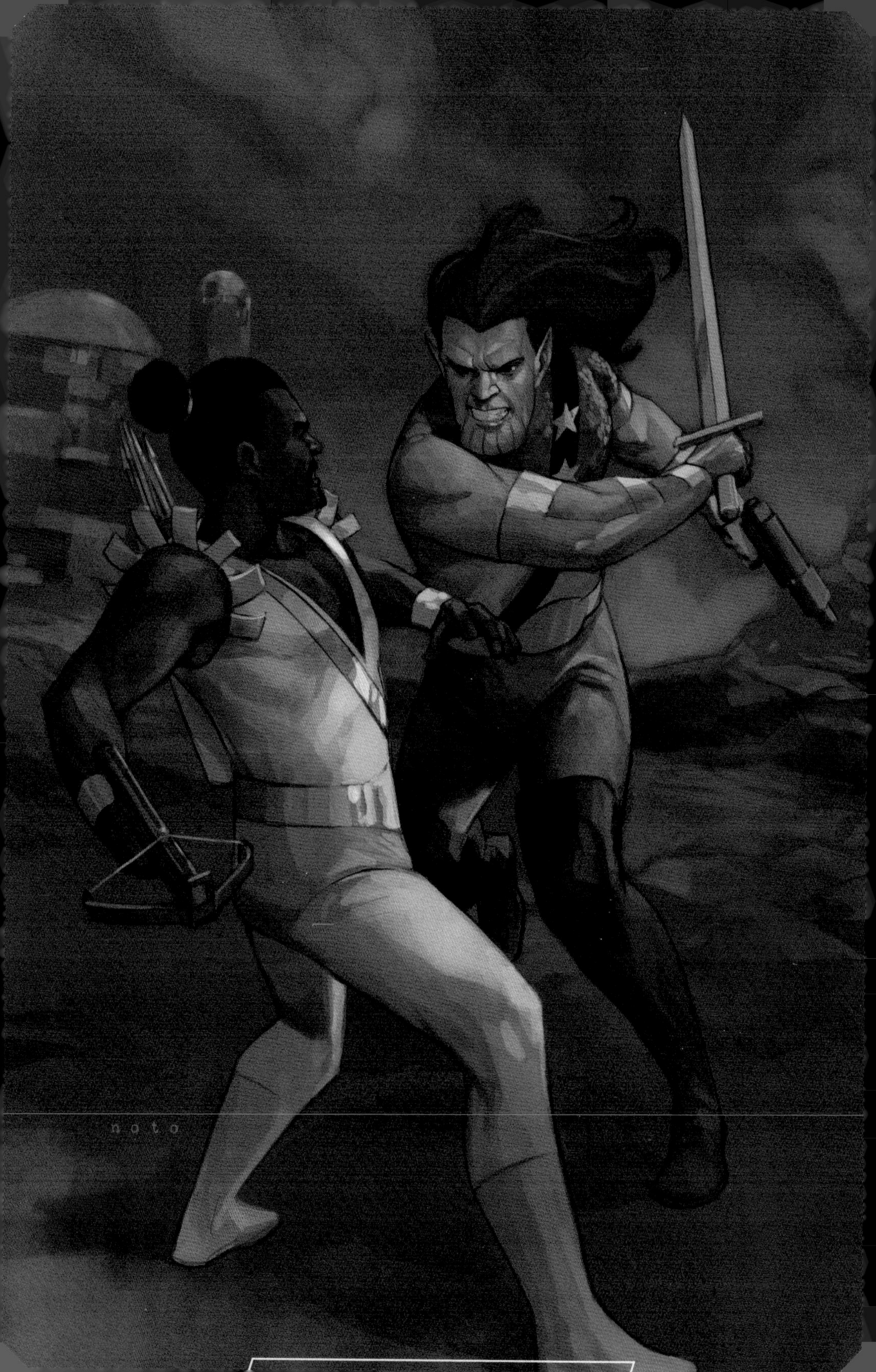

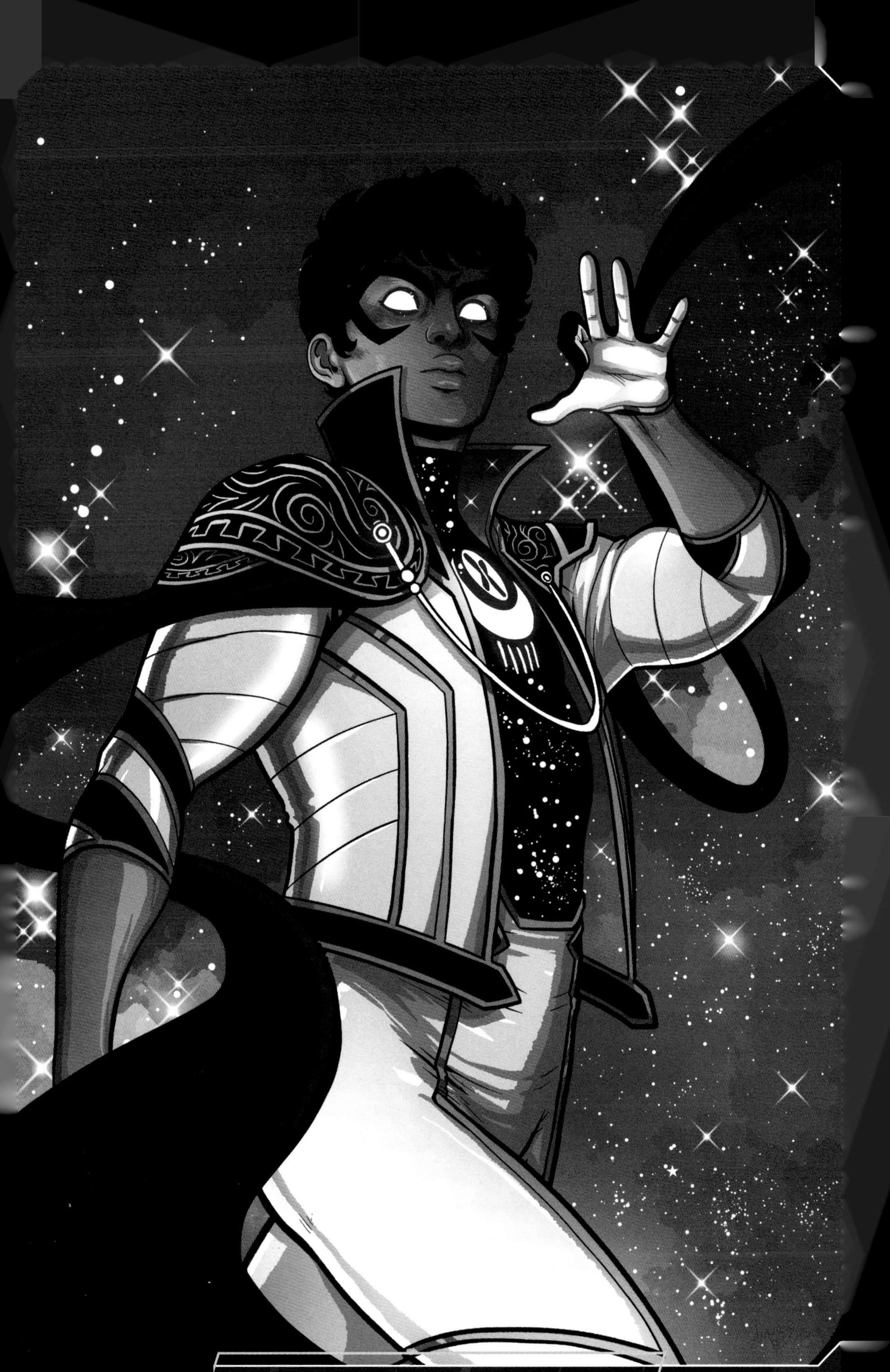

#7 PRIDE VARIANT BY LUCIANO VECCHIO

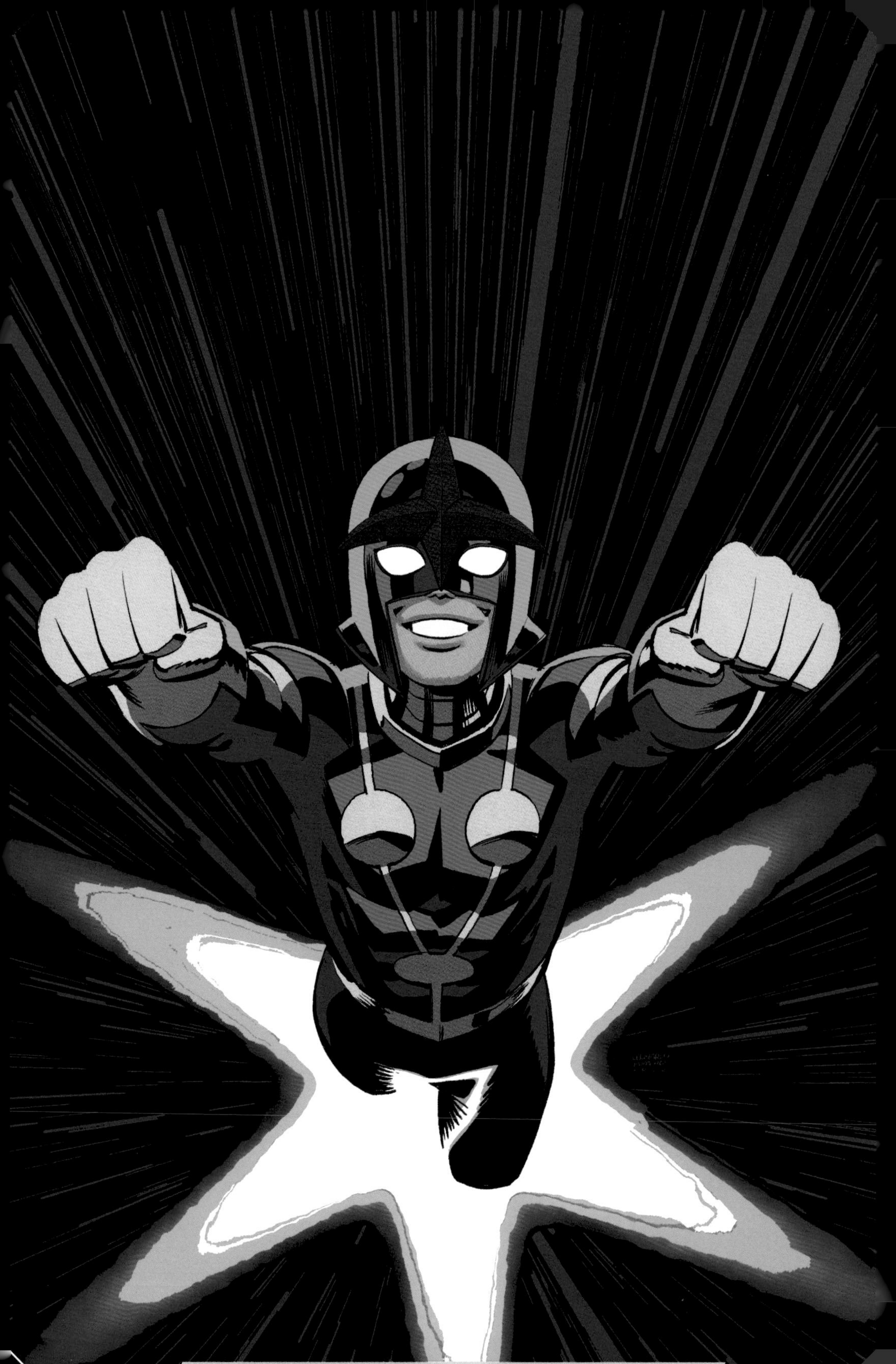

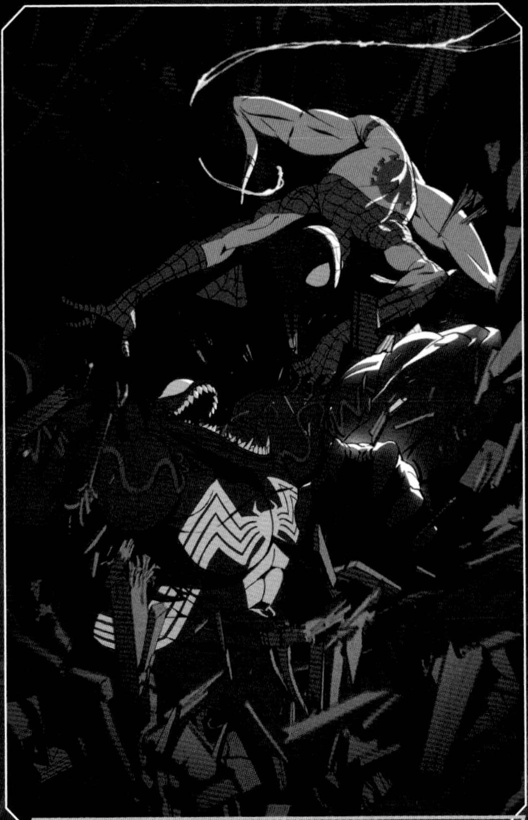

#9 BEYOND AMAZING SPIDER-MAN VARIANT BY
CHASE CONLEY

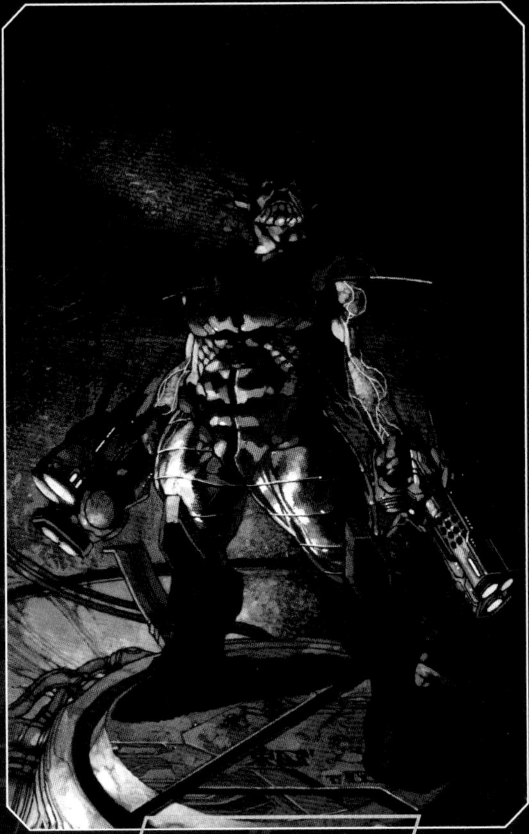

#10 VARIANT BY
SIMONE BIANCHI

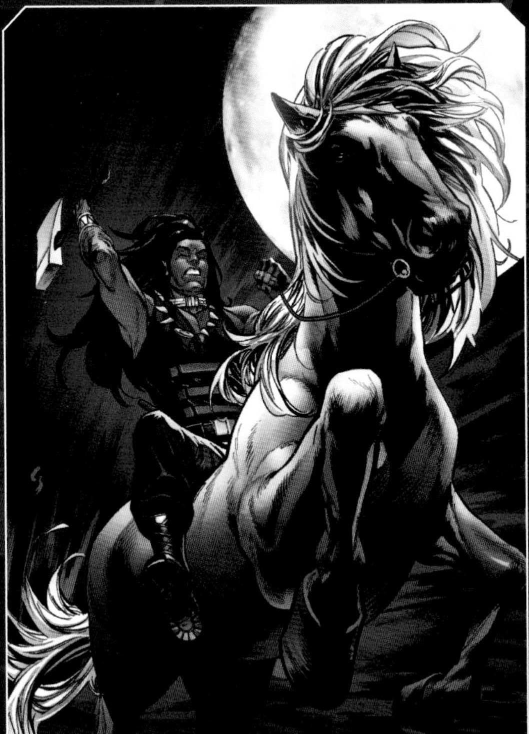

#11 RED WOLF VARIANT BY
GEOFF SHAW & DAVID CURIEL

CHARACTER DESIGNS BY AARON KUDER

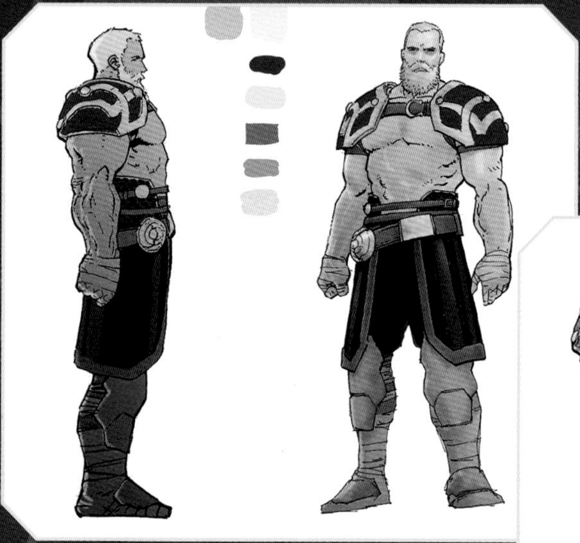

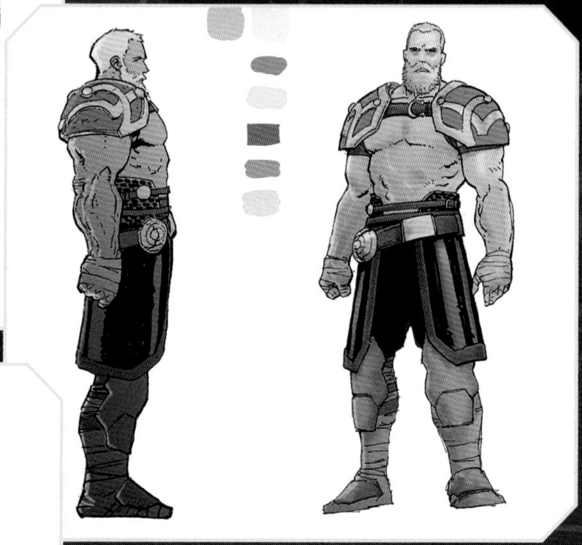

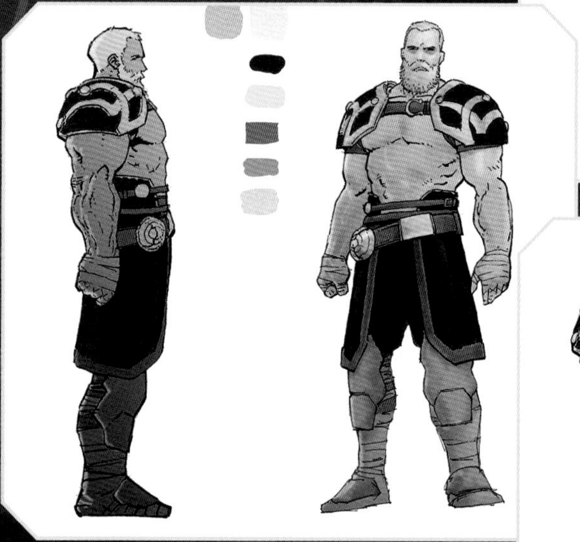

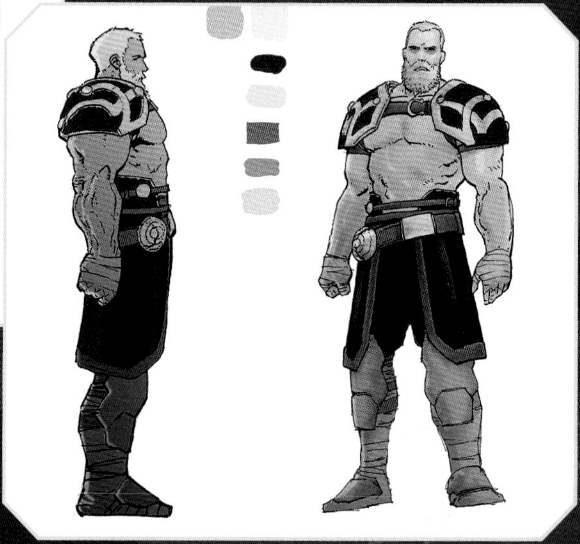

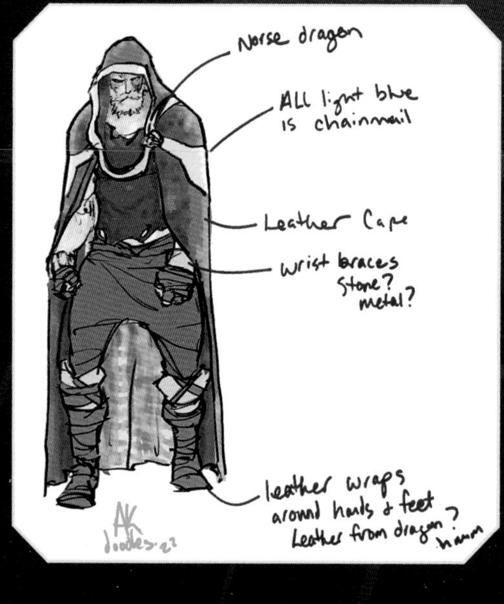
Norse dragon
ALL light blue is chainmail
Leather Cape
wrist braces stone? metal?
leather wraps around hands & feet Leather from dragon? hmmm